Documentary History
of
Eastern Europe

by

ALFRED J. BANNAN

and

ACHILLES EDELENYI

University of Dayton

TWAYNE PUBLISHERS, INC.

NEW YORK

Preface

In the years since World War II, American scholars have shown a much greater interest in the history of those areas usually designated as East-Central Europe and the Balkans. The creation there of socialist states allied to Soviet Russia seemed a great tragedy in the late 1940's. But in 1969 it appears that national feeling has not been thoroughly repressed and that the national genius of any given nation occasionally finds the means of free and articulate expression. More and more, it becomes evident that the proper historical study of Eastern Europe should not begin with the Russian occupation of 1945, but that a true understanding must probe further back.

The Communization of seven East European states has, of course, created a superimposed unity, which though expressed in such agreements as the Warsaw Pact or Comecon, might not seem valid when applied to past centuries. To be sure, all such categorizations are somewhat tenuous and sometimes ludicrous, but a study of many different periods of East European history easily points up the continuous interdependence of these states. Sometimes this interdependence found expression in temporary alliances against the Byzantines, Ottoman Turks and Austrian Hapsburgs; on other occasions, the interdependence was still apparent in great national rivalries. All too often, East European history is studied from an imperfect focus, be it Vienna, Istanbul, Berlin or Moscow. The great need is that Eastern Europe be understood as it was and is, an entity unto itself with special problems and special ways of coping with these problems.

The study of Eastern Europe, as with that of almost every large area composed of different states, must often take the form of national histories which almost necessarily lead to overly-sympathetic accounts of past national glories. The historiography of some East European states is still in a parlous state, and generalized studies have only of late reached a high level of reliability. As more scholars enter the field and adopt a sophisticated approach unbiased by nationalistic, religious, or social interests, the study of Eastern Europe will doubtless begin to lose the character that it seemed to suggest to many people in the past.

But the great amount of intense spade work now in progress must always be accompanied by popularization of Eastern Europe's history. As courses and institutes dealing with Eastern Europe proliferate on the graduate level, some heed must be taken so that all this scholarship might have more impact on undergraduates. Future teachers of history in secondary schools should be reached, and those bright students who will enter graduate study should at least have the opportunity to choose a brief survey course that will acquaint them with an area where they could be of future value to scholarship. More courses are needed on Eastern Europe, to be sure. But among almost all the areas of general historical interest, Eastern Europe is one of the few that still does not possess adequate books that could be used for a comprehensive undergraduate course.

With the proliferation of books of documents, there has not been one work that truly covered East-Central Europe and the Balkans. Ours is the first work to present significant documents and descriptions from the area's history. And following the belief that East European history did not begin in 1945, we decided that the limit must be pushed back as far as possible, to the time of the first Slavic invasions. Even for East European specialists, the medieval period has been terra incognita. But at least on a popular level, this history can be made manageable.

In gathering together these documents, the medieval period required the greatest number of translations on our part. Even documents of major significance had never been translated before. But the documents have been right at hand, thanks to the great collections begun at the end of the nineteenth century in the various East European countries. And it would seem that students should peruse a good number of these documents before they begin to make generalizations about East European history.

In every case, we have tried to make this collection as interesting as possible. The dull character of so many collections of documents neither captures the student's imagination nor stimulates his thought. If this collection seems a bit irreverent at times, the editors will be gratified.

University of Dayton

ALFRED J. BANNAN
ACHILLES EDELENYI

Contents

Documentary History
of
Eastern Europe

CHAPTER 1

Early Slavic Migrations

The "Laurentian Chronicle" is one of the few early sources that tells us of events in Russia before 1000 A.D. Many events described by the Chronicle are based on unreliable legends, but the compilers of the Chronicle display great knowledge, especially of the movements of various peoples in southern Russia. Since the Chronicle was put into a finished form in the early twelfth century, it was possible to make use of non-Russian, especially Byzantine, sources. There are also indications in the Chronicle of a slight use of western sources.

Samuel Hazzard Cross and Olgerd Sherbowitz-Wetzor (translators), THE RUSSIAN PRIMARY CHRONICLE, LAURENTIAN TEXT (Cambridge, 1953), pp. 53–56. Reprinted by permission of The Medieval Academy of America.

Over a long period the Slavs settled beside the Danube, where the Hungarian and Bulgarian lands now lie. From among these Slavs, parties scattered throughout the country and were known by appropriate names, according to the places where they settled. Thus some came and settled by the river Morava, and were named Moravians, while others were called Czechs. Among these same Slavs are included the White Croats, the Serbs and the Carinthians. For when the Vlakhs attacked the Danubian Slavs, settled among them, and did them violence, the latter came and made their homes by the Vistula, and were then called Lyakhs. Of these same Lyakhs some were called Polyanians, some Lutichians, some Mazovians, and still others Pomorians. Certain Slavs settled also on the Dnieper, and were likewise called Polyanians. Still others were named Derevlians, because they lived in the forests. Some also lived between the Pripet' and the Dvina, and were known as Dregivichians. Other tribes resided along the Dvina and were called Polotians on account of a small stream called the Polota, which flows into the Dvina. It was from this same stream that they were named Polotians. The Slavs also dwelt about Lake Il'men', and were known there by their characteristic name. They built a city which they called Novgorod. Still others had their homes along the Desna, the Sem', and the Sula, and were called Severians. Thus the Slavic race was divided, and its language was known as Slavic.

When the Polyanians lived by themselves among the hills, a trade-route connected the Varangians with the Greeks. Starting from Greece, this route proceeds along the Dnieper, above which a portage leads to the Lovat'. By following the Lovat', the great lake Il'men' is reached. The river Volkhov flows out of this lake and enters the great lake Nevo. The mouth of this lake opens into the Varangian Sea. Over this sea goes the route to Rome, and on from Rome overseas to Tsar'grad. The Pontus, into which flows the river Dnieper, may be reached from that point. The Dnieper itself rises in the upland forest, and flows southward. The Dvina has its source in this same forest, but flows northward and empties into the Varangian Sea. The Volga rises in this same forest but flows to the east, and discharges through seventy mouths into the Caspian Sea. It is possible by this route to the eastward to reach the Bulgars and the Caspians, and thus attain the region of the Shem. Along the Dvina runs the route to the Varangians, whence one may reach Rome, and go from there to the race of Ham. But the Dnieper flows through various mouths into the Pontus. This sea, beside which taught St. Andrew, Peter's brother, is called the Russian Sea.

When Andrew was teaching in Sinope and came to Kherson (as has been recounted elsewhere), he observed that the mouth of the Dnieper was near by. Conceiving a desire to go to Rome, he thus journeyed to the mouth of the Dnieper. Thence he ascended the river, and by chance he halted beneath the hills upon the shore. Upon arising in the morning, he observed to the disciples who were with him, "See ye thes hills? So shall the favor of God shine upon them that on this spot a great city shall arise, and God shall erect many churches therein." He drew near the hills, and having blessed them, he set up a cross. After offering his prayer to God, he descended from the hill on which Kiev was subsequently built, and continued his journey up the Dnieper.

He then reached the Slavs at the point where Novgorod is now situated. He saw these people existing according to their customs, and on observing how they bathed and scrubbed themselves, he wondered at them. He went thence among the Varangians and came to Rome, where he recounted what he had learned and observed. "Wondrous to relate," said he, "I saw the land of the Slavs, and while I was among them, I noticed their wooden bathhouses. They warm them to extreme heat, then undress, and after anointing themselves with an acid liquid, they take young branches and lash their bodies. They actually lash themselves so violently that they barely escape alive. Then they drench themselves with cold water, and are thus revived. They think nothing of doing this every day, and though tormented by none, they actually inflict such voluntary torture upon themselves. Indeed, they make of the act not a mere washing but a veritable torment." When his hearers learned this fact, they marveled. But Andrew, after his stay in Rome, returned to Sinope.

While the Polyanians lived apart and governed their families (for before the time of these brothers there were already Polyanians, and each one lived with his gens on his own lands, ruling over his kinsfolk), there were three brothers, Kiy, Shchek, and Khoriv, and their sister was named Lybed. Kiy lived upon the hill where the Borichev trail now is, and Shchek dwelt upon the hill now named Shchekovitsa, while on the third resided Khoriv, after whom this hill is named Khorevitsa. They built a town and named it Kiev after their oldest brother. Around the town lay a wood and a great pine-forest in which they used to hunt wild beasts. These men were wise and prudent; they were called Polyanians, and there are Polyanians descended from them living in Kiev to this day.

Some ignorant persons have claimed that Kiy was a ferryman, for near Kiev there was at that time a ferry from the other side of the river, in consequence of which people used to say, "To Kiy's ferry." Now if Kiy had been a mere ferryman, he would never have gone to Tsar'grad. He was then the chief of his kin, and it is related what great honor he received from the Emperor in whose reign he visited the imperial court. On his homeward journey, he arrived at the Danube. The place pleased him and he built a small town, wishing to dwell there with his kinfolk. But those who lived near by would not grant him this privilege. Yet even now the dwellers by the Danube call this town Kievets. When Kiy returned to Kiev, his native city, he ended his life there; and his brothers Shchek and Khoriv, as well as their sister Lybed, died there also.

After the deaths of these three brothers, their gens assumed the supremacy among the Polyanians. The Derevlians possessed a principality of their own, as did also the Dregovichians, while the Slavs had their own authority in Novgorod, and another principality existed on the Polota, where the Polotians dwell. Beyond them reside th Krivichians, who live at the head waters of the Volga, the Dvina, and the Dnieper, and whose city is Smolensk. It is there that the Krivichians dwell, and from them are the Severians sprung. Ab Beloozero are situated the Ves', and on the lake of Rostov, the Merya, and on Lake Kleshchino the Merya also. Along the river Oka (which flows into the Volga), the Muroma, the Cheremisians, and the Mordva preserve their native languages. For the Slavic race in Rus' includes only the Polyanians, the Derevlians, the people of Novgorod, th Polotians, the Dregovichians, the Severians, and the Buzhians, who live along the river Bug and were later called Volhynians. The following are other tribes which pay tribute to Rus': Chud', Merya, Ves', Muroma, Cheremis', Mordva, Perm', Pechera, Yam', Litva, Zimegola, Kirs', Narva, and Liv'. These tribes have their own languages and belong to the race of Japheth, which inhabits the lands of the north.

Now while the Slavs dwelt along the Danube, as we have said, there came from among the Scythians, that is, from the Khazars, a people called Bulgars who settled on the Danube and oppressed the Slavs. Afterward came the White Ugrians, who inherited the Slavic country. These Ugrians appeared under the Emperor Heraclius, warring on Chosroes, King of Persia. The Avars, who attacked Heraclius the Emperor, nearly capturing him, also lived at this time. They made war upon the Slavs, and harassed the Dulebians, who were themselves Slavs. They even did violence to the Dulebian women. When an Avar made a journey, he did not cause either a horse or a steer to be harnessed, but gave command instead that three of four or five women should be yoked to his cart and made to draw him. Even thus they harassed the Dulebians. The Avars were large of stature and proud of spirit, and God destroyed them They all perished, and not one Avar survived. There is to this day a proverb in Rus' which runs, "They all perished like the Avars." Neither race nor heir of them remains. The Pechenegs came after them, and the Magyars passed by Kiev later during the time of Oleg....

CHAPTER 2

Bogomils in Byzantium

In the *Alexiad*, Anna Comnena, the eldest daughter of the Byzantine Emperor Alexius I (1081–1118), portrays her father's reign in an adulatory style. Her story of the Bogomil, Basil, is very unfair to the accused "heretic," but she indicates Bogomilian tendencies toward egalitarianism in the conversation between Basil and Emperor Alexius. At the same time, her story reveals the superstitious nature of eleventh century Byzantium and the religious fanaticism that motivated not only monks but emperors.

Elizabeth A. S. Dawes (translator), THE ALEXIAD OF THE PRINCESS ANNA COMNENA (London: Kegan, Paul, Trench, Trubner and Co., Ltd., 1918), pp. 412–415.

After this in the course of the years of his reign, a very great cloud of heretics arose, and the nature of their heresy was new and hitherto unknown to the church. For two very evil and worthless doctrines which had been known in former times, now coalesced; the impiety, as it might be called, of the Manichæans, which we also call the Paulician heresy, and the shamelessness of the Massalians. This was the doctrine of the Bogomils compounded of the Massalians and the Manichaeans. And probably it existed even before my father's time, but in secret; for the sect of the Bogomils is very clever in aping virtue. And you would not find any long-haired wordling belonging to the Bogomils, for their wickedness was hidden under the cloak and cowl. A Bogomil looks gloomy and is covered up to the nose and walks with a stoop and mutters, but within he is an uncontrollable wolf. And this most pernicious race, which was like a snake hiding in a hole, my father jured and brought out to the light by chanting mysterious speels. For now that he had rid himself of much of his anxiety about the East and the West he turned his attention to more spiritual matters. For in all things he was superior to other men; in teaching he surpassed those whose profession was teaching; in battles and strategy he excelled those who were admired for their exploits. By this time the fame of the Bogomils had spread everywhere. (For Basil, a monk, was very wily in handling the impiety of the Bogomils; he had twelve disciples whom he called 'apostles,' and also dragged about with him some female disciples, wretched women of loose habits and thoroughly bad, and he disseminated his wickedness everywhere.) This evil attacked many souls like fire, and the Emperor's soul could not brook it, so he began investigating the heresy. He had some of the Bogomils brought to the palace and all proclaimed a certain Basil as the teacher and chief representative of the Bogomilian heresy. Of these, one Diblatius was kept in prison, and as he would not confess when questioned, he was subjected to torture and then informed against the man called Basil, and the disciples he has chosen. Accordingly the Emperor entrusted several men with the search for him. And Sotanael's arch-satrap, Basil, was brought to light, in monk's habit, with a withered countenance, clean shaven and tall of stature. The Emperor, wishing to elicit his inmost thought by compulsion under the disguise of persuasion, at once invited the man on some righteous pretext. And he even rose from his chair to greet him, and made him sit by him and share his table, and threw out his whole fishing-line and fixed various baits on the hooks for this voracious whale to devour. And he made this monk, who was so many-sided in wickedness, swallow all the poison he offered him by pretending that he wished to become his discliple, and not he only, but probably his brother, the Sebastocrator Isaac, also; he pretended too to value all the words he spoke as if they came from a divine voice and to defer to him in all things, provided only that the villain Basil would effect his soul's salvation. "Most reverend father," he would say (for the Emperor rubbed sweets on the rim of the cup so that this demoniac should vomit forth his black thoughts), "I admire thee for thy virtue, and beseech thee to teach me the new doctrines thy Reverence has introduced, as those of our Churches are practically worthless and do not bring anybody to virtue." But the monk at first put on airs and he, that was really an ass, dragged about the lion's skin with him everywhere and shied at the Emperor's words, and yet was puffed up with his praises, for the Emperor even had him at his table. And in all this the Emperor's cousin [?] the Sebastocrator, aided and abetted him in the play; and finally Basil spued out the dogmas of his heresy. And how was this done? A curtain divided the women's apartments from the room where the two Emperors sat with the wretch who blurted out and openly declared all he had in his soul; whilst a secretary sitting on the inner side of the curtain committed his words to writing. And the nonsense-monger seemed to be the teacher while the Emperor pretended to be the pupil, and the secretary wrote down his doctrines. And that man, stricken of God, spun together all that horrible stuff and did not shun any abominable dogma, but even despised our theology and misrepresented all our ecclesiastical administration. And as for the churches, woe is me he called our sacred churches the temples of devils, and our consecration of the body and blood of our one and greatest High Priest and Victim he considered and condemned as worthless. And what followed? the Emperor threw off his disguise and drew the curtain aside; and the whole senate was gathered together and the military contingent mustered, and the elders of the church were present too. The episcopal throne of the Queen of Cities was at that time occupied by that most blessed of patriarchs, Lord Nicholas, the Grammarian. Then the execrable doctrines were read out, and proof was impossible to attack. And the defendant did not deny anything, but immediately bared his head and proceeded to counter-demonstrations and professed himself willing to undergo fire, scourging and a thousand deaths. For these erring Bogomils believe that they can bear any suffering without feeling pain, as the angels forsooth will pluck them out of the fire. And although all . . . and reproached him for his impiety, even those whom he had involved in his own ruin, he remained the same Basil, an inflexible and very brave Bogomil. And although he was threatened with burning and other tortures he clung fast to his demon and embraced his Satanael. After he was consigned to prison the Emperor frequently sent for him and frequently exhorted him to forswear his impiety, but all the Emperor's exhortations left him unchanged. But we must not pass over in silence the miracle which happened to him. Before the Emperor had begun to take severe measures against him, after his confession of impiety he would occasionally retire to a little house which had recently been prepared for him situated fairly close to the royal palace. It was evening and the stars above were shining in the clear air, and the moon was lighting up that evening, following the Synod. When the monk entered his cell about midnight, stones were automatically thrown, like hail, against his cell, and yet no hand threw them, nor was there any man to be seen stoning this devil's abbot. It was probably a burst of anger of Satanael's attendant demons who were enraged and annoyed because he had betrayed their secrets to the Emperor and roused a fierce persecution against their heresy. A man called Parasceviotes who had been appointed guard over that infatuated old man to prevent his having intercourse with others and infecting them with his mischief, swore most solemnly that he had heard the clatter of the stones as they were thrown on the ground and on the tiles, and that he had seen the stones coming in successive

showers but had not caught a glimpse anywhere of anyone
throwing the stones. This throwing of stones was followed
by a sudden earthquake which had shaken the ground, and
the tiles of the roof had rattled. However Parasceviotes,
as he asserted, was quite unafraid before he suspected it
was the work of demons, but when he noticed the stones
seemed to be poured down like rain from above and that
the old heresiarch had slunk inside and had shut himself
in, he attributed the work to demons and was not able
to . . . whatever was happening.

IX Let this be sufficient about that miracle. I wished
to expound the whole heresy of the Bogomils, but 'modesty
prevents me,' as the beautiful Sappho says somewhere, for
though a historian, I am a woman and the most honourable
of the Porphyrogeniti and Alerius' eldest scion, and what
is the talk of the vulgar had better be passed over in silence.
I am desirous of writing so as to set forth a full account
of the Bogomilian heresy; but I will pass it over, as I
do not wish to defile my tongue. And those who wish to
understand the whole heresy of the Bogomils I will refer
to the book entitled *Dogmatic Panoply,* which was compiled
by my father's order. For there was a monk called Zyga-
benus, known to my mistress, my maternal grandmother,
and to all the members of the priestly roll, who had pursued
his grammatical studies very far, was not unversed in rhetoric, and was the best authority on ecclesiastical dogma;
the Emperor sent for him and commissioned him to expound
all the heresies, each separately, and to append to each
the holy Father's refutations of it; and amongst them too
the heresy of the Bogomils, exactly as that impious Basil
had interpreted it.

CHAPTER 3

The Sinodik Tsaria Borisa—Anti-Bogomil Fulminations

Boril, Tsar of the Bulgars, called a council in 1211 to

deal with the Bogomil problem. The council met at Tirnovo and in its condemnation of the Bogomils, indicated some of the sect's main teachings. While Bogomilism did partake of Manichaean dualism, with its belief in the world's evilness and the positive nature of evil, the sect also created disturbances by the fact that it especially appealed to the lower classes. There were overtones of social protest in Bogomilism, but Boril probably found it expedient to make only limited reference to the Bogomils' quest for freedom and justice (article 18). Bogomilism died hard in the Balkans, and when the Turks entered Europe in the fourteenth century, many Bogomils either supported them or became converts to Islam.

Victor N. Sharenkoff, A STUDY OF MANICHAEISM IN BULGARIA WITH SPECIAL REFERENCE TO THE BOGOMILS (New York: Carranza and Co., Inc 1927), pp. 81–83.

1. 'Because our guilful foe spread the Manichaean heresy all over the Bulgarian land and mixed it up with Messalianism, let him and all the leaders of this heresy be accursed.

2. The priest Bogomil, who during the reign of the Bulgarian Tsar Peter adopted the Manichaean heresy and spread it all over into the Bulgarian countries, and also his disciples who believe that our Lord Jesus Christ was seemingly born, seemingly separated from the body which He threw into the air; and all those that call themselves his apostles, let them be cursed.

3. Cursed by everything of the heretics: their customs, meetings at night, sacraments, and their pernicious teachings, and those that follow them.

4. Cursed be those who are associated to them, who eat and drink with them, and accept gifts from them as their co-religionists.

5. Cursed be those who on the twenty-fourth of June, the Birthday of John the Baptist, practice magic and ceremonials with fruits, and perform foul sacraments at night, similar to Hellenistic ceremonies.

6. Cursed be those who call Satan the creator of all visi-

ble things, and assert that he is the steward of rain and hail and of everything that comes from the earth.

7. Cursed be those who say that a woman becomes pregnant in her womb through the act of Satan, who assists her constantly even until the birth of her child, and who cannot be driven away by Holy Baptism, prayer, and fasting.

8. Cursed be those who blaspheme John the Baptist and say that he together with his baptism, was from Satan; and who have an aversion to baptism, baptize themselves without water, reciting only the "Our Father."

9. Cursed be those who have an aversion to the church, to the hymns, and to the house of God, and who simply recite "Our Father," singing it on the corners of the streets.

10. Cursed be those who reject and abuse the Holy Liturgy and the sacred orders, saying that these are an invention of Satan.

11. Cursed be those who reject and abuse the Eucharist with the venerated body of our Lord Jesus Christ, and also reject salvation through the sacrament.

12. Cursed be those who reject the reverence of the honored cross and the holy icons.

13. Cursed be those who admit such heretics into the church of God before they repent of their accursed heresy.

14. Cursed be Basil, the physician, who spread this thrice-accursed heresy into Constantinople during the reign of the Orthodox Emperor Alexis Comnenus.

15. Cursed be Constantine of Bulgaria, the ex-metropolitan of Kerkir who instructed falsely and wickedly about the true God Our Savior Jesus Christ.

16. Cursed be all the adherents of Constantine of Bulgaria and those who grieve and mourn because of his deposition.

17. Cursed be Peter of Cappadocia, the 'elder' (*dedets*) of Sredets.

18. Cursed be those who either by herbs, magic, entranchments, devilish witchcraft or by poison try to injure the tsar, anointed by God.

19. Cursed be those who busy themselves with magic, enchantments, and predictions.

20. Cursed be the thrice-accursed Bogomil, his disciples
Michael, Theodore, Dobri, Stephan, Basil, Peter, and his
other disciples and adherents, who babble that Christ was
not born of the Holy Virgin, Mother of God, and that he
became flesh only in appearance.

CHAPTER 4

A Medieval Chronicler Describes Early Bohemia

Cosmas of Prague (1045?-October 21, 1125) is the main
source of information for the early history of the Bohemians. He was a cleric, well traveled and educated, who
became dean of the cathedral chapter of St. Vitus in Prague.
As our selection from his *Bohemian Chronicle* indicates,
he had to rely too heavily on popular tradition. Cosmas
earned the title, the "Herodotus of Bohemia," and while
some would stress his accuracy, it seems apparent that
his art was more that of an excellent story-teller.

We do know that the Bohemians entered their future
homeland circa 500 A.D., that they probably had a leader
named Czech, and that they differentiated themselves from
their closest Slavic neighbors, the Moravians and the
Lusatians (ancestors of the modern Wends, a very small
group but one whose two dialects are of linguistic significance). An Asiatic invader, the Avars, conquered Bohemia
later in the sixth century, and they ruled Bohemia for
one century. Eventually, in the seventh century, a strong
Bohemian leader, Samo, defeated them. But the period of
Avar rule blotted out many memories of the earlier period,
and thus made the task of Cosmas all the more difficult.
Still, Cosmas would have to be regarded as one of the
finest medieval chroniclers, certainly a fore-runner of the
witty Frenchman, Joinville.

F. M. Pelcl and J. D. Dobrovsky (editors), COSMAE
ECCLESIAE PRAGENSIS DECANI CHRONICON BOHEMORUM,

from the series, SCRIPTORUM RERUM BOHEMICARUM (Prague: Widtmann, 1783), Vol. I, pp. 2–6. Translated by the editors.

Whoever might have originally come into an uninhabited Bohemia—and we certainly do not know how numerous they were—they were definitely looking for a pleasant place to live. They must have first examined the pleasing aspects of the land, the valleys and the mountains. And as I presume, they must have put up their first buildings near Mount St. George between the River Eger and the River Moldau. And it must have been with joy that they implanted the banner that they had carried over a great distance....

Pure water was their wholesome drink. The rays of the sun, the water of the streams, the fields and the forest, even the women, all were common property. Like the animals of the forest, they had another partner each night, and with the coming of the dawn, they dissolved their sacred tie of love. Whenever the night surprised one of them alone, he threw himself down on the grass and slumbered peacefully under the shelter of a tree. The use of wool, linen and any other sort of clothing was unknown to them. Only in winter would they clad themselves with the skin of sheep or wild animals. They did not know the word 'mine'. Theirs was like a monastic life, and they regarded everything they had, in word and deed, as 'ours'. On their abodes, there were no locks, and their doors were never closed to anyone in need. They need not fear for there were no thieves, robbers or destitute people. No crime was more grave for them than theft or robbery. They did not use any other weapon than the arrow, and the arrow was only used to kill game. But their happiness turned into pain. Public property turned into private property. The property that they formerly loved they now despised like a worthless tool. As Boethius said: Greed rages in all like the fire of Mt. Aetna.

In the meantime, other evils ensued and everything became worse. Before, nobody became angry over any seeming insult, and if any reproach was made, it was accepted with equanimity. There was then no judge or duke to whom complaints were carried and punishments meted out. Later, without any compunction, the leading men of the tribe—those of strong personality, good character and many possessions—came together to form a council to debate about controversial cases and suspected crimes. Among these leading men there was one named Crocco. From him, the fortress of Cracow received its name. The fortress of Cracow, which is now covered with growth, is in the forest which is close to the district of Stibrone. Crocco was a perfect man for his time, rich in temporal goods and sharp-minded in forming judgments. He was one to whom not only his own tribe but men of other groups came to ask his counsel on disputed questions. This great and excellent man had no male heirs, but on the other hand, he was the father of three daughters upon whom nature had conferred a wisdom that only men are usually wont to possess. The oldest of the daughters was Kazi. Kazi was not deficient in any respect in her knowledge of plants and sorcery. She was like another Media. Nor was she behind Master Paonius in her knowledge of medicine. When she helped someone, even the fates did not carry out their deadly work....

Similar praise can be given to Tetzka, who, although she never married, was a woman of great intelligence. She built the fortress named after her, Tethen. The fortress was built on a steep precipice overlooking the River Msa. This same woman instructed the ignorant and simple people in how they should worship and adore the pagan gods, and she introduced customs that were completely superstitious and blasphemous to God. There are even today peasants who live like pagans, and they worship water, fire, trees or rocks. Some sacrifice on a mountain of hill, another adores home-made idols that they may protect him and his house.

The third and youngest sister was named Lubossa. She excelled the others even more so in wisdom. She built the most powerful fortress of the time, and she built it in a place adjacent to the district of Stebecna....But because nobody is completely happy, as Horace said, this praiseworthy woman was not free of human weakness, and she practiced fortune-telling. Because she often predicted the future, after the death of her father, she was chosen to be a judge.

CHAPTER 5

The Conversion of Bohemia and Moravia

Sts. Cyril and Methodius, Byzantine missionaries to
Moravia and Bohemia, brought with them the Slavonic
script to which they adopted the Slavic tongue for
the liturgy. The Moravian Duke who had called for them
in 863, Rostislav, hoped that by their assistance the work
of conversion would be taken out of the hands of German
bishops eager for power. Despite German pressure, the
brothers visited Rome in 868 and received a warm welcome
from Pope Nicholas V. Cyril died in Rome but Methodius
was consecrated as Archbishop of Moravia. After many
troubles consequent upon the overthrow of Rostislav by
his nephew, Svatopluk, Methodius retrieved his position.
Rostislav, in league with the Germans, persuaded Pope John
VIII that he should summon Methodius to Rome for judgment. Methodius was well received at Rome, and the Pope
graciously issued the Bull of 880 reconfirming Methodius'
Archbishopric and allowing for the use of the Slavic tongue
in the liturgy. All was lost after his death, for in 885,
Pope Stephen V banned the Slavic liturgy. But still a means
of written language had been created which would be used
later by Serbians, Bulgarians and Russians. And at the
same time, Slavic consciousness had been created to the
extent that some historians see this whole series of episodes
as the beginning of Pan-Slavism.

Antonii Boczek (editor), CODEX DIPLOMATICUS ET EPISTO-
LARIS MORAVIAE (Olomuch: Ex Typographia Aloysii
Skarnitzi, 1836), Vol. I, pp. 42–44. Translated by the
editors.

Pope John VIII recommends Archbishop Methodius to
Svatopluk, Duke of Moravia, and permits the use of the
Slavic language in the liturgy.

We asked this venerable brother, your archbishop Methodius in the presence of our bishops, whether he believes in the orthodox faith and whether he sings during the mass as does the holy Roman church. He declared that he believes and sings the psalms, according to the evangelical and apostolic doctrine, as the holy Roman church does and as it is transmitted by the fathers. We have found him in all ecclesiastical doctrines and practices orthodox and useful, and we send him back again to govern the church to which he is commissioned. You should receive him as your own pastor with honor, reverence and joyful spirit, for we have confirmed his privileges as archbishop with the precept of our apostolic authority and ordered that it should remain, God-pleasing, forever.

We rightly praise the Slavonic letters, which were invented by Constantine and by which God should be praised properly. And in the same language, we order that the praises and works of our Lord Christ should be recited; for we are admonished by sacred authority to praise the lord not only in three but in all languages: "Praise the Lord all nations, praise the Lord all peoples." And the apostles, filled with the holy Spirit spoke in all languages about the greatness of God. Thus Paul, the heavenly trumpeter, admonished: "All language should confess that our Lord Jesus Christ is in the glory of God the Father." And he also enlightens us in the first epistle to the Corinthians when he says that we should enrich the church of God by using different languages. It is not against the true faith or doctrine when masses are sung in the Slavonic language. Nor is it against the faith to use Slavonic for the divine lessons of the Old or New Testament (well translated and interpreted) or for reciting the hours of the divine office. For He who made the 3 principal languages, namely Hebrew, Greek, and Latin, He also created all the others to the praise and glory of himself. Nevertheless, we order, that in all churches of your land, because of the dignity it confers, the gospel should be read first in Latin and then afterward Slavonic translations should be read to the people who do not understand Latin. And if, on the other hand, it pleases you and your court to hear the Masses in the Latin language, we order that the solemnities of the Masses should be celebrated for you in Latin.

Dated in the month of June, 880.

CHAPTER 6

Events in the Late Ninth Century

The Chronicle, as quoted below, mixes together two stories, that of the Magyars' westward movement into Europe and that of the missionary activities of Cyril and Methodius. Although the two stories are unrelated, and the dates are confused (the activities of Cyril and Methodius took place before 888 A.D.), still there was a reasonable proximity in time of the two events. The story of Cyril and Methodius is rather confused, but the Chronicle is more accurate on the activities of the Magyars.

Samuel Hazzard Cross and Olgerd Sherbowitz-Wetzor (translators), THE RUSSIAN PRIMARY CHRONICLE, LAU-RENTIAN TEXT (Cambridge, 1953), pp. 62–64. Reprinted by permission of The Medieval Academy of America.

(888–898). The Magyars passed by Kiev over the hill now called Hungarian, and on arriving at the Dnieper, they pitched camp. They were nomads like the Poloycians. Coming out of the east, they struggled across the great mountains, and began to fight against the neighboring Vlakhs and Slavs. For the Slavs had settled there first, but the Vlakhs had seized the territory of the Slavs. The Magyars subsequently expelled the Vlakhs, took their land, and settled among the Slavs, whom they reduced to sub-mission. From that time this territory was called Hun-garian. The Magyars made war upon the Greeks, and seized the Thracian and Macedonian territory as far as Salonika.

They also attacked the Moravians and the Czechs.

There was at the time but one Slavic race including the Slavs who settled along the Danube and were subjugated by the Magyars, as well as the Moravians, the Czechs, the Lyakhs, and the Polyanians, the last of whom are now called Russes. It was for these Moravians that Slavic books were first written, and this writing prevails also in Rus' and among the Danubian Bulgarians. When the Moravian Slavs ad their princes were living in baptism, the Princes Rostislav, Svyatopolk, and Kotsel sent messengers to the Emperor Michael, saying, "Our nation is baptized, and yet we have no teacher to direct and instruct us and interpret the sacred scriptures. We understand neither Greek nor Latin. Some teach us one thing and some another. Furthermore, we do not understand written characters nor their meaning. Therefore send us teachers who can make known to us the words of the scriptures and their sense." The Emperor Michael, upon hearing their request, called together all the scholars, and reported to them the message of the Slavic princes. The scholars suggested that there was a man in Salonika, by name Leo, who had two sons familiar with the Slavic tongue, being learned men as well. When the Emperor was thus informed, he immediately summoned the sons of Leo from Salonika, directing him to send to court forthwith his sons Methodius and Constantine. Upon receipt of this message, Leo quickly sent forth his sons. When they came before the Emperor, he made known to them that the Slavs had communicated to him their desire for teachers who could interpret the holy scriptures to them. The Emperor prevailed upon them to undertake the mission, and sent them into the Slavic country to Rostislav, Svyatopolk, and Kotsel. When they arrived, they undertook to compose a Slavic alphabet, and translated the *Acts* and the Gospel. The Slavs rejoiced to hear the greatness of God extolled in their native tongue. The apostles afterward translated the Psalter, the *Oktoechos*, and other books.

Now some zealots began to condemn the Slavic books, contending that it was not right for any other nation to have its own alphabet apart from the Hebrews, the Greeks, and the Latirns, according to Pilate's superscription, which he composed for the Lord's cross. When the Pope at Rome heard of this situation, he rebuked those who murmured against the Slavic books, saying, "Let the word of the Scripture be fulfilled that 'all nations shall praise God' (*Ps. lxxi*, 17), and likewise that 'all nations shall declare the majesty of God according as the Holy Spirit shall grant them to speak' (*cf. Acts, ii*, 4). Whosoever condemns the Slavic writing shall be excluded from the Church until he mend his ways. For such men are not sheep but wolves; by their fruits ye shall known them and guard against them. Children of God, hearken unto his teachings, and depart not from the ecclesiastical rule which Methodius your teacher has appointed unto you." Constantine then returned again, and went to instruct the people of Bulgaria; but Methodius remained in Moravia.

Prince Kotsel appointed Methodius Bishop of Pannonia in the see of St. Andronicus, one of the Seventy, a disciple of the Holy Apostle Paul. Methodius chose two priests who were very rapid writers, and translated the whole Scriptures in full from Greek into Slavic in six months between March and the twenty-sixth day of October. After completing the task, he appropriately rendered praise and honor to God, who had bestowed such a blessing upon Bishop Methodius, the successor of Andronicus. Now Andronicus is the apostle of the Slavic race. He traveled among the Moravians, and the Apostle Paul taught there likewise. For in that region is Illyricum, wither Paul first repaired and where the Slavs originally lived. Since Paul is the teacher of the Slavic race, from which we Russians too are sprung, even so the Apostle Paul is the teacher of us Russians, for he preached to the Slavic nation, and appointed Andronicus as Bishop and successor to himself among them. But the Slavs and the Russes are one people, for it is because of the Varangians that the latter became known as Rus', though originally they were Slavs. While some Slavs were termed Polyanians, their speech was still Slavic, for they were known as Polyanians because they lived in the fields. But they had the same Slavic language.

(899–902). The Emperor Leo incited the Magyars against the Bulgarians, so that they attacked and subjugated the whole Bulgarian country. When Symeon heard this news, he turned upon the Magyars who attacked him and conquered the Bulgarians so that Symeon took refuge in Silistria....

CHAPTER 7

The Creation of Hungary

Our most thorough account of the early Hungarians was written at the court of King Bela IV in the thirteenth century. Legend is interwoven with fact, and much of the story is inaccurate. The Magyars' migration into Pannonia was probably due to pressure put on them by the fierce tribe of Petchnegs. The Byzantine-Bulgarian struggle had, even before 896, brought the Magyars into the western orbit as the Byzantines made use of them as auxiliaries. The chronicle of the Anonymous makes a connection between the Magyars and the Huns which is generally not accepted today.

Stephanus Ladislaus Endlicher (editor), RERUM HUNGARI-CARUM MONUMENTA ARPADIANA (Sankt Gallen, 1849; Reissued Leipzig: Verlag Karl W. Hiersemen, 1931), pp. 1–16. Translated by the editors.

In the year of our Lord, 819, Ugek of the Magog dynasty, was the most eminent prince of Scythia. At Dentumoger, he took as his wife the daughter of the Unidubelian duke, Emesu. She gave birth to a son, Almus....
When Almus grew to manhood, the gift of the Holy Spirit was in him even though he was a pagan. And he was more powerful and wise than all the other rulers of Scythia. All matters in the government required his advice, help, and aid before there was any action. When Duke Almus was still young, he married a woman of his own country, the daughter of a noble prince, and she begot a son, Arpad. The brave and warlike Hungarians descended from the

Scythian people.... Their country had become too crowded and they had neither sufficient food nor space. Therefore, the seven princes decided that they could no longer rely on the meager resources of the country. They counselled together, decided to leave their homeland, and conquer a country where they might then dwell. And they decided to leave for the land of Pannonia since this land had once belonged to Attila, an ancestor of Almus and Arpad.

The seven princes, after much deliberation, recognized that they would not be able to carry out their desired venture without a supreme leader. Therefore, the seven princes chose as their leader the son of Ugek, Almus.... In unison they said to Almus: 'From this day, we choose you as our duke and leader. And wherever your destiny leads you, we shall follow."

After pagan custom, the seven princes opened their veins and let their blood flow into a cup which they presented to Duke Almus. Thus they confirmed their oath, and although they were pagans, they still kept any contract that had been confirmed by an oath.

Duke Almus and his princes listened to the entreaties of the Ruthenes and concluded with them an agreement guaranteeing eternal peace. When the Hungarians marched through their land, the Ruthenes gave to them countless presents, among them their sons as hostages. For all these presents, the Ruthenes hoped in return not to be driven from their land. The Ruthenian duke of Galicia ordered two thousand archers and three thousand peasants to go forward and construct a road through the forest that would go as far as Pannonia. The Duke of Galicia loaded all the animals with foodstuffs and donated many animals for the Hungarians to eat. Then they assembled, the seven princes or the Magyars, the seven princes of the Cumans, with all their relatives, serfs, and maids, and with the guidance of the Duke of Galicia, they set out for Pannonia. And having marched over the Carpathians, they descended into Hungary, and when they arrived there, they called their first stopping-place Munkacs (Worker) because it had been only through hard labor that they reached their destination. For forty days they stayed at Munkacs. There they assuaged their fatigue, and they began to love the country beyond what they had imagined as possible.

The Slavs, however, who were the native inhabitants, were very greatly frightened when they heard of the newly arrived Magyars. They willingly submitted to Duke Almus for they had heard that he was descended from the line of King Attila. And although the Slavs were the subjects of Duke Salan, they nevertheless served Duke Almus with great awe and fear and gave him everything that he required, for this was fitting toward their recognized lord....

In the year of the Incarnation, 903, Duke Arpad sent his armies forth and won the whole country between the Tisza and the Budrug, up to Ugocsa. After three days and forced the soldiers of Duke Salan to walk back in chains to the fortress of Hung. And when Duke Arpad and his people had been at Ugocsa for several days, they marveled at the fertility of the soil, the abundance of wild animals, and the large number of fish in the Tisza and Budgrug.

When Duke Salan finally heard the bad news from Slavs who had fled before the Hungarian onslaught, he became fearful of raising his hand against them. But following the usage of the Bulgarians, Salan instructed his ambassador to go to Arpad and threaten the Hungarian leader.... of fighting, Arpad took Ugocsa. He had its walls destroyed The envoy of Salan was to order Arpad and his followers to make recompense for their shameful deeds and retreat beyond the Budrug. Otherwise, Salan would come upon them himself with Greek and Bulgarian cohorts, and as a reward for their evil actions, he would leave but hardly one man who might return home, thankful for his escape....

Duke Arpad listened to the message from the proud Salan, and did not answer it in the same tone but with the following humble words: "Although my ancestor, the powerful King Attila, possessed all the land between the Danube and the Tisza down to the border of Bulgaria, I would like to claim only a part of this land for pasturing my herds. I make this humble claim not out of fear of the Bulgars and the Greeks but out of friendship for Duke Salan. I would also request of your duke that he send me two bottles of water from the Danube and some grass from the sand dunes of Olpara that I may determine whether the grass is sweeter than that of Scythia and whether the

water of the Danube is better than the water of the Don."
And then with many rich presents, Duke Arpad dismissed
the envoys who were now very favorably disposed toward
him. Then he held counsel with his own people and sent
messengers to Duke Salan....

His envoys found Duke Salan in the fortress of Olpar
on the Tisza. They greeted him in the name of Arpad,
and on the second day of their arrival at his court, they
showed him all the presents they had brought. Duke Salan
marvelled at the presents, and he listened to the messages
of his envoys and the Hungarian envoys. Upon hearing
them, he was jubilant. He was friendly to the envoys of
Arpad and gave them rich presents. Then he fulfilled the
request of Arpad. On the twelfth day Oundu and Ketel
obtained permission to take leave of Duke Salan, and they
returned to their own people. And Salan gave them with
some disdain two bottles of Danube water, a bunch of hay
from the sand of Olpar, and multitudinous presents for
Arpad. Along with these presents, he allowed them to have
all the land up to the river Soujou with all its inhabitants.
Then Oundu and Ketel hurriedly returned to Arpad with
the envoys of Salan and they handed over the presents
of the Duke and said that land would be donated with
all its inhabitants. Consequently, there was great joy at
the court of Duke Arpad, and for three days there was
great feasting. Then Duke Arpad confirmed the peace and
sent the envoys of Duke Salan home with rich presents.

After a while Arpad and his nobles held counsel and
sent messengers to Salan to tell him, as a joyful event,
of the victories of Thosu, Bulsu, and Tuhutum and to ask
of him further land up to the river Zogea. And thus it
had indeed happened. The envoys this time were Etu and
Vogta. They found Salan at Olpar and reported to him
their message. Salan was very fearful and allowed to Arpad
all the land up to the Zogea and gave the envoys many
presents. On the seventh day Etu and Vogta took leave
and returned to their ruler. Duke Arpad received them
back with favor and their message created great joy at
the court of the Duke. And Arpad started to grant great
estates to his faithful followers.

And after a while Duke Salan pondered over the recent

deeds of the Hungarians. Then he began to have an ever greater fear that the Hungarians, in anger, might force him off his own land. Then he held counsel with his people, and sent messages to the Bulgars and to the Greeks requesting aid so that he might fight Arpad. And they, in turn, sent him a great army. When the army arrived for Duke Salan at Tetel, the court of Duke Salan was in great transports of joy. On the second day, he sent messengers to Arpad to tell him that he should leave here and go back where he came from. When Arpad and his nobles heard this, they became angry, and sent back this message to Salan: "The land between the Danube and the Tisza, and the water of the Danube that flows from Regensburg to Greece, we bought with our money. Shortly after we arrived here, we purchased all this with the twelve white steeds and the other items we sent to you. And then Salan sent us back with praise of his own fertile fields and Danube water. Therefore, we order your lord to leave our country and posthaste go back to Bulgaria from where his ancestor had come after the death of Attila. Otherwise, we will without delay start a campaign against him." With sadness the envoys returned with this decision to Salan. The Hungarians then left the river Zogea and first camped with their entire army between Mt. Tetevelen and the Tisza. From there they traveled along side the banks of the Tisza to Olpar.

Duke Salan set out, in a great fury, from the Tetel with his Greeks and Bulgarians to do battle with Arpad. And when both armies had come close together, and night fell, not a man dared to sleep. Each man had always close at hand his fully saddled horse. Before sunrise both armies readied themselves for battle. But Duke Arpad, confident of the aid of the War God, put on his armor, gave orders to his army, and, emitting many tears, prayed to the lord. He then spoke words of encouragement to his soldiers.... And after he had inspired them to perform courageous deeds, Lelu, the son of Tosu, blew the battle horn. Bolsu, the son of Bogat, raised the battle flag. The first line went into battle. And the two enemy armies struck at each other, starting to fight without giving quarter. And as the entire army of Arpad committed itself to battle, the army of the

Greeks and Bulgars fell in large numbers. And as Salan saw his forces being beaten, he fled into Bulgaria in order to save his life. The Greeks and Bulgars, due to their fear of the Hungarians, were unable to retrace their steps, and in order to save their lives, they tried to swim the Tisza as if it were a small stream. But because of their panic, so many of them drowned in the river that scarcely any escaped to report the bad news to their emperor. Therefore, the place where the Greeks perished is called to this day, "Haven of the Greeks."

CHAPTER 8

Of the Croats and Of the Country They Now Dwell In

Constantine Porphyrogenitus VII (905–959), son of Leo VI, ruled the Byzantine Empire from 913 to 959. His reign was generally successful, but Constantine enjoyed little credit for its success because he delegated so many responsibilities to subordinates. He was a patron of the arts and devoted his main efforts to scholarship. His account of early Slavic history is one of our best sources and well it might be because he had access to the imperial records. Byzantine pride is of course apparent in his account, but the veracity of his narrative is beyond heavy reproach.

Gy. Moravcsik and R. J. H. Jenkins (translators), CONSTANTINE PORPHYROGENITUS. DE ADMINISTRANDO IMPERIO (Budapest: Pazmany Peter Tudomanyegy. 1949), Chapter 31, pp. 146–153. Reprinted by permission of R. J. H. Jenkins.

The Croats who now live in the region of Dalmatia are descended from the unbaptized Croats, also called 'white', who live beyond Turkey and next to Francia, and have for Slav neighbors the unbaptized Serbs. 'Croats' in the

Slav tongue means 'those who occupy much territory'. These
same Croats arrived to claim the protection of the same
emperor Heraclius, at that time when the Avars had fought
and expelled from those parts the Romani whom the
emperor Diocletian had brought from Rome and settled
there, and who were therefore called 'Romani' from their
having been translated from Rome to those countries, I
mean, to those now called Croatia and Serbia. These same
Romani having been expelled by the Avars in the days
of this same emperor of the Romans Heraclius, their countries were made desolate. And so, by command of the emperor Heraclius these same Croats defeated and expelled
the Avars from those parts, and by mandate of Heraclius
the emperor they settled down in that same country of
the Avars, where they now dwell. These same Croats had
at that time for prince the father of Porgas. The emperor
Heraclius sent and brought priests from Rome, and made
of them an archbishop and a bishop and elders and deacons,
and baptized the Croats; and at that time these Croats
had Porgas for their prince.

This country in which the Croats settled themselves was
originally under the dominion of the emperor of the Romans, and hence in the country of these same Croats the
palace and hippodromes of the emperor Diocletian are still
preserved, at the city of Salona, near the city of Spalato.

These baptized Croats will not fight foreign countries
outside the borders of their own; for they received a kind
of oracular response and promise from 'the pope of Rome
who in the time of Heraclius, emperor of the Romans, sent
priests and baptized them. For after their baptism the
Croats made a convenant, confirmed with their own hands
and by oaths sure and binding in the name of St. Peter
the apostle, that never would they go upon a foreign country and make war on it, but rather would live at peace
with all who were willing to do so; and they received from
the same pope of Rome a benediction to this erect, that
if any of the pagans should come against the country of
these same Croats and bring war upon it, then might the
God of the Croats fight for *the Croats* and protect them,
and Peter the disciple of Christ give them victories. . . .

The prince of Croatia has from the beginning, that is,

ever since the reign of Heraclius the emperor, been in servitude and submission to the emperor of the Romans, and was never made subject to the prince of Bulgaria. Nor has the Bulgarian ever gone to war with the Croats, except when Michael Boris, prince of Bulgaria, went and fought them and, unable to make any headway, concluded peace with them, and made presents to the Croats, and received presents from the Croats. But never yet have these Croats paid tribute to the Bulgarians, although the two have often made presents to one another in the way of friendship. . . .

Great Croatia, also called 'white', is still unbaptized to this day, as are also the Serbs who are its neighbours. They muster fewer horse and fewer foot than does baptized Croatia, because they are more constantly raided, by the Franks and Turks and Pechenegs. Nor have they either galleys or cutters or merchant-ships, for the sea is far away; for from those parts to the sea it is a journey of 30 days. And the sea to which they come down after the 30 days is that which is called 'dark'.

CHAPTER 9

Of the Serbs and Of the Country They Now Dwell In

The following selection is another chapter from the *De Administrando Imperio* of Constantine Porphyrogenitus. As is the case with the Croats, here is one of the best sources for the early history of the Serbians.

Gy. Moravcsik and R. J. H. Jenkins (translators) CONSTANTINE PORPHYROGENITUS. DE ADMINISTRANDO IMPERIO (Budapest: Pazmany Peter Tudomanyegy. 1949), Chapter 32, pp. 152–161. Reprinted by permission of R. J. H. Jenkins.

The Serbs are descended from the unbaptized Serbs,

also called 'white' who lived beyond Turkey in a place called
by them Boiki, where their neighbour is Francia, as is
also Great Croatia, the unbaptized, also called 'white'; in
this place, then, these Serbs also originally dwelt. But when
two brothers succeeded their father in the rule of Serbia,
one of them, taking a moiety of the folk, claimed the protection of Heraclius, the emperor of the Romans, and
the same emperor Heraclius received him and gave him
a place in the province of Thessalonica to settle in, namely
Serbia, which from that time has acquired this denomina-
tion. 'Serbs' in the tongue of the Romans is the word for
'slaves', whence the colloquial 'serbula' for menial shoes,
and 'tzerboulianoi' for those who wear cheap, shoddy foot-
gear. This name the Serbs acquired from their being slaves
of the emperor of the Romans. Now, after some time these
same Serbs decided to depart to their own homes, and the
emperor sent them off. But when they had crossed the
river Danube, they changed their minds and sent a request
to the emperor Heraclius, through the military governor
then governing Belgrade, that he would grant them other
land to settle in. And since what is now Serbia and Pagania
and the so-called country of the Azchlumi and Terbounia
and the country of the Kanalties were under the dominion
of emperor of the Romans, and since these countries had
been made desolate by the Avars (for they had expelled
from those parts the Romani who now live in Dalmatia
and Dyrrachium), therefore the emperor settled these same
Serbs in these countries, and they were subject to the emperor of the Romans; and the emperor brought elders from
Rome and baptized them and taught them fairly to perform the works of piety and expounded to them the faith
of the Christians. And since Bulgaria was beneath the dominion of the Romans * * * when, therefore, that same
Serbian prince died who had claimed the emperor's protection, his son ruled in succession, and thereafter his grand-
son, and in like manner the succeeding princes from his
family. And after some years was begotten of them Boise-
slav, and of him Rodoslav, and of him Prosigois, and of
him Blastimer; and up to the time of this Blastimer the
Bulgarians lived at peace with the Serbs, whose neighbours
they were and with whom they had a common frontier,

and they were friendly one toward another, and were in servitude and submission to the emperors of the Romans and kindly entreated by them. But, during the rule of this same Blastimer, Presiam, prince of Bulgaria, came with war against the Serbs, with intent to reduce them to submission; but though he fought them three years he not merely achieved nothing but also lost very many of his men. After the death of prince Blastimer his three sons, Muntimer and Stroimer and Goinikos, succeeded to the rule of Serbia and divided up the country. In their time came up the prince of Bulgaria, Michael Boris, wishing to avenge the defeat of his father Presiam, and made war, and the Serbs discomfited him to such an extent that they even held prisoner his son Vladimer, together with twelve great boyars. Then, out of grief for his son, Boris perforce made peace with the Serbs. But, being about to return to Bulgaria, and afraid lest the Serbs might ambush him on the way, he begged for his escort the sons of prince Muntimer, Borenas and Stephen, who escorted him safely as far as the frontier at Rasi. For this favour Michael Boris gave them handsome presents, and they in return gave him, as presents in the way of friendship, two slaves, two falcons, two dogs and eighty furs, which the Bulgarians describe as tribute. A short while after, the same three brothers, the princes of Serbia, fell out, and one of them, Muntimer, gained the upper hand and, wishing to be sole ruler, seized the other two and handed them over to Bulgaria, keeping by him and caring for only the son of the one brother Goinikos, Peter by name, who fled and came to Croatia, and of whom we shall speak in a moment. The aforesaid brother Stroimer, who was in Bulgaria, had a son Klonimer, to whom Boris gave a Bulgarian wife. Of him was begotten Tzeeslav, in Bulgaria. Muntimer, who had expelled his two brothers and taken the rule, begat three sons, Pribeslav and Branos and Stephen, and after he died his eldest son Pribeslav succeeded him. Now, after one year the aforesaid Peter, son of Goinikos, came out of Croatia and expelled from the rule his cousin Pribeslav and his two brothers, and himself succeeded to the rule, and they fled away and entered Croatia. Three years later Branos came to fight Peter and was defeated and captured by him, and blinded.

Two years after that, Klonimer, the father of Tzeeslav, escaped from Bulgaria and he too came and with an army and entered one of the cities of Serbia, Dostinika, with intent to take over the rule. Peter attacked and slew him, and continued to govern for another 21 years, and his rule began during the reign of Leo, the holy emperor, of most blessed memory ,to whom he was in submission and servitude. He also made peace with Symeon, prince of Bulgaria, and even made him god-father to his child. Now, after the time that this lord Leo had reigned, the then military governor at Dyrrachium, the protospatharius Leo Rhabduchus, who was afterwards honoured with the rank of magister and office of foreign minister, arrived in Pagania, which was at that time under the control of the prince of Serbia, in order to advise and confer with this same prince Peter upon some service and affair. Michael, Prince of the Zachlumi, his jealousy aroused by this, sent information to Symeon, prince of Bulgaria, that the emperor of the Romans was bribing prince Peter to take the Turks with him and go upon Bulgaria. It was at that time when the battle of Achelo had taken place between the Romans and the Bulgarians. Symeon, mad with rage at this, sent against prince Peter of Serbia Sigritzis Theodore and the notorious Marmais with an army, and they took with them also the young prince Paul, son of Branos whom Peter, prince of Serbia, had blinded. The Bulgarians proceeded against the prince of Serbia by treachery, and, by binding him with the relationship of god-father and giving a sworn undertaking that he should suffer nothing untoward at their hands, they tricked him into coming out to them, and then on the instant bound him and carried him off to Bulgaria, and he died in prison. Paul, son of Branos, entered into his room and governed three years. The emperor, the lord Romanus, who had in Constantinople the young prince Zacharias, son of Pribeslay, prince of Serbia, sent him off to be prince in Serbia, and he went and fought, but was defeated by Paul; who took him prisoner and handed him over to the Bulgarians and he was kept in prison. Then, three years later, when Paul had put himself in opposition to the Bulgarians, *they* sent this Zacharias, who had previously been sent by the lord Romanus the emperor, and he expelled Paul and himself took possession of the rule over the Serbs; and therupon, being mindful of the benefits of the emperor of the Romans, he broke with the Bulgarians, being not at all wishful to be subjected to them, but rather that the emperor of the Romans should be his master. And so, when Symeon sent against him an army under Marmaim and Sigritizis Theodore, he sent their heads and their armour from the battle to the emperor of the Romans as tokens of his victory (for the war was still going on between the Romans and the Bulgarians); nor did he ever cease, just as the princes also that were before him had been used to send missions to the emperors of the Romans, to be in subjection and servitude to them. Again, Symeon sent another army against prince Zacharias, under Kninos and Himnikos and Itzboklias, and together with them he sent also Tzeeslva. Then Zacharias took fright and fled to Croatia, and the Bulgarians sent a message to the 'zupans' that they should come to them and should receive Tzeeslav for their prince; and, having tricked them by an oath and brought them out as far as the first village, they instantly bound them, and entered Serbia and took them away with them the entire folk, both old and young, and carried them into Bulgaria, though a few escaped away, and entered Croatia; and the country was left deserted. Now, at that time these same Bulgarians under Alogobotour entered Croatia to make war, and there they were all slain by the Croats. Seven years afterwards Tzeeslav escaped from the Bulgarians with four others, and entered Serbia from Preslav, and found in the country no more than fifty men only, without wives or children, who supported themselves by hunting. With these he took possession of the country and sent a message to the emperor of the Romans asking for his support and succour, and promising to serve him and be obedient to his command, as had been the princes before him. And thence forward the emperor of the Romans continually benefited him, so that *The* Serbs living in Croatia and Bulgaria and the rest of the countries, whom Symeon had scattered, rallied to him when they heard of it. Moreover, many had escaped from Bulgaria and entered Constantinople, and these the emperor of the Romans clad and comforted and sent to Tzeeslav. And from the rich gifts of the emperor of the Romans he organized and populated the country, and is, as before, in servitude and subjection to the emperor of the Romans; and through the cooperation and many benefits of the emperor he has united this country and is confirmed in the rule of it.

The prince of Serbia has from the beginning, that is, ever since the reign of Heraclius the emperor, been in servitude and submission to the emperor of the Romans, and was never subject to the prince of Bulgaria.

In baptized Serbia are the inhabited cities of Destinikon, Tzernabouskei, Megyretous, Dresneik, Lesnik, Salines; and in the territory of Bosona, Katera, and Desnik. . . .

CHAPTER 10

Russia Chooses Orthodox Christianity

The following story attempts to put a good light on Russia's conversion to Christianity. The conversion appears to have been part of a political bargain with the Byzantines.

Samuel Hazzard Cross and Olgerd Sherbowitz-Wetzor (translators), THE RUSSIAN PRIMARY CHRONICLE, LAURENTIAN TEXT (Cambridge, 1953), pp. 110–117. Reprinted by permission of The Medieval Academy of America.

(987). Vladimir summoned together his boyars and the city-elders, and said to them, "Behold, the Bulgars came before me urging me to accept their religion. Then came the Germans and praised their own faith; and after them came the Jews. Finally the Greeks appeared, criticizing all other faiths but commending their own, and they spoke at length, telling the history of the whole world from its beginning. Their words were artful, and it was wondrous

to listen and pleasant to hear them. They preach the existence of another world. 'Whoever adopts our religion and
then dies shall arise and live forever. But whosoever em-
braces another faith, shall be consumed with fire in the
next world.' What is your opinion on this subject, and what
do you answer?" The boyars and the elders replied, "You
know, oh Prince, that no man condemns his own possessions, but praises them instead. If you desire to make certain, you have servants at your disposal. Send them to
inquire about the ritual of each and how he worships God."
     Their counsel pleased the prince and all the people, so
that they chose good and wise men to the number of ten,
and directed them to go first among the Bulgars and inspect
their faith. The emissaries went their way, and when they
arrived at their destination they beheld the disgraceful actions of the Bulgars and their worship in the mosque; then
they returned to their country. Vladimir then instructed
them to go likewise among the Germans, and examine their
faith, and finally to visit the Greeks. They thus went into
Germany, and after viewing the German ceremonial, they
proceeded to Tsar'grad, where they appeared before the
Emperor. He inquired on what mission they had come, and
they reported to him all that had occurred. When the Emperor heard their words, he rejoiced, and did them great
honor on that very day.
     On the morrow, the Emperor sent a message to the Patri-
arch to inform him that a Russian delegation had arrived
to examine the Greek faith, and directed him to prepare
the church and the clergy, and to array himself in his
sacerdotal robes, so that the Russes might behold the glory
of the God of the Greeks. When the Patriarch received
these commands, he bade the clergy assemble, and they
performed the customary rites. They burned incense, and
the choirs sang hymns. The Emperor accompanied the
Russes to the church, and placed them in a wide space,
calling their attention to the beauty of the edifice, the chanting, and the pontificial services and the ministry of the
deacons, while he explained to them the worship of his
God. The Russes were astonished, and in their wonder
praised the Greek ceremonial. Then the Emperors Basil
and Constantine invited the envoys to their presence, and

said, "Go hence to your native country," and dismissed them with valuable presents and great honor.

Thus they returned to their own country, and the Prince called together his boyars and the elders. Vladimir then announced the return of the envoys who had been sent out, and suggested that their report be heard. He thus commanded them to speak out before his retinue. The envoys reported, "When we journeyed among the Bulgars, we beheld how they worship in their temple, called a mosque, while they stand ungirt. The Bulgar bows, sits down, looks hither and thither like one possessed, and there is no happiness among them, but instead only sorrow and a dreadful stench. Their religion is not good. Then we went among the Germans, and saw them performing many ceremonies in their temples; but we beheld no glory there. Then we went to Greece, and the Greeks led us to the edifice where they worship their God, and we knew not whether we were in heaven or on earth. For on earth there is no such splendor or such beauty, and we are at a loss how to describe it. We only know that God dwells there among men, and their service is fairer than the ceremonies of other nations. For we cannot forget that beauty. Every man, after tasting something sweet, is afterward unwilling to accept that which is bitter, and therefore we cannot dwell longer here." Then the boyars spoke and said, "If the Greek faith were evil, it would not have been adopted by your grandmother Olga who was wiser than all other men." Vladimir than inquired where they should accept baptism, and they replied that the decision rested with him.

After a year had passed, in 6496 (988), Vladimir proceeded with an armed force against Kherson, a Greek city, and the people of Kherson barricaded themselves therein. Vladimir halted at the farther side of the city beside the harbor, a bowshot from the town, and the inhabitants resisted energetically while Vladimir besieged the town. Eventually, however, they became exhausted, and Vladimir warned them that if they did not surrender, he would remain on the spot for three years. When they failed to heed this threat, Vladimir marshalled his troops and ordered the construction of an earthwork in the direction of the city. While this work was under construction, the inhabitants dug a tunnel under the city-wall, stole the heaped-up earth, and carried it into the city, where they piled it up in the center of the town. But the soldiers kept on building, and Vladimir persisted. Then a man of Kherson, Anastasius by name, shot into the Russ camp an arrow on which he had written, "There are springs behind you to the east, from which water flows in pipes. Dig down and cut them off." When Vladimir received this information, he raised his eyes to heaven and vowed that if this hope was realized, he would be baptized. He gave orders straightway to dig down above the pipes, and the water-supply was thus cut off. The inhabitants were accordingly overcome by thirst, and surrendered.

Vladimir and his retinue entered the city, and he sent messages to the Emperors Basil and Constantine, saying, "Behold, I have captured your glorious city. I have also heard that you have an unwedded sister. Unless you give her to me to wife, I shall deal with your own city as I have with Kherson." When the Emperors heard this message they were troubled, and replied, "It is not meet for Christians to give in marriage to pagans. If you are baptized, you shall have her to wife, inherit the kingdom of God, and be our companion in the faith. Unless you do so, however, we cannot give you our sister in marriage." When Vladimir learned their response, he directed the envoys of the Emperors to report to the latter that he was willing to accept baptism, having already given some study to their religion, and that the Greek faith and ritual, as described by the emissaries sent to examine it, had pleased him well. When the Emperors heard this report, they rejoiced, and persuaded their sister Anna to consent to the match. They then requested Vladimir to submit to baptism before they should send their sister to him, but Vladimir desired that the Princess should herself bring priests to baptize him. The Emperors complied with his request, and sent forth their sister, accompanied by some dignitaries and priests. Anna, however, departed with reluctance. "It is as if I were setting out into captivity," she lamented; "better were it for me to die at home." But her brothers protested, "Through your agency God turns the land of Rus' to repentance, and you will relieve Greece from the danger of grievous war. Do you not see how much harm the Russes have already brought upon the Greeks? If you do not set out, they may bring on us the same misfortunes. It was thus that they overcame her hesitation only with great difficulty. The Princess embarked upon a ship, and after tearfully embracing her kinfolk, she set forth across the sea and arrived at Kherson. The natives came forth to greet her, and conducted her into the city, where they settled her in the palace.

By divine agency, Vladimir was suffering at that moment from a disease of the eyes and could see nothing, being in great distress. The Princess declared to him that if he desired to be relieved of this disease, he should be baptized with all speed, otherwise it could not be cured. When Vladimir heard her message, he said, "If this proves true, then of a surety is the God of the Christians great," and gave order that he should be baptized. The Bishop of Kherson. together with the Princess's priests, after announcing the tidings, baptized Vladimir, and as the Bishop laid his hand upon him, he straightway received his sight. Upon experiencing this miraculous cure, Vladimir glorified God, saying, "I have now perceived the one true God." When his followers beheld this miracle, many of them were also baptized. . . .

CHAPTER 11

Polish Interference in Russia and its Aftermath

The Polish state created by Miezko in the tenth century showed great strength under his successor, Boleslav. In 1017, Boleslav marched into Russia in order to restore his son-in-law, Svyatopolk, to control of Kiev. Boleslav succeeded, but his son-in-law became restive at his presence and fomented a rebellion against Boleslav. Boleslav withdrew in disgust, and Svyatopolk was subsequently overthrown by his brother, Jarislav, in 1019. Despite its ulti-

mate failure, the Russian campaign was the most notable
exhibition of Polish power until that time.

Samuel Hazzard Cross and Olgerd Sherbowitz-Wetzor
(translators), THE RUSSIAN PRIMARY CHRONICLE, LAU-
RENTIAN TEXT (Cambridge, 1953), pp. 132–133.
Reprinted by permission of The Medieval Academy of
America.

(1018). Boleslav attacked Yaroslav with Svyatopolk and
his Lyakhs. After collecting Russes, Varangians, and Slavs,
Yaroslav marched forth against Boleslav and Svyatopolk,
and upon arriving at Volyn', they camped on either side
of the Bug. Now Yaroslav had with him his guardian and
general, Budy by name. He scoffed at Boleslav, remarking,
"We shall pierce your fat belly with a pike." For Boleslav
was big and heavy, so that he could scarcely sit a horse,
but he was crafty. So Boleslav said to his retainers, "If
you do not avenge this insult, I will perish alone," and
leaping upon his horse, he rode into the river and his retainers after him, while Yaroslav had no time to align
his troops, so that Boleslav vanquished him.

Then Yaroslav fled with four men to Novgorod, and Boleslav entered Kiev in company with Svyatopolk. Boleslav
ordered that his force should be dispersed to for-
age throughout the cities, and so it was done. When Yaroslav arrived at Novgorod in his flight, he planned to escape overseas, but the lieutenant Constantine, son of
Dobrynya, together with the men of Novgorod, destroyed
his boat, protesting that they wished to fight once more
against Boleslav and Svyatopolk. They set out to gather
funds at the rate of four *kuny* per commoner, ten *grivny*
from each elder, and eighteen *grivny* from each boyar.

With these funds they recruited Varangians whom they
imported, and thus collected for Yaroslav a large army.

While Boleslav was settled in Kiev, the impious Syvato-
polk ordered that any Lyakhs found in the city should
be killed, and so the Lyakhs were slain. Then Boleslav
fled from Kiev, taking with him the property and the boyars of Yaroslav, as well as the latter's two sisters, and
made Anastasius steward of the property, for the latter

had won his confidence by his flattery. He took with him a large company, and having appropriated to himself the cities of Cherven, he returned to his native land. Svyatopolk thus reigned alone in Kiev, but Yaroslav attacked him again, and Svatopolk fled among the Pechenegs.

(1019). Svyatopolk advanced with a large force of Pecheneg supporters, and Yaroslav collected a multitude of soldiery, and went forth against him to the Al'ta River. Yaroslav halted at the site were Boris had been slain and, lifting up his hands to heaven, exalimed, "The blood of my brother cries aloud to thee, oh Lord. Avenge the blood of this just man. Visit upon this criminal the sorrow and terror that thou didst inflict upon Cain to avenge the blood of Abel." Then he prayed and said, "My brethren, although ye be absent in the body, yet help me with your prayer against this presumptuous assassin." When he had thus spoken, the two armies attacked, and the plain of the Al'ta was covered with the multitudinous soldiery of both forces. It was then Friday. As the sun rose, they met in battle, and the carnage was terrible, such as had never before occurred in Rus'. The soldiers fought hand to hand and slaughtered each other. Three times they clashed, so that the blood flowed in the valley. Toward evening Yaroslav conquered, and Svyatopolk fled.

As he fled a devil came upon him and his bones were softened so that he could not ride, but was carried in a litter. His retainers bore him to Brest in his flight, but he still cried out, "Fly with me, they are pursuing us!" His servants sent back to see who was pursuing them, and there was actually no one following their trail, but still they fled on with him. He lay in a faint, and when he recovered, he still cried out, "Run, they are pursuing us!" He could not endure to stay in one place, but fled through the land of the Lyakhs, pursued by the wrath of God. Upon reaching the wilderness between Poland and Bohemia, he died a miserable death. When judgment thus rightly fell upon him as a sinner, torments seized this impious prince after his departure from this world. That is clearly proved by the fatal wound which was dealt him and which mercilessly drove him to his end; and since his death he abides in bonds and in torment everlasting.

His tomb is in the wilderness even to this day, and an evil odor issues forth from it. . . .

CHAPTER 12

The Mission of St. Gerard in Hungary

St. Gerard of Csanád gained fame for his successful organization of the church in eleventh-century Hungary. Born in northern Italy, he entered the Benedictine Order and served as abbot of the Abbey of San Georgio at Venice. In 1015, he became the tutor of Emeric, the son of King Stephen I of Hungary. In 1035, the Diocese of Csanad was established with Gerard as its first bishop. As bishop, he founded many parishes and monasteries that were often staffed by foreigners. After the death of King Stephen, Gerard was martyred at Buda on September 24, 1046. The *Lessons of St. Gerard*, in a liturgical context, relate the story of the revered saint's life and martyrdom.

Stephanus Ladislaus Endlicher (editor), RERUM HUNGARICARUM MONUMENTA ARPADIANA (Sankt Gallen, 1849; Reissued Leipzig: Verlag Karl W. Hierseman, 1931), pp. 202–204. Translated by the editors.

Lesson I . . . This man (St. Gerard) was born of Venetian parents, and through the grace of God, he was entirely devoted to Jesus Christ and followed from his earliest years the commandments laid down in Holy Scripture. And this was so because he took the religious habit as a boy and did not succumb to the sinfulness of the first parents. He followed that way by which the new man is formed to the wishes of God and having avoided the temptation to disobey God, he tried to love the joys of divine contemplation even as a young man. . . .
Lesson III. Finally, he arrived in Pannonian parts in

the reign of Stephen, the most Christian king, whom the humble man of the Lord sought out beseechingly and told the cause of his journey. And he was received by the king with a special love and affection. When the king saw that he was of high morals and great discipline, one who had the odour of sanctity, the king secretly dismissed, against St. Gerard's will, those who had accompanied him on his journey; St. Gerard had to remain behind, and he was put under custody. When the servant of the Lord found that he was alone, avoiding the people, he went into a hermitage commonly called Beel where for seven years he devoted himself to fasting and prayer. And he lived completely alone with the exception of the monk, Maurice.

Lesson IV. In the meantime, king Stephen, like a most powerful Joshua, suppressed the impiety of his subjects and overcame the bad morals of the pagans, and prepared the hearts of many for the seeds of the Holy Faith. When the king saw that his kingdom had acquired the tranquility of peace, he called the servant of the Lord from the hermitage, gave him bishop's regalia, and asked him to preach to the people. To St. Gerard, the supernatural piety confirmed such a grace that all the inhabitants of the place started to love him uniquely and worshipped him like a father. And quickly, this father of many was considered like the patriarch, Abraham.

Lesson V. When the number of the faithful increased, he built houses of worship in each town. The main church was dedicated to St. George, the most precious martyr of Christ, and it was built on the side of the river Maros. Therefore, the see was called Maros to which the holy king, Stephen, donated many great and noble gifts. In this church, in honor of the Saviour's Mother, he erected a holy altar before which a silver censer was placed. And he employed two old men to be vigilant that not even for one hour should the incense not be distributed.

Lesson VI. After the death of the holy king, Stephen, a rebellion broke out in Pannonia. The holy man, St. Gerard, left the town of Alba, and arrived at the church of Saint Sabina where he told the brothers then at dinner: "Our friends, tomorrow we will be called to the dinner of the Lamb, and therefore, without excuse, we should not

hesitate to die for Christ." The next day, after he celebrated Mass, he joyfully proceeded toward martyrdom.
When, therefore, he arrived at the river Danube, a large
crowd of evil men surrounded him. They threw rocks at
him as he sat in a chariot. Then, trying to hold his horses
in check, the chariot overturned and the bishop fell to the
ground. But, kneeling on the earth, he shouted with a clear
voice: "Lord Jesus Christ, do not blame them for they
know not what they do." And when he said this, he was
struck in the breast by a lance, and became the first martyr
of Pannonia and died in the Lord. Amen.

CHAPTER 13

The Advice of St. Stephen to His Son, Duke Imre

On Christmas Day, 1000 A.D., Stephen, with the blessing
of Pope Sylvester II, was crowned as the first King of
Hungary. Baptized by St. Adalbert of Prague in 985, Stephen succeeded his father, Geza, as ruler of the Magyars
in 997. A member of the Arpad dynasty, Stephen laid the
foundations of an important medieval state, and his saintli-
ness and practicality made him the most revered figure
in Hungarian history.

Stephen's *Instructions* to his son represent the most re-
vealing view of his insights and the way that he ruled.
He was obviously acquainted with theology. His admoni-
tions against anti-Trinitarians make one suspect that he
was dusting off some bits of information that had more
relevance in the time of the Arians, but even the newly
converted Magyars may have questioned the doctrine of
the Trinity.

Stephen also appreciated the unique position of Hungary,
a land without enough people and yet surrounded by po-
tentially troublesome neighbors. While he counselled that
foreigners should be allowed to settle in Hungary, he did
not think of building an empire. When he said that "the

presence of foreigners is good because the country of only one language and one custom is weak and frail," he not only meant to "curb the arrogance of enemies," but to enhance the cultural diversity of the realm.

Stephanus Ladislaus Endlicher (editor), RERUM HUNGARI-CARUM MONUMENTA ARPADIANA (Sankt Gallen, 1849; Reissued Leipzig: Verlag Karl W. Hierseman, 1931), pp. 299–309. Translated by the editors.

Chapter 1

Because nobody can succeed to the royal dignity except those instructed in and faithful to the Catholic faith, therefore, in our instructions we give the first place to the holy faith. First, I advise and command, my dearest son, that if you wish to have the royal crown enhanced by honesty, you should conserve and observe the Catholic and Apostolic faith with such diligence that you will become an example to all those subjected to you by God. And thus, all men of the church will call you a genuine son of the Christian faith; if this be not so, you cannot be called a Christian and a son of the church.

Those with a false faith, those who do not fulfill and elaborate the faith with good works because faith dies without good works—those neither rule on earth honestly nor do they participate in the crown of the eternal kingdom. And on the other hand, if you retain the shield of the faith, you will also have the helmet of salvation. With these weapons, you will be able to fight legitimately against visible and invisible enemies. For, as the apostle says, "Nobody will be crowned who did not wage the good fight."

If you find any among your subjects—and I hope this will not be the case—who tried to divide, diminish, or increase belief in the Holy Trinity, you should realize they are followers of the arch-heretic and they are not children of the Holy Church. You should not support or defend them else you will appear to be an enemy of God.

Chapter 2

In the royal palace, after the faith, the church which was first instituted by Christ is given our next consideration. Afterwards, through its members who were the apostles and the Holy Fathers, the Church was transplanted, firmly established, and spread over the entire world. And although it always has new converts, in other places, nevertheless, it is considered something ancient. But here, my most beloved son, in our monarchy, still it is young and new as when first preached. Therefore, it needs custodians who are more careful and watchful that the good which was conceded by divine clemency, through His immense mercy—conceded to us who do not deserve it—through your inefficiency, negligence, and sloth not be destroyed and annihilated. For he who diminishes and disfigures the dignity of the Holy Church is one who wants to mutilate the body of Christ. The Lord Himself told Peter whom he placed as custodian and master of the Holy Church: "You are Peter and upon this rock I will build my Church." If some unhappy person scandalizes the members of the children of this Holy Church, according to the gospel, it is ordered that a millstone, carried by the donkeys, should be placed on his neck, and he should be thrown into the depths of the sea. That is, he should be expelled from the power of dignity and should stay outside the church of the just. In that worldly misery, he should be like a pagan and a tax collector. Therefore, my son, with great vigilance, you must be watchful for the Holy Church, from day to day, that it may increase rather than decrease. The kings were called august ones (augusti) because they added to the Church. You should do likewise so that your crown may be more praiseworthy and that life may be happier and more abundant.

Chapter 3 About the Honor That Should Be Given to the Bishops

The royal throne is glorified through the power of the bishops. The bishops are therefore our third consideration in the question of the royal dignity. My dear son, you should treat them as your superiors. You should respect them and protect them as you would your own eyesight. If you have their goodwill, you will not fear any adversaries. When they watch over you, you will be safe. In everything, their prayer will recommend you to Almighty God because God made them the custodians of the human race, the bishops who safeguard souls, who are the formulators and givers of all the ecclesiastical dignities and divine sacraments. Without this, neither kings nor principalities are truly constituted. Through them, by their intervention, the sins of man are forgiven. If you love them in a perfect way, no doubt you will purify yourself, and you will govern your kingdom in an honorable way. In their hands is placed the power to leave us in our sins or absolve us from sins. God placed them in an everlasting testament, God made them aloof from the mass of humanity and made them participants in sharing His own name and holiness. And God forbade that they should be reprehended and corrected by man thriugh the divinely-appointed king, David: "You should not touch My annointed ones." Anyone who touches the anointed of God, the man of the most sacred order, in such wise that the bishop loses dignity through false accusations and the faithful are scandalized; that evil man proceeds both against divine and canonical institutions. I absolutely forbid you to ever act like this, my son. If you wish to live happily, if you wish to have a pure reign, you should remember that when you offend the bishops, you offend God Himself. If it still happens that any of them act in such a manner as to deserve criticism, and of course, I hope no such thing ever happens, admonish him three of four times, according to the precept of the Bible, while giving no general publicity to the problem. If he does not wish to listen to your counsel and corrections given diplomatically, you must therefore use public means. If he does not heed you, let the whole church know. For if you observe the divinely-ordered position, you will **perfectly exalt your glorious crown.**

Chapter 4 On the Honor of Princes and Soldiers

The fourth adornment of monarchy is the fidelity, fortitude, efficiency, brotherly love, and wisdom of the princes, counts and soldiers. They are the strength of the realm, defenders of the weak, fighters of enemies, and the augmenters of the marks (boundaries or border areas). They are, my son, brothers and fathers. None of them should you place in servitude or treat as servants. They should fight for you, not serve you. You should rule them without anger, pride, or envy, but peacefully, humbly, with meekness, remembering that all men are human. And while your humility will inspire them, pride and envy will make them despair. If you will be peaceful, then you will deserve the name of king—and be called the son of the king—and the soldiers will love you. If you are angry, proud, envious, unpacific, and if you are haughty to the counts and princes, without doubt, the strength of the soldiers will then be a weakness of the crown, and your kingdom will be given to others. Being fearful of this, you should virtuously direct the counts that they may be chained through your love, always be solicitous for the kingdom's welfare, and never commit crimes. And thus your kingdom should always remain tranquil.

Chapter 5 On the Observance of Justice and Patience

The fifth ornament of the royal crown is the observance of patience and justice. David, the king and prophet, says: "God, give Your judgment to the king," and on another occasion, he says: "The honor of the king loves Your judgment." About patience, the Apostle Paul said: "Be patient to everybody." And Our Lord in the gospel: "In your patience, you will possess your souls." You should be attentive to this, my son, for if you wish to have the honor of the kingdom then you should love justice. If you want to save your soul, practice patience. Anytime, my most beloved son, if a cause comes before you for judgment or if somebody is guilty of a capital crime, do not behave impatiently. You will punish him—whose oath must be unstable and frail—because stupid pledges should be broken. Neither should you judge by yourself lest your regal dignity be stained by dealing with insignificant matters, but rather you should delegate such matters to the judges whose duty it is to deal with them according to the laws. Be afraid to be a judge; enjoy being a king and deserving of the royal name. Patient kings rule, impatient kings tryannize. If something arises that is worthy of being judged by you, you should handle the case with patience and mercy. Thus, your crown may be praised and honored.

Chapter 6 On Accepting and Supporting Foreigners

In aliens and newcomers there is such a great usefulness that worthily it may be called the sixth ornament of the royal dignity. The Roman Empire increased thuswise, and the rulers became great and glorious because many noble and wise men from other lands came under their rule. Rome would have been still like a slave if Aeneas had not freed her. Since foreigners come from different parts and provinces, they bring with them different languages, habits, laws, and weapons which all decorate and augment the royal power and curb the arrogance of enemies. And the presence of foreigners is good because the country of only one language and one custom is weak and frail. Therefore, my son, I order that you should feed them and honor them with goodwill so that they will prefer to live in your realm rather than any other place. If you destroy what I have built or you dissipate what I have brought together, without doubt, your realm will suffer the consequences of your actions. That this should not happen, daily do something that increases your kingdom so that your crown may be held in high esteem by all.

Chapter 7 About the Importance of Counsel

In royal tribunals, counsel should hold seventh place. Through counsel are the kings selected, kingdoms determined, the country defended, wars decided, victory won, enemies repelled, allies found, cities founded, and camps of enemies destroyed. However, under what conditions is counsel useful? Dull-witted, arrogant and mediocre men, it seems, cannot enrich counsel given to the king, which good counsel comes from better, more significant men. Good ministers are completely honest and wise seniors who give counsel that is articulate and can be refined.

Therefore, my son, don't ask advice of young people and others lacking in wisdom but ask advice of older people whose views, because of their age and wisdom, are more gracious. Because the counsels of the king are locked in the minds of wise men, they cannot be obtained from the minds of the young or less wise. If you follow wise men, you become a wise man yourself. And if you converse with inferior minds, you will become similar to them. And the Holy Spirit said it to Solomon, and David sings: "With the holy man, you will be holy, with the innocent man, you will be innocent, with the distinguished man, you will be distinguished, and with the perverse man, you will be perverse." And besides this, whatever is appropriate to a certain age, those of that age should do. Accordingly, young men should be adept with weapons, older ones in the giving of counsel. However, young men should not be completely neglected when it is a matter of accepting their counsel. But, when you speak with them, even if the counsel is good, that counsel should be told to older men so that you may measure all your actions by the standard of wisdom.

Chapter 8 Elders Should Be Imitated and Children Should Be Obedient to Their Parents

The imitation of elders in the royal dignity must occupy the eighth place. It is the greatest royal ornament to follow the laws of predecessors and to imitate honest parents. He who despises the decrees of his ancestors despises the laws of his fathers, nor does he observe divine laws, either. Fathers, therefore, are to nourish their sons, and children, therefore, are to be obedient to their parents. He who is disobedient to his father is an enemy of God. In effect, all in a state of disobedience resist the will of God. The spirit of disobedience scatters the launch of the crown. Disobedience is the scourge of the entire kingdom. Therefore, my most beloved son, the decrees of your father, my orders, should be for you, decrees that you are prompt to fulfill. Thus, your prosperity will always be directed by royal reins. My behavior, which you see is appropriate to the royal dignity, you should imitate without any trace of ambiguity. It is difficult for you to have royal rule over this country if you are not an imitator of those kings who preceded you. What Greek would rule the Latins with Greek customs, or what Latin would rule the Greeks with Latin customs? Therefore, follow my manner of acting so that among your people you will be held in esteem, and among foreigners, you will be held as praiseworthy.

Chapter 9   On the Observation of Prayer

The observation of prayer is the greatest sign of royal health and therefore, is the ninth point. And so in the ninth rule of dignity, the following is said: You, my son, who will many times go into the church to adore God, should always say, as did Solomon, the son of a king, who was himself the son of a king: "Show, oh Lord, wisdom from the seed of your greatness, that it may stay with me and work with me, that I may know what is acceptable to you for all time." And again: "Lord, father and God of my life, do not let me fall into your disfavor. Don't give me proudness in my vision and evil desire, turn away from me. Lord, take from me concupiscence and do not let me have traffic with a soul that is irreverent and perverse." The ancients used to recite this prayer. You should use the same prayer, so that will relieve you of all vices, that you may be called by all the king without any defects. Pray also that God will drive from you sloth and instability and that he replace these vices with the virtues with which you will be able to defeat all visible and invisible enemies, and make you always secure against all incursions of your adversaries. Thus with all your subjects, you may finish the course of your life in peace.

Chapter 10 On Piety, Mercy, and the Other Virtues

The measure of virtues is the finishing touch on the royal crown, and in the precepts, is placed tenth. Because the lord of virtues is the King of Kings Himself, and as the celestial armies' fullness consists in the ten choirs, so, the course of your life should follow ten commandments. It is necessary that the king be pious and merciful and endowed with the other virtues. The king who is stained with impiety and cruelty, will, in vain, try to be called a king for all will call him a tyrant. Therefore, my most beloved son, the sweetness of my heart, the hope of the future generation, I pray, I order that in every matter at every time you will be supported by piety. Not only before immediate and future relationships, but before princes and dukes, and before neighbors and subjects. You may be merciful with aliens and everyone else who comes to you, because pious works lead to the greatest happiness. Be merciful to all who are oppressed always having this example in your heart: "I want mercy and not sacrifice." Be patient to all, not only to the powerful persons but also to those who lack power. Finally, be strong so that prosperity will not blow you up with pride. And neither should adversity make you despair. Be also humble so that God may place you in a high place both here and in the future. Be truly moderate so that you punish nobody beyond measure. Be meek so that you will never resist justice. Be honest so that you will not hurt anybody with an impulsive affront. Be chaste so that you will avoid all the unclean features of passion that bring death.

All the things enumerated above constitute the royal crown. Without them nobody is able to rule here nor arrive at the eternal kingdom.

CHAPTER 14

The Treatment of Jews in Medieval Hungary

This law of King Coloman (1095–1116) represented one of his many attempts to bring order to his kingdom. While the law seems to be directed against the Jews, they are given some protection against unscrupulous Christians.

Stephanus Ladislaus Endlicher (editor), RERUM HUNGARI-CARUM MONUMENTA ARPADIANA (Sankt Gallen, 1849; Reissued Leipzig: Verlag Karl W. Hierseman, 1931), pp. 371–372. Translated by the editors.

1. Henceforward, no Jew should presume to buy or sell a Christian slave, no matter what might be the Christian's language or nationality. Neither may any Jew retain a Christian slave in his service. If any Jew violates this law, he should pay damages to the Christian slave found in his service.

2. If a Christian loans money to a Jew, or vice versa, and the amount of the loan is two or three pensos then the borrower should receive from the loaner a vadimonium. Also, Christians and Jews should be brought forth as witnesses so that if one party denies the loan, it should be proved not by the vadimonium but by the witnesses of both parties.

3. But if it is so that more than three pensos were loaned, then the vadimonium and the witnesses must be the same as before. And the names of witnesses and the amount should be written on a paper to which should then be affixed the seal of both the loaner and the borrower. Thus, if one wishes to use force against the other, the truth should be confirmed by the paper to which the seals have been affixed.

4. If a Jew wishes to buy something from a Christian, or vice versa, the transaction should take place before reli-

able Jewish and Christian witnesses, the transaction should be recorded with the names of the witnesses, and then should be properly sealed. Thus, if someone should later be accused of theft, the document should be produced by the accused one. And if the document is correct and the witnesses uphold it, the accused person cannot be punished.

5. If the accused one cannot produce the original owner of the apparently stolen object, he must show the document with the names of the witnesses therein inscribed. Thus, through the oaths of the witnesses, he should escape punishment.

6. If the accused did not have Christian witnesses and the Jew produced suitable witnesses, then the Jew, because of the witnesses, is considered correct and the accused should pay as settlement four times the value of the stolen object.

7. If the accused cannot find the owner of the object in question, nor produce the document properly sealed, after being judged according to the custom of the country, he must pay as a fine twelve times the value of the stolen object.

CHAPTER 15

Hungary's Magna Carta—The Golden Bull of 1222

The Golden Bull of 1222 is one of the most important constitutional documents of Hungarian history. Extracted from a weak king, Andrew II, it did not tremendously diminish the monarch's power. The aim of those who sought the Golden Bull was to increase their power vis-à-vis the great nobles, the common people and the king. In our translation, we use the word 'noblemen' to indicate the class that gained greater privileges through the Golden Bull. In the document, the term used is 'servants of the king.'

Stephanus Ladislaus Endlicher (editor), RERUM HUNGAR-
ICUM MONUMENTA ARPADIANA (Sankt Gallen, 1849; Reissued Leipzig: Verlag Karl W. Hierseman, 1931),
pp. 420-423. Translated by the editors.

In the name of the Holy Trinity and Undivided Unity,
Andrew, hereditary successor, king by the grace of God
of Hungary, Dalmatia, Croatia, Bosnia, Serbia, Galicia, and
Lodomeria. As the liberty instituted by St. Stephen, of
many nobles of our kingdom as of others also, has been
arbitrarily diminished on many points by some kings who
on occasion satisfied their personal feelings and at other
times listened to the advice of disloyal men who only sought
their own interest; our nobles themselves have many a
time asked the ears of our serenity and those of their kings,
our predecessors, to give audience to their requests and
numerous demands with regard to bringing about reforms
in our kingdom and thus wishing to satisfy their repeated
entreaties in all things as we are held to do especially
since there is aroused between us and you on such occasions great bitterness which it is expedient to avoid in
order to keep more fully the royal dignity (for this cannot
be done any better than by them [the nobles]), we grant
to them as well as to the other dwellers of our kingdom
the liberty given by the holy king, and we regulate with
regard to the reform of the state of our kingdom, the following salutary measures:

1. We establish that we shall be obliged to hold a solemn
assembly at royal Albe every year on the feast of the holy
king unless we are hindered by some urgent business or
by sickness; and if we cannot attend in person the palatine
will without fail take our place and will listen to the cases
in our stead and all the nobles who wish it will freely
gather there.

2. We also wish that neither we nor our successors at
any time arrest noblemen, nor ruin them in favor of some
powerful magnate if they had not previously received a
summons or been convicted by means of judicial forms.

3. Moreover, we shall not levy any taxes or head money
on the estates of the nobles, and we shall only stay at

their house or in their domain when they invite us to do so. We shall neither levy taxes on clerics.

4. If a nobleman dies without a son, his daughter shall have a quarter of his possessions, he shall dispose of the rest as he sees fit, and if death prevents him of the deposition of his goods, they will go to his nearest relatives. And if he has absolutely no posterity, they will belong to the king.

5. The counts will not have the authority to pass any judgment on the goods of the nobles, unless it be cases concerning legal tender or tithes. The lieutenants of the counts will not have the authority to judge anybody except their own people. Thieves and highwaymen will be judged by royal judges but under the personal presidency of the count.

6. Furthermore he will not have the right to initiate an inquiry with regard to the denunciation of thieves, as is the custom, by the oath of the gathered populace.

7. If the king intends to lead an army out of the kingdom, the nobles will not be obliged to go with him unless it be at his own expense. And upon his return he will not have the right to impose upon them a fine by means of a royal military declaration. But if an enemy army threatens the safety of the kingdom all will be obliged to render military service. Item, if we should wish to lead an army out of the kingdom and we march in person with the army all those who hold a county will be under obligation to accompany us at our own expense.

8. The palatine will judge without discrimination all the inhabitants of the kingdom, but cases involving the noblemen's lives or the confiscation of their goods will not be decided without the consent of the king. He will not be replaced by anyone to enforce justice except for one designated person at his own court.

9. Our curial count, as long as he remains at court, will have the right to judge everybody at any place and bring to a finish a case started at court. But when he is residing on his lands he will neither be empowered to give a commission to a bailiff nor start judicial proceedings.

10. If a man who received land for military service dies while in the army, his son or his brother will be bestowed

a similar dignity. And if a nobleman dies in the same fashion, his son will be rewarded as it pleases the king.

11. If foreigners, men of worth come into the kingdom, they will not be promoted to high positions without the concurrence of the diet of the kingdom.

12. The wives of the deceased, those given the death penalty, or those who perish in judicial combat will not be stripped for any reason of their dowry.

13. When the vassals follow the court or when they go to wherever it may be, the poor will neither be oppressed nor despoiled by them.

14. Item, if a count does not behave honorably as the duty of his charge demands it, or if he oppresses the people under his administration, having been convicted of this, he will be dishonorably discharged from his position in the presence of the entire kingdom and condemned to restore that which he had taken away.

15. Our squires, hound masters, and falconers will not have the right to penetrate into the lands of the nobles.

16. We shall not confer any entire county nor any high position with an hereditary title nor as anyone's private property.

17. No one will ever be stripped of goods that he acquired in return for rendering genuine services.

18. Item, the nobles can with our permission appear before our son, from the greatest to the least, and they will not, for this, risk the loss of their goods. We shall not receive any man who is constantly condemned by our son, nor any trial that was started under him and not terminated. Our son for his part will act the same way.

19. The vassals will maintain the privileges that were established by the king, St. Stephen: the same holds for foreign colonists of all nations; privileges that were given to them initially will be maintained.

20. The tithes will not be redeemed in money but will be rendered by means of farm produce such as wine or grain, and if the bishops set themselves against this, we will not help them.

21. The bishops will not be obliged to give for our cavalry the same tithes provided by the nobles nor will their people (servants) be obliged to bring their tithes to the royal domains.

22. Item, our hogs will not be allowed to graze in the forests and meadows of the nobles without their consent.

23. Item, our new currency will be in effect for one year from Easter to Easter and the coins will be such as they were in the time of king Béla.

24. The count of the chamber of legal tender and those in charge of the salt taxes and customs will be nobles of our kingdom. They will be taken neither from the Ismaelites nor the Jews.

25. Item, the salt will not be stored in the interior of the country, but only at Szabolcs, Regécz, and on the borders.

26. Item, no domains can be transferred to foreigners; if some have been conferred or sold, they must be offered to the people of the kingdom who may purchase them.

27. The tax on skins of marten will be paid according to the custom established by king Coloman.

28. If someone has been regularly condemned by legal action, no power will be able to protect him.

29. The counts will benefit only from the revenues of the county. The king will collect all the other revenues which belong to him such as wine, customs, cattle, and two-thirds of the revenues of cities.

30. Item, with the exception of four vassals, the palatine, the ban, and the curial counts of the king and the queen, no one will be invested with a double dignity.

31. And so that this concession and ordinance may last forever during our own lifetime and also those of our successors, we have set it down in seven copies and sealed them with our golden seal: so that one may be sent to the lord, the Pope, so that he may file it among his records; the second to the hospitalers; the third to the templars; the fourth to the king; the fifth to the chapter at Esztergom; the sixth will go to Kalocsa; the seventh will be kept by the palatine in office so that having the text right under his eyes, he may not deviate from any of the prescriptions contained within, nor suffer that the king, the nobles, or others violate it, so that they may enjoy their privileges and thus remain faithful to us and also to our successors without refusing the legitimate obedience to the royal crown. If we or any of our successors ever

wish to subtract from this ordinance, the bishops, the other
vassals and nobles of our kingdom, all together or separately, in the present or the future, will have in virtue
of this ordinance, and without running the risk of appearing unfaithful, the freedom to resist us or contradict us
and our successors.

Given by the hands of Cletus, chancellor of our court
and provost of the church of Eger, in the year of the
Incarnation, 1222, when the venerable John was archbishop
of Esztergom, the reverend Ugrin of Kalocsa; Desider, bishop of Csanád; Robert of Veszprém; Thomas of Eger; Stephen of Alba Julia; Bartholemew of Pécs; Cosmos of Györ;
Bereck of Vácz; Vincent of Nyitra; the seventeenth year of
our reign.

CHAPTER 16

The Position of the Saxon Minority in Transylvania

In this document, King Andrew II reconfirmed the rights
given to the Saxons of Transylvania in the twelfth century.
It is apparent from the document that Magyar magnates
were depriving the Saxons of their freedom. And just as
the lower nobility had done in 1222, the Saxons were able
to sway Andrew to take their side. The Saxons had been
settled in Transylvania to serve as a militia force against
possible Byzantine invasions and had performed this role
quite successfully in the middle of the twelfth century. In
return for their services, the Saxons were given a privileged
status which they jealously guarded.

Stephanus Ladislaus Endlicher (editor), RERUM HUN-
GARICARUM MONUMENTA ARPADIANA (Sankt
Gallen, 1849; Re-issued Leipzig: Verlag Karl W. Hierse-
man, 1931), pp. 420–423. Translated by the editors.

In the name of the Holy Trinity, Three Persons in One God, Andrew, by the grace of God, king forever of Hungary, Dalmatia, Croatia, Bosnia, Serbia, Galicia, and Lodomeria. As it belongs to the crown to combat the stubbornness of proud individuals, so it belongs to the royal benevolence to mercifully give relief to those who are oppressed, reward the service of those who have been faithful, and give justice to all as they deserve it. Our loyal guests, Germans in Transylvania, come to us on their knees humbly presenting their grievances that they have lost all the freedom which enticed them to come to Transylvania at the invitation of the pious king Geza. And unless we open our eyes in our customary kindness, it is evident that because of extreme poverty, these people cannot render us any service. We, therefore, deem it necessary to follow our usual path of kindness and listen to their just complaints. We will that it come to the notice of all, now and in the future, that we, adhering to the laws of our ancestors and moved by kindness, give back to the Saxons their former freedom. And that freedom is given according to these regulations:

1. That all the people from Vaross to Baralt, with the land of Székely, and the lands called Szebus and Daraus should constitute one people, under one judge and all counties besides Czeben should cease completely their existence.

2. The Count of Czeben should not presume to appoint as a judge in the above mentioned counties anyone who is not a resident thereof, has not been elected by the people thereof, and is not capable. In the county of Czeben, nobody should dare to buy the office of judge....

5. They should not refuse to give to royal nuncios sent to collect taxes, for each day of their stay, three lotones for their daily expense.

6. Five hundred soldiers for use in the kingdom must be given, one hundred for outside the kingdom if the king personally leads the army. But if a king's servant is sent out of the kingdom, either to help his friend, or on his own business, only 50 soldiers should be sent by the Saxons to accompany him.

7. They should freely elect their priests and those elected should be paid tithes. And with regard to any case involving ecclesiastical law, age-old custom should be followed.

8. We will and order firmly that nobody should judge the churchmen, only ourself or the Count of Czeben, whom we will appoint to do so at a suitable place and time.

9. If it happens that they were judged by any other, they are obliged only to sentencing on minor cases. Nobody can cite them before us unless their case could not have been terminated before their own judge.

10. We grant them only one seal that will be validly recognized by ourself and our magnate.

11. If somebody in a case involving money sues someone else, he can use as witnesses only persons who live within their boundaries. . . .

14. We will and order, with royal authority, that none of our servants may demand a villa or landed estate. If somebody makes such a demand on the people, it should thus be refused to them by the Saxons.

15. Besides this, we order that the Saxons, when we visit them, must offer us hospitality at three places. But if the Voivoda goes through their land on royal service, they should offer hospitality at two places, when he arrives and when he leaves.

16. We add further to the above freedoms that their merchants may go freely everywhere in our kingdom, asserting their rights on account of this royal grant. Further, we order that all their business transactions may be accomplished without paying levies.

That the above statement may hold true for posterity, the present document is confirmed by our double seal— 1224.

CHAPTER 17

The Tartar Menace in the Thirteenth Century

Kievan Russia suffered a severe reversal of fortunes with the Tartar occupation of the thirteenth century. The following story shows the cruelty and religious intolerance of the Tartars whose ferocity was so great that it virtually paralyzed European opposition. The Tartars invaded both Poland and Hungary in 1241. Though only 30,000 attacked Poland, they succeeded in occupying most of the country. Hungary suffered the same fate at the hands of Batu Khan's army despite all the efforts of King Bela IV (1235–1270). No aid was given to Poland and Hungary by their western neighbors, and both nations were only saved by the death of the Golden Horde's Khan, Ogotai. In 1242, Batu Khan withdrew his troops so that he might participate in the contest for power over the Horde in Asia. The easy triumphs of the Tartars demonstrated the fragile character of the Polish and Hungarian states and may have contributed to a more responsible quest for centralized authority.

Robert Michell and Nevill Forbes (translators), THE CHRONICLE OF NOVGOROD, 1016–1471 (London: Camden Society, 1914), Camden Third Series, Vol. XXV, pp. 88–92.

Tsar Baty killed *Knyaz* Mikhail of Cherigov and his *Voyevoda* Fedor in the Horde on September 18. And the killing of them was like this. There was an invasion of pagan Tartars into the Russian Land; and these shut themselves in the towns. And envoys came from *Tsar* Baty to Mikhail, who then held Kiev; and he, seeing their words of deceit, ordered them to be killed and himself fled with his family to Hungary; and some fled to distant parts; and others hid in caves and forests, and few of them stayed behind; and these after some time settled in the towns; and they counted their number and began to levy tribute upon them. And *Knyaz* Mikhail having heard this, he brought back the people who had fled on all sides to strange lands, and they came to their own land. And the Tartars began to summon them with insistence to go to Baty, saying of them: "It is not meet for you to live in the land of the *Khan* and of Baty without doing homage to them." And many having gone bowed. And Baty had this custom of the *Khan's:* If any one came to do obeisance, he would not order him to be brought before him, but wizards used to be ordered to bring them through fire and make them bow to a bush and to fire; and whatever anyone brought with him for the *Tsar*, the wizards used to take some of everything and throw it into the fire, and then they used to let them go before the *Tsar* with their gifts. And many *Knyazes* with their *Boyars* passed through the fire, and bowed to the bush, their idols, for the glory of this world, and each asked of them power and they used to give it to them without dispute, that they might deceive them with the glory of this world. And the most reverend *Knyaz* Mikhail being then in Chernigov, and seeing many deceived by the glory world, God sent grace and the gift of the Holy Spirit upon him; He put into his heart to go before the *Tsar* Baty and to denounce his deceit with which he deceived the Christians. And he came to his spiritual father and told him saying: "I wish to go to *Tsar* Baty." His spiritual father answered him: "Many having gone have done the will of the pagan *Tsar* Baty, deceived by the glory of this world; went through the fire and bowed to the sun and to the bush, and destroyed their souls and bodies. And thou, my son, Mikhail, if thou wilt go, do not thus, as the others; go not through the fire; bow not to their idols, nor eat their food, nor take their drink between thy lips, but confess the Christian faith, for it becometh not Christians to bow to anything, but only to our Lord Jesus Christ." And Mikhail and his *Voyevoda* said to him: "By they prayer, father, as God wills so be it; I would like to pour out my blood for Christ and for the Christian faith." His *Voyevoda* Fedor spoke likewise. Their spiritual father said to them: "You two will be fresh holy martyrs

in the present generation for the confirmation of faithful people, if you do thus." Mikhail and Fedor his *Voyevoda* promised to do thus and were blessed by their spiritual
father. Then their father gave them the holy communion
for the journey, calling it pre-sanctified and having blessed
them, dismissed them and said to them: "May God give
strength to you and may God for whom you are eager
to suffer send you help." Then Mikhail came to his house,
and took from his goods what he needed. And going
through many lands they yet reached *Tsar* Baty. And they
told Baty: "The Russian *Veliki Knyaz* Mikhail has come
to bow to thee." And *Tsar* Baty ordered them to bring
his wizards; and the wizards having come before the *Tsar*,
the *Tsar* said to them: "As it is according to our custom,
do to *Knyaz* Mikhail, and then bring him before me." And
they having gone to Mikhail, saying to him: "The *Tsar*
Baty summons thee." And he having taken his *Voyevoda*
Fedor, went with him, and having reached the place where
fire was laid on both sides, many pagans were going through
the fire, and were bowing to the sun and to the idols.
And the wizards led Mikhail and his *Voyevoda* Fedor
through the fire. Mikhail said to them: "It does not become
Christians to go through fire and to bow to the idols, to
which these bow; such is the Christian religion, not to
bow to any thing nor to idols, but to bow to the Trinity:
to the Father, the Son, and the Holy Ghost." And Mikhail
said to his *Voyevoda* Fedor: "Better it is for us not to
bow to the things to which these bow." And they having
left them at the place to which they had been brought,
went to tell *Tsar* Baty: "Mikhail the *Veliki Knyaz* does
not listen to thy command, does not go through the fire
and does now bow to thy gods: he says, it does not become Christians to go through the fire, nor do they bow
to things, neither to the sun nor to idols, but they bow
to the Father who made all things, to the Son, and to
the Holy Ghost." And *Tsar* Baty grew very angry, he
sent one of his nobles, his steward named Eldega, and he
said: "Why hast thou made nought of my command, and
hast not bowed to my gods, but from this moment choose
for thyself life or death; if thou keepest my command thou
shalt both live and shalt receive all they princedom, but

if thou wilt not go through the fire, nor bow to the bush and to the idols then thou shalt die by a cruel death." Then Mikhail answered: "To thee, *Tsar*, I bow, since God hath granted thee the sovereignty of this world, but to the things to which these bow I shall not bow." And Eldega, the *Tsar's* steward, said to him: "Mikhail, beware: thou art dead." And Mikhail answered him: "Indeed, I wish to suffer for Christ and to shed my blood for the true faith." Then said Boris, *Knyaz* of Rostov, to Mikhail with much weeping: "My lord father, do the *Tsar's* will." Then likewise the *Boyars* of Boris also said: "We will all receive public penance for thee with all our power." Then Mikhail answered: "Brothers, I do not wish to call myself a Christian by name only and to do the work of pagans; but on the contrary I believe in Christ the only God." When Mikhail had said this, his *Voyevoda* Fedor began to think in himself saying: "What if Mikhail should grow weak by the prayer of these men, remembering the love of his wife and the caresses of his children?" Then remembering the words of his spiritual father, Fedor said to Mikhail: "Dost thou remember the word of our spiritual father which he taught us from the holy gospels? The Lord said: 'he that desireth to save his soul shall destroy it, and he that destroyeth his soul shall save it.' And again, he said: 'what shall it profit a man if he receive the sovereignty of all this world and lose his soul? and what will he get in exchange for his soul? for whosoever shall suffer shame for me and for my words and shall confess me before men, I too will confess him before my Father which is in Heaven, and whosoever shall deny me before men I also will deny him before my Father who is in Heaven.'" And Mikhail and Fedor saying this, they began to pray them urgently, that they would listen to them. And Mikhail said to them: "I will not listen to you, nor will I destroy my soul." Than taking off his mantle Mikhail threw it to them, saying to them: "Receive the glory of this world if you desire it." And Eldega having heard that they were unable to persuade him, then went to inform the *Tsar* of what Mikhail had said; for there was a quantity of Christians and pagans in that place, and they were listening to what Mikhail answered to the *Tsar*. Then the blessed Mikhail and Fedor began to sing, and having finished singing they took holy communion, the body and blood of Christ, which their father had given them who had blessed them for this to suffer for Christ. And those who stood by said: "Mikhail, the executioners are coming from the *Tsar* to kill you; bow, and you will live." And Mikhail and Fedor answered as with one mouth: "We will not bow, and will not listen to you , for the sake of the glory of this world," and began to sing: "Thy martyrs, O Lord, did not deny Thee, nor did they turn away from Thy commandments, but rather suffered for Thy sake, O Christ, and endured many tortures and received perfect crowns in heaven," and so forth. And then the executioners having arrived, and having jumped off their horses, they seized Mikhail, they stretched him out and holding his arms, began to strike him with their hands over the heart, and threw him prone on to the ground and struck him with their heels. And when he had been overpowered a certain man who had been a Christian and then become pagan having denied the Christian faith, and become a pagan transgressor of the law, named Doman, this man cut off the head of the holy *Veliki Knyaz* Mikhail, and hurled it away. And at that minute they said to Fedor: "Bow thou to our gods and thou wilt received the whole *Knyazdom* of they *Knyaz*." And Fedor said to them: "I do not desire the *Knyazdom* and do not bow to your gods; but I wish to suffer for Christ like my *Knyaz*." Then again they began to torture Fedor as before they had Mikhail, and then they cut off his honoured head too. Thus, these men thanking the Lord suffered for Christ, and gave over their holy souls to the Lord into the hands of God, new holy martyrs. And their holy bodies were thrown to the dogs to eat, but on the contrary, the holy bodies having lain many days were by the grace of God preserved and in no way injured. And our merciful God the Lord, who loves mankind glorifying His holy and obedient servants who had suffered for Him and for the Orthodox faith, a pillar of fire appeared from earth to heaven over their honourable bodies, shining with exceeding bright rays for the confirmation of Christians and for the conviction of the faithless who leave God and bow to things, and for the terrifying of the pagans. And

their holy and honourable bodies were saved by some God-
fearing Christians. The killing of them was on the 20th
day of September; through whose prayers and through the
supplication of these sufferers of pain and martyrs, Mikhail and Fedor, we shall be worthy to find mercy and
remission of our sins at the hands of our Lord Jesus Christ,
in this and in the future life, together with the Father,
the Son and the Holy Ghost, now and for ever and ever,
Amen. . . .

CHAPTER 18

Serbia's Medieval Law Code

Stephan Dusan (1331–1355) was the most renowned of
the medieval Serbian rulers. Through conquest and alliances, Stephan succeeded in controlling most of southeastern Europe. The law code of 1349 was another ornament
for the career of Stephan who in 1346 had been so audacious
as to style himself "Emperor of the Serbs and the Romans."
The law code is rather unenlightened, but it does serve
to give a reasonably accurate picture of Serbian mores in
the fourteenth century. Although Stephan could carry on
a careful diplomacy with Rome, Latin Christianity was rig-
idly legislated against. Some rights were acknowledged for
those of noble status, and their social privileges were recognized in the way that fines were fixed in a hierarchical
fashion.

Malcolm Burr (translator), *"The Code of Stephan Dusan,"*
SLAVONIC AND EAST EUROPEAN REVIEW, Vol. 28 (1959),
pp. 198–217. By permission of the editors of the
SLAVONIC AND EAST EUROPEAN REVIEW.

Article 6. Of the Latin Heresy

And concerning the Latin heresy, any Christians who have turned to unleavened bread, let them return to Christianity. And if anyone fails to obey and does not return, let him be punished as it is written in the laws of the holy fathers.

Article 7. Of the Latin Heresy

And the Great Church shall appoint protopops in all cities and market towns to bring back Christians from the Latin heresy, who have turned to the Latin faith, to give them spiritual instruction, and that every man return to Christianity.

Article 8. Of Latin Priests

And if a Latin priest convert a Christian to the Latin faith, let him be punished according to the laws of the holy fathers.

Article 10. Of Heretics

And if any heretic be found living among Christians, let him be branded on the face and driven forth: and whoso shall harbour him, he too shall be branded.

Article 39. Of the Lords and Gentry

And to the lords and gentry, who live within my state, both Serbs and Greeks, to whom was given land as a patrimony and in chrysobuls before my reign and who held it up to the day of this council, those patrimonies are confirmed.

Article 41. Of Lords' Hereditary Estates

If any lord have no child, or if he have and it die, then upon his death the inheritance remains empty until there be found someone of his kin up to the third cousin, and to him shall the inheritance fall.

Article 42. Of Free Hereditary Estates

And all hereditary estates are free of all works and tribute to my majesty, save that they shall pay the corn-due and provide soldiers to fight, according to the law.

Article 45. If Free Estates

And when lords and other people have hereditary churches upon their estates, neither the Lord Tsar, nor the Patriarch, nor any biship may subject those churches to the Great Church, but the hereditary owner is free to appoint his own monk and to take him for ordination to the bishop in whose diocese it is, and in that church the bishop shall control only ecclesiastical affairs.

Article 46. Of Slaves

And whoso hath slaves, let him have them as an inheritance. And only the lord himself, or his wife, or his son, may free them and none other.

Article 48. Of Lords and Horses

And when a lord dies, his good horse and arms shall be given to the Tsar, and his great robes of pearls and golden girdle, let his son have them and let them not be taken by the Tsar: and if he have no son, but have a daughter, then his daughter is free to sell or give it freely.

Article 60. Of the Tsar's Maintenance

Everyone shall provide for the Tsar wherever he goes. From every town to the district, from district to district. And again from district to town.

Article 85. Of Heretical Utterance

Whoso utters heretical words, if he be noble let him pay one hundred perpers: and if he not be noble, let him pay twelve perpers and be flogged with sticks.

Article 92. Of Horse-stealing

If any man recognize his own horse under another man and it be in the mountains or in the wilderness, let him take him to the nearest village and hand him to the village and call upon it to deliver him to the tribunal: and if the village do not deliver him to the tribunal, let that village pay so much as the tribunal shall direct.

Article 94. Of Lords and Commoners

If a lord kill a commoner, whether in a city, county or in a mountain district, he shall pay one thousand perpers. But if a commoner kill a baron, he shall pay three hundred perpers and both his hands shall be cut off.

Article 95. Of Insulting and Killing Clerics

Whoso insulteth a bishop, monk, or priest, he shall pay one hundred perpers. But if a man kill a bishop, monk or priest, let him be killed and hanged.

Article 97. Of the Lord's Beard

Whoso shall pluck the beard of a lord or good man, both his hands shall be cut off.

Article 98. Of Commoner's Plucking

If two commoners pluck, the fine is six perpers.

CHAPTER 19

The Final Declaration of Jan Hus

In the fifteenth century, Bohemia was in a religious turmoil that occasionally forced all Europe to take note. The teachings of the English reformer, John Wycliffe, deeply influenced the Czech professors at the University of Prague and when the German professors, representing the majority, condemned Wycliffe's doctrines in 1403, a great controversy began. After 1403, Jan Hus, revered as a priest and teacher, assumed leadership of the pro-Wycliffe, anti-German faction. Despite condemnations from Zbynek, Archbishop of Prague, and the anti-pope, John XXIII, Wenceslaus IV of Bohemia took a somewhat tolerant view of the Hussites.

The brother of Wenceslaus IV, Sigismund (the King of Hungary who shared the imperial dignity with Wenceslaus), co-sponsored the Council of Constance that judged Hus. Sigismund granted Hus a safe conduct for the trip to Constance. When Hus came to Constance in 1414, prior to the arrival of Sigismund, he gave some sermons to friendly groups. But the enemies of Hus had him imprisoned, and while Sigismund was angry when he discovered that his safe conduct had been ignored, he gave way and allowed Hus to undergo trial and an execution that took place on July 6, 1415. The execution settled nothing and caused the Hussites in Bohemia to take a stronger stand. At Constance itself, many, including the eminent Italian humanist, Poggio, judged the proceedings against Hus a barbaric act unworthy of the Council that ended the Great Schism and tried to enact religious reforms.

Herbert B. Workman and R. Martin Pope (editors), THE LETTERS OF JOHN HUS (London: Hodder and Stoughton, 1904), pp. 275–276.

I, John Hus, in hope a priest of Jesus Christ, fearing to offend God, and fearing to fall into perjury, do hereby profess my unwillingness to abjure all or any of the articles produced against me by false witnesses. For God is my witness that I neither preached, affirmed, nor defended them, though they say that I did. Moreover, concerning the articles that they have extracted from my books, I say that I detest any false interpretation which any of them bears. But inasmuch as I fear to offend against the truth, or to gainsay the opinion of the doctors of the Church, I cannot abjure any one of them. And if it were possible that my voice could now reach the whole world, as at the Day of Judgment every lie and every sin that I have committed will be made manifest, then would I gladly abjure before all the world every falsehood and error which I either had thought of saying or actually said. I say I write this of my own free will and choice.

Written with my own hand, on the first day of July.

CHAPTER 20

The Battle of Varna

The Ottoman Turks had been in Europe for nearly a century before 1444. While initial victories were won in

Greece, Bulgaria, Serbia and Albania, the tide turned in the 1440's. In Albania, a great popular leader, George Castriota (Scanderbeg), began anti-Turkish operations that lasted for twenty-five years. The Serbian ruler, George Brankovic, joined the Hungarian in 1443 for a rather successful campaign against the Ottomans.

In 1444, the Turks were forced to sign a treaty (Szegedin) whereby they lost most of their power in Serbia and Wallachia. There was dismay in Rome that the Turks had not been entirely driven out of Europe, and the papal legate, Cardinal Julian Cesarini, advised the Hungarian king, Vladislav, that he should renounce the Treaty of Szegedin and launch a campaign in 1444.

With the hope of aid from the Venetian fleet, the Hungarian army advanced toward the Black Sea. Their leader was John Hunyadi (Corvinus) who held the title, Voivoda of Transylvania. George Brankovic refused to help the Hungarians, and the Venetian fleet was of no assistance. On November 10, the battle of Varna took place on the shore of the Black Sea. The Hungarians, without allies and greatly outnumbered by the Turkish forces, were defeated after a protracted struggle. It was obvious that Rome had asked for too much, and its gamble back-fired. The Turks, after Varna, had substantial control of southeastern Europe.

Nic Densusianu (editor), *Documente Privitóre La Istoria Romanilor* (Bucharest: Socecu and Teclu, 1890), Vol. I, Part 2, pp. 715–717.

Most Holy Father.

Although I did not have the opportunity to report personally to your Holiness, I now confidently do so by letter. And I send you news of the late conflict, in which it was not so much our strength, but our misfortune that was betrayed. . . . Having had wide experience in warfare since my early years, I easily admit that the wheel of military fortune is such that, according to the slightest movement of the Supreme Spectator, it rolls to favorable or calamitous conclusions. God may be the judge of those who

were the cause of such a great distress for the Christian
people. Many neighboring princes, of Wallachia, of Bulgaria, of Albania as well as Constantinople, promised ample
military aid, and told us to fly to their aid with feathered
feet, because everything had been provided there for us.
We answered their call after such great encouragement,
marched with our army, crossing into the territory of the
Turks. And since all that we needed was the promised
help, we confidently penetrated farther each day into enemy
territory. Some hostile units surrendered without resistance, some we defeated. But after a time it was clear that
we could not rely on past promises of assistance. We had
to face a situation that we had not anticipated since the
friendship of the above-mentioned princes at its best was
worse than insufficient and since the promised alliance
actually turned out to be an insidious deception. Thus, while
neglecting the defense of our own land, we found ourselves
ill-armed in enemy country. However, before our perilous
situation became evident, we obtained many spoils,
slaughtered many Turks, and inflicted great damage. We
were able to avoid open battle, but we were ashamed to
give up the campaign that we had started for Christ's
sake. . . . Therefore, a pious boldness overcame us and
we resolved to take a venturesome course. An unequal battle
took place which was fiercely fought, and only the sunset
stopped the carnage. But the battle became a losing one
because of the continuous waves of an endlessly attacking
multitude, from which we receded not so much defeated
than rather overrun and separated from each other.

Nevertheless, we saw it with our own eyes and know
it from many documents, that we did not inflict fewer
wounds to the enemy than we received. We left them with
the remains of a bloody and funestuous victory. Further
it is worthwhile to lament with great sighs the deplorable
casualties we suffered. For there perished at Varna the
king, our most illustrious prince and leader, and the venerable father, the Lord-Legate, Julian, whose character was
virtuous and solid. . . . Our defeat was not caused by our
weakness, or the superior bravery of the Turks, but it
was divine justice which administered the defeat to us for
we were ill equipped and almost unarmed; the barbarians

won the day because of our sins. Therefore, recognizing
rather the weight of our guilt than that of our wounds,
we have a firm hope that the One who administered the
defeat as a revenge for our sins will give a remedy to
those who hope, and will move the mind of Your Holiness
to strengthen the unbroken but bent power of the Christian
people. . . .

CHAPTER 21

The Fall of Constantinople—1453

This contemporary account describes quite vividly the
taking of Constantinople by the Ottoman Turks in 1453.
The event produced a profound shock in Europe, but the
Byzantine Empire had been on its death-bed for nearly
a century before 1453. The unbounded ferocity of the Ottoman troops won Mehmed a place in the history of infamy,
at least as told by Europeans.

Kritovoulos, translated by *Charles T. Riggs,* HISTORY OF
    MEHMED THE CONQUEROR (Princeton, 1954), pp. 69–73.
    By permission of Princeton University Press.

229. Giustinianni with his men, and the Romans in that
section fought bravely with lances, axes, pikes, javelins,
and other weapons of offense. It was a hand-to-hand encounter, and they stopped the attackers and prevented them
from getting inside the palisade. There was much shouting
on both sides—the mingled sounds of blasphemy, insults,
threats, attackers, defenders, shooters, those shot at, killers
and dying, of those who in anger and wrath did all sorts
of terrible things. And it was a sight to see there: a hard
fight going on hand-to-hand with great determination and
for the greatest rewards, heroes fighting valiantly, the one
party struggling with all their might to force back the

defenders, get possession of the wall, enter the City, and fall upon the children and women and the treasures, the other party bravely agonizing to drive them off and guard their possessions, even if they were not to succeed in prevailing and in keeping them.

230. Instead, the hapless Romans were destined finally to be brought under the yoke of servitude and to suffer its horrors. For although they battled bravely, and though they lacked nothing of willingness and daring in the contest, Giustinianni received a mortal wound in the breast from an arrow fired by a crossbow. It passed clear through his breastplate, and he fell where he was and was carried to his tent in a hopeless condition. All who were with him were scattered, being upset by their loss. They abandoned the palisade and wall where they had been fighting, and thought of only one thing—how they could carry him on to the galleons and get away safe themselves.

231. But the Emperor Constantine besought them earnestly, and made promises to them if they would wait a little while, till the fighting should subside. They would not consent, however, but taking up their leader and all their armor, they boarded the galleons in haste and with all speed, giving no consideration to the other defenders.

232. The Emperor Constantine forbade the others to follow. Then, though he had no idea what to do next—for he had no other reserves to fill the places thus left vacant, the ranks of those who had so suddenly deserted, and meantime the battle raged fiercely and all had to see to their own ranks and places and fight there—still, with his remaining Romans and his bodyguard, which was so few as to be easily counted, he took his stand in front of the palisade and fought bravely.

233. Sultan Mehmed, who happened to be fighting quite near by, saw that the palisade and the other part of the wall that had been destroyed were now empty of men and deserted by the defenders. He noted that men were slipping away secretly and that those who remained were fighting feebly because they were so few. Realizing from this that the defenders had fled and that the wall was deserted, he shouted out: "Friends, we have the City! We have it! They are already fleeing from us! They can't stand it any

longer! The wall is bare of defenders! It needs just a little more effort and the City is taken! Don't weaken, but on with the work with all your might, and be men and I am with you'."

Capture of the City

234. So saying, he led them himself. And they, with a shout on the run and with a fearsome yell, went on ahead of the Sultan, pressing on up to the palisade. After a long and bitter struggle they hurled back the Romans from there and climbed by force up the palisade. They dashed some of their foe down into the ditch between the great wall and the palisade, which was deep and hard to get out of, and they killed them there. The rest they drove back to the gate.

Death of Emperor Constantine

235. He had opened this gate in the great wall, so as to go easily over to the palisade. Now there was a great struggle there and great slaughter among those stationed there, for they were attacked by the heavy infantry and now a few others in irregular formation, who had been attracted from many points by the shouting. There the Emperor Constantine, with all who were with him, fell in gallant combat.

236. The heavy infantry were already steaming through the little gate into the City, and others had rushed in through the breach in the great wall. Then all the rest of the army, with a rush and a roar, poured in brilliantly and scattered all over the City. And the Sultan stood before the great wall, where the standard also was and the ensigns, and watched the proceedings. The day was already breaking.

Great Rush and Many Killed

237. Then a great slaughter occurred of those who happened to be there: some of them were on the streets, for they had already left the houses and were runnning toward the tumult when they fell unexpectedly on the swords of the soldiers; others were in their own homes and fell victims to the violence of the Janissaries and other soldiers, without any rhyme or reason; others were resisting, relying on their own courage; still others were fleeing to the churches and making supplication—men, women, and children, everyone, for there was no quarter given.

238. The soldiers fell on them with anger and great wrath. For one thing, they were actuated by the hardships of the siege. For another, some foolish people had hurled taunts and curses at them from the battlements all through the siege. Now, in general they killed so as to frighten all the City, and to terrorize and enslave all by the slaughter.

Plunder of the City

239. When they had had enough of murder, and the City was reduced to slavery, some of the troops turned to the mansions of the mighty, by bands and companies and divisions, for plunder and spoil. Others went to the robbing of churches, and others dispersed to the simple homes of the common people, stealing, robbing, plundering, killing, insulting, taking and enslaving men, women, and children, old and young, priests, monks—in short, every age and class.

Here, too, a Sad Tragedy

240. There was a further sight, terrible and pitiful beyond all tragedies: young and chaste women of noble birth and well to do, accustomed to remain at home and who had hardly ever left their own premises, and handsome

and lovely maidens of splendid and renowned families, till then unsullied by male eyes—some of these were dragged by force from their chambers and hauled off pitilessly and dishonorably.

241. Other women, sleeping in their beds, had to endure nightmares. Men with swords, their hands bloodstained with murder, breathing out rage, speaking our murder indiscriminate, flushed with all the worst things—this crowd, made up of men from every race and nation, brought together by chance, like wild and ferocious beasts, leaped into the houses, driving them out mercilessly, dragging, rending, hauling them disgracefully into the public highways, insulting them and doing every evil thing.

242. They say that many of the maidens, even at the mere unaccustomed sight and sound of these men, were terror-stricken and came near losing their very lives. And there were also honorable old men who were dragged off by their white hair, and some of them beaten unmercifully.

243. There were priests who were driven along, and consecrated virgins who were honorable and wholly unsullied, devoted to God alone and living for Him to whom they had consecrated themselves. Some of these were forced out of their cells and driven off, and others dragged out of the churches where they had taken refuge and driven off with insult and dishonor, their cheeks scratched, amid wailing and lamentation and bitter tears. Tender children were snatched pitilessly from their mothers, young brides separated ruthlessly from their newly-married husbands. And ten thousand other terrible deeds were done. . . .

CHAPTER 22

The Defense of Belgrade by John Hunyadi

In this extract from a letter to one of the Burgundian bishops, Pope Calixtus III relates the story of John

Hunyadi's successful efforts to hold Belgrade against the Turks in 1456. The unsuccessful siege of Belgrade by the Ottomans surprised a Europe which had become accustomed to Turkish victories. The Pope's exuberance and high hopes for the future were misplaced. Although the Pope understood the mighty financial burdens involved in defeating the Turks, he tended to be too sanguine in his predictions of total Christian victory. Even Hunyaddi could not push the Turks back to Constantinople.

A. *Theiner* (editor) VETERA MONUMENTA HISTORICA HUNGARIAM SACRAM ILLUSTRANTIA (Rome: Vatican Press, 1860), Vol. II, pp. 280–281. Translated by the editors.

Oh admirable empire of our Savior! The insane Turks, burning with anger and with a most powerful army, occupied the plains and the mountains. They pressed hard upon the fortress of Belgrade which is the key to the Hungarian Empire. They destroyed the walls and other defenses and thought themselves to be in possession of the fortress. If this fortress had been lost, the very existence of the entire Christian republic would have been in danger. Then would the way be open, and the Turks could have entered Hungary without opposition. In this case the Turks would have gained the opportunity to put to the test the entire Christian world.

But the Supreme Lord did not allow his religion to be covered with such darkness. Neither did he permit such a shame to be showered upon the true faith.... The barbarians were routed by the most powerful Athlete of Christ, Prince John Hunyadi, and a small army of plebians and unarmed soldiers.... With joy in our hearts we were in a state of exhaltation after this memorable victory. We lost our old apathy which had been caused by the inaction of the Christian princes. And we gave thanks and honor to God and ordered that all Christendom should pray and rejoice at this great victory.... We give you our Encyclical naming prayers that we asked for.... We now nurture the hope, based on our inviolate faith, that we will not only reconquer Constantinople, but we will free Europe, Asia, and the Holy Land.

The Catholic princes should follow us, and they should toil for the faith of Christ, their foremost obligation. And because we are presently burdened with unbearable expenses..., we exhort you and your princes to obtain more funds in addition to what you were already obliged to collect.

We cannot perform such a great task unless the Christians assist us. Besides, we send to those parts our beloved son, Peter Clerici....

Made in Rome, under the ring of the Fisherman, at St. Peter's, August 14, 1456. In the Second Year of our Pontificate.

CHAPTER 23

The Battle of Mohács

The Turkish expedition of 1526 which brought about the conquest of the greater part of Hungary was carefully considered by the sultan, Suleiman the Magnificent. Louis II of Hungary was the brother-in-law of Charles V and Ferdinand, Duke of Austria. Ferdinand could see that the Turkish conquest of Hungary would threaten his own territory, and the evidence shows that he did try to provide help for Hungary albeit too late. So while Suleiman knew that Austrian forces might face him, he also had obtained a western ally, France. And the French had specifically asked for the expedition that Suleiman undertook in 1526.

The Hungarians had some forewarning of the Turks' coming, but adequate defensive measures were not taken. The battle of Mohács, on August 29, 1526, was an impossible attempt by Louis II to hold back the Turks. The Hungarian defeat was inevitable. Thus fell one of the proudest states of medieval Europe, and the subsequent history of Hungary would be even more horrible than that of Serbia and Bulgaria because Hungary would become the western frontier of the Ottoman Empire, the arena of many later wars that would cause remarkable devastation. Western Europe had been short-sighted in not giving aid, but the Hungarian nobles' quest for power had so weakened the monarchy that a determined fight against the Turks was impossible. But even after Mohács, there was some chance that Hungary would not be swallowed up by the Turks. Suleiman was astonished at the ease with which Hungary had been conquered, but even the Ottoman Empire did not have enough troops to permanently garrison such a large territory. And doubtless, the Turks knew that permanent occupation in 1526 would probably provoke a strong reaction from Austria.

Istvan Brodarics, "Die Schlacht von Mohacs," in Julius von Farkas (editor), UNGARNS GESCHICHTE UND KULTUR IN DOKUMENTEN (Wiesbaden, 1955), pp. 45–49. Translated by the editors with permission of O. Harrassowitz.

King Louis discovered that Suleiman had concluded peace treaties with all his neighbors for several years, and with both his army and naval forces would soon attack Hungary. The king was shocked when he learned of this, and because the coming of the Turks was confirmed by many sources, he called together the Hungarian Diet on the feast of St. George April 23, 1526.... At this Diet, all ranks of the Hungarian nobility from every part of the country appeared and concurred in all the necessary preparations for the defense of the country. Among other preparations, the Diet decided that all the high magnates, ecclesiastical and secular, plus the lower nobility with a determined number of serfs, should appear on July 2 at Tolna. From Tolna they would proceed toward the enemy. In the meantime, the king would make any other preparations for the war. It was decided that the king should send forth envoys to neighboring states in order to warn them of the coming danger. In particular, he should urgently admonish the Pope to increase the amount of money formerly given to Hungary in times of danger so that the king might raise mercenary troops for defense.

Immediately after the dissolution of the Diet, the king devoted every effort to the coming crisis. He informed all the Christian rulers of the danger, asked all for help, especially the Holy Roman Emperor, Charles V, and the French king, Francis I. He also sent envoys to his brother-in-law, Duke Ferdinand of Austria, and to the other imperial dukes, who were assembled at Speyer for a meeting of the Imperial Diet. He contacted the Papal Nuncio, Alexander Burgio, to urge him to intervene with the Pope in order to persuade him to send a larger amount of money for the enormous war expenses. In the meantime, letters and envoys of the Archbishop of Kalocsa and the Voyvodas of Transylvania arrived with the news that the Turks were approaching Belgrade. An advance force of the Turks had already crossed the Save River. Despite the fact that no aid had yet arrived from Bohemia or any other country, and although only a few Hungarian troops were at his disposal, he set out from Buda on July 23, and moved slowly along the Danube toward Tolna. At Mohács they assembled together with twenty-four to twenty-five thousand troops. Naval forces were not present, but would have been of no use since the Turks were assembled only two miles away with three hundred thousand troops.

On the day of battle, August 29, the Hungarian strategy was to spread out their force in such a way that they would not be encircled. The army was divided into two columns. In the first column stood the army commanders, but they did not have a determined place; thus, they could move to wherever they were needed. The second column, where the king took his place, was meant to be the more stationary one, and it consisted mainly of cavalry flanked by some infantry. The king took his place in the fourth line of the second column. In the three lines in front of the king, there stood mainly royal court officials and the high nobility. Surrounding the king in the fourth line was the royal body guard. The king's appearance, his character, and his courage were praiseworthy. Had destiny permitted it, he would have been one of our greatest kings.

The place where the army had assembled was one mile from Mohács and a half-mile from the Danube. A large plain stretched out before them with neither forests, bushes, streams nor hills. But between the Danube and Mohács there was an expanse of marshland heavily overgrown with reeds, a place where many were about to perish.

On the far side of the plain lay a chain of hills forming a half-circle, and on the other side was the camp of the Turkish Sultan. At the foot of the hills, on the far side, was a small village with a church, and in this village called Földvar, the Turks placed their heavy cannon.

On August 29, the army assembled in battle-line shortly after sunrise. The weather was very clear and beautiful. The palatine led the king through the ranks of the army, showing him to all: "See, here is your king." For some of them had doubted that he was present. "The king is here. He is ready to suffer anything including death for his country, for his Saviour, for the wives and children of all of you. And so, every man should be of courage and not forget that he is an Hungarian. Think of your fore-fathers, heroes, brave Christian fighters who won many brilliant victories over this same enemy, the Turk. Their numbers should not frighten you. Victory does not depend on numbers but on the courage of the troops. God in Heaven will give aid to all who fight for His Holy Faith. Victory lies in His hands," said the palatine, "and not only the fate of Hungary but the fate of all Christendom." After the king and the palatine had spoken to the troops at various places, then the king returned to his appointed station.

We spent the greater part of the day waiting for the enemy's advance. It was already after three o'clock. Some magnates, weary from waiting, recommended that the trumpets should sound an end to the state of alert and that all should return to the camp. Then the Archbishop of Kalocsa discovered the magnates' desire, hurried to the king, and admonished him not to delay the battle under any circumstances because it would be less dangerous to wage battle against only part of the enemy's troops than to wait until the next day when the entire Turkish army would be assembled. "Victory is certain today." Hearing these words, the king immediately gave the signal to attack. Mixed with the loud sound of horns and trumpets was the rallying cry of the soldiers invoking, as was their ancient custom, the name of the Saviour. As we attacked, we saw the enemy troops descending, in large numbers, from the hills on the other side of the plain and among their host was the Sultan himself. A helmet was placed on the king's head. At this instant, one could see a certain paleness on the face of the king. It seemed as though he sensed a possible catastrophe.

As the signal to attack was given, those in the first line engaged strenuously with the Turks. All batteries were fired.

The battle lasted about one and a half hours. Many found their graves in the swampy marshland. The corpse of the king was found one mile away from the village of Csele, in a low-lying section where the Danube had temporarily overrun its banks. Here drowned horse and rider, both clad in battle armour. The Archbishop fell also, standing in the first line, after what was said to have been a brave fight. His head was separated from his body, put on the end of a lance, and on the next day was carried about triumphantly in the camp of the Turks. It was said that his head was later placed before the tent of the Sultan. The day after the battle, 1500 prisoners were decapitated while the Turkish army looked on. For the most part, they were magnates. The Sultan sacrificed their blood to his gods. Few of the prisoners were allowed to remain alive.... Out of the infantry, only three or four thousand survived of the twelve to thirteen thousand who marched into the battle.

The Turkish Sultan remained for several days in the neighborhood of Mohács. Then he started out for Buda, and on his way he plundered and burned everything in his path. He found Buda unprotected and had the city set afire. Then, with fire and sword, he devastated everything from the Danube to Lake Balaton. However, Eztergom was successfully defended by a man of the lower classes, Andreas Nagy, who had been commander of infantry in the district of Eztergom. Visegrad, where the crown of St. Stephen was kept, also did not fall because it was stoutly defended by monks and peasants.

After he had devastated Transdanubia from the delta of the Drava River to the Raba River, even people far away, as those in Vienna, were greatly frightened. Then the Sultan crossed the Danube near Pest over a bridge that he had had built, and he traveled into the Danube-Tisza Plain. From there he sent his troops in every direction to devastate the land as they had done in Transdanubia, and he ordered that all those who had had not fled across the Tisza

River were to be massacred or enslaved. After he had thus
vented his fury, he marched back to his own lands for a
rebellion that had broken out in Asia Minor required his
return.

CHAPTER 24

A comparison of Turkish and Christian Soldiers (Sixteenth
    Century)

As envoy of the Austrian Hapsburgs, Ogier Ghiselin de
Busbecq had the opportunity to observe the Turks during
their greatest period of power. He shows much admiration
for the Turkish troops and compares them most favorably
with western armies.

Edward Seymour Forster (translator), THE TURKISH
LETTERS OF OGIER GHISELIN DE BUSBECQ, IMPERIAL
AMBASSADOR AT CONSTANTINOPLE (Oxford: Clarendon
Press, 1927), pp. 109–112.)

The Sultan when he sets out on a campaign, takes as many
as 40,000 camels with him, and almost as many baggage-
mules, most of whom, if his destination is Persia, are loaded
with cereals of every kind, especially rice. Mules and camels
are also employed to carry tents and arms and warlike
machines and implements of every kind. The territories
called Persia which are ruled by the Sophi, as we call him
(the Turkish name being Kizilbash), are much less fertile
than our country; and, further, it is the custom of the
inhabitants, when their land is invaded, to lay waste and
burn everything and so force the enemy to retire through
lack of food. The latter, therefore, are faced with serious
peril, unless they bring an abundance of food with them.
They are careful, however, to avoid touching the supplies
which they carry with them as long as they are marching

against their foes, but reserve them as far as possible, for their return journey, when the moment of retirement comes and they are forced to retrace their steps through regions which the enemy has laid waste, of which the immense multitude of men and baggage animals has, as it were, scraped bare, like a swarm of locusts. It is only then that the Sultan's store of provisions is opened and just enough food to sustain life is weighed out each day to the Janissaries and the other troops in attendance upon him. The other soldiers are badly off, if they have not provided food for their own use; most of them, having often experienced such difficulties during their campaigns—and this is particularly true of the cavalry—take a horse on a leading-rein loaded with many of the necessities of life. These include a small piece of canvass to use as a tent, which may protect them from the sun or a shower of rain, also some clothing and bedding and a private store of provisions, consisting of a leather sack of two of the finest flour, a small jar of butter, and some spices and salt; on these they support life when they are reduced to the extremes of hunger. They take a few spoonfuls of flour and place them in water, adding a little butter, and then flavour the mixture with salt and spices. This, when it is put on the fire, boils and swells up so as to fill a large bowl. They eat of it once or twice a day, according to the quantity, without any bread, unless they have with them some toasted bread or biscuit. They thus contrive to live on short rations for a month or even longer, if necessary. Some soldiers take with them a little sack full of beef dried and reduced to a powder, which they employ in the same manner as the flour, and which is of great benefit as a more solid form of nourishment. Sometimes, too, they have recourse to horseflesh; for in a great army a large number of horses necessarily dies, and any that die in good condition furnish a welcome meal to men who are starving. I may add that men whose horses have died, when the Sultan moves his camp, stand in a long row on the road by which he is to pass with their harness or saddles on their heads, as a sign that they have lost their horses, and implore his help to purchase others. The Sultan then assists them with what ever gift he thinks fit.

All this will show you with what patience, sobriety, and

economy the Turks struggle against the difficulties which beset them, and wait for better times. How different are our soldiers, who on campaign despise ordinary food and expect dainty dishes (such as thrushes and beccaficoes) and elaborate meals. If these are not supplied, they mutiny and cause their own ruin; and even if they are supplied, they ruin themselves just the same. For each man is his own worst enemy and has no more deadly foe than his own intemperance, which kills him if the enemy is slow to do so. I tremble when I think of what the future must bring when I compare the Turkish system with our own; one army must prevail and the other be destroyed, for certainly both cannot remain unscathed. On their side are the resources of a mighty empire, strength unimpaired, experience and practice in fighting, a veteran soldiery, habituation to victory, endurance of toil, unity, order discipline, frugality, and watchfulness. On our side is public poverty, private luxury, impaired strength, broken spirit, lack of endurance and training; the soldiers are insubordinate, the officers avaricious; there is contempt for discipline; licence, recklessness, drunkenness, and debauchery are rife; and, worst of all, the enemy is accustomed to victory, and we to defeat. Can we doubt what the result will be? Persia alone interposes in our favour; for the enemy, as he hastens to attack, must keep an eye on this menace in his rear. But Persia is only delaying our fate; it cannot save us. When the Turks have settled with Persia, they will fly at our throats supported by the might of the whole East; how unprepared we are I dare not say!...

CHAPTER 25

A Contemporary Compares Suleiman the Magnificent and the Emperor Ferdinand

This evaluation by Ogier Ghiselin de Busbecq is favorable to Ferdinand, but at the same time exhibits a highly sophis-

ticated understanding of the new situation created by the
proximity of the Turks.

Edward Seymour Forster (translator), THE TURKISH
 LETTERS OF OGIER GHISELIN DE BUSBECQ, IMPERIAL
 AMBASSADOR AT CONSTANTINOPLE (Oxford: Clarendon
 Press, 1927), pp. 238–241.

There may, perhaps, be some who regret that the Emperor
[Ferdinand] has not shown more zeal for warlike achievements and has not sought laurels in that field. The Turks, it
may be urged, have raged over Hungary for many years,
laying it waste far and wide, and we have never come to the
rescue, as our reputation demands; we ought long ago to
have marched against them and, massing all our forces
together, decided in a pitched battle which nation fortune
desired should rule. Such advice is bold, but I doubt whether
it is wise. Let us consider the matter rather more closely.
In my opinion we ought to judge of the capacity of generals
and emperors rather by their plans than their fortune and
the results which they achieve. In their plans they ought to
take reckoning of their opportunities, their own strength,
and the nature and resources of their enemy. If an ordinary
enemy, well known to us, and lacking the prestige of
victory, were to attack our territory, and our forces were
equal to his, it would, I fear, be imputed to cowardice if we
did not face him and check his advance in a pitched battle.
But if our enemy were a scourge sent against us by the
anger of Heaven (such as was Attila in the olden time,
Tamerlane within the recollection of our grandfathers, and
such as the Ottoman Sultans are in our own days), to whom
nothing is an obstacle, and before whose advance everything falls—to hurl oneself precipately against such a foe
with a small and hastily levied army would deserve, I am
afraid, the imputation not merely of rashness but even of
madness.

Soleiman stands before us with all the terror inspired by
his own successes and those of his ancestors; he overruns
the plain of Hungary with 200,000 horsemen; he threatens
Austria; he menaces the rest of Germany; he brings in his
train all the nations that dwell between here and the

Persian frontier. He is at the head of an army equipped with the resources of many kingdoms; of the three continents into which our hemisphere is divided; each contributes its share to achieve our destruction. Like a thunderbolt he smites, shatters, and destroys whatever stands in his way; he is at the head of veteran troops and a highly trained army, which is accustomed to his leadership; he spreads far and wide the terror of his name. He roars like a lion along our frontier, seeking to break through, now here, now there. Before now nations threatened by much less serious peril have often left their native land before the pressure of a powerful foe and sought homes elsewhere. There is little credit in remaining calm in the face of trifling dangers; but not to be alarmed by the approach of such an enemy as ours, while kingdoms crash in ruin around us, seems to me to betoken Herculean courage. Yet the heroic Ferdinand stands his post, and refuses to retreat from the position which he holds. He would fain possess such resources that he could take his all on the hazard of a battle at his own risk and without incurring the charge of madness; but prudence tempers these generous impulses. He sees what ruin any failure in so mighty an enterprise would entail upon his own faithful subjects, nay, upon Christianity in general, and deems it wrong for an individual to harbour designs for his private gratification which can only be carried out by calamitous sacrifices on the part of the State. He reflects how unequal the struggle will be if 25,000 or 30,000 infantry, together with a small force of cavalry, join battle with 200,000 cavalry supported by veteran infantry. What he must expect from such a contest is clear to him from the precedents of the past—the disasters of Nicopolis and Varna, and the plains of Mohacs still white with the bones of slaughtered Christians....

The Emperor Ferdinand's plan was the same as that of Fabius Maximus; after estimating his own Soleiman's resources, he judged that the last thing which a good general ought to do was to tempt fortune and encounter the attack of so formidable an enemy in a pitched battle. He, therefore, resolved to throw all his energies into the other alternative, namely to delay and check the tide of invasion by the construction of dykes and ramparts and every kind of fortification.

It is now about forty years since Soleiman captured Belgrade, slew King Louis, and reduced Hungary, and so secured the prospect of possessing himself not only of this province but also of territory farther north. In this hope he besieged Vienna; then, renewing the war, he captured Güns and again threatened Vienna, but this time only at a distance. But what has he achieved by his mighty array, his unlimited resources, his countless hosts? He has with difficulty clung to the portion of Hungary which he had already captured. He who used to make an end of mighty kingdoms in a single campaign, has won, as the reward of his expeditions, some scarcely fortified citadels and unimportant towns and has paid dearly for the fragment which he has gradually torn away from the vast mass of Hungary. He has once looked upon Vienna, it is true, but it was for the first and last time.

It is said that Soleiman has set before himself the achievement of three ambitions: namely, to see the completion of his mosque, which is indeed a sumptuous and splendid structure; to restore the ancient aqueducts and give Constantinople a proper water supply; and to capture Vienna. His first two objects have been achieved; in his third ambition he has been baulked—I hope, forever....

CHAPTER 26

Venality of the Polish Nobles

Piotr Skarga Powéski achieved fame for his courageous sermons to the Polish Diet. Although the Polish gentry gained power in the sixteenth century at the expense of the magnates, still the Polish peasantry were the real victims. The gulf between the gentry and peasants widened to the point where Skarga saw that were really two people, those who were free amid those in slavery. He saw this gulf as a possible sign of Polish weakness, and as happened in Hun-

gary, this development did not lend strength to the kingdom. The Polish peasant and country gentleman alike went
their own way unconcerned, except in moments of grave
crisis, for the nation's welfare. The jealous pride of the
gentry curtailed royal authority at the same time that national solidarity was undermined. Poland never solved these
problems that finally contributed to the partition of
1792, and 1795. The Catholic priest, Piotr Skarga, thus
achieved a legendary reputation for being the prophet of
Poland's doom.

Manfred Kridl, Wladyslaw Malinowski and Józef Wittlin
(editors), FOR YOUR FREEDOM AND OURS (New York,
1943), pp. 45–47. By permission of Frederick Ungar
Publishing Co., Inc.

On the Love of the Motherland

O powerful lords, o earthly gods, keep a generous and
open heart for the weal of your brethren, and your peoples,
and all the souls which this kingdom and its territories en-
compass within themselves. Do not confine and cramp your
chambers and treasure chests. Release its flow from you,
great mountains, on the whole populace, as a river flows to
the flat fields. Follow that Christian king who, having set
out with his army, had painted on his banner a bird which
with its blood enlivened the little birds poisoned by the
snake, thus manifesting that he was prepared to die for his
people, promising death unto himself and life unto them.

There are those who say: What is the use of the Kingdom
and of the Commonwealth if I fare ill and do not have what
I desire? It is a thief's heart that wishes riches to the
detriment of others. Do not seek riches, ask the Lord for
your needs, and be content with your condition, and be not
squanderers or idlers, and do not seek to destroy scores of
thousands of people, your brethren, for your own sake.
Lord, grant that there be few such monsters, who, worse
than the beasts of the field are bereft of humanity or
mercy.

It is said that there are such who do not wish to serve the Commonwealth if they cannot expect advantage for themselves, or if they are not to be recompensed. They are indeed stupid who do not know that virtue seeks only its own decency for reward, who do not see that true rewards stem not from earthly kings but from the Monarch of the world itself. Only God is so powerful and rich and we should seek our rewards with Him. . . . Who serves his country, serves himself, for in it, as we have said before, all goodness is contained. Who will say: pay me for I protect my health, and my home, and my wife and my children; the protection itself is thy reward, why dost thou clamor? When thou eatest, drinkest, carest for thy health, dost thou seek a reward for this?

On Unjust Laws

All things require that the laws be just, useful to all, implanting virtues, and most of all fear of God, protecting God's glory and worship, and finally be well executed and disciplined. For laws which want no justice are distorted as human wrong; they are not laws but evils, for justice is the foundation of the whole Commonwealth. The kingdoms that lack it, says St. Augustine, may truly be called thiefdoms not kingdoms.

The law which serves one party or one estate and harms and injures the other should not be called law. For the laws should be universal, for the advantage of all citizens. As the head does not bid one hand to do what would harm the other, but what is useful to both, so the Apostle says: "One limb in the body has the care of the other; and what one suffers all suffer with it"; so also in the Commonwealth, which is one body, nothing should help one estate that would harm another, for thus the whole body would harm itself.

Also that evil law must be mentioned which makes yoemen, freeborn men, Poles and Christians subject, and poor men slaves, as if they were bought or captured in a just war; whereby others do with them as they please, giving them no protection of their possessions or life and providing them with no court of justice to plead against

their intolerable wrongs.... and exercising over them a
supreme domination at which we ourselves shudder.

Whether that be proper and whether there be a little
justice in this law one must ask of the laws and customs,
spiritual and temporal, of the whole of Christendom. If they
be neither bought nor captured, if they are Poles of the
same blood, not Turks or Tartars, why do they groan in
slavery? Why should we use them not as hirelings but as
slaves? He sits on thy soil, and if he misbehaves, drive him
away from thy soil, but do not take his natural and
Christian freedom away from him, or make thyself, without
a judge, supreme master over his life. The ancient Christians, who when they were pagans had bought slaves; gave
freedom to all, as brothers in Christ, when they released
themselves from the devil's bondage through holy baptism.
And we, faithful and holy Christians, forcefully coerce
Poles of the same nation who have never been slaves; and
when like bartered cattle, they must flee from their misery
we search for them; and when they, poor and miserable,
seek their food elsewhere we exact ransom on them as
Turks on prisoners. This is unheard of in the whole of
Christendom. I know that not all in our country do this, but
according to an evil and savage and unjust law they may do
so, which God forbid, to their own damnation. How is it
possible not to feel shame before all Christendom for such
a law? How is it possible not to fear lest the pagans use such
force and absolute domination over us as a consequence of
God's vengeance?

For God's sake let us avoid this curse and misery with
which the Lord threatens us through his Prophets. Abolish
evil unjust laws that obstruct justice; do ye not know that
their purpose is the general weal, and when they harm, they
must be changed? Not only are these mentioned here which
have always been evil and harmful, which never contained
any justice in them, but also those which may have been
good for our ancient fathers, but are harmful to us at the
present time....

CHAPTER 27

The Intervention of Bethlen Gabor in the Thirty Years War, 1623-1624

Gabriel Bethlen (Bethlen Gabor) reigned as prince of Transylvania for only sixteen years (1612-1628), but the stability and prosperity that characterized this period were so noteworthy that the era came to be known as Transylvania's Golden Age. Both the Viennese Hapsburgs and the Ottoman Turks had enough problems of their own that Bethlen was able to establish a strong position for himself. Anything that might weaken the two super-powers was to his advantage, and when the Thirty Years War first started, Bethlen threw his weight behind the anti-Hapsburg Bohemians. He would have to subsequently retrace his steps, but as he was a man of brilliant diplomatic skill, turns of fortune were easily weathered.

Sir Thomas Roe, THE NEGOTIATIONS OF SIR THOMAS ROE IN HIS EMBASSY TO THE OTTOMAN PORTE, FROM THE YEAR 1621 TO 1628 INCLUSIVE (London: Samuel Richardson, 1740), pp. 206–210.

Bethlem Gabor having with great expedition marched over Hungary, and reduced most part thereof to his obedience, except the townes of Presburgh, Rab. Komaza, and some fewe other forts, his army constituting of 33000 Transilvanians and Hungars, and almost as many Turks and Tartars voluntarily following for booty, mett with no showe of resistance, until he approached Tornavia, within 4 dayes march of the border of Moravia; whither sending before some regiments of his horse, to the nomber of 4000, to summon the towne, they discovered some imperiall troopes, sent to make garrison therein, beeing 2300 foote, and 200 cavallarye, and arrived within halfe an English mile, between whom and the citty they thrust themselves.

These troopes, perceiving they were sodainly prevented, and not knowing how farr the princes whole army was behind, tooke downe a small brook to a village, and fortified themselves in a church, and church-yard walled. The commander of the Hungars dispatched away a currier to Gabor, with advise, That hee should send him some foote with expedition, relating the mannor how hee had enclosed this garrison. In the meane tyme he summons them, and tells them, that hee had taken possession of Tornavia for his master; and at the same tyme summons the towne, and tells them, That their succours sent had yielded to him, keeping all intelligence from one another, and both from attempting anything. The next day the prince, with his vantguard, arrives in fight; and then his collonell sends some troupes to make guard before one of the ports, very neare the wall. These Germans, shutt upp in the church-yard, seeing the enemyes horse under the comaund of the towne, and no shott made at them, beleeved that it was true, that the place was rendred; so, before the foote came upp to force them, they yeelded themselves, and tooke pay of the prince; all, except 36 of the principall, that had licence to depart. These beeing now wonne, the cittizens, the next day, opened their ports, and received Bethlem for their lord: thus these were gayned, without any stroke. From hence he marcheth directly towards Moravia, and sends before him, a dayes journey, 8000 horse, to discover and spoile. The emperour, finding these beginnings urgent, orders the brother of the prince of Lichestein to drawe downe his garrisons of Bohemia and Moravia to the frontire; and sends the marquiss of Monte Negro, with Collalto, Don Balthaser de Marades, the count Slickc, Volstein, Tiffen-bach, conte Torquato kinsman to the pope, Sampach, and all his principall capteynes, to meete them, and to forme an army for defence. It is said, they were gathered together 15000, besides the baggage; who beeing lodged at the foote of an hill, in the borders of Moravia, and many of their soldiers straggling to gather grapes, were by these avant corriers of Gabor discovered, and presently besett, who tooke and slewe 700; some escaped, and gave the allarum, or else the whole imperiall campe had bene surprised without centinell or guard, having proved as serviceable as

the geese in the capitoll. The Hungars having gotten the top
of the hill, seeing the Bohemian and German army so neare
in the bottom, and in some confusion, resolved to make
tryall how they were provided, and make show of a charge;
but finding them in better order to receive them, retyred;
one capten only, adventuring too meare, was taken prisoner, and carried to the imperiall quarter; who beeing
examined, told them, That the prince with a mighty army
would, the next night, bee in fight; and therefore hee
advised them to prepare for their safety; for that he came
with resolution to fight, and over-matching them in
nomber, there was no probability other then death or
captivity. The Imperialls rather scorned than beleeved these
threatenings; butt the capteyne assuring them, it was no
tyme to jest with his owne life and theirs, they removed the
next morning, and marched towards a towne called
Hodoline, or Ghoding, upon the river of Moraw, that
divides Hungary from Moravia; about which was a small
trench, and within it a castle of some defence. The horse of
Gabor, seeing them move toward that place, pressed in a
gallopp before them, and sett all the houses on fire, which
burned a day and a night, untill the whole was consumed:
In this meane tyme Bethlem arrives with his army, and the
Imperialls stand in battalion to expect their fortune; butt
the fire beeing ended, gave them leave to enter among the
ruynes and ashes, and to make the best of necessity; where
they fortified themselves, having no store of provision. In
this estate, beeing enclosed about 13 dayes, it was discovered by a prisoner, that they were in great want; and that
the soldiours beganne to mutyny, demanding of their
capteynes, either to lead them out to fight and dye like men,
or to make such a party for them as their present condition
would admitt. Don Balthasar, generall of all the horse, in
the name of all the commanders, gathered the army
together; and acknowledging to them, first, the great virtue
they had showed, to abide at once the assaults of perill and
famine for their honor; and protesting, that their cafe and
their generalls was all one, for matter of allowance,
entreated them to strengthen themselves with hope and
constancy; and required of them an universal promise, that
they would abide with patience untill about the end of

October, then at hand: if, in that tyme, neither God nor the emperer sent them succours, they would make some composition for them, not doubting but to find Gabor a christian and a soldiour, though an enemy: and to this proposition they all gave their words and faith. The reason of this short obteyned tyme proceeded not from any thought of supply from the emperour; butt from an opinion and custome, that the *Turks would break upp their camp upon St. Demetrius-day, the 26. of that moneth,* they having never used to stay longer in the field, for the incommodityes of winter; and that now they served in a nature of voluntaries, and gotten their prey, it was very likely noting could hold them from rising: butt if that hope failed them, they then resolved to give the soldiers leave to make quarter for themselves; the generalls and commanders purposing to retyre into the castle with some competent numbers, which they doubted not to keepe, until supplyes, or weather, should force the enemy to dislodge. The prince of Transilvania, knowling likewise, that at that thme hee should have trouble enough to stay his succours, and if they stayed, hee feared they would prove ill wynter guests, and discreditt him with his Hungars, whom they indifferently spoiled, tooke councell either to force them before that day, or to wynne them by policy. Butt this latter beeing the safer way, and, it *seemes, hee had no desire to putt so many persons of quality into power of the Turks, whose prisoners by agreement they must remayne,* and having also intelligence upon what hopes the Imperialls held out, hee counterworks *with the Turks to give him a promise to abide with him 15 dayes after St. Demetrius;* in which tyme hee pretended to *deliver the fort and all into their hands;* conjecturing, as it seemes, that before that day the Germans would make some overture, out of which hee might work his owne advantage, and abteyne his owne ends, and they would admire and fear his power and creditt in the Turkish army: for, doubtless, hee might *have forced them, if hee had pleased*; butt then hee had made his estate *desperate of any reconciliation with the emperour,* and must resolve to continue the warr, uncerteyne of the constancy *of the Turks*; assured, they being once retyred, would very late drawe againe into the field: and perhapps he doubted the various success of warre, and of the setling of *this state in Asia*, where all things were in distemper; and was somewhat carefull of his reputation in Christendome, which hee knew was farr adventured in this action, for which above 20000 poore soules lost their liverty, and endangered their faith; therefore hee makes use of his tyme and his witt. And the Imperialls, finding themselves deseived in the hope of breaking up of the campe, now no longer able to susteyne their wants, send commissioners to him, in the emperours name, to treat some agreement. Hee seeing his *15 dayes weare out apace*, and the *Turks* beginning to dislodge, accepts the offer; and that very day, to give satisfaction to this *port*, dispeeds one of his chamber, post; to make knowne to *the vizier (a man not uneasy to abuse)* that hee had done his uttmost to deteyne the *Turks to winter in Hungary*; butt beeing not able longer to hold them together, hee was forced to come to treaty; for to advanture to assualt the trenches, was full of perill; to rise without some conclusion, were to quitt the place, and honor to the enemy, and to weaken his owne reputation; to continue the seege after the departure of his succours, would hazard his owne army into mutiny: therefore, that hee was resolved to make a truce for 8 moneths, that seeing the grand signor had received the emperours ambassador, tyme might bee allowed for treaty and finall conclusion: that as then hee had not fully agreed; but gave him commission to say, it was resolved on to bee done, only with a *formall reservation*, of the approvement of the *viziers*, without which it should bee held as not done; that hee should require the finall resolution of the port, Whether the grand signor would continue constant, and maynteyne him in the warre, or not? If they resolved upon warre, then to demand provision of munition, money, soldiours, and all other necessaries, in season; and *in a measure, in these tymes, impossible:* if they desire peace, that they should give a draught of what conditions they affected; butt withall, an absolute power to himselfe, to mittigate them, and to make such other, at his discretion, as the necessity of the affaires and tyme required, for the profitt of this empire. The prince, at the first arrival of these deputies at his quarter, discovered some jealousy and discontent in some of his followers: whereuppon hee called most of his commanders, and desired them not to mistrust him; hee shewed some reasons why hee might bee enforced to make a truce; butt protected hee would never depose armes, not conclude a finall peace with the emperour, except hee would also disarme, and leave Germany in quiett; for though it were a hard choice for him, *to bee bitten by a woolfe, or by a dogge, yet seeing hee could better trust the one then the other, he would make use of one to curb the other.* This gave not dull satisfaction, butt the words of a prince are currant payment, because they beare stampe; for his meaning, nor what hee treated, hee trusted none withall butt his owne breat. The messenger here arrived play'd his part so well and secretly, as hee gave good satisfaction to the state, ready enough to beleeve well, and procures a ratification of the truce now supposed to bee made; and for instructions in the intended treaty, receives three articles, and one commission: first, That the emperour should disclayme all right and title to Hungary, and should leave the people free, and Gabor to governe them. 2dly, That the prince elector, and all the provinces that had sent their ambassadors and presents to this port, and had made league, and taken the imperiall protection should bee restored to their pristine liberty and estates. 3dly, That the emperour should pay a tribute of 40000 dollars for Austria, pretended to bee granted in the dayes of sultan Selymus. Butt the commission of the key of the worke; whereby the prince, with the councell of the bassa of Buda, hath obteyned *plenam potentiam* at his owne discretion, if hee find peace convenient, to make and conclude it. This last beeing, as wee suppose; the end and scope of Gabors desires; the others only a garnishing, to *make the Turks beleeve, that hee is very carefull of their service*, and the emperour, that hee is very powerfull, and much cared for here, wee think, will produce an end of these warrs: and I am of this opinion, *because hee hath chosen by this truce rather to oblige the emperour, and his commanders, by so great a benefitt as their liberty, and their whole army, then to make them enemyes irreconcyleable.* And to this *agrees* his owne *profession*, That hee *drewe not in the Turks for any neede hee had of their succour*, nor for any *benefitt intended to them*; butt to make *a glorious show to the emperour of his creditt in this court, thereby to facilitate his ends*, which, what they are, tyme only must, as a mistery, reveale.

What the articles and arrests of this truce are, wee not know nothing, butt that it is taken untill July or September, 1624. And I have bene more large in the particulars of this matter, then may seeme needful; butt I desired, that from the lynes, parts, and wayes of his actions, your honor might *judicare virum*, and make some conjecture what may bee expected from him hereafter.

To the emperours ambassadour I gave the first advice of this truce, to his great joy; who as constantly affirmes, that hee hath assurance the grand signor will have noe breach with his master; which proceeds more of necessity than affection.

CHAPTER 28

Turkish Power in the 1630's

Blount was a perceptive observer of Turkish manners. His travels in the Turkish Empire were adventurous, and he, more than most travelers, delighted in the exuberance displayed by his various hosts. His observations on the orderliness of Turkish armies are instructive. The Ottoman Empire was still of great consequence when Blount made his journey in the 1630's.

(Blount, Henry, *A Voyage into the Levant* (Written in 1634), John Pinkerton editor of *A General Collection of the Best and Most Interesting Voyages and Travels in All Parts of the World* (London: Longman, Hurst, Rees, Orme & Brown, 1811), Vol. X, pp.230–231.)

At length we reached Vallivoh, a pretty little town upon the confines of Hungary; where the camp staying some days, we left them behind, and being to pass a wood near the Christian country, doubting it to be (as confines are) full of thieves, we divided our caravan of six score horse in two parts; half with the persons, and goods of least esteem, we sent a day before the rest, that so the thieves, having a booty, might be gone before we came, which happened accordingly; they were robbed; one thief, and two of ours slain; some hundred dollars worth of goods lost. The next day we passed, and found sixteen thieves in a narrow passage, before whom we set a good guard of harquebuzes and pistols, till the weaker fort passed by; so in three days we came safe to Belgrada.

The city, anciently called Taurunum, or Alba Graeca, was the metropolis of Hungary, till won by sultan Soliman the second, in the year 1525. It is one of the most pleasant, stately, and commodious situations that I have seen; it stands most in a bottom, encompassed eastward by gentle and pleasant ascents, employed in orchards or vines; southward is an easy hill, part possessed with buildings, the rest a burying-place of well nigh three miles in compass, so full of graves as one can be by another; the west end yields a right magnificient aspect, by reason of an eminency of land jetting out further than the rest, and bearing a goodly strong castle, whose walls are two miles about, excellently fortified with a dry ditch and out works. This castle on the west side is washed by the great river Sava, which on the north of the city loses itself in the Danubius, of old called Ister, now Duny, and is held the greatest river in the world, deep and dangerous for navigation, runs eastward into the Euxine or Black Sea, in its passage receiving fifty and odd rivers, most of them navigable. Two rarities, I was told of this river, and with my own experience found true; one was, that at mid-day and mid-night, the stream runs slower by much than at other times; this they find by the noise of those boat-mills, whereof there are about twenty, like those upon the Rhoane at Lions; their clackers beat much slower at those times than else, which argues like difference in the motion of the wheel, and by consequence of the stream; the cause is neither any reflux, nor stop of current by wind or otherwise, for there is no increase of water observed. The other wonder is, that where those two great currents meet, their waters mingle no more than water and oil; not that either floats above other, but join unmixed; so that near the middle of the river, I have gone in a boat, and tasted of the Danuby as clear and pure as a well; then putting my hand not an inch further, I have taken of the Sava as troubled as a street channel, tasting the gravel in my teeth; yet it did not tast unctious, as I expected, but hath some others secret ground of the antipathy, which though not easily found out, is very effectual; for they run thus threescore miles together, and for a day's journey I have been an eye witness thereof.

The castle is excellently furnished with artillery, and at the entrance there stands an arsenal with some forty or fifty fair brass pieces, most bearing the arms and inscription of Ferdinand the emperor. That which to me seemed strangest in this castle (for I had free liberty to pry up and down) was a round tower called the Zindana, a cruelty not by them devised, and seldom practiced; it is like old Rome's Gemoniae: the tower is large and round, but within severed into many squares of long beams, set on end about four feet asunder; each beam was stuck frequently with great flesh hooks; the person condemned was naked, let fall amongst those hooks, which gave him a quick or lasting misery, as he chanced to light; then at the bottom the river is let in by grates, whereby all the putrefaction was washed away. Within this great castle is another little one, with works of its own; I had like to have miscarried with approaching the entrance, but the rude noise, and worse looks of the guard, gave me a timely apprehension with sudden passage, and humiliation, to sweeten them, and get off; for, as I after learned, there is kept great part of the Grand Seignior's treasure, to be ready when he wars on that side the empire: it is death for any Turk or Christian to enter; and the captain is never to go forth without particular license from the emperor. Here the bashaw of Temesuar, joining the people of Buda, and his own with those of Belgrade and Bosnah, they were held encamped on the south side of the town, yet not so severely, but the Spahies, Janisaaries, and Venturiers, had leave to go before to the general rendezvous, as they pleased, though most of them staid to attend the bashaws; they there expected Murath bashaw; he, five days after our arrival, came in with a few foot, but four thousand horse, of the Spahy Timariot's; such brave horses, and men so dexterous in the use of the launce, I had not seen. Then was made public proclamation to hang all such Janissaries as should be found behind these forces. With them the next day we set forward for Sophia, which in twelve days we reached. The bashaws did not go all in company, but setting forth about an hour one after another, drew out their troops in length without confusion, not in much exact order of file and rank, as near no enemy. In this and our former march, I much admired that we had a caravan loaded with clothes, silks, tissues, and other rich commodities, were so safe, not only in the main army, but in straggling troops, amongst whom we often wandered, by reason of recovering the Jews sabbath; but I found the cause to be the cruelty of justice; for thieves upon the way are empaled without delay; or mercy; and there was a Saniack, with two hundred horse, who did nothing but coast up and down the country, and every man who could not give a fair account of his being where he found him, was presently strangled, though not known to have offended; for their justice, although not so rash as we suppose, yet will rather cut off two innocent men, than let one offender escape; for in the execution of an innocent, they think if he be held guilty, the example works as well as if he were guilty indeed; and where a constant denial makes the fact doubted, in that execution, the resentment so violent terrifies the more: therefore to prevent disorders sometimes, in the beginnings of war, colourable punishments are used, where just ones are wanting. This speedy and remorseless severity makes that when then their great armies lie about any town or pass, no man is endamaged or troubles to secure his goods; in which respect it pretends more effect upon a bad age than our Christian compassion, which is so easily abused, as we cannot raise two or three companies of soldiers, but they pilfer and rifle wheresoever they pass; wherein the want of cruelty upon delinquents, causes much more oppression of the innocent, which is the greatest cruelty of all. Yet without their army there want not scandals, for in the way we passed by a Palanga, which is a village fortified with mud walls against thieves, where we found a small caravan to have been assaulted the day before, and divers remaining sore wounded; for through all Turkey, especially in desart places, there are many mountaineers, or outlaws, like the Wild Irish, who live upon spoil, and are not held members of the state, but enemies, and used accordingly. In all our march, though I could not perceive much discipline, as not near an adverse party, yet I wondered to see such a multitude so clear of confusion, violence, want, sickness, or any other disorder; and, though we were almost three score thousand, and sometimes found not a town in seven or eight days, yet was there such plenty of good bisket, rice, and mutton, as wheresoever I passed up and down to view the Spahies and others in their tents, they would often make me sit and eat with them very plentifully and well....

CHAPTER 29

Wallachia in 1657—Time of Troubles

Depicted in this selection is the plight of two travelers in a time of trouble. The Patriarch of Antioch and his son, who relates the story, passed through Wallachia in 1657, the year that the rule of Constantine Serbar as hospodor came to an end. Constantine, successor to the illustrious Matthew Bessarab, allowed himself to be drawn into the anti-Polish, anti-Turkish intrigues of the Transylvanian ruler, George Rákóczy II. The Turks, aided by Tartar reinforcements, invaded Wallachia and caused much damage. Much of this story is paraphrased by the translator, but the chaos and destruction in 1657 are well conveyed.

Paul, Archdeacon of Aleppo, THE TRAVELS OF MACARIUS, PATRIARCH OF ANTIOCH, *F. C. Belfour*, translator (Oxford: University Press, 1836), pp. 96–109.

Other causes for anxiety alarmed the travellers; for a report reached Tergovist that the Turks, in alliance with the Tatars, were marching against Hungary; and that they might make a punitive expedition through Wallachia and Moldavia on account of the Cral of Hungary having forced the Beys of those countries to furnish him with troops. (Hungary was fighting in alliance with Sweden against the Emperor of Russia.) The seething condition of the country make Kyr Macarius and his son desire to put themselves within reach of the Hungarian mountains where the Wallachians were accustomed to take refuge in time of need. The proposed visitations of the convents gave an ostensible reason for their movements towards this goal.

On June 18 they set out, taking all their luggage with them. Their route followed the bank of the great river Aluta and led them to the famous Monastery of Kozia, by a narrow pass overhanging the river, through a deep ravine full of rocks and roaring waters. On the farther side were vast, impassable, wooded mountains. "As we ascended the ravine we passed under a perpendicular rock, the side of a high mountain. A wooden bridge, resting on the frightfully steep bank, stretched over the river. It was nailed on one side to two tall trees and rested on the other on the mountain precipice. When any danger threatens the convent the monks remove the bridge, leaving an impassable gulf. We were afraid to cross it on horseback, so we alighted and crossed on foot. The road was very narrow and close to the edge of the precipice. It led to a large open plain of fields, gardens and vineyards, in the midst of which stood the convent, a handsome strong edifice, guarded by the river and high mountain summits and pathless woods. It is situated at the extremity of Wallachia, and Hungary lies north and south of it. Its name Kozia means natural fortress."

The travellers reached the convent on June 28 and there deposited their luggage by command of the Bey. A visit to this convent had been specially planned, because they had heard that there was deposited a most valuable book from the imperial collection of S. Sophia at Constantinople, viz. an exposition of the Psalms of David, compiled by S.

Nicetas in the eleventh century from all the holy doctors of the Church and others, 300 folio pages. This book was believed to be unique, as no copy of it existed in the Pope's library nor in that of any European city library.

The Archdeacon wrote: "Having heard the praises of this book, I exerted myself to the utmost; and by the aid of my father, I got it home to our lodgings, and having found a priest, Papa Yani from Scio, a fine writer of Greek, we engaged him to make a copy.

"As the love of wine is an innate propensity of every Greek I did not cease to steal away his senses till we had carried him up to this convent of Kozia, where we forced him to stay and write. Each day we sent him an allowance of two *okas* of wine for his dinner and supper; his senses were sobered and his powers of mind shone forth in all their brightness, and he completed his copy of the book... Our design was, if it pleased God, sooner or later to send the book to be printed in the country of the Franks, as well for our own benefit as for that of the whole Church of Christ.

"We obtained from the aforesaid Metropolitan of Gaza leave to copy another book, the contents of which he had gathered in every country and from many authors perfectly unique, as no other copy of it existed. He had named it the *Book of Prophesies*. He consented with difficulty to its being copied. But afterwards, in the war, he was robbed of it and of everything that he possessed, and he wrote to Kyr Macarius, entreating us to get a copy written out for him, from ours."

With visits to several more convents in ravines and on lakes, the tour of eighty-two days ended by the travellers' return to Tergovist on September 10. There the Bey Constantine still detained them. On November 8 the Patriarch married him to a Circassian slave, whom they named at her baptism Nadala. The ceremony was performed within the palace, in the harem.

Two months later Constantine received the news from Constantinople that he was deposed from his governship, with the result that Wallachia was reduced to utter desolation and ravaged by the invasions of its enemies.

The deposition of the Bey Constantine was an act of

revenge of the Grand Vizir, as punishment for the successful appeal to the Sultan, made in the previous year by the
Beys of Moldavia and Wallachia, against the Vizir's exorbi-
tant demands on them for tribute. They had paid the full
tribute in 1657, but the Vizir repeated his demand for
additional payment of five hundred thousand sheep, three
hundred horses and an increase of the money tribute. While
negotiations were going on, he cut them short by deposing
Constantine and appointing in his place a son of the late
Radzivil Voivode. He also despatched one of his officers to
the Khan and his Tatars, enjoining them to march on
Moldavia and Wallachia.

Constantine, hearing this, sent warning to all his subjects, "The whole country, in consequence, was thrown into
confusion, the wretched inhabitants fleeing from their
farms and villages in the severe frost and deep snow." This
was followed by an order from the dreaded Turks to
Constantine to depart immediately from the principality.
The Bey and his grandees determined to offer resistance to
their tyrants. Troops were enrolled. The Metropolitan,
standing from morning to night in the church, swore them
on the holy gospel and the cross. These additional troops
brought the number of soldiers available up to a hundred
and ten thousand.

Constantine proved a despicable leader of his army. His
vacillating policy led him to retreat from Tergovist, leaving
the town to be defended by twelve thousand of his troops to
whom he gave permission to seize all provisions and liquors
left in the town. These miserable defenders, in an intoxi-
cated condition, were seized with panic at the approach of
three hundred Tatars and fled, leaving the city at the mercy
of this handful of invaders. After plundering, they set fire
to it, carrying away a vast number of its inhabitants into
captivity. They slew one hundred and sixty of the monks at
Stalia Convent, and burned its church, that was packed
with possessions of the people, among which was the
property of Kyr Macarius. They broke open the tombs of
the late Bey and his family and of Constantine's domina,
stripped the bodies and flung them naked to the winds.
Other tombs were also desecrated. The fire did not cease its
ravages till the greater part of the city was destroyed.

The new Bey, accompanied by the Pasha, entered Ter-govist on February 23. After setting its walls on fire (in retribution for Constantine's having ordered Bucharest to be burned before the Turks could advance upon it), they marched to that stricken city.

"As for Constantine, he fled to Hungary to a castle in the city of Brashob, where he remained with all his adherents. May God deny him eternal salvation for the deeds he perpetrated. His situation was very ignominious because of his running away without fighting.

"As soon as we were assured of Constantine's flight, we departed in haste from Kimpolung on February 21, and fled to a small ancient convent called Gharadas and there deposited all we had brought away with us. The carriages, too, we gave up to be burried in the thickets. Our horses we kept saddled day and night. A hiding place was found for us in the heart of the woods. Notwithstanding the depth of the fallen snow and the intense frost no one dared to light a fire for fear of the smoke betraying our presence.

"Then we heard that Michael Voivode, the new Bey, had taken up his residence in Bucharest, and that the people and military were tendering him their allegiance, and he was readily pardoning them. He sent letters throughout the province, proclaiming peace and pardon and calling on the fugitives to return to their homes. We, like the rest of the people, took courage and returned to Kimpolung, though we still left most of our goods with the peasants of Gharadas. It cost all the money we had to pay the expenses on them.

"I rode with a number of others to Tergovist, where we saw bodies of the slain lying strewed about the streets....We heard that the Tatars had gone off with their captives, reported as being from seventy thousand to a hundred and fifty thousand. Many were redeemed by the new Bey, who did not allow the Turks to make a single captive....Our Lord the Patriarch sent a letter of congratulation to the new Bey, which he received most graciously. We were told that he had resided twenty-five years within the Sultan's seraglio among the Turks; yet no one had seduced him to deviate from his Christian creed. He was a student of ecclesias-tical writings, and a linguist in the Polish, Hungarian, Greek, Turkish, Persian and his native Wallachian tongues.

"Encouraged by these tidings we went to Bucharest. After the burning of it, nothing remained but the churches; and in them the people of rank were lodged. On Pentecost Sunday, May 30, 1658, the Patriarch crowned the Bey, according to the form in the great Prayer Book. On the altar was laid a braided girdle and a gilt mace; also a crown made for the Bey at Constantinople, resembling the head-dress of the Seleucians. It was decorated with a plume of feathers, in crystals and jewels.

When the Bey entered the church the great Ban and the logothete (Chancellor) took him by the arms, the clergy preceding him, and advanced to the royal doors, whence came forth two bishops who, taking the Bey by the arms, conducted him to the Sanctuary. There he knelt, with his head uncovered, while I said the liturgical formula, 'Let us Attend'. Our master then laid a part of his pallium on the Bey's head, saying: 'The grace of God, which ever heals what is weak and supplies what is deficient, promotes the Christian Prince Michael, son of Radzivil Voivode, to the rank of a Sovereign. Let us, therefore, pray for him, that the grace of the all-holy spirit may come upon him.'

"The Patriarch then raised him up and invested him with the girdle, hanger and sword. He clothed him with the robe of sovereignty, a brocaded mantle trimmed with sable fur, and crowned him with the Constantinople crown. Then he blessed and kissed him, and the two bishops delivered him to the two archons at the door of the Sanctuary, who led him up to his throne. Our master first, then the bishops, the twelve great archons, priests, monks, deacons and the rest of the State archons all congratulated, blessed and prayed for him. The concourse of the people was very great."

The Bey was immediately plunged into preparation for war, having received orders from Constantinople to march with the Sultan's army against the Majars. Despite these activities he spent his mornings and evenings in the company of Kyr Macarius, discussing all manner of religious and other matters with him.

Meanwhile ex-Bey Constantine, with a fresh army, was threatening to re-enter Wallachia; while the Pasha of Silistria and his Tatar troops invaded the country. This renewal of war brought fresh anguish upon the unfortunate people, who again quitted their homes and fled for refuge to the mountains.

The Archdeacon wrote: "Despairing of our personal safety, we could see nothing for it but to quit Wallachia; even if we had to leave our property behind. On July 9, 1658, the Bey left for the camp, and our perplexity was extreme. His deputy found for me two carriages, which we loaded with our heavy luggage and goods and I went with them to Galatz, where we found a vessel from Trebizond about to return. On it I shipped our goods and our companions with a store of provisions and they set sail.

"Then I hired some men with muskets and set out on my return, fearing lest I should come across the Turks, who were on their march, robbing and murdering on their way. I found not a single person, not even a dog or any other animal, between Galatz and Bucharest. I stumbled on some dead bodies in my path. The whole world was a blank. I reached Bucharest on July 31, but did not find the Patriarch there, he having retreated, in fear and alarm, to Piteshti, where I joined him.

"After spending nearly two months on horseback, going hither and thither, recovering all I could of our property, we started from Bucharest on September 9 for Galatz, reaching it on September 17. We stopped there twenty-two days, seeking for a ship to take us to Sinope, but found that the Vizir had taken all the ships to carry his stores and munitions to the Danube.

"Through our fears of traversing the Black Sea, we had waited these two years, hoping to be able to travel by way of Roumelia; and thence by good fortune to embark on some ship belonging to Christians on the White Seas. But to go by that route had, up to the present time, been utterly impossible. We saw from Galatz the fires on the mountains of the Majars and knew what they meant.

"At length we found a ship belonging to a Christian from Sinope, laden with barley; and we agreed to give him two hundred piastres [about £3] to take us to that port. We could scarce credit our senses when we had, at last, stowed our luggage on board the ship and found ourselves embarked clear of immediate danger from the invaders.

"We left Galatz on October 13, and passed down the

Danube to Kilia, a large castle at the mouth of the channel of the Black Sea. Here we heard the Mahometan *azan* (call to prayer), having for six years heard only bells. Here they catch sturgeons.

"At the opening into the Black Sea we found about seventy vessels that had been waiting more than two months for a wind to sail forth. On October 24 a favourable wind sprang up, and we got out to sea. In two days and a night we sailed two hundred and fifty miles to Kavarna Port. Here we passed a most wretched night ready to die of sea-sickness, for it blew a gale. At break of day we went on shore and stayed with a priest till the 29th, when the people of the ship fetched us back and we went with them, as going to the slaughter. The wind had changed and we sailed four hundred miles, crossing the channel of Constantinople from the Roumelian side to the coast of Anatolia, to Heraclea, where S. Theodore, a commander-in-chief, suffered martyrdom."...

CHAPTER 30

The Turkish Defeat at Vienna—1683

The Vienna expedition of 1683 was the brainchild of the Grand Vizier, Kara Mustapha, son-in-law of Sultan Mohammed IV (1648–1687). Kara Mustapha did not have to worry about French or Russian interference, and because the Hapsburgs had been autocratic toward Royal Hungary, the Turks had the support of a Magyar army led by Imre Tököli.

But the great mistake of Kara Mustapha was his neglect of Poland. History seemed to prove the divergence of Hapsburg and Polish interests, yet King John Sobieski of Poland signed a pact with Emperor Leopold in March, 1683. When the defenders of Vienna were about to capitulate, Sobieski appeared with an army of 80,000 on September 11.

The battle turned into a Turkish disaster and signalled the beginning of Ottoman decline.

M. Delerac (translator), POLISH MANUSCRIPTS: OR THE SECRET HISTORY OF THE REIGN OF JOHN SOBIESKI, THE III OF THAT NAME, KING OF POLAND (London: D. Rhodes, 1700), pp. 355–364.

The Victory which the King of *Poland* hath obtained over the Infidels, is so great and so compleat that past Ages can scarce parallel the fame; and perhaps future Ages will never see any thing like it. All its Circumstances are as profitable to Christendom in general, and to the Empire in particular, as glorious to the Monarch. On one hand we see *Vienna* besieged by three hundred thousand Turks; reduced to the last extremity; its Outworks taken; the Enemy fixed to the Body of the Place; Masters of one Point of the Basions, having frightful Mines under the Retrenchments of the besieged: We see an Emperor chased from his Capital; retired to a Corner of his Dominions; all his Country at the mercy of the Tartars, who have filled the Camp with an infinite Number of unfortunate Slaves that had been forcibly carried away out of Austria. On the other hand, we see the King of *Poland*, who goes out of his Kingdom, with part of his Army, and hastens to succour his Allies, who abandons what is dearest to him, to march against the Enemies of the Christian Religion willing to act in Person on this Occasion, as a true Buckler of Religion; and will not spare his eldest Son, the Prince of *Poland*, whom he carries with him, even in a tender Age, to so dangerous an Expedition as this was. That which preceded the battle is no less surprizing. The Empire assembles on all sides, the Elector's of *Saxony* and *Bavaria* come in Person to join their Troops with the *Imperialists* under the command of the Duke of *Lorrain*. Thirty other Princes repair out of Emulation, to one another, to the Army, which nevertheless, before they will enter upon Action, stay for the presence of the K of *Poland*, whose presence alone is worth an Army.

They all march with this Confidence. The King passes the *Danube* first, and leaves no Troops on the other side to cover Moravia from the Incursions that the Malecontents under Count *Teckley* might make into the same, as the Duke of *Lorrain* had proposed; because, says the King, he had wrote to that Hungarian Lord, that if he burnt one Straw in the Territories of his Allies, or in his own, he would go and burn him and all his Family in his House, so that this was enough to protect that Country during the distance of the Army. He leads them afterwards through unfrequented Defiles to the tops of the Hills of *Vienna*, and in fight of the Turks, who drew out of their Camp to put themselves in order, and even attack'd the Imperialists by break of Day on Sunday the 12th of *September*, before the King of *Poland* had made an end of forming his Order of Battle, and extending his Lines, in which his Majesty has mixed his Hussars, and other Polish Troops among those of the Empire.

In the mean time, the Turks leave their Trenches well provided with Janisaries, with a considerable Body at the Posts and at the Attacks, to hinder the besieged from sallying out; hoping to continue the Siege at the same time as the Army should make head against the Succours of the Christian Princes; and truly they had wherewith all to back this proud Revolution; having above 30000 Men, according to the King's Account, who found above 100000 small tents in their Camp, wherein apparently according to the manner of disposing their Men, there were at least three Men in each, and his Polish Majesty has reduced the common Report of 300000 Tents which would infinitely augment the number of Soldiers to that of 100000.

The Battle was fought on the 12th, it lasted 14 or 15 Hours; the slaughter was horrible, and the loss of the Turks inestimable, for they left upon the Field of Battle, besides the Dead and Prisoners, all their Canon, Equipage, Tents and infinite Riches that they had been six Years gathering together throughout the whole Ottoman Empire. There was found in their Camp above a Million of Powder, Bullets, Balls and other Ammunition, without reckoning the Powder that the Servants burnt by inadvertancy in several Places of the Park of the Artillery the flame whereof made an Emblem of the terrible day of Judgment, with the Earthquakes that will accompany it; and that thick Mass of

Clouds that will obscure the Universe: A Loss nevertheless which ought to be called a great Misfortune, seeing 'tis above a Million more, as the King assures us in his Letter, that he wrote himself to the Queen, from which all these Particulars are extracted.

The Battle ended by the Infantry of the Trenches, and of the Isle of the *Danube*, where the Turks had a Battery. The Night was spent in slaughter, and the unhappy Remnant of this Army saved their Lives by flight, having abandoned all to the Victors; even an infinite Number of Waggons, loaden with Ammunition, and some Field pieces, that designed to have carried with them; and which were found next Day upon the Road they had taken; which makes us suspect that they'l not be able to rally again, as neither having where withal to incamp themselves nor Cannon to shoot with.

So soon as the Grand Visier knew the Defeat of his first Lines, he caused a red Tent to be pitched at the Head of his Main Body, where he resolved to dye for the Ottoman Empire, but his Last Efforts were to no purpose; and the Wing of the Imperialists, which he attacked with all his might, was so opportunely succoured by the presence of the King, who brought part of the Troops of his left Wing thither; that all fled before him. So soon as he perceived the red Tent, knowing by it that the Visier was there in Person, he caused all his Artillery to fire upon that Pavillion, encouraging the Activity of the Gunners by considerable Recompenses promising them fifty Crowns for each Cannon-shot; and these leveled their small Pieces so well, that they brought down the Tent of the Grand Visier; and the Troop of Prince *Alexander* his second Son, had the Advantage to break through that Body of Cavalry, at the very Place where the Visier was, who was dismounted, and had much ado to save himself upon another Horse; having left, among the slain, his *Kiayia*, that is, his *Lieutenant General, and the second Person of the Army;* with abundance of considerable Officers; all the Standards; the Marks of his Dignity that are carried before him, or that are set up before his Pavillions; even the great Standard of Mahomet, which the Sultan had put into his Hands when he set out upon this Expedition; and which the King has sent to *Rome* by the Sieur *Talenti,* one of his Secretaries, to be a Testimony to the Pope, of this great Victory.

The King understood afterwards by Deserters, who come every hour in Troops to surrender themselves to him, as well as the Renegadoes, that the Visier, seeing the defeat of the Army, called his Sons to him, imbraced them, bitterly bewailed their Misfortune, and turned towards the Han of the Tartars, and said, *And thou, wilt not thou succour me?* To whom the Tartar Prince replied, That he knew the King of *Poland* by more than one Proof, and that the Visier would be very happy if he could save himself by flight, as having no other way for his Security, and that he was going to show him Example.

The Grand Visier being this abandoned, took the same-way, and retired in Disorder with only one Horse; that which he had in the Battle, and was armed all over with Steel, having fallen into the Hands of the King with all the Equipages of that Ottoman General; who has left his Majesty Heir to all his Riches. In effect, his Letters were dated from the Tents of the Grand Visier, the Park whereof was of as large Extent as the City of *Warsaw* or that of *Leopold;* inclosing his Baths, Fountains, Canals, a Garden, a kind of Menagerie or Place for strange Beasts and Birds, with Dogs, Rabbets and Parrots. There was found an Ostridge of an admirable Beauty, which had been taken from one of the Emperor's Country-Houses, and whose Head the Visier's Men cut off in their Retreat, that it might not serve to adorn the King's Menagerie. This Precaution would have been of greater use if they had taken it with Respect to the Standard of Mahomet, and of that prodigious Quantity of Riches, Bows, Quivers, Sabres set with Rubies, and Diamonds, precious Moveables and Equipages of great Value, that were left with the Tents to the King of *Poland;* which made that Monarch say very pleasantly in his Letter to his Queen, *You will not tell me at my return, what the Tartarian Women tell their Husbands when they see them return from the Army without Booty; Thou are not a Man, seeing thou returnest empty handed; for doubtless he was the first in the Battle, who returns loaden with the Spoils of the Enemy; the Grand Visier having made me his Universal Legatee.* The Booty that was taken in this Action is infinite and inestimable: The Field of Battle was sowed with Gold Sabres, with Pieces of Stuff, and such a prodigious Quantity of other things that the Pillage which has already lasted three Days, will scarce be over in a whole Week, although the Besieged are come out of the Town in great Companies to partake of the Booty with the victorious Soldier; both the one and the other being scarce able as yet to perswade themselves that this happy success is real, it is so extraordinary: Insomuch that the whole Army, which nevertheless has done its duty very couragiously, can't forbear to attribute this great Victory to the mighty God of Battles, who would make use of the Hands of the King of *Poland* to overthrow the Enemies of his Name; for which let him be honoured and glorified for ever and ever....

CHAPTER 31

The Last Letter of a Hungarian Patriot

Ferencz Rákóczy II (1676–1735) came from a distinguished family that had produced three princes of Transylvania in the seventeenth century. His early years were chaotic, but while he was educated in Bohemia under the care of the Austrians, he kept the patriotism taught him by his family.

In 1703, Rákóczy returned to Hungary and took the leading place in an anti-Austrian rebellion. Without adequate equipment, money, or support from the Magyar nobility, Rákóczy still managed to keep up a resistance until 1711. In February of 1711, Rákóczy left Hungary and after wandering through Poland and France, he settled in the Turkish Empire where he lived from 1717 until his death in 1735.

Ráth Károly and Thaly Kálmán (editors), II RAKOCZY FERENCZ FEJEDELEM EMLEKIRATAI (Pest: Kiadja Rathmor, 1868), pp. 343–346. Translated by the editors.

Farewell Letter of Ferencz Rákóczy II to Ali Pasha

No doubt you will be amazed, my dear friend, when you receive this letter with the report of my death. But the frailty of man makes death unavoidable. Love of God calls me and while I prepare for death, I must express my gratitude to the Invincible Emperor....I have given orders to the officers of my court that when I die they will report it to you. They will send at the same time this letter to my dear friend. May the last word of his true friend move his heart, and may he show to the emperor, to my gracious lord, the last speech of my grateful heart.

My arrival in this glorious empire I attributed always to God's inscrutable wisdom....My mind was ruled by confidence in God and by the hope that the Sublime Porte would not let me down. And now in this last hour of my life I can say that I was not disappointed because my person was honored and I was given support. I am grateful that I was protected from the evil intentions of my enemies.

Many times it was a consolation during my life that my good intentions were recognized by the ministers of the sublime Porte who were good and amiable toward me. And thus, living in quiet tranquility, I prepared myself for liberation from all my miseries....I love my followers as my sons and directed by Christian feelings, I distributed everything among them which is under my control. But I am not ashamed to confess that I am living in such poverty that I could not leave anything as a suitable reward for all those officers whom the mighty emperor offered to me and who served me faithfully and with diligence.

Regarding this matter, if I can attribute to myself any merit in the face of the invincible emperor: that he may show his gracious goodness toward all those who served me according to his orders.

But because through so many years I was rather a burden than an advantage to the Sublime Porte, I recommend each of them to the gracious goodness of the mighty emperor but especially Abraham Effendi, my faithful interpreter. May almighty God reward him with his choicest blessings for the good deeds he performed for me. And I ask the Sultan, in the name of God, to make it certain that my few followers will not be as sheep left without a shepherd.

Prince Ferencz Rákóczy

CHAPTER 32

The Phanariot Rulers of Moldavia

Thornton gives a very dismal picture of the situation in Moldavia at the beginning of the nineteenth century. For him the Greek rulers (Phanariots) are bad enough, the native Roumanian princes (boyars) are even worse. Although there is some truth in Thornton's account, it is obvious that his excess of puritanism blinds him to a more profound analysis of the Moldavian political structure.

Thomas Thorton, THE PRESENT STATE OF TURKEY (London: Joseph Mawman, 1809), Vol. II, pp. 369–371.

The education of the *boyars* is little superior in point of real utility to that of the common people. The children are instructed by priests in the houses of their parents, and are surrounded by *chinganehs*, who corrupt them by abject servility and a base compliance with all their caprices. Formed by such tutors, they pass into a world of hypocrisy and vice, without one just principle to regulate their conduct, without one generous purpose, or one honourable sentiment. They adopt indiscriminately the vices, without inheriting the vivacity, of the Greeks, or veiling them with that delicacy which the Greeks have not wholly relinquished. They confound whatever is most degrading in luxury with the fair fruit of civilization, and in their rude adoption of European manners, they plunge into promiscuous debauchery, and indulge to excess in an unprincipled passion of gaming. Like the Poles and Hungarians the *boyars* inherit a taste for magnificent dresses and splendid equipages: they love balls and public entertainments, but their assemblies are rude and tumultuous. Their tables are open to every person of their acquaintance, but are inelegantly served. In the cities they are forbidden to form connexions of intimacy, or even to keep up intercourse, with strangers; but I have occasionally lodged for a night in their country seats, and was always received and treated by them with a plain but decent hospitality.

The Greeks adopt a more than Asiatic luxury: they sleep after dinner on their sophas, whilst a female servant fans away the flies and refreshes the air which they breathe: They exact from their attendants the respect and homage which they have seen paid to the Turkish grandees; but feeling within themselves no consciousness of personal worth or importance, they cannot command with Turkish dignity, the petulance of vanity betrays itself in harsh expressions, and insulting behaviour, to their inferiors.

On the death or deposition of a prince the divan assembles, and immediately assumes the administration of public affairs. All the creatures or dependents of the prince are removed from office, and other persons are appointed, who are continued in authority until the arrival of his successor. The *caimacam*, or lieutenant of the newly created prince announces the nomination of his master, but does not interfere in the affairs of government, further than in superintending the collection of the prince's revenues. The fallen sovereign is immediately forsaken by his courtiers, is always treated with neglect, and sometimes with insult and abuse. He returns privately, and without pomp, to Constantinople, where he retires to his seat in the Fanal or on the shores of the Bosphorus. With the usual modesty of *rayahs* the princes resume their habits of submission, and the exterior of humility. They are followed only by a single servant; but at home they are surrounded by a princely and titled household: they allot to particular officers distinct portions of service, and pass the day in planning new schemes of ambition, or in receiving the secret homage of their clients and vassals....

CHAPTER 33

The Court at Bucharest—Early Nineteenth Century

This description by MacMichael is typical of many others that tended to see the Phanariot class in Roumania as extremely decadent. William MacMichael (1784–1839) was a student fresh out of Oxford (M.D., 1816) when he made his second trip into Eastern Europe. He possessed no great insight, but his portrayal of life in Wallachia and Moldavia adequately conveys the malaise felt by some inhabitants who chafed under the restrictions of Turkish rule. After his book was published in 1819, MacMichael embarked on a distinguished career as a physician and did not resume the romantic voyage of his younger days.

William MacMichael, JOURNEY FROM MOSCOW TO CONSTAN-TINOPLE (London: John Murray, 1819), pp. 117–119.

The inhabitants of Buchorest are as much addicted to the vice of gambling, and the love of dissipation in general, as those of the capital of Moldavia. There was, however, no theatre open, and their chief public amusement consisted in the jolting promenade along the streets, similar to that described at Jassy. But as we were here during the carnival, there were public balls two or three times a week at one of the principal inns, and we were present one evening at a sort of theatrical exhibition resembling the feats of horsemanship at Astley's; the entertainment, which was given by some itinerant Germans, in a public building called *"The Club,"* began with a dance executed on stilts, and concluded with a ludicrous scene in imitation of our popular farce of the "Tailor riding to Brentford." The dialogue was in German, a language much spoken here; and it gave a laughable air of dignity to the representation, to listen to the calpaked courtiers of the Hospodar, translating into modern Greek parts of the ridiculous conversation of the players. When, for instance, the inexperienced rider asks the innkeeper in the farce, if he has any steady horse he can recommend to him, the Wallachian gentry thought it a very good joke to surround the officer of the Prince, who is at the head of the department of the post at Buchorest, and teaze him with the question, "Have you good horses." Many of the tricks of the performers were of the coarsest description; but the Princess and her daughters who were present at the entertainment, seated on sofas at the upper end of the room, and dressed with a profusion of jewels, seemed highly delighted, and laughed immoderately at jests, not much distinguished by good breeding. As a proof of the state of morals in the capital, the son of the Hospodar (dressed like a Turk, and wearing a turban, in which he would not have dared to be seen at Constantinople,) entered the club, where sat his mother and sisters, having on his arm his mistress, a beautiful Wallachian lady, who had lately deserted her husband and six children; there appeared to be nothing extraordinary, or that was considered indelicate, in his conduct. The Prince himself was not at the club, but most of the officers of his court, and many of the principal nobles of Wallachia were assembled in the room; they were uniformly dressed in huge calpaks, with long flowing robes, and many were smoking Turkish pipes; in short, every thing was Eastern in the appearance of the men, though in the costume of the ladies, who were sitting cross-legged on sofas, there was an evident admixture of French and Oriental attire; their coiffures were richly ornamented with jewels, and they wore French silk dresses, probably made at Vienna, together with the Greek zone and Turkish slippers. Under the jealous eye of the suspicious government of Turkey, the article of dress is a matter of no small importance; and the use of the costume of civilized Europe would be considered as dangerous an innovation, as the adoption of the most enlightened views of modern policy.

During the occupation of the country by the Russians, the boyars eagerly laid aside this loose attire, and wore the French dress; but on their return to Turkish authority, they were obliged to resume the robe and the calpak. It was with reluctance they saw themselves revert to their former masters; and, it is said, they envy the lot of the inhabitants of that part of Moldavia, who are so happy as to enjoy the protection of the autocrat of all the Russias. When the imperial head-quarters were at Buchorest, the army spent considerable sums of money in the town, a circumstance which makes the inhabitants regret still more their absence.

It would seem, therefore, that the lapse of a century has made a great change in the political feelings of the natives of these countries, as may be inferred from their conduct in 1711, at the most critical period of the war carried on by Peter the Great against the Turks. Cantemir, the Prince of Moldavia, who, in addition to his boasted descent from the great Tamerlane, was distinguished by talents worthy of the antient Greeks, possessing alike a knowledge of letters and arms, had thrown off his allegiance to the- Porte and joined the army of the Czar, which was encamped on the north bank of the Pruth. The tents of the Grand Vizier were on the opposite side of the river; and the fate of the campaign might depend, in a great measure, on the decision of the people, in the centre of whose territory the hostile troops were assembled. But neither the example, nor the entreaties, of the accomplished Prince of Moldavia were able to shake the former attachment of his subjects; and they, as well as their neighbours, the inhabitants of Wallachia, espoused the party of the Grand Vizier, and abundantly supplied the Turkish camp with provisions. "Tant," says Voltaire, "l'ancienne idée de la barbarie Muscovite avoit aliéné tous "les esprits." . . .

CHAPTER 34

Wallachia and Moldavia in the Early Nineteenth Century

Neale's description of the Roumanian principalities is exaggerated, but the exotic character of the land is well evoked. Visitors at this time seemed to delight in describing the absurdities of the rulers in Wallachia and Moldavia, making rash generalizations which probably delighted readers in their homelands. It is notable that while Neale castigates the many Hospodars of whom he knew nothing, he speaks highly of the only one that he met, Prince Alexander Mourousi, Hospodar of Wallachia.

Adam Neale, TRAVELS THROUGH SOME PARTS OF GERMANY, POLAND, MOLDAVIA, AND TURKEY (London: Longman, Hurst, Rees, Orme and Brown, 1818), pp. 161–163.

The exhalations from the numerous marshes around Jassy, render the inhabitants very unhealthy, and cause annually a great mortality amongst them from the severe intermittent and remittent fevers of which they are the cause. At any time likewise when the plague has entered for example, in 1771, during the plague before alluded to, Moldavia, Jassy has been found to suffer most severely; the Russian garrison here lost a prodigious number of men, including the general in command, named Stoffeln, who by his foolish prejudices, over-ruled the precautionary measures which the army surgeons wished to enforce, and contributed to propagate the contagion more widely amongst his troops, till at length it was introduced into Poland and Russia, and reached Moscow, which capital it almost depopulated. Besides the calamities of pestilence, Jassy is subject from its locality to other ravages, arising from troops of hungry wolves, which pour down during the long winter nights from the forests of the adjoining mountains, and carry off the domestic animals, and sometimes even women and children. To repel these invaders, every family is provided with a brace or two of large wolf-dogs, which keep up during the night a terrific baying, and banish sleep from the eye-lids of visitors, unused to these canine watchmen. Those trusty guardians quite murdered by sleep during my stay, and made me often feel the force of the words of the Roman poet, *"vigilum canum tristes excubiae;"* for no sounds can be more melancholy than that of 10,000 or 12,000 wolf-dogs baying the moon at intervals all night, while the distant hamlets at the foot of the mountains re-echoed the sound. During the day-time, the clatter of the wooden mallets beating the tablets at the doors of the Greek churches, calling the people to prayers, the use of bells being prohibited in the Turkish provinces, produces a most disagreeable effect.

Russia has been gradually acquiring a domination over the provinces of Moldavia and Wallachia, by efforts efforts which have been slowly but progressively renewed. She first obtained a right of interfering in their internal administration by the treaty of Kainargik in 1774, which granted the right of appointing consuls in any port or city in the Ottoman empire. In 1781, Russian residents were appointed at the courts of Jassy and Bukarest; and in 1802 by the influence of the Russian court, the Greek Prince Ipsilanti was promoted to the government of Wallachia, and Prince Mourousi to that of Moldavia, with the express condition that neither of them should be removed from their principalities, unless proved guilty of an offense which the Russian minister at Constantinople should deem sufficent to justify their deposal. Trusting to Russian protection, Prince Mourousi, at the time of our visit seemed to consider his government as a family fief, only to be terminated by his life, and was employed in erecting a stately palace in a commanding situation, which his son-in-law pointed out to our notice, with some exultation, as a token of the prosperity and permanency of the Mourousi dynasty. But how fallacious were these hopes. This family were not long permitted to enjoy their new residence; for after my return to England, I observed by the journals, that Prince Mourousi had died the death of most of his predecessors. It was on the 7th November 1812, that Prince Demetri Mourousi, ci-devant Hospodar of Wallachia, and one of the Ottoman plenipotentiaries at the congress of Bukarest, who signed the treaty of peace with Russia, was decapitated at Schumla, the head-quarters of the grand vizier, agreeably to orders transmitted by the Grand Seignor. We are generally assured that he suffered this catastrophe because it was known that he was a partisan of Russia. Such was the fate of Demetri Mourousi, a fate which commonly terminates the lives of these faithless and intriguing men the Greek Hospodars. After passing several years in dangling at the levees of the Turkish viziers, flattering, lying, bribing, and undermining their rivals by malignant slanders, they become Court Dragomans, and afterwards succeed on vacancies to the principalities of Wallachia and Moldavia. They set out for their seat of government loaded with debts, contracted in bribing the members of the Turkish divan, and surrounded by a host of needy relatives and hungry parasites, who are to be maintained and provided for by draining the peasantry of these devoted provinces. The most oppressive exactions are enforced, to wrest from these wretched peasants the wealth required to pay the Grand Seignor's revenue and keep the divan in good humour; and often on returning to the shores of the Bosphorus to enjoy their ill-acquired fortunes, the bowstring or scimitar puts a period to their career. Our kind host Prince Alexander Mourousi seemed an honourable exception to this character. He was about thirty years of age, had accompanied a Turkish embassy to Paris, was well informed, and seemed to have profited from his intercourse with the enlightened society of the French capital; was a kind husband, and the happy father of two promising children. The hospitality and attention which he showed towards Colonel Gillespie and myself, and the grateful sense he evinced of some professional attentions which I had it in my power to show him, were sufficient to prove to me that in his bosom existed a high feeling of gratitude, which we often in vain look for in a more cultivated mind; and this induces me to speak of and to remember him with much esteem. . . .

CHAPTER 35

Greek Independence

In 1821, after years of ferment and preparation, a revolt occurred in Greece against Turkish rule. Although the initial uprising led by Alexander Ypsilantis failed in early

1821, wide-spread revolt followed the call to arms by the Greek hierarchy on March 25, 1821. At first, the Greeks were able to wrest control of much of Greece from the Turks with very little outside assistance. The great powers stood aside despite the religious sympathy harbored by the Russians and the cultural feelings held by western Europe.

In 1825, the Sultan secured the assistance of the Egyptian ruler, Mehemet Ali, who successfully invaded the Peloponnesus. The Greeks were divided into quarreling factions, and it appeared that the revolt would be snuffed out. At this juncture, foreign assistance was necessary. The British foreign minister, George Canning, decided that if the western powers did not intercede on the Greek's behalf, Russia might take unilateral action that would upset the balance of power in the east. The Treaty of London, engineered by Canning, aimed to settle the Greek problem without Russia gaining undue power.

The Greeks quickly accepted the mediation offer of London, but the Turks refused. The Turkish refusal led to naval maneuvers in the Levant by the British and French fleets which resulted in the decisive defeat of the Turkish-Egyptian fleet in the battle of Navarino (Oct. 20, 1827). After Navarino, it was almost a certainty that Greek independence would be recognized. In the Treaty of Adrianople (Sept. 24, 1829) which ended the brief war between Russian and the Turks, the Sultan accepted the provisions of the Treaty of London with regard to Greece. The later Protocol of London (Feb. 3, 1830) recognized Greece as an independent state under the protection of France, Russia and Britain.

Reprinted in *Edward Hertslet* THE MAP OF EUROPE BY TREATY (London: Harrison and Sons, 1891), Vol. I, pp. 769–774.

TREATY BETMEEN GREAT BRITAIN, FRANCE, AND RUSSIA, FOR THE PACIFICATION OF GREECE. (LONDON) JULY 6, 1827

In the Name of the Most Holy and Undivided Trinity.

His Majesty the King of the United Kingdom of Great

Britain and Ireland, His Majesty the King of France and Navarre, and His Majesty the Emperor of All the Russias, penetrated with the necessity of putting an end to the sanguinary struggle which, while it abandons the Greek Provinces and the Islands of the Archipelago to all the disorders of anarchy, daily causes fresh impediments to the commerce of the States of Europe, and gives opportunity for acts of Piracy which not only expose the subjects of the High Contracting Parties to grievous losses, but also render necessary measures which are burthensome for their observation and suppression;

His Majesty the King of the United Kingdom of Great Britain and Ireland, and His Majesty the King of France and Navarre, having moreover received from the Greeks an earnest invitation to interpose their Mediation with the Ottoman Porte; and, together with His Majesty the Emperor of All the Russians, being animated with the desire of putting a stop to the effusion of blood, and of preventing the evils of every kind which the continuance of such a state of affairs may produce;

They have resolved to combine their efforts, and to regulate the operation thereof, by a formal Treaty, for the object of re-establishing peace between the contending parties, by means of an arrangement called for, no less by sentiments of humanity, than by interests for the tranquillity of Europe.

For these purposes, they have named their Plenipotentiaries to discuss, conclude, and sign the said Treaty, that is to say;—

His Majesty the King of the United Kingdom of Great Britain and Ireland, the Right Honourable John William Viscount Dudley, a Peer of the United Kingdom of Great Britain and Ireland, a Member of His said Majesty's Most Honourable Privy Council, and his Principal Secretary of State for Foreign Affairs;

His Majesty the King of France and Navarre, the Prince Jules, Count de Polignac, a Peer of France, Knight of the Orders of His Most Christian Majesty, Maréchal-de-Camp of his Forces, Grand Cross of the Order of St. Maurice of Sardinia, &c., &c., and his Ambassador at London;

And His Majesty the Emperor of All the Russias, the

Sieur Christopher Prince de Lieven, General of Infantry of His Imperial Majesty's Forces, his Aide-de-Camp General, his Ambassador Extraordinary and Plenipotentiary to His Britannic Majesty, &c.;

Who, after having communicated to each other their Full Powers, found to be in due and proper form, have agreed upon the following Articles:

Offer of Mediation.

ART. I. The Contracting Powers shall offer their Mediation to the Ottoman Porte, with the view of effecting a reconciliation between it and the Greeks.

This offer of Mediation shall be made to that Power immediately after the Ratification of the present Treaty, by means of a joint Declaration, signed by Plenipotentiaries of the Allied Courts at Constantinople; and, at the same time, a demand for an immediate Armistice shall be made to the Two Contending Parties, as a preliminary and indispensable condition to the opening of any negotiation.

Bases of Arrangement.

ART. II. The Arrangement to be proposed to the Ottoman Porte shall rest upon the following bases:

Greece to be a Dependency of Turkey and Pay Tribute. Appointment of

Greek Authorities.

The Greeks shall hold under the Sultan as under a Lord paramount; and, in consequence thereof, they shall pay to the Ottoman Empire an annual Tribute, the amount of which shall be fixed, once for all, by common agreement. They shall be governed by authorities whom they shall choose and appoint themselves, but in the nomination of whom the Porte shall have a defined right.

Greeks to become Possessors of all Turkish Property on Payment of Indemnity.

In order to effect a complete separation between the individuals of the two nations, and to prevent the collisions which would be the inevitable consequence of so protracted a struggle, the Greeks shall become possessors of all Turkish Property situated either upon the Continent, or in the Islands of Greece, on condition of indemnifying the former proprietors, either by an annual sum to be added to the tribute which they shall pay to the Porte, or by some other arrangement of the same nature.

Details of Arrangement and Boundaries to be settled by Negotiation.

ART. III. The Details of this Arrangement, as well as the Limits of the Territory upon the Continent, and the designation of the Islands of the Archipelago to which it shall be applicable, shall be settled by a negotiation to be hereafter entered into between the High Powers and the Two Contending Parties.

Pacification of Greece.

ART. IV. The Contracting Powers engage to pursue the salutary work of the Pacification of Greece, upon the bases laid down in the preceding Articles, and to furnish, without the least delay, their Representatives at Constantinople with all the Instructions which are required for the execution of the Treaty which they now sign.

Equal Advantages to be Conferred on All Nations.

ART. V. The Contracting Powers will not seek, in these Arrangements, any augmentation of territory, any exclusive influence, or any commercial advantage for their subjects, which those of every other nation may not equally obtain.

Guarantee of 3 Powers.

ART. VI. The arrangements for reconciliation and Peace which shall be definitively agreed upon between the Contending Parties, shall be guaranteed by those of the Signing Powers who may judge it expedient or possible to contract that obligation. The operation and the effects of such Guarantee shall become ths subject of future stipulation between the High Powers.

Ratifications.

ART. VII. The present Treaty shall be ratified, and the Ratifications shall be exchanged in 2 months, or sooner if possible.

In witness whereof, the respective Plenipotentiaries have signed the same, and have affixed thereto the Seals of their Arms.

Done at London, the 6th day of July, in the year of Our Lord, 1827.

> (L. S.) DUDLEY.
> (L. S.) LE PRINCE DE POLIGNAC.
> (L. S.) LIEVEN.

(translation.)

ADDITIONAL ARTICAL

In case the Ottoman Porte should not, within the space of one month, accept the Mediation which is to be proposed to it, the High Contracting Parties agree upon the following measures:

Commercial Relations to be entered into with Greece in case of Turkish

Refusal of Mediation.

I. It shall be declared to the Porte, by their Representatives at Constantinople, that the inconveniences and evils described in the patent Treaty as inseparable from the state of things which has, for six years, existed in the East, and the termination of which, by the means at the command of the Sublime Ottoman Porte, appears to be still distant, impose upon the High Contracting Parties the necessity of taking immediate measures for forming a connection with the Greeks.

It is understood that this shall be effected by establishing commercial relations with the Greeks, and by sending to and receiving from them, for this purpose, Consular Agents, provided there shall exist in Greece authorities capble of supporting such relations.

Measures to be adopted by Allied Powers in case of Nonobservance of

Armistice.

II. If, within the said term of one month, the Porte does not accept the Armistice proposed in Article I of the patent Treaty, or if the Greeks refuse to carry it into execution, the High Contracting Powers shall declare to either of the Contending Parties which may be disposed to continue hostilities, or to both of them, if necessary, that the said High Powers intend to exert all the means which circumstances may suggest to their prudence, for the purpose of obtaining the immediate effects of the Armistice of which they desire the execution, by preventing, as far as possible, all collision between the Contending Parties; and in consequence, immediately after the above-mentioned declaration, the High Powers will, jointly, exert all their efforts to accomplish the object of such Armistice, without, however, taking any part in the hostilities between the Two Contending Parties.

Immediately after the signature of the present Additional Article, the High Contracting Powers will, consequently, transmit to the Admirals commanding their respective squadrons in the Levant, conditional Instructions in conformity to the arrangements above declared.

Measures to be adopted in case of Refusal of Ottoman Porte.

III. Finally, if, contary to all expectation, these measures do not prove sufficient to produce the adoption of the propositions of the High Contracting Parties by the Ottoman Porte; or if, on the other hand, the Greeks decline the conditions stipulated in their favour, by the Treaty of this date, the High Contracting Powers will, nevertheless, continue to pursue the work of pacification, on the bases upon which they have agreed; and, in consequence, they authorize, from the present moment, their Representatives at London, to discuss and determine the future measures which it may become necessary to employ.

The present Additional Article shall have the same force and validity as if it were inserted, word for word, in the Treaty of this day. It shall be ratified, and the Ratifications shall be exchanged at the same time is those of the said Treaty.

In witness whereof the respective Plenipotentiaries have signed the same, and have affixed thereto the Seals of their Arms.

Done at London, the 6th day of July, in the year of Our Lord, 1827.

> (L. S.) DUDLEY.
> (L. S.) LE PRINCE DE POLIGNAC.
> (L. S.) LIEVEN.

[The Porte declared its Entire adhesion to the Stipulations of this Treaty, by a Declaration signed on the 9th September,1829, and in Art. X of the Treaty of 14th September, 1829.]

CHAPTER 36

The New Order in Poland—The Reign of Nicholas I

Czar Nicholas I succeeded the more liberal Alexander I in 1825. Poland still had its own Diet, the existence of which Nicholas, from the outset of his reign, found odious. International problems with the Turks and Austria forced Alexander to be somewhat diplomatic toward the Poles.

But still, in 1830, when it appeared that Polish troops might be used by the Czar to crush the July Revolution in France, great dissatisfaction began to brew. The Polish revolt started in Warsaw on November 29. For nearly a year, Polish resistance was able to survive, but in October of 1831, the revolt was crushed.

Cultural, political, and religious persecutions were carried out by the Czar's agents. The Manifesto of March 25, 1832 included some freedoms that had previously existed, but all parliamentary forms were actually suppressed. Even the Universities of Wilno and Warsaw failed to survive Nicholas' reforms of 1832.

Reprinted in *Joseph Hordynaki,* HISTORY OF THE LATE POLISH REVOLUTION AND THE EVENTS OF THE CAMPAIGN (Boston: Printed for Subscribers, 1833), pp. 424–428.

Imperial Manifesto of March 25, 1832

"By the grace of God, Nicholas I., Emperor of Russia, King of Poland, etc. When, by our Manifesto of Jan. 2, last year, we announced to our faithful subjects the march of our troops into the kingdom of Poland, which was momentarily snatched from the lawful authority, we at the same time informed them of our intention to fix the future fate of this country on a durable basis, suited to its wants, and calculated to promote the welfare of our whole empire. Now that an end has been put by force of arms to the rebellion in Poland, and that the nation, led away by agitators, has returned to its duty, and is restored to tranquillity, we deem it right to carry into execution our plan with regard to the introduction of the new order of things, whereby the tranquillity and union of the two nations, which Providence has entrusted to our care, may be forever guarded against new attempts. Poland, conquered in the year 1815 by the victorious arms of Russia, obtained by the magnanimity of our illustrious predecessor, the Emperor Alexander, not only its national existence, but also special laws sanctioned by a Constitutional Charter. These favors, however, would not satisfy the eternal enemies of order and lawful power. Obstinately persevering in their culpable projects, they ceased not one moment to dream of a separation between the two nations subject to our sceptre, and in their presumption they dared to abuse the favors of the restorer of their country, by employing for the destruction of his noble work the very laws and liberties which his mighty arm had generously granted them. Bloodshed was the consequence of this crime. The tranquillity and happiness which the kingdom of Poland had enjoyed to a degree till then unknown, vanished in the midst of civil war and a general devastation. All these evils are now passed. The kingdom of Poland, again subject to our sceptre, will regain tranquillity, and again flourish in the bosom of peace, restored to it under the auspices of a vigilant government. Hence we consider it one of our most sacred duties to watch with paternal care over the welfare of our faithful subjects, and to use every means in our power to prevent the recurrence of similar catastrophes, by taking from the ill-disposed the power of disturbing public tranquillity. As it is, moreover, our wish to secure to the inhabitants of Poland the continuance of all the essential requisites for the happiness of individuals, and of the country in general, namely, security of persons and property, liberty of conscience, and all the laws and privileges of towns and communes, so that the kingdom of Poland, with a separate administration adapted to its wants, may not cease to form an integral part of our empire and that the inhabitants of this country may henceforward constitute a nation united with the Russians by sympathy and fraternal sentiments, we have, according to these principles, ordained and resolved this day, by a new organic statute, to introduce a new form and order in the administration of our kingdom of Poland.

"St. Petersburgh, February 26, 1832.

"NICHOLAS . . .

"Art. 1. The kingdom of Poland is forever to be reunited to the Russian empire, and form an inseparable part of that empire. It shall have a particular administration conformably to its local necessities, as well as a civil and military code. The statutes and the laws of cities and towns remain in full vigor.

"Art. 2. The Crown of the kingdom of Poland is hereditary in our person and in our heirs and successors, agreeably to the order of succession to the throne prescribed by all the Russias.

"Art. 3 The Coronation of the Emperors of all the Russias and Kings of Poland shall be one and the same ceremonial, which shall take place at Moscow, in the presence of a deputation from the kingdom of Poland, which shall assist at that solemnity with the deputies from the other parts of the empire.

"Art. 4. In the possible event of a regency in Russia, the power of the regent or regentess of the empire will extend over the kingdom of Poland.

"Art. 5. The freedom of worship is guarantied; every one is at liberty to exercise his religion openly, under the protection of Government; and the difference of Christian faiths shall never prove a pretext for the violation of the rights and privileges which are allowed to all the inhabitants. The Roman Catholic religion, being that of the majority of our Polish subjects, shall be the object of especial protection of the Government.

"Art. 6. The funds which the Roman Catholic clergy possess, and those of the Greek church united, shall be considered as the common and inviolable property of the hierarchy of each of those creeds.

"Art. 7. The protection of the laws is assured to all the inhabitants without distinction of rank or class. Each shall be empowered to assume dignities or to exercise public functions, according to his personal merits or talents.

"Art. 8. Individual liberty is guarantied and protected by the existing laws. No one shall be deprived of his liberty, or called to justice, if he be not a transgressor of the law in all the forms prescribed. Every one detained shall be apprised of the motive of arrest.

"Art. 9. Each person arrested must submit to a delay of three days to be heard and judged of, according to the forms of law, before competent tribunals: if he be found innocent, he will instantly obtain his liberty. He will be equally restored to liberty who shall furnish a sufficient surety.

'Art. 10. The form of judicial inquests directed against

the superior functionaries of the kingdom, and against persons accused of high treason, shall be determined by a particular law, the foundation of which shall be accordant with the other laws of our empire.

"Art. 11. The right of property of individuals, and of corporations, is declared sacred and inviolable, inasmuch as it will be conformable to the existing laws. All the subjects of the kingdom of Poland are perfectly free to quit the country, and to carry away their goods, provided they conform to the regulations published to that effect.

"Art. 12. The penalty of confiscation shall not be enforced but against state crimes of the first class, as may be hereafter determined by particular laws.

"Art. 13. Publication of sentiments, by means of the press, shall be subjected to restrictions which will protect religion, the inviolability of superior authority, the interests of morals, and personal considerations. Particular regulations, to this effect, will be published according to the principles which serve as a basis to this object in the other parts of our empire.

"Art. 14. The kingdom of Poland shall proportionably contribute to the general expenditure and to the wants of the empire. The proportion of taxes will be stated hereafter.

"Art. 15. All contributions and taxes which existed in November, 1830, shall be levied after the manner formerly settled till the new fixing of taxes.

"Art. 16. The treasury of the kingdom of Poland, and all the other branches of the administration, shall be separated from the administration of the other parts of the kingdom.

"Art. 17. The public debt of Poland, acknowledged by us, shall be guaranties as formerly, by the government, and indemnified by the receipts of the kingdom.

"Art. 18. The bank of the kingdom of Poland, and the laws respecting credit, shall continue under the protection of Government.

"Art. 19. The mode of commercial transactions between the Russian empire and the kingdom of Poland shall be regulated according to the respective interests of the two countries.

"Art. 20. Our army in the empire and in the kingdom shall compose one in common, without distinction of Russian or Polish troops. We shall reserve to ourselves a future decision of this, by an especial law, by what arrangement, and upon what basis, the kingdom of Poland shall participate with our army. The number of troops which shall serve as the military defence of the kingdom will be also ultimately determined upon by a law.

"Art. 21. Those of our subjects of the empire of Russia, who are established in the kingdom of Poland, who possess or shall possess, real property in that country, shall enjoy all the rights of natives. It shall be the same with those of our subjects of the kingdom of Poland, who shall establish themselves, and shall possess property, in the other provinces of the empire. We reserve to ourselves to grant hereafter letters of naturalization to other persons, as well to strangers as to Russians, who are not yet established there. Those of our subjects of the Russian empire who may reside for a certain time in Poland, and those of our subjects of the kingdom of Poland who may sojourn in the other parts of the empire, are subject to the laws of the country where they reside.

"Art. 22. The superior administration of the kingdom of Poland is confided to a council of administration, which shall govern the kingdom in our name, under the presidency of the governor of the kingdom.

"Art. 23. The council of administration is composed of the governor of the kingdom, of superior directors, who superintend the commissions, and among whom are divided the interests of the administration, of comptroller, presiding over the supreme Chamber of Finance, and of other members, who we shall appoint by special orders."

CHAPTER 37

The Transformation of Hungary—Early Nineteenth Century

Quin's account gives an over-view of the problems that

faced responsible Hungarian leaders such as Count Szechenyi. Education, industry, parliamentary government, development of the Hungarian language, and exploitation of natural resources were discussed against a background of
primitive conditions, apathy, and Viennese inertia. But conditions were worse in the Turkish lands as the presence
of the Lazaretto testifies. Quin (1796–1843) was a lawyer
and litterateur, who founded the Dublin Review in 1836,
and usually exhibited progressive views on the questions
of his time.

Michael J. Quin, A STEAM VOYAGE DOWN THE DANUBE
(London: Richard Bentley, 1836), Vol. I, pp. 167–171.

At two o'clock I went to dine with the Count. A rude
sort of a gate opened to a court-yard through which I
passed to a staircase, or rather a wide step-ladder, and
soon to a gallery leading to a suite of rooms genteely
furnished. On the table in the Count's sitting apartment
I recognised as old friends the *Edinburgh* and *Quarterly
Reviews,* several of our "Annuals," and other English and
French periodical publications. Besides the Count, a Hungarian magnate of considerable property, was present, who
coincides in most of the prudent views which the Count
entertains with reference to the civilization of Hungary.
Mr. Popovicz was also of the party, as well as a sensible
young barrister from Pesth, named Tasner, who accompanied the Count as his secretary. We had an excellent
dinner of vermicelli soup, bouilli, haricot mutton, beef rag-
out, roast fowl, and pudding, following by a desert of sweet
cake and grapes. The wines were champagne and the ordinary white vintage of the country, the best I had yet tasted
in Hungary. Our conversation at dinner turned chiefly on
the enterprize in which the Count was engaged, and in
which all his faculties seemed to have been absorbed.

I collected from what was said that it was intended to
construct a road wide enough for carriages, along the whole
of the left bank of the Danube, and that canals were to
be formed parallel to the rapids and other rocky passages,
where the river was liable to be reduced much below its
ordinary level during the summer and autumn. These works

necessarily required a large expenditure, which the returns of the Steam Navigation Company were not expected to repay. The Austrian government, therefore, actuated by an impulse of public spirit which it too rarely acknowledges on other subjects, has taken upon itself the entire outlay which these undertakings will require, and has, moreover, with peculiar propriety, intrusted to Count Szechenyi the superintendence of the whole, as well as an unlimited supply of funds, for which he accounts directly to the emperor. It is especially understood that a certain percentage is secured by the Austrian government to the Navigation Company upon its capital, provided the returns should fall below a stated amount: in point of fact the returns have for some time exceeded the amount agreed upon, so that the government is not likely to have any further responsibility in that respect.

The enterprize was originated by the Count, who, at an early period of his life (he is at present about forty-four years of age), plainly perceived the great advantages that would accrue to Hungary, if the Danube were rendered navigable for steam-boats to the Black Sea. Adopting the English system for procuring a large capital in small shares, he formed a list of subscribers at Presburg, consisting of magnates, members of the lower chamber of the diet, bankers, and merchants, which he brought over to this country. Here, also, he obtained a few distinuished names, and made himself master of all the details of steam navigation. Having ordered the engines for three boats to be sent from Birmingham to Trieste, he had the vessels built in that port, and then a petition was presented to the diet, on behalf of the subscribers, praying its sanction to the undertaking. This was the first instance in which the diet was called upon to take into its consideration a measure peculiar to Hungary in its national character, and involving, therefore, consequences of a vast political as well as commercial tendency. If the diet took this enterprize under its auspices, the popularity and the sense of independence which the assembly would thus acquire, might lead to other measures still more conducive to the reestablishment of the Hungarian nation. Prince Metternich immediately sent for Count Szechnyi, whose brother is married to a sister of the prince's wife, and sought explanations of this treasonable proceeding. The Count's answer was very simple and unequivocal.—"If you have no wish that the diet should adopt the petition and act upon it, do the thing yourselves, for the Danube at all events cannot be long without steam-boats." The hint was taken, the petition was cushioned, the plans of the Count were not only accepted but improved upon a most magnificent scale, and given back to himself for execution. The Count is the most distinguished leader of the opposition party in the diet, but he took care to have it thoroughly understood, that though, for the benefit of Hungary, he charged himself with the commission offered to him by Prince Metternich, he was still free to follow up his political principles in every way that he thought advantageous to his country.

CHAPTER 38

A Moderate Nationalist—Count Szechenyi

Count Istvan Szechenyi (1791–1860) holds a very revered place in Hungarian history. He became known as the foremost moderate critic of Kossuth and consistently favored an equitable attitude toward the national minorities in Hungary. Before 1848, Szechenyi had a career distinguished by his support of commercial and cultural progress. In 1848, after the revolt began in Hungary, he briefly held the portfolio of ways and communications. But the turmoil of 1848 and his intense dislike for Kossuth finally drove him to nervous exhaustion. For the next twelve years of his life, he was insane. In April of 1860, he committed suicide. The following Address to the Academy presents the spirit of his ideas.

Julius von Farkas (editor), UNGARNS GESCHICHTE UND KULTUR IN DOKUMENTEN (Wiesbaden: O. Harrassowitz,

1955), pp. 117–121. By permission of the publisher. Translated by the editors.

Would it not be wonderful if everybody were ordered to be Hungarian or at least decided to become Hungarian. Or failing that, would it not seem a pleasing project if we could say that a man is Hungarian even though the Hungarian tongue is only one of the languages he is able to speak. But, of course, this is not an easy matter to accomplish. In one single cultured intellect, there are more attractive and consistent qualities than in a thousand empty and disorganized minds. Similarly, only superiority and nothing else can spread nationality. When, on the other hand, the holiest zeal, the most laudable heroism, the strongest will are present, I agree that these qualities can win a thousand battles. But when it comes to the problem of spreading Hungarian nationality, these martial virtues are not even slightly helpful. On the contrary, these qualities can only cause the greatest anxiety and present us with ominous pitfalls. These extremely praiseworthy characteristics must have as their foundation the enchanting power of discernible civilization combined with the irresistible weight of moral superiority. . . .

The Hungarian language cannot be equated with Hungarian personality. A man, just because he is an Hungarian, is therefore not a virtuous man. And that man who marches along with the Hungarian flag wrapped around himself is therefore not a patriot. And how many, under the guise of patriotism, are working toward the destruction of the country. These people, who have really nothing to commend themselves but their blind fanaticism, are placed on pedestals. These fanatics cast suspicion on the genuine patriotism of others, staining them with their dirty brush. Yes, and they even cause antipathy and hatred toward those, who, pure of heart and free of any possible reproach, work with an honest love for their country. Finally, the very name, patriot, will become one open to suspicion. Let us face it, this is why Hungarian patriotism is looked upon by foreigners as of little value, and is even seen as something far from pure. And because of this suspicion towards us, not even the greatest Hungarian citizen is able to elicit sympathy for the Hungarian civilization and win them over to our side. Yes, there is a sort of false patriotism applauded here and worshipped as an idol, which is imputed by foreigners to even our greatest citizens and thus discredits them.

We should turn away from this abominable picture where poisoned glory celebrates its usurped feast. And although we can only view this sorry picture with terror, seeing how many signs of rottenness our nation carries in itself, nevertheless we should not become despondent. We should still retain confidence in ourselves and turn our eyes toward a more hopeful possibility which stands open before us. Although we are few in number, and not all of us are above reproach, nevertheless, we have not yet given up. Many faithful souls with noble virtues are guarding the nation's prosperity.

Let us have confidence in our strength. But let us never enter any struggle without complete preparation. We must economize our strength better than in the past. . . . In the rebirth of a nation, time is of the essence. The humble bee and the industrious ant are more effective than bombastic words and loud noises. Let us be convinced that the more we approach the ideal that I have spoken of, the more we shall reach our earthly salvation.

On the contrary, the most sure and speedy way to destruction is to disassociate ourselves from that ideal. Accordingly, we must be very careful that each one of us does no harm, so that each person may work with uncompromising perseverance. Thus, each one may be useful. Every son will be a saviour of our nation, a benefactor of our people, and a glory to Hungary. Such care is a joyful consciousness, and therefore, may each Hungarian accept his task and faithfully carry it out.

And if everything we do is of no avail, if all our hopes must be dashed to the ground, and even our memory effaced from the record of humanity, still let us at least demonstrate to any invisible witnesses, witnesses before whom the question is not victory or defeat but those values that glorify humanity, that among our generation there were some who deserved a better fate because they fought untiringly for national survival and self-improvement with their very last breath.

CHAPTER 39

Suppression of the Hungarian Revolt—1848

Up until September of 1848, the Austrian government had not given up on hopes of peacefully settling the problem of Hungarian disaffection. But while the chief minister in Vienna, Wessenberg, tried to make a settlement with the leaders in Budapest, events outstripped all calculations. The minority groups in Hungary, the Serbs, Roumanians and Croats grew restive, and Hungarian rule seemed to them quite unpromising. A regular militia for the borderlands, centuries old, existed in Croatia, and these troops under Jellachich became fired up against the Hungarians.

On September 11, 1848, the troops of Jellachich began to move without imperial sanction against the Hungarians. On September 29, at Pakozd-Velencze, the Croatians failed to win a victory, and Jellachich ordered a retreat to the north. He was courting imperial disapproval, and if Vienna disavowed him, the Hungarian troops would have a good pretext to annihilate his armies. In a seemingly untenable position, Jellachich could save himself only by earnestly courting Vienna's favor. Jellachich was saved by the fact that on September 29, at Pest, the imperial mediator, Count Lamberg, was murdered by a large crowd. At Vienna, it seemed no longer possible to deal peacefully with the Hungarians. If Kossuth and the independent-minded Hungarians had control of the country, Vienna had no choice but to seek any possible allies, including Jellachich's descrepid army.

Reprinted in Phineas Camp Headley, THE LIFE OF LOUIS KOSSUTH *(Auburn: Derby and Miller, 1852), pp. 128–129.*

"We, Ferdinand I., Constitutional Emperor of Austria, &c., King of Hungary, Croatia, Sclavonia, Dalmatia the Vth of this name, to the Barons, to the High-Dignitaries of the Church and State, to the Magnates and Representatives of Hungary, its dependencies, and the Grand Duchy of Transylvania, who are assembled at the Diet, convoked by ourselves in our free and royal town of Pesth, our greeting:

"To our deep concern and indignation the House of Representatives has been seduced by Kossuth and his adherents to great illegalities; it has even carried out several illegal resolutions against our royal will, and has lately, on the 27th of September, issued a resolution against the commission of the Royal Commissary, our Lieutenant Field-Marshal, Count Francis Lamberg, appointed by ourselves to re-establish peace. In consequence of which, this our Royal Commissary, before he could even produce his commission, was in the public street violently attacked by the furious mob which murdered him in the most atrocious manner. Under these circumstances, we see ourselves compelled, according to our royal duty, for the maintenance of the security and the law, to take the following measures, and to command their enforcement:

"First. We dissolve the Diet by this our decree; so that after the publication of our present Sovereign Rescript, the Diet has immediately to close its sessions.

"Secondly. We declare as illegal, void, and invalid, all the resolutions of the Diet, which we have not sanctioned.

"Thirdly. All troops and armed bodies of every kind, whether national guards, or volunteers, which are stationed in Hungary, and its dependencies, as well as in Transylvania, are placed by this our decree, under the chief command of our Ban of Croatia, Sclavonia and Dalmatia, Lieutenant Field-Marshal Baron Joseph Jellachich.

"Fourthly. Until the disturbed peace and order in the country shall be restored, the Kingdom of Hungary shall be subjected to martial law; in consequence of which, the respective authorities are meanwhile to abstain from the celebration of congregations, whether of the counties, of the municipalities, or of the districts.

"Fifthly. Our Ban of Croatia, Sclavonia and Dalmatia, Baron Joseph Jellachich, is hereby invested and empowered as Commissary of our Royal Majesty; and we give him full power and force, that he may, in the sphere of Executive Ministry, exercise the authority, with which as Lieutenant of our Royal Majesty, we have invested him in the present extraordinary circumstances.

"In consequence of this our Sovereign plenipotence, we declare that whatsoever the Ban of Croatia shall order, regulate, determine and command, is to be considered as ordered, regulated, determined and commanded by our royal authority. In consequence of which, we likewise by this graciously give command to all our ecclesiastical, civil and military authorities, officers, and High Dignitaries of our Kingdom of Hungary, its dependencies, and Transylvania, as also all their inhabitants, that all the orders signed by Baron Jellachich as our empowered Royal Commissary, shall be by them obeyed, and enforced, in the same way as they are bound to obey our Royal Majesty." . . .

CHAPTER 40

Palacky on the Slav-German Question

Frantisek Palacky (1798–1876) was the leading figure in the modern revival of Czech national feeling. He gained scholarly fame with his five volume *History of Bohemia*. In 1848, when it appeared that the Austrian Empire might disintegrate, Palacky took the position that an Austrian state could continue to exist if it were composed of nationalities with equal rights. Even the moderate ideas of Palacky were found unacceptable at the court of the Emperor Franz Josef. While twentieth century Czech nationalists held to the idea of independence, Palacky continued to be revered by his own people.

Translated in Hans Kohn, PAN-SLAVISM, ITS HISTORY AND IDEOLOGY
(Notre Dame, 1953), pp. 65–69. Repinted by permission of the Notre Dame Press.

I am a Czech of Slav descent and with all the little I own and possess I have devoted myself wholly and for ever to the service of my nation. That nation is small, it is true, but from time immemorial it has been an independent nation with its own character; its rulers have participated since old times in the federation of German princes, but the nation never regarded itself nor was it regarded by others throughout all the centuries, as part of the German nation. The whole union of the Czech lands first with the Holy German Empire and then with the German Confederation was always a purely dynastic one of which the Czech nation, the Czech Estates, hardly wished to know and which they hardly noticed. . . .

If anyone asks that the Czech nation should now unite with the German nation, beyond this heretofore existing federation between princes, this is then a new demand which has no historical legal basis, a demand to which I personally do not feel justified in acceding until I receive an express and valid mandate for it. The second reason which prevents me from participating in your deliberations is the fact that from all that has been so far publicly announced of your aims and purposes you irrevocably are, and will be, aiming to undermine Austria forever as an independent empire and to make its existence impossible— an empire whose preservation, integrity and consolidation is, and must be, a great and important matter not only for my own nation but for the whole of Europe, indeed for mankind and civilization itself. Allow me kindly to explain myself briefly on this point.

You know, gentlemen, what power it is that holds the whole great eastern part of our continent; you know that this power which now already has grown to vast dimensions, increases and expands by its own strength every decade to a far greater extent than is possible in the Western countries; that being inaccessible at its own center to almost every attack, it has become, and has for a long time been, a threat to its neighbours; and that, although it has an open access to the north, is nevertheless always seeking, led by natural instinct, to expand southwards and will continue to do it; that every further step which it will take forward on this path threatens at an ever accelerated pace to produce and found a *universal monarchy,* that is to say, an infinite and inexpressible evil, a misfortune without measure or bound which I, though heart and soul a Slav, would nonetheless deeply regret for the good of mankind even though that monarchy proclaimed itself a Slav one.

Many people in Russia call and regard me as an enemy of the Russians, with as little justice as those who among the Germans regard me as an enemy of the Germans. I proclaim loudly and publicly that I am in no way an enemy of the Russians: on the contrary, I observe with joyful sympathy every step by which this great nation within its natural borders progresses along the road of civilization: but with all my ardent love of my nation I always esteem more highly the good of mankind and of learning than the good of the nation;for this reason the bare possibility of a Russian universal monarchy has no more determined opponent or adversary than myself, not because that monarchy would be Russian but because it would be universal.

You know that in south-east Europe, along the frontiers of the Russian empire, there live many nations widely different in origin, language, history and habits—Slavs, Rumanians, Magyars, and Germans, not to speak of Greeks, Turks and Albanians—none of whom is strong enough by itself to be able to resist successfully for all time the superior neighbour to the east; they could do it only if a close and firm tie bound them all together. The vital artery of this necessary union of nations is the Danube; the focus of its power must never be removed far from this river, if the union is to be effective at all and to remain so. Certainly, if the Austrian state had not existed for ages, we would be obliged in the interests of Europe and even of mankind to endeavor to create it as fast as possible.

But why have we seen this state, which by nature and history is destined to be the bulwark and guardian of Europe against Asiatic elements of every kind—why have we seen it in a critical moment helpless and almost unadvised in the face of the advancing storm? It is because in an unhappy blindness which has lasted for very long, Austria has not recognized the real legal and moral foundation of its existence and has denied it: the fundamental rule that all nationalities united under its scepter should enjoy complete equality of rights and respect. The right of nations is truly a natural right; no nation on earth has the right to demand that its neighbour should sacrifice itself for its benefit, no nation obliged to deny or sacrifice itself for the good of its neighbour.

Nature knows neither ruling nor subservient nations. If the union which unites several different nations is to be firm and lasting, no nation must have cause to fear that by that union it will lose any of the goods which it holds most dear; on the contrary each must have the certain hope that it will find in the central authority defense and protection against possible violations of equality by neighbours; then every nation will do its best to strengthen that central authority so that it can successfully provide the aforesaid defense. I am convinced that even now it is not too late for the Austrian empire to proclaim openly and sincerely this fundamental rule of justice, the *sacra ancora* for a ship in danger of floundering, and to carry it out energetically in common and in every respect: but every moment is precious; for God's sake do not let us delay another hour with this. . . .

When I look behind the Bohemian frontiers, then natural and historical reasons make me turn not to Frankfurt but to Vienna to seek there the center which is fitted and destined to ensure and defend the peace, the liberty and the right of my nation. Your efforts, gentlemen, seem to me now to be directed as I have already stated, not only towards ruinously undermining, but even destroying that center from whose might and strength I expect the salvation not only of the Czech land. . . .

And if Hungary following its instincts severs its connections with the (Austrian) state or, what would amount almost to the same, concentrates within itself—will then Hungary which does not wish to hear of national equality be able to maintain itself free and strong in the future? Only the just is truly free and strong. A voluntary union of the Danubian Slavs and Rumanians, or even of the Poles themselves, with such a state which declares that a man must first be a Magyar before he can be a human being is entirely out of the question; and even less thinkable would be a compulsory union of this kind. . . .

"In conclusion I must briefly express my conviction that those who ask that Austria (and with it Bohemia) should unite on national lines with the German empire, demand its suicide . . . Nothing remains for the Austrian and German Empires but to organize themselves side by side on a footing of equality, to convert the existing ties into a permanent alliance of defense and defiance, and should it be advantageous to both sides perhaps to create also a customs union. I am ready at every moment gladly to give a helping hand in all activities which do not endanger the independence, integrity and growth in power of the Austrian empire."

CHAPTER 41

Wolves in the Night—Perils of Travel in the Nineteenth Century

The following is a typical story of the hazards of travel that still existed in the mid-nineteenth century. Very few provisions were made for the almost non-existent tourists through Moldavia and Bukovina, and the incredible stories brought back to western Europe conveyed a primitive and exotic picture of this area. Captain Spencer's story and others like it helped to create a somewhat unfavorable image in the minds of those not interested in the sociological or political reasons for Roumania's primitive character.

Captain Spencer, TURKEY, RUSSIA, THE BLACK SEA (Lon-George Routledge and Co., 1854), pp. 138–143.

On leaving Jassy, the frost having set in with increased severity, we rolled onward with great rapidity, as if our postilion was running a race against time; and although the horses were small, they went at the rate of fifteen *wersts* an hour. While we remained within a few miles of the town, cultivated fields, villages and hamlets, neat gardens and vineyards, alternately met the view; but these pleasing objects once past, there was the same want of population we before observed, and the country increased in solitary wildness when we entered the mountain district.

At one time our route lay through a dense forest, then along the banks of a charming lake; now we wound round a steep precipice, then plunged into a dark and dismal abyss, to emerge into a beautiful valley, watered with the meandering stream or rushing torrent, given by the bountiful hand of nature to fertilize the soil.

What might not be done here, if this highly favoured country were occupied by a colony of our scientific husbandmen from Western Europe! Every one of these sunny slopes would then be laid out in vineyards; the valley in cornfields, pastures and meadows; and the hills and mountains stripped of their impenetrable forests, to make way for numerous herds of cattle and flocks of sheep. Still, the desolate aspect of the country does not prevent many a Boyar from adding considerable to his revenue by the sale of leeches, which are found in some of the rivers and marshes of this mountain district.

Hitherto our journey had been most prosperous, till arriving at the vast forest that separates Moldavia from the Bukowina, we were overtaken by one of those sudden snow storms so fatal to the traveller in this wild inhospitable district. Happily our postilion, prognosticating from the lowering aspect of the heavens to the danger that threatened us, galloped madly toward a ruined chalet, the usual resting-place of such caravans as journey in this direction.

On arriving at our place of refuge, we found it to be a miserable wooden hut, surrounded by a dilapidated paling, filled with travellers, their packs, horses, and a flock of sheep,and as continuing our route to Boyana, the next post-station, was completely out of the question, we made preparations to pass the night. Our poor horses being badly off for shelter, our first care was to repair the shed with a quantity of loose timber, in which operation we were aided by the snow when making a roof, for it froze as fast as it fell.

With respect to provender for man and beast, we had taken good care to provide an ample supply in case of an accident, and as the other travellers felt inclined to be merry, a fat sheep was selected and roasted for the occasion; we were moreover favoured by a change in the weather, for the night became clear and bright, though it still continued to freeze hard.

The reader must now suppose we had supped, and smoked the chibouque, but before retiring to rest we took precautions, lest any stray wolf should pay us a visit during the night—and to guard against this mishap, it was determined that our whole party should in turn mount guard, and replenish the blazing fire we had made in the centre of the enclosure, intented for the twofold purpose of keeping our cattle warm, and scaring away any dangerous intruder.

Things went on very well till about the middle of the night, when we were awoke from the land of dreams by the discharge of firearms, and, lo! our young *pandour* rushed into the hut, exaliming he had fired at a wolf and wounded him, and that the animal fled howling back to the forest.

"Rash, foolish boy!" cried our of our fellow travellers, jumping up from his lair of sheepskins, "we shall have the whole hungry pack down upon us in less than half an hour, for they will devour him, and then track his blood to the place where he was wounded." Unfortunately for our slumbers the old man was right, and now we had to make preparations as quickly as possible for the encounter.

We have already said that our night quarters was a miserable hut, a few feet from the ground; consequently our first object was to barricade it with pieces of wood, so as to render it, in case of need, sufficiently strong to resist any attack that might be made upon it by the wolves; but our poor horses and the flock of sheep in the open shed were exposed to certain destruction, and our next care was to take measures in their defense.

On inspecting our fortress, we found several breaches had been made in the paling of the enclosure; these we filled up with piles of wood, and then placed our little garrison as sentinels at different points, to beat back our enemies should they attempt to climb over the enclosure. Our party consisted of seven; a butcher and his help, the owner of the flock of sheep, from Tchernowitz; two caravan rivers with their packs of wool, on their way to Jassy; the postilion, the *pandour*, and ourselves. As to weapons of defence, our fellow-travellers had none other than the long knife and light hatchet they carried in their belt; this we remedied by converting pieces of wood into ponderous clubs. As for the *pandour* and ourselves, we were armed to the teeth, with plenty of ammunition at hand if necessary.

Half an hour or more had probably elapsed, when we first perceived the enemy, in greater force than we considered agreeable, stealthily marching around the glare of the immense fire we kept blazing in the centre of the enclosure, as if debating whether it would be prudent to cross the gleaming boundary.

At length a powerful fellow made his appearance, probably the commander-in-chief, who, after reconnoitering our position, being no doubt strongly tempted by bleating sheep and neighing horses—the unerring instinct of the poor animals telling them that danger was near—dashed boldly forward, followed by the whole pack, and with a bound attempted to clear the paling. Stout hearts and strong clubs, however, soon drove them back, laying many sprawling on the ground; we reserved our fire, in obedience to the advice of our captain, the old shepard, who recommended us not to use our firearms unless an opportunity should be afforded of inflicting certain death, in order that none might escape again to the forest, and bring back a reinforcement.

Our ferocious assailants, not liking the blows from our clubs, retreated, and apparently, after holding a consultation, it was resolved to attack the enclosure in different directions, and in some places where it was weak two or three succeeded in climbing over the fence, when they were instantly despatched by our firearms and the long knives and hatchets of our fellow combatants, when we hurled them over the fence to be devoured by their famishing comrades beneath. The fate of our first invaders, however, did not deter others from following their example, and in the morning we counted the skeletons of eight or nine who had become the victims of their temerity.

Happily the dawn of day caused our unwelcome visitors to return to their woods, leaving us at liberty to pursue our journey, and with mutual congratulations for our providential escape our party separated. The day was fine, the snow as hard as a bed of ice, and after a drive of a couple of hours we came to the long-wished-for Boyana.

CHAPTER 42

The Polish Revolt of 1863

1863 was the greatest year of Polish revolutionary activity. Although the revolt against Czarist rule failed, world attention was directed to events in Poland. The rebellion could not succeed without foreign assistance, but despite strenuous efforts by Polish nationalists in England and France, no help of significance was obtained. The two manifestoes below made an effort to enlist both the peasantry and the Ruthenian minority in the Polish Kingdom created by the Congress of Vienna. Although there was a pure idealism in these appeals, Europe had entered an age of realism in which success rested on power rather than romantic notions of unity. The West did not help and Bismarck's Prussia gave its favor to the Russian government.

Manfred Kridl, Wladyslaw Malinowski, and Józef Wittlin (editors), FOR YOUR FREEDOM AND OURS (New York, 1943), pp. 87–89. Reprinted by permission of Frederick Ungar Publishing Co., Inc.

Whereas, the emancipation of the peasants has so far in spite of the general desire of the nation, and due to the obstacles put in this way by the aggressor government, not been effected; moreover,

Whereas, the acquisition by farmers of lands which heretofore they have held by right of rents, statute labor or other obligations diminishes the property of those who have hitherto been the owners.

The Central National Committee, acting as the Provisional National Government, resolves and decrees that:

Art. 1. All landed property which any farmer has held hitherto by right of statute labor, rent or by any other right, together with gardens, houses and farm buildings, as well as the rights and privileges attached thereto, shall become from the date of the present decree the exclusive and hereditary property of the hitherto holder without any obligations, tributes, statutes, labor or rent whatsoever, with only the condition that taxes due from it be paid and the appropriate national services be rendered.

Art. 2. The hitherto owners of the land ceded to the farmers shall receive indemnities corresponding to its value from national funds, through the state debt.

Art. 3. The principles for defining the amount of the appraisal of the land and the kind of the credit to be instituted shall be indicated in separate decrees.

Art. 4. All ukases, and rescripts issued by the aggressor government concerning so-called peasant relations are abolished and therefore binding to one one.

Art. 5. The present decree shall apply to private properties and to government, donative, ecclesiastic and any other properties.

Art. 6. The Central National Committee, acting as the Provisional National Government, charges the military and country chiefs with the promulgation and execution of the present decree.

Issued in Warsaw, January 22, 1863

TO OUR RUTHENIAN BROTHERS!

The banner of insurrection has been planted on the soil of Poland. The struggle for the independence and liberty of Poland, Lithuania and Ruthenia has already been begun by the youth of Warsaw who resist the violence of the

Muscovite conscription. Masses of the people hasten from all directions to the national standards, and many a blow has already been dealt by weapons wrested from the very hands of the enemy and by the scythes of the peasants. The insurrection spreads and gathers strength, for its watchword is the liberty and happiness of the nation, and its first act shall bring justice to the numerous peasant class. Through the decree of emancipation issued by the National Government we have won millions of new citizens in the whole area of the Commonwealth who, despite differences of faith and language, shall enjoy equal rights in the free determination of their fate.

Ruthenian brothers! Your land, which for so many centuries has shared good fortune and bad with the rest of the Commonwealth, must today also reverberate with the cry of freedom! Blood spilled on your soil, on your fields will bring victory to the insurrection. The Czarist armies will meet the grave under your cairns, and your scythes united with the Lithuanian and Polish scythes will achieve independence and liberty for Poland, Lithuania, and Ruthenia.

We shall mold a guarantee of victory out of unity, endurance and stubborn, intrepid and decisive struggle. Ruthenians, we summon you to the struggle! Your negligence, your hesitation, may postpone the moment of general happiness. Do not be guilty of impeding the regeneration of our common homeland.

We are faced by a strong foe, but the Czar's bayonets and guns, his frauds and deceptions which seek to incite the peasants against the insurrection which gives them liberty, property and citizenship, his intrigues which aim to disrupt the brotherhood of the peoples of the Commonwealth, will splinter and fall before the banner of justice which we carry.

To arms, to arms, we call you, brothers, and the first act of your insurrection shall be the immediate emancipation of the peasants!

Issued in Warsaw, February 5, 1863

CHAPTER 43

Saxon Traditions in Transylvania—Nineteenth Century

This description of German towns in Transylvania conveys their quaint, tradition-laden character. The legends are hardly credible, and these isolated towns were rather somnolent places in the century before radical German nationalism would give their people a cause. Still, even when Roumania expatriated so many Germans after World War II, most of them preferred to remain behind and live in the old way. Since the Germans were either merchants or the equivalent of country gentry, they enjoyed as good a life as was possible in Transylvania. Transported there to be frontier guards in the twelfth and thirteenth centuries, they had taken advantage of the frontier's freedom to entrench themselves as a privileged class. They added to the multi-national conglomeration that constituted the eastern borderland of Historic Hungary.

Andrew F. Crosse, ROUND ABOUT THE CARPATHIANS (Edinburgh: William Blackwood and Sons, 1878), pp. 178–181.

I remained several days at Hermannstadt, principally for the sake of resting my hores, which unfortunately had been rubbed by the saddle-bags on my ride from Petroseny. I spent the time agreeably enough, exploring the neighbourhood and making chance acquaintances. I bought here Bishop Teusch's *History of Transylvanian Saxons, a* handybook in two volumes. It interested me very much, especially reading it in the country itself where so many stirring scenes had been enacted.

Wishing to see some of the neighbouring villages, I set off one fine day on a walking expedition. I chose Sunday, because on that day one can see to best advantage the costume of the peasants. Hammersdorf is a pretty enough village, "fair with orchard lawns," but not so charming as Heltau, which, standing on high ground, commands an extensive view of the whole plain, with the old "Red Town" in the foreground of the picture. The church in this village is a very fine specimen of the fortified churches, which are a unique feature of the Transylvanian borderland. The origin of this form of architecture is very obvious; it was necessary to have a defence against the incursions of the Tartars and Turks, who for centuries troubled the peace of this fair land. In every village of the Saxons in the south and east of Transylvania the church is also a fortified place, fitted to maintain a siege if necessary. The construction of these buildings varies according to circumstances: the general character is that the sacred edifice is surrounded, or forms part of a strong wall with its watchtowers; not infrequently a second and even a third wall surround the place. In every case a considerable space of ground is enclosed around the church, sufficent to provide accommodation for the villagers; in fact every family with a house outside had a corresponding hut within the fortified walls, Here, too, was a granary, and some of the larger places had also their school-tower attached to the church. It happened not unfrequently that the villagers were obliged to remain for some weeks in their sanctuary.

Heltau is an industrious little place. Here is manufactured the peculiar white frieze so much worn by the Wallacks. Nearly every house has its loom, but I was told the trade is less flourishing than formerly. The woollencloth manufacturers of Transylvania have suffered very much from the introduction of foreign goods; but, on the other hand, if they would bestir themselves they might enormously increase their exports. Heltau is a market-place, and reserves many old privileges very jealously. Its inhabitants were often in dispute with the burghers of Herrmannstadt, and on one occasion they had the audacity, in rebuilding their church-tower, to place four turrets upon it. Their neighbours regarded this with great indignation, for are not four turrets the sign and symbol of *civic* authority? The burghers of Herrmannstadt hereupon obliged the men of Heltau to sign a bond, saying that "they were but humble villagers", and promising to treat their haughty neighbours with all due "honour, fear, and friendship."

From Heltau I went on to Michaelsburg, an extremely curious place. In the centre of a lovely valley rises a conical rock of gneiss, protruding to the height of 200 feet or more. This is crowned by the ruins of a Romanesque church. There are, I believe, only two other specimens of this kind of architecture in the country. The time of the building of Michaelsburg is stated to be between 1173 and 1223. Before the use of artillery this fortified church on the rock must have really been impregnable. Inside the walls I found a quantity of large round stones—the shot and shell of those days; these stones were capable of making considerable havoc amongst a besieging party I should say. The custom was in the old time that no young man should be allowed to take unto himself a wife till he had carried one such stone from the bed of the river where they are found, to the summit of the rock within the church walls. As these stones weigh between two and three hundred-weight, and the ascent is very steep, it was a test of strength. The villagers were anxious to prevent the weaklings from marrying lest they should spoil the hardy race.

CHAPTER 44

The Accession of Prince Charles in Roumania

Alexander Cuza, prince of Moldavia and Wallachia since February 5, 1859, was overthrown by a military-political coup d'état on February 23, 1866. Cuza had been found unsuitable by Roumanian leaders for many reasons, but his refusal to make republican reforms was the most important. At the same time, it was hoped that another ruler, from an important western family, could bring the connections and prestige necessary to fend off the Turks, Russians, and Austrians. The Liberal party leader, Ion Bratianu, smoothed the path for acceptance of Charles of Hohenzollern-Siegmaringen as the new prince. With some support from his relatives, King William of Prussia and Napoleon III of France, Charles decided to accept the Roumanian invitation. On May 22, 1866, after traveling incognito through Austrian territory, Charles reached Bucharest. In June, the Paris Conference of principal powers discussed the Roumanian question. The Porte was furious, because the turn of events in Roumania portended the complete loss of Ottoman sovereignty over land they had controlled for centuries. But Austria, also opposed to a strong Roumanian state, was unable to help the Turks (the Austro-Prussian War prevented that), and the Russians were not sufficiently aroused to act. Finally, the Porte had to accept the fait accompli. This Firman of October 23, 1866 is a bit slighting to the Roumanians and masks the fact that an independent Roumanian state had now been created.

Firman of Investitue of Prince Charles of Hohenzollern as prince of the United Principalities of Moldavia and Wallachia. Constantinople, October 23, 1866.

Reprinted in Edward Hertslet, THE MAP OF EUROPE BY TREATY (London: Harrison and Sons, 1891), Vol. III, pp. 1783–1787.

To Prince Charles of Hohenzollern, who has been invested with the dignity of Prince of the United Principalities of Moldavia and Wallachia.

Having nothing more at heart than putting an end to the disturbances which have for some time past taken place in the United Principalities of Moldavia and Wallachia, an important part of my Empire, and to see their prosperity developed, as well as the happiness and well-being of their inhabitants, and that object being only attainable by the establishment of solid and lasting order;

Recognising, on the other hand, the wisdom, the high intelligence, and the capabilities which distinguish you, I confer on you the Rank and Prerogatives of Prince of the United Principalities on the following conditions, which have been specified in the Vizieral Letter addressed to you on the 19th October of the present year, which you accepted by your answer dated on the 20th of the same month, and by which

Recognition of Rights of Turkey to Sovereignty over the United Principalities.

1. You engage, in your own name and in the name of your successors, to respect in their Integrity my Rights of Sovereignty over the United Principalities, which form an Integral Part of my Empire within the limits fixed by the stipulations of ancient Conventions and by the Treaty of Paris of 1856.

Armed Force not to exceed 30,000 Men.

2. Not to exceed, under any pretext whatever, without previous understanding with my Government, the number of 30,000 men, to which the Armed Force of every description of the United Principalities may be raised.

Coinage.

3. Authority having been granted on our part to the United Principalities to have a special Coin bearing a mark of our Government, which shall be hereafter decided between my Sublime Porte and you, to consider that authority as of none effect so long as that decision has not been come to.

Treaties and Conventions with Foreign Powers to be binding on United Principalities. Principalities not to conclude Treaties or Conventions with Foreign Powers. Principalities to be consulted on Treaties and Conventions bearing upon their Laws and Commerce.

4. To consider as binding on the Principalities all Treaties and Conventions existing between my Sublime Porte and other Powers, in so far as they do not infringe on the Rights of the United Principalities established and recognised by the Acts which concern them; also to maintain

and respect the principle that no Treaties or Conventions can be directly concluded by the United Principalities with Foreign Powers. My Imperial Government will nevertheless not fail in future to consult the United Principalities on the stipulations of any Treaty or Convention which might bear upon their Laws and Commercial Regulations.

Above Restrictions not to bear upon Arrangements of an Unofficial or Non-Political Character.

Arrangements of local interest between two neighbouring Administrations, and not having the form of an Offical Treaty, or of a political character, shall continue to remain excluded from the above restrictions.

Not to create any Order of Decoration.

5. To abstain from creating any Order of Decoration intended to be conferred in the name of the United Principalities.

Rights of Sovereignty.

6. Always to respect my Rights of Sovereignty over the United Principalities in the proportion which shall hereafter be fixed in concert with you.

Tribute.

7. To increase the Tribute paid to my Government by the Principalities in the proportion which shall hereafter be fixed in concert with you.

Disturbers of the Peace not to be allowed in the United Principalities.

8. Not to permit that the Territory of the United Provinces shall serve as a focus for Ringleaders of Disturbances, such as would endanger the tranquillity either of the other parts of my Empire or of neighbouring States.

Security to Turkish Subjects trading in the Principalities.

9. To come to an understanding hereafter with my Imperial Government for the adoption of practical measures necessary to secure the assistance and protection due to those of my subjects who from other parts of my Empire shall proceed to the United Principalities with the object of entering into commercial transactions.

Hereditary Title of Prince of the United Principalities.

Considering the conditions enumerated above, and the engagements contained in the before-mentioned answer to the letter of my Grand Vizier, the Rank and Prerogatives of Prince of the United Principalities are conferred upon you as a Hereditary Title for you and your heirs in a direct line, with the reservation, in case of a vacancy, that Rank shall be conferred upon the eldest of your heirs by an Imperial Firman.

Fulfilment of Engagements.

You will therefore watch that no Act shall be allowed contrary to the preceding conditions and to the fundamental dispositions of the Treaties and Conventions concluded with friendly and Allied Powers of my Empire, referring to the United Principalities, and you will devote your attention in perfecting and ensuring the good administration of the United Principalities, and in developing the well-being and prosperity of their inhabitants in conformity with my Imperial wish.

Given at Constantinople, the 14th Djemasɪ-ul-Akhir, 1283 (23rd October, 1866).

CHAPTER 45

Ferencz Deak—Speech to the Hungarian Diet

Ferencz Deak (1803–1876) gained fame by consistently advocating the view that Austria must recognize the ancient rights of the Hungarian nation. Possessed of a strong background in law and opposed to the use of violence, he became the dominant political leader in Hungary during the 1860's.

After the Austrians were humiliated by a Prussian army in 1866, the Austrians decided that an accomodation must be made with Hungary. Deak, who boasted that he did not raise his demands when Austria was in an embarassing situation, saw his program accepted in the Compromise (Ausgleich) that created the Austro-Hungarian monarchy in 1867. His success gained him the title, "Sage of the Nation."

Reprinted in Julius von Farkas (editor), UNGARNS GESCHICHTE UND KULTUR IN DOKUMENTEN (Wiesbaden, 1955), pp. 168–173. By permission of O. Harrassowitz. Translated by the editors.

Hard times and dangerous years have just passed. Our nation has stood at the brink of complete annihilation. But Divine Providence, which has visited upon us such great anxiety, also awakened in our hearts such an inherent strength that we did not lapse into despair. Thus, we were able to embrace our country with a greater love in the most perilous moments of its existence. May Heaven allow that these hard days will teach us something and that we who were united in sufferings will also unite for the great tasks before us.

The Diet has now constituted itself and we have to consult and decide on the form and content of our first solemn declaration. . . .

I do not wish to bore you by just listing, cne by one, the points in our declaration. What I wish to do is to show the grand design of our declaration, to demonstrate the logic and interrelationships of the many singular statements in the declaration.

The last twelve years have been for us a time of great suffering. Our age-old constitution was suppressed, and we were burdened with the foreign system of a limitless power. The weight of this oppressive system was made even greater by those persons who ran this administration with obvious hostility for us, with little understanding of our problems, and even with outright malice. With such people administering our government, it seemed to them a crime that we should feel free and that we should identify with our nation. And an even greater crime was pure, unselfish love for our country. They exhausted the resources of our country, and their expropriations were made with hardly any pretence of legality. And our very nationality as Hungarians became a reason for persecuting us. Every day brought new suffering, and each new calamity tore from our heart any shred of faith or confidence that we might possess.

God perhaps desired that we should thus suffer but not despair, that we should not be unfaithful to ourselves. And He wished, too, that twelve years of experience should bring the Hapsburg ruler to the conclusion that the system of absolutism could not bring happiness to the peoples of the monarchy. In fact, he has realized that this system of absolutism could bring utter ruin to the people of the monarchy. Therefore, His Majesty wanted to enter the constitutional path after eliminating the system by which he formerly governed. And he wanted to put the nations's destiny in the hands of its own people.

Thus, we have assembled here as the representatives of the Hungarian nation in order to commence our constitutional activity, but our first step is a painful declaration. This declaration must be made not because of past sufferings over which we would rather spread a veil of forgetfulness, but because of illegalities that still persist and without the immediate elimination of which, neither the reestablishment of our constitutional life and our national existence is the legal sovereignty and independence of our country. Our first and most holy duty is accordingly to use our entire strength and capabilities to make certain that Hungary remains Hungary and its constitutional sovereignty and independence remain uninfringed upon. When this sovereignty is attacked, when it is threatened through any danger, we know no more important task, no more urgent imperative than that we should protest without delay.. . . .

Therefore, we hold it as necessary to declare in a solemn manner that Hungarian sovereignty and independence were unalterably guaranteed by past laws respecting the rights of Hungary, and also by treaties, royal edicts and coronation oaths. These documents that guarantee our independence cannot be sacrificed because of lame excuses proffered by special interests. And we must uphold our sovereignty as the basic prerequisite for our national existence. Therefore we can never agree that questions of public taxation and military service should be decided other than by the Hungarian Diet. We cannot share our power over legislation with anyone other than the King of Hungary. As we do not wish to exercise legislative power over any other country, so we do not wish to share power over ourselves with anyone other than the King of Hungary. We, the government and administration of Hungary, can make ourselves dependent on no person other than the King of Hungary. And we do not wish, in any way, to unite our powers with any other country. We do not wish to participate in the imperial council Reichsrat nor in any other body that brings together representatives of other countries. And we cannot recognize the right of these councils to dispose of matters pertaining to Hungary. We are willing, only if the situation arises, to communicate with the constituent peoples of the Empire on a unilateral basis where our complete sovereignty is preserved. . . .

A parliamentary government, a system of ministers responsible to the Diet, freedom of the press, and the jury system as well as the right of the Diet to levy taxation; all these are the strongest guarantees of constitutional liberty. Our past laws gave us these guarantees, and we will never consent to their limitation or suspension. We will always object to any suspension of these laws as a suspension of constitutional liberty, and we will consider such a suspension as a denial of the constitutional principle itself.

The final goal of government is not power or magnificence. Power is only a means; the final goal is the happiness of the citizens. When the ruler, who once held that absolutism promoted the happiness of his people, saw, after twelve years, that absolutism did not promote that goal, then he decided to enter the path of constitutional government. If the monarch wishes that the uprooted confidence of the past should be restored, then he will learn to sympathize with our ideas and interests to the fullest extent.

The king of Hungary becomes its legal king only through the ceremony of coronation. And the coronation is legal only if certain prescribed conditions have been completely fulfilled. These preliminary conditions are the following: the uninfringed right to our constitutional sovereignty, the territorial and political integrity of the country, the complete restoration of our basic laws, the reinstatement of our parliamentary government and of our system of ministerial responsibility as well as the elimination of any traces of absolutism. Without agreement to these pre-conditions, any discussion, much less any agreement, is impossible.

This is what I want to be said in our first declaration. I do not presume to think that this declaration, proposed today, will obliterate all dangers and evils. I do not pretend that this declaration will be a universal panacea. It is even probable that the usual policy of the Austrian statesmen will make them dictate to us impossible demands, and because of their intransigeance we shall probably come to the breaking point. But we shall not be the ones to precipitate the breach, and if we cannot avoid a split, we must make certain that we will not be blamed for it. When we say to our people and all Europe that we, in moderation, did everything possible, all will see that they demanded the sacrifice of our constitutional sovereignty by taking away our rights over taxation and military service. All will see that they robbed us of parliamentary government and the system of responsible ministers. It will be evident to all that they desired that Hungary be no longer a sovereign and independent Hungary, that they wanted Hungary to be nothing but a constituent province of Austria. Therefore, all will see that because we would not accept these conditions and could not agree to the political destruction of the country, it came to a split. Then, if all this comes to pass, we will stand vindicated. Nobody will be able to fault us and in truth, we shall not be in an unenviable position where even the slightest blame for the split could be imputed to us. . .

There will undoubtedly be some who will object that this policy is not bold enough. There may even be those who will consider it too timid. Yes, gentlemen, this policy is not one of boldness that would risk everything on one stroke. But is is not a timid policy either. It is a sound policy that realizes our unique strength and position. In warfare and great adventures, boldness is a necessity because it gives greater strength and thus helps to insure success. But in debate on public affairs, I prefer a determination that is accompanied with caution. Boldness in politics is only suitable when that boldness behind it has a considerable amount of strength. If that strength is not present, the bold statesman is nothing more than a foolhardy gambler.

Timid, even cowardly, is the person who worries only about himself when the fate of his country is at stake. But that person who does not worry about himself, who is only concerned for his nation's well being, is therefore cautious that no harm come to himself or that he be placed in a restricted position where he cannot help his country. Such a person is not timid and is certainly not a coward.

We can always control our personal destiny, and when we gamble with our future, we must, of course, suffer all the damaging consequences. Yet we must always remember that we have in our hands not just our lives, but the fate of multitudes who with all confidence placed in us a sacred trust. The fate of our country is far more precious to us than our own existence. We must guard our nation from any danger, and we must have a love for our nation that is always clear-sighted. We can sacrifice everything for our nation. But we will not sacrifice the nation for anything.

CHAPTER 46

The Creation of the Dual Monarchy

The creation of the Dual Monarchy was necessary if the Austrian Empire wished to remain a European power of consequence. After being defeated by the Germans in 1866, Emperor Francis Joseph, obviously dissatisfied with imperial policy, appointed Count von Beust as foreign minister. He advised the emperor that an agreement with Hungary was possible and would strengthen the empire.

After negotiations in which Ferencz Deak and Gyula Andrassy were the Hungarian participants, the Compromise (Ausgleich) was adopted by the Hungarian Diet in March of 1867. While there would be unity in questions of war and foreign policy, decisions about internal matters were delegated to the Hungarian Diet and ministers. The Compromise of 1867 was resented by the other minorities of the empire, but the system lasted until World War I. It obviously increased the number of exploiters in the empire whose loyalty henceforward could be unquestioned.

Reprinted in Herbert Wright (editor), THE CONSTITUTION OF THE STATES AT WAR, 1914–1918 (Washington, D.C.: Government Printing Office, 1919), pp. 4–10.

AUSTRIAN LAW OF 21 DECEMBER 1867.

Law Concerning the Affairs Common to all of the Countries of the Austrian Monarchy, and the Manner of Managing Them, Supplementary to the Constitutional Law on the Representation of the Empire.

Article 1. The following affairs are declared common to Austria and Hungary:

a. Foreign affairs, including diplomatic and commercial representation abroad, as well as measures relating to international treaties, reserving the right of the representative bodies of both parts of the Empire (Reichsrat and Hungarian Diet) to approve such treaties, in so far as such approval is required by the Constitution.

b. Military and naval affairs; excluding the voting of contingents and legislation concerning the manner of performing military service, the provisions relative to the local disposition and maintenance of the army, the civil relations of persons belonging to the army, and their rights and duties in matters not pertaining to the military service.

c. The finances, with reference to matters of common expense, especially the establishment of the budget and the examination of accounts.

Art. 2. Besides these, the following affairs shall not indeed be administered in common, but shall be regulated upon uniform principles to be agreed upon from time to time:

1. Commercial affairs, especially customs legislation.

2. Legislation concerning indirect taxes which stand in close relation to industrial production.

3. The establishment of a monetary system and monetary standards.

4. Regulations concerning railway lines which affect the interests of both parts of the empire.

5. The establishment of a system of defense.

Art. 3. The expenses of affairs common to both Austria and Hungary shall be borne by the two parts of the Empire in a proportion to be fixed from time to time by an agreement between the two legislative bodies (Reichsrat and Diet), approved by the Emperor. If an agreement can not be reached between the two representative bodies, the proportion shall be fixed by the Emperor, but for the term of one year only. The method of defraying its quota of the common expense shall belong exclusively to each of the parts of the Empire.

Nevertheless, joint loans may be made for affairs of

common interest; in such a case all that relates to the negotiation of the loan, as well as the method of employing and repaying it, shall be determined in common.

The decision as to whether a joint loan shall be made is reserved for legislation by each of the two parts of the Empire.

Art. 4. The contribution towards the expense of the present public debt shall be determined by an agreement between the two parts of the Empire.

Art. 5. The administration of common affairs shall be conducted by a joint responsible ministry, which is forbidden to direct at the same time the administration of the joint affairs and those of either part of the Empire.

The regulation of the management, conduct, and internal organization of the joint army shall belong exclusively to the Emperor.

Art. 6. The legislative power belonging to the legislative bodies of each of the two parts of the Empire (Reichsrat and Hungarian Diet) shall be exercised by them, in so far as it relates to joint affairs, by means of delegations.

Art. 7. The delegation from the Reichsrat shall consist of 60 members, of whom one third shall be taken from the House of Lords and two thirds from the House of Representatives.

Art. 8. The House of Lords shall choose its 20 members of the delegation from among its own members by a majority vote.

The 40 members to be chosen by the House of Representatives, shall be so elected that the deputies from each provincial diet may elect, in conformity with the following apportionment, a certain number of delegates, who may be chosen from among themselves or from the House at large.

By majority vote the deputies from the Kingdom of Bohemia shall elect 10; the Kingdom of Dalmatia, 1; the Kingom of Galicia and Lodomeria, with the Grand Duchy of Cracow, 7; the Archduchy of Lower Austria, 3; the Duchy of Styria, 2; the Duchy of Carinthia, 1; the Duchy of Carniola, 1; the Duchy of Bukowina, 1; the Margravate of Moravia, 4; the Duchy of Upper and Lower Silesia, 1; the Princely County of Tyrol, 2; the Territory of Vorarlberg, 1; the Margravate of Istria, 1; the Princely County of Gorz and Gradiska, 1; the city of Triest with its territory, 1.

Art. 9. In the same way each house of the Reichsrat shall elect substitutes of delegates, of whom 10 shall be chosen by the House of Lords and 20 by the House of Representatives.

The number of substitutes to be chosen by the House of Representatives shall be so apportioned that there shall be one substitute for every one to three delegates, and two substitutes for every four or more delegates. The election of each substitute shall take places separately.

Art. 10. Delegates and their substitutes shall be elected annually by the two houses of the Reichsrat.

The delegates and substitutes shall retain their functions until the new election.

Members of the delegation are eligible for reelection.

Art. 11. The delegations shall be convened annually by the Emperor, who shall determine the place of their meeting.

Art. 12. The delegation from the Reichsrat shall elect a president and vice president from among its own members, and choose also its secretary and other officers.

Art. 13. The powers of the delegations shall extend to all matters concerning common affairs.

All other matters shall be beyond their power.

Art. 14. The projects of the government shall be submitted by the joint ministry to each of the delegations separately.

Each delegation shall also have the right to submit projects concerning affairs which are within its competence.

Art. 15. For the passage of a law concerning matters within the power of the delegations the agreement of both delegations shall be necessary, or in default of such agreement, a vote of the full assembly of the two delegations sitting together; in either case the approval of the Emperor shall be necessary.

Art. 16. The right to hold the joint ministry to its responsibility shall be exercised by the delegations.

In case of the violation of a constitutional law in force regarding common affairs, either of the delegations may present charges to the other against the joint ministry or against any one of its members.

The impeachment shall be legally effective when resolved upon separately by each of the delegations, or in a joint meeting of the two.

Art. 17. Each delegation shall propose, from among the independent and legally trained citizens of the country which it represents, but not from among its own members, 24 judges, of whom 12 may be rejected by the other delegation. The accused, or all of them when there are several, shall have the right to reject 12 of those named by the two delegations, but only in such a manner that an equal number of judges be rejected from the lists proposed by each delegation.

The remaining judges shall form a court for the trial of the impeachment.

Art. 18. A special law on the responsibility of the joint ministry shall regulate the details concerning the impeachment, the procedure of trial, and the judgment.

Art. 19. Each delegation shall act, deliberate and vote in separate session. Article 31 indicates an exception to this rule.

Art. 20. The decisions of the delegation of the Reichsrat shall require for their validity the presence of not less than 30 members besides the president, and every decision shall require the vote of a majority of those present.

Art. 21. The delegates and substitutes from the Reichsrat shall receive no instructions from their electors.

Art. 22. The delegates from the Reichsrat shall personally exercise their right to vote; Article 25 determines when a substitute shall take the place of a delegate.

Art. 23. The delegates from the Reichsrat shall enjoy in that capacity the same immunity which they have as members of the Reichsrat by virtue of Article 16 of the fundamental law concerning the representation of the Empire.

If the Reichsrat is not in session, the above-mentioned rights shall be enforced by the delegation itself with respect to its members.

Art. 24. One who ceases to be a member of the Reichsrat shall cease at the same time to be a member of the delegation.

Art. 25. If a vacancy occurs in the delegation or among the substitutes a new election shall be held.

If the Reichsrat is not in session the substitute shall take the place of the retiring delegate.

Art. 26. When the House of Representative is dissolved the powers of the delegation of the Reichsrat shall come to an end. The newly assembled Reichsrat shall elect a new delegation.

Art. 27. The session of the delegation shall be closed, after the completion of its work, by the president with the consent of the Emperor or by his order.

Art. 28. The members of the joint ministry shall have the right to take part in all the deliberations of the delegation, and to present their projects personally or through a deputy.

They shall be heard whenever they desire.

The delegation shall have the right to address questions to the joint ministry or to any one of its members, to require answers and explanations and to appoint committees to whom the ministers shall furnish all necessary information.

Art. 29. The sessions of the delegation shall as a rule be public.

Exceptionally the public may be excluded if it is so decided by the assembly in secret session, upon the request of the president or of not less than five members.

Every decision, however, shall be made in public session.

Art. 30. Each delegation shall communicate to the other its decisions and, if the case requires it, the reasons therefor.

This communication shall take place in writing, in German on the part of the delegation of the Reichsrat, in the Hungarian language on the part of the delegation of the Diet; in each case there shall be annexed a certified translation into the language of the other delegation.

Art. 31. Each delegation shall have the right to propose that a question be decided by a vote in joint session, and this proposal can not be declined by the other delegation after the exchange of three written communications without result.

The two presidents shall agree upon the time and place

of the joint meeting of the two delegations for the purpose of voting together.

Art. 32. In the joint sessions the presidents of the delegations shall preside alternately. It shall be determined by lot which of the two presidents shall preside in the first place.

In all subsequent sessions the presidency at the first joint meeting shall belong to the president of the delegation which has not had the presidency at the meeting immediately preceding.

Art. 33. In order to transact business in joint session the presence of not less than two thirds of the members of each delegation shall be necessary.

Decisions shall be reached by a majority vote.

If one delegation has more members present than the other, so many members shall abstain from voting as shall be necessary to establish an equality of the number of votes from each delegation.

It shall be determined by lot which members shall abstain from voting.

Art. 34. The joint sessions of the two delegations shall be public.

The minutes shall be kept in the two languages by the secretaries of the two delegations and attested by both.

Art. 35. Further details regarding the procedure of the delegation of the Reichsrat shall be regulated by an order of business to be adopted by the delegation itself.

Art. 36. Agreement concerning matters which, though not managed in common, yet are to be regulated upon the same principles, shall be reached in one of the following ways: (1) The responsible ministries by an agreement between themselves shall prepare a project of law which shall be submitted to the representative bodies of the two parts of the Empire and the project agreed upon by the two representative bodies shall be submitted for the approval of the Emperor. (2) Each representative body shall elect from its members a deputation composed of an equal number of members, which shall prepare a project upon the initiative of the respective ministries; such project shall be submitted to each of the legislative bodies by the ministires, shall be regularly considered, and the identical law of the two assemblies shall be submitted for the approval of the Emperor. The second procedure shall be followed especially in reaching an agreement concerning the distribution of the cost of affairs administered in common. . . .

CHAPTER 47

Greece in the Later Nineteenth Century

The following passage, written by a contemporary observer in the 1870's, gives a good picture of the problems faced by Greece after nearly four decades of independence. Underneath a superficial picture of some governmental ineptitude, wretched diet and extreme poverty, the author perceived, especially in his description of the university students at Athens, some of the perennial vivacity of the Greek personality.

Charles K. Tuckerman, THE GREEKS OF TODAY (New York: G. P. Putnam's Sons, 1878), pp. 143–157.

The first blow for Greek independence was struck in April 1821. The fires of revolution had been kindled for many years, but the inflammatory materials were collected and dispersed with such secresy and vigilance-the chief instruments being the orthodox clergy, who whispered of hope and freedom in the pauses of their prayers-that when the venerable Bishop of Patras raised and sanctified the banner of revolt, it was responded to from every quarter of the Turkish dominion. The Porte heard the cry of battle with a smile of derision. What were poorly armed and undisciplined Greeks to accomplish against the glittering phalanxes of the Sultan? Europe heard it, and looked on with apathy at the hopelessness of the struggle. It was the United States which first responded, in the words of President Monroe, Webster, Clay, Everett, Dwight, Poinsett, and hun-reds of lesser voices, to the resolution of the Greek Senate at Calamata, which declared "that having deliberately resolved to live or die for freedom, they were drawn by an irresistible sympathy to the people of the United States."

The assertion in Webster's great speech on Greece, that her "sacrifices and suffering ought to excite the sympathy of every liberal-minded man in Europe," was not supported by facts—at least during the early period of the conflict. The Greeks fought single-handed, with valor in their hearts, wretched flint locks in their hands, and dissensions in their midst. As a Greek historian puts it, "David, scarcely armed with a sling, attacked the formidable Goliath." After a conflict corresponding to that of our seven years' war, not only in duration, but in many of its hardships, England and France came to the aid of the wretched and worn-out revolutionists, and, at the eleventh hour, by the naval battle of Navarino, accomplished the independence of a small portion of Greek territory. This result was unpremediated, and Wellington pronounced it an "untoward event." Doubtless this is the opinion of many to this day; but I will not believe that Gladstone's nobler sentiment, uttered in Parliament in 1870, and in the fact of the then humiliated Greek people, is not the prevailing sentiment of all sound and unprejudiced English minds, namely, that "to crush Greece, would be to strike a blow at the hopes of mankind."

But, although the semi-centennial anniversary of Greek Independence has passed, fifty years of Greek autonomy have not yet passed. The disorders, and dispersions and corruption of the revolution did not give place to any form of systematized order for many years subsequent to the conclusion of actual warfare. A career of self-government cannot be said to have been fairly inaugurated until the Greeks recovered from the terrible exhaustion of the seven years' war, say in 1830, when Greece was declared an independent State by the Protocol of London. Indeed, it was not until 1835, when the seat of government was transferred from Nauplia to Athens—then a collection of miserable Turkish tenements—that much in the way of practical progress was attainable. Thirty-six years then, is the period upon which the political critic should pass judgement. What, it may with propriety be asked, has Greece

accomplished during these thirty-six years of political autonomy?

I do not propose to review the work, or even to record
more than a handful of statistics. Although "figures never
lie," they often deceive. The man who builds but one house
in a life time may have given stronger evidences in that
achievement of the triumph of resolute faith over despair,
than the builder of a city, although each may have begun
his work without a penny in his pocket. The Greeks were
worse than beggars when the seven-years' flood of the revolution rolled back and left them naked on the almost barren
sands of the land they had fought so long to reach. Then
they looked around them to behold but little in the way
of resources within their reach, while the high, fertile plains
of Thessaly and Epirus, which had formed the most significant portion of their land of promise, lay within sight,
but cut off from them by diplomacy, a worse enemy, because a more subtle one, than the Turk, whose might was
visible and could be met hand to hand.

The Greeks were worse than beggars, because they had
begged before, and disgusted the lenders by their inability
to pay the interest. The first loan was contracted in London in the excitement of the Greek revolution, through
the efforts of a few interested and disinterested Philhel-
lenes. Out of £2,300,000 borrowed and for which the whole
Hellenic nation expected to become responsible and easily
to pay off under a solid government of their own, but
£924,800 reached the Greeks, the loan having been negotiated "like a hopeless affair" at fifty nine and fifty-five
per cent. This sum was immediately expended in the purchase of materials for carrying on the war, and when the
war was ended but a little more than one-fifth of the people
who had looked for freedom received it; but a little more
than a third of the territory fought for received it, and
less than a million of people found themselves responsible
for the payment of a debt which had been contracted by
many millions. When Saint Denis was reported to have
picked up his own head and walked several miles with
it under his arm, the celebrated Ninon observed that the
number of miles was nothing, it was only the first step
that cost. Greece was worse off than Saint Denis for she

had no legs left to walk off with. The head with its inventive energies was left, and the weak and wounded arms managed to pick up a scanty sustenance, and this, to her thinking, was, under the circumstances, miraculous enough. Much of the first loan was subsequently bought by Dutch speculators at five or six per cent, and might now be liquidated at a low rate but for subsequent loans—the outgrowth of the first. The united debt of Greece amounts today ot nearly $42,000,000. The revenue, according to the budget for 1870, amounted $5,544,866 and the expenditure to $6,-063,112. This was not an exceptional year, as the revenue, owing to difficulties in collecting and negligence in enforcing the payment of taxes, shown an annual deficit of a million of dollars. Under such circumstances the national debt stands a poor chance of redemption; and Greece being excluded from the money markets of Europe, has an onerous work to support herself under the disadvantages of a small territory and sparse population. About a fourth part of the population live by agricultural pursuits. Her merchant marine is actively engaged in the trade with Turkey and the ports of the Levantine which it largely controls. In these occupations lies her only material strength, and under circumstances of great discouragement; the poverty of her people—feeble resources-inexperience-the enervating influences of old customs and habits of thought, Greece has failed to fulfill the exaggerated and unreasonable expectations of the enthusiastic Philhellenes. But Greece has nevertheless done much in the way of real progress. Briefly enumerated she has, in these thirty-five or forty years of freedom, doubled her population and increased her revenues five hundred per cent. Eleven new cities have been founded on sites formerly deserted. More than forty towns, reduced to ruins by the war, have been rebuilt, restored to regular proportions, and enlarged, presenting at present the aspect of prosperous and progressive cities. Some roads have replaced the foot and saddle paths which were the sole avenues of communication under the Turks, and telegraphic communication extends over the kingdom. Eight or ten ports have been cleared, deepened and opened to communication. Light houses and bridges have been erected. From four hundred and forty vessels,

measuring 61,640 tons, her merchant fleet has increased
to more than five thousand vessels of 330,000 tons. Nearly
a hundred thousand vessels enter Greek ports yearly, of
which more than three quarters are engaged in the coasting
trade. The united value of imports and exports exceeds
twenty-five millions of dollars. Greece has five Chambers
of Commerce, numerous insurance companies, and a national bank, the associated capital of which exceeds eight
millions of dollars. In 1830 the small dried grape of Cor-
inth-of which the word "currant" is a corruption, and which
forms the chief article of export-sold at about $150 the ton.
It now sells at from $40 to $50, which indicates the enormous increase in the production of this one article of commerce, from about ten millions of pounds now. The vines
have increased from 25,000 stremmes—a stremma being
about a third of an English acre—to 700,000; the fig trees
from 50,000 to 300,000; the olives from 2,300,000 to 7,500,-
000 and the value of the silk and cotton production shows
also an increase. The population of the chief towns at the
last census, was: Athens, 48,107; Patras, 90; Corfu,
24,091; Syra 20.996; and Zante, 20,480. the army, newly
organized in 1867, consists of 14,300 troops of the line,
but every Greek is a soldier in the hour of need. The Fleet
is composed of a frigate of fifty guns; two corvettes, together of forty-eight guns; one side-wheel steamer of six
guns; six screw steamers, together of ten guns; two new
iron clads; and twenty-six smaller vessels and gunboats.

The agriculturalist in Greece plods on, a patient, ceaseless
laborer for what, at its best, produces only a simple subsistence. He is temperate and frugal, and—not looking beyond his domestic resources—a tolerably happy man. He
neither neglects his religious observances nor his children's
education; and if he sits down to lament anything, it is
that his taxes are not lighter, his crops not more profitable,
and his country only a fraction of that which he believes
to be his by right of nationality, religion, language, and
hereditary claims. The Greek sailor, on the other hand,
finds some compensation for his national afflictions in the
buoyant bound of the billows beneath his staunch, well-
laden little craft, with which he coasts his native shores
or scours the waters of Turkey and its provinces, and brings

home bags of drachmas for his cargoes of fruits and grains; for he, too, although unhappily deprived of the golden atmosphere of London, has "the genius which knows how to venture." But what becomes of that large body of young men, who with the pride of a somewhat higher birthright than the peasant or the seafaring man, with the energy and ambition of youth, endowed with mental qualities which, if profitably directed, would place them on a level with the best intellectual society of Europe, but without a shilling in their pockets, have to make their way in the world? The life of one such man will very nearly illustrate the life of many hundreds. He finds himself at an age when the pressure of existence begins to be felt, and the necessity for self-support is painfully apparent, a helpless youth in his father's house. The household is respectably but barely held together by the over-taxed industry of his parent, who without the educational advantages which the era of national independence has afforded to her children, digs the soil and trims his vines, or perhaps exists on the uncertain and meager salary of a public office. With a natural love for learning, the son has attended the "gymnasia," and perhaps dreamed that in something better than the tillage of the soil ought to lie his lot in life. But if, discarding books, he finds himself willing to resort to manual labor, the prospect is anything but cheering. The land is probably rented from the Government and at best offers few resources for the large and growing-up family which now manage to exist upon its produce. To go abroad and seek from a cold world—especially cold to one of his nationality—a position of usefulness, is like casting one's only shilling on the generosity of the gambling table, and probably he has not the shilling to venture. There is business at home; many Commercial houses ennoble the cities of Athens, Patras, Syra, etc., but they have been of slow growth and have hundreds of applicants for the first vacancy which may occur in the poorest paid clerk-ships. He bows his head in despair with but a single forlorn hope. That hope is Athens. Surely, in the Capital of the Kingdom, bustling with politicians, lawyers, doctors, journalists, something must offer to a man, sensible of his own merits and ready to devote mind and body to the general or to the personal weal. To the Capital he manages to pay or beg his way, and there drifts, insensibly, perhaps, into the whirlpool of the University—where a thousand others, mostly like himself, find a few years of something like happiness in the excited hum of social and political companionship, with the common object in view of mental culture. He attends the lectures on law, medicine, science, philosophy and belles lettres—devouring knowledge—and, as a hungry child, ignorant of the world around it, sucks the nipple of the Alma Mater. He takes his books home to his little scantily furnished lodging, and pores over them till his eyes ache and his shrunken stomach craves for something more substantial. At a cheap eating house he satisfies his hunger with a few olives and bread, washed down with the resined wine of the country, which is barely sufficent to sustain him until the next repast. Probably he passes the evenings at a cafe—sitting for hours with three or four companions over a single cup of coffee and innumerable cigarettes, discussing—what? The last opera?—the scandal of the day? the lascivious life of cities? It is more than probably that the conversation is earnest; it relates to the morning lecture at the University, or it discusses a classical problem; or what, is sure to come in, and with more or less vehemence, before the evening is over—the political question which is that day the topic of the newspapers, or the subject of debate in the arena of Parliament. In their enthusiasm, these political and literary roysterers heed not the passing hour, and still less heed the presence of the foreigner, who, if by chance, "taking notes" of Athenian society, will be sure to put them down as a parcel of degenerate and drunken blackguards, fit representatives of the national life of Greece. But his university career comes at last to an end. The young man has arrived at the years of manhood. Through unremitting labor of the brain and bodily self-denial, he obtains his degree, and finds himself standing where several roads part, uncertain which of them take. He is fit for the practice of the law, and is not without the ambition which takes delight in gazing upon one's own signboard as he goes into his office lined with the bound-up authorities of his craft. But the profession is full. The city of Athens may be proud of the legal talent which finds exercise at her various bars; but to the few who gather the laurels and wear them in marble dwelling houses, there is a hopeless, swaying crowd, briefless, nameless, and a hunger. The same may be said of every other profession. Thousands gather at the fountain, but the slender stream fills only the nearest pitchers, and that but slowly. People cannot be all of them at loggerheads, or stretched on beds of sickness. There is one road—and an honorable one it is, too—which takes many of the graduates of the University, in spite of its uninviting aspect and poorly paid occupation. Our young man can, if he chooses, go where many of his fellows go, into the benighted provinces of Turkey, and along the Danube, and open, or teach in schools. The stream of the University at Athens meanders through the Greek provinces of Turkey, and gives to no small portion of them all the intellectual freshness and growth they possess. But one of the chief qualities of a teacher of youth is patience, and an absolute disregard to the claims of personal ambition-qualities which are eminently the reverse of those which animate the average Greek mind. Penury may be endured; but patience and obscurity are incompatible with the activity of brain and national self-esteem, which characterize the modern Greek. The young man cannot ponder long at the angle of the professional roads, for his nature abhors mental immobility. He who judges him as he saunters through the streets or sits dreamily at the table of a cafe, judges him wrongly. The brain is working in some direction or other, however passive may be the outward man. If the tongue is not tripping with volubility of speech, it is because no fellow tongue is by to challenge argument. There is but one other road, or rather highway, of occupation open to him; and down that he advances with the rushing crows. The reading of newspapers, the gasconade of the cafe, the warmth of daily debate on public affairs in the corridor of the University, has already made him a political partisan. He has his favorite statesman, and enrolls himself in the ranks of the supporters or denouncers of the existing ministry. In a word, he becomes an embryo politician, scribbles for the journals, and hangs around the camp of the Minister or ex-minister from whom he hopes

to catch, in time, a loaf of fish of party patronage. He
knows that when it comes, it will barely support life for
the brief period that the ministry hold office, but he fills
the interregnum with hopes which may shape themselves
to realities to come. That first political crust is a magic
portion. He dreams of one day becoming Prime Minister
himself, when fame and a sense of personal power shall
fill up the crevices of his physical necessities. If for a
moment he realizes the absolute barrenness of the occupation he has accepted for life, it is but for a moment, for
he sees no other alternative. Thus Athens becomes sur-
charged with an element, for the most part unproductive
and unwholesome to the body politic, and yet one which
seems to result from natural causes, for which there is
no immediate remedy. Let him who laments as I do, that
so much mental culture and absolute talent should be squan-
dered in the political arena, where so seldom are seen the
strength of self-sacrificing statesmanship, point out a practical remedy, that is not born of national self-experience,
as sooner or later it must be born in Greece. As men
look everywhere but to themselves to discover the majesty
of the State, so the Greek, with his eager intellect and
restless ambition, looks all around him for a sphere of
development, unmindful that in his own arms and hands
lie the germs of national prosperity. He does not believe
in the "nobility of labor," nor is it to be wondered at
in a country where, through generations of foreign domination, labor was but the synonym of servitude.

CHAPTER 48

Bishop Strossmayer and Slavic Nationalism

In the nineteenth century, churchmen often played a role
in the development of national feeling. Bishop Joseph
George Strossmayer, although German and Catholic, carried on a vigorous campaign to obtain solidarity among

the various South Slavic peoples. He was a prophet of the Yugoslav idea and made the city of Zagreb the great center of South Slavic culture. His letter to Gladstone could have no immediate effect since Gladstone did not become Prime Minister, replacing Disraeli, until 1880. Storssmayer, in this letter, makes some overly facile generalizations, but it is evident that beneath the rhetoric, he had a rather clear picture of political developments in the Balkans. Letter of Bishop Strossmayer to Mr. Gladstone, Oct. 1, 1876.

Reprinted in R. W. Seton-Watson, THE SOUTHERN SLAV QUESTION AND THE HAPSBURG MONARCHY (London: Constable and Co., Ltd., 1911) pp. 417–421.

Allow me to thank you from my inmost soul for the generous initiative you have taken, before your own glorious nation and the whole civilized world, for the rights of humanity and freedom, for which the unfortunate Southern Slavs are suffering so much and are pouring forth their blood in an unequal conflict. We have rejoiced at it the more, because of our sincere admiration for your country, which has succeeded so well in reconciling order and stability with liberty and with every description of progress, and the noble movement which has recently taken possession of a part of the English people fills us with hope, because the force of public opinion is irresistible when it is directed towards noble ends, and is guided by men of your services and reputation. Therefore I thank you again heartily, and will add a few words, not to say anything that is new, but to relieve the pressure that is on my heart.

The Koran has manifested before God and man its absolute incapacity to govern Christian nations, by making itself the basis not only of religious but of social and political life. Its fatal purpose is either to force Islamism upon them, or to deprive them for ever of political rights, and to plunge them into an intolerable oppression. No power in the world can change this inherent mission of the Koran, for it comes, in the belief of the Moslem, from God Himself. To rule and aggrandise, and to indulge undisturbed in all those unnatural vices which, before they bring about the death of nations, are always the source of dreadful cruelities, that is the appointed mission which the Musselman has received from God. Between the slavery of the Koran and all other slavery there is this difference, that the one is commonly the result of evil custom, of vice and passion, of causes that are destitute of divine sanction, whilst the other claims to be directly sanctioned by God Himself, and must therefore be unchangeable and perpetual. Hence the evident truth, that all attempted reforms are fruitful of nothing but increase of suffering to the Christian. The Turks have the right to say that they must obey the voice of God rather than the precepts of human policy. They regard compulsory reforms as sacrilegious follies, calculated to disturb the rights and enjoyments assured to them by Heaven, and take their revenge on the Christians who occasion the demand for reform. They are cunning enough to abound with treacherous promises in the hour of trouble; but we can truly say of such hollow pledges—"mentita est iniquitas sibi" and "quae societas lucis cum tenebris aut Christi cum Belial." It is impossible that their promises should ever be sincere. It is pitiful that there should be men who have the courage to allow themselves to be so openly deceived; and it is sad especially that the European diplomacy should be among them. Diplomacy ought to be the highest and safest tribunal, full of wisdom and experience; but it exhibits itself now in a light that does not deserve the confidence of the world. Instead of simplifying problems it makes them obscure, and supplies solutions which instead of peace and tranquillity produce new complications, new delusions, new animosities and new conflicts. Of this kind are assuredly all the reforms now spoken of.

To make the situation of the Christians in some measure bearable, it is requisite that the Turkish Government should be able to give them securities for their personal safety, for intellectual progress, and for a decently upright administration. Turkey is manifestly unable to satisfy any one of these requirements. Not the first, for Turkey cannot grant to Christians the right of serving with Mohammedans in the regular army. The Christian cannot remain a slave whose liberty, property and life are at the disposal of his

Turkish master. He must be unarmed, because he is not his own master, and has no country of his own. In consequence of the undeserved protection it enjoys, and perhaps of secret suggestions, Turkey intends to create an universal militia or Landwehr, to deliver it once and for all from European influence and from proposals of reform. If, to the disgrace of Europe, this should be accomplished, then woe to the Christians! God knows whether in that event the self-constituted protectors and advisers would not afterwards suffer for it themselves.

Turkey cannot satisfy the second requirement, because it absolutely contradicts its nature and its divinely appointed mission to pay for Christian schools and institutions. Islam regards this as the greatest crime, whereas the destruction of the Alexandrian library was a holy and religious work. Lastly, the Turkish administration is the incurable spot in the Turkish State. We know by our own experience, the character of the Asiatic bureaucracy which the Turks have, for many years, sent into our Slavonic provinces. They have not an atom of the laboriousness and integrity necessary to a decent administrative system. They are so covetous and so vicious that they can only be compared to swarms of locusts that devastate a country, and leave nothing but desolation and disease behind; and I cannot help observing the contrast between the Arabs, who left splendid traces of their mental activity in Europe, and the Turkish race, which is utterly incapable of creating anything and is only skilful to destroy. They will leave nothing behind them in the fairest regions of Europe, after four centuries of occupation, but destitution and misery, without a sign of any loftier or better purpose. All that is spoken about reform is an illusion, founded very often on bad faith. For there are men who foolishly conceive that the resurrection of the Slavonic race in these parts would be the ruin of their own people. Hence the cry, that the Slavonians must not be free, that the germs of an independent commonwealth must not be suffered to take root in that country. These men are blind to the truth that, by a providential law, the deliverance and revival of an oppressed nation is a pledge of future benefit for others. That is the true secret of solidarity of nations. That must

be a truly wretched and intolerable existence, which requires as its condition, that a neighbouring people should
be crushed and enslaved. There is a process of union going
on among the Slavonian people, which, in spite of many
obstacles and errors, God seems to have taken in His hands.
The issue is a secret of Providence. But I hope with my
whole heart that it will be for the advantage of the state
to which I belong, and which seems to have the exalted
mission of interponing between great nations, to prevent
conflict and to bring about a solution of the most intricate
questions, that shall be for the advantage and happiness
of Europe. The result depends on this: whether that Power
remains true without swerving to that law of Justice which
is the daily bread of the nations that live for the achievement of great ends. We Croasts can truly say, that in this
little group of Slavonian brethren, we represent the Tuscan
element. Under great difficulties and in a short course of
years, we have called into existence institutions which justify us in claiming the lead in the path of intellectual progress and of high ideals. We have a great duty to perform,
and we are conscious of our function in this region, and
in the questions which are stirring the world. It is in the
power of others either to frustrate our action, or to free
and consolidate us.

The Bulgarians are an extremely quiet, sensible and hard-
working people, rich in domestic virtues. A moral and
hard-working people is *eo ipso* fit for self-government. An
independent administration, if it was granted to this fine
Slavonian race, would set free forces that would soon do
much for material and for moral civilization; and ecclesiastical self-government, partially introduced, would serve
them as a school for political self-government.

The Servians are a warlike and very enterprising race,
full of vitality. It would be a just reward of their sanguinary sacrifices in a sacred cause, to put the autonomy of
Bosnia under the protection of their energy and their fifty
years experience. A valuable security for the success of
Bosnian self-government would be due provision for the
moral influences which are never more important than in
a primitive condition of society. A good Catholic and Orthodox Bishop could do a great work in that country.

Such a system of self-government in its European provinces would suit the true interest of Turkey far better than the continual intervention of Europe in its internal affairs, which is injurious to its honour and reputation. I am thoroughly convinced that any solution of the Eastern question which does not include full administrative autonomy in the European provinces of Turkey will increase the confusion and the danger.

Once more I thank you most sincerely, and hope that I shall soon be able to thank you personally and to shake you warmly by the hand. Two distinguished Englishmen, Dr. Liddon and Mr. Malcolm MacColl, visited me lately, and gave me courage to write to you. I need not say that if you should ever visit this country, you will find the heartiest and most fraternal reception at my house.

STROSSMAYER, *Bishop of Bosnia*

DIAKOVO, *October 1, 1876*

CHAPTER 49

The Revolt at Stara Zagora in 1875

The abortive Bulgarian uprising of 1875 is well recounted in this episode written by one of the participants. Those Bulgarians willing to challenge Turkish rule were not numerous enough, although most Bulgarians paid lip service to the idea of independence. The romantic patriotism of the Bulgarians contrasts strikingly with the realism of other European nationalistic movements in the later nineteenth century. The young Stefan Stamboloff, so daring and resourceful in 1875, managed to survive the Turkish massacres and became a great leader of independent Bulgaria. As this selection begins, the group of patriots are already aware that the revolt may have failed because the people of nearby towns apparently have not taken to arms. Their only hope is to find some support in the small town of Nova Mahala.

Zachary Stoyanoff, PAGES FROM THE AUTOBIOGRAPHY OF A BULGARIAN INSURGENT, Translated by M. W. Potter (London: Edward Arnold, 1913), pp. 54–61.

It was not yet dusk when we left the thicket and started towards Nova Mahala, about half an hour's walk. Before entering the village we sent two scouts (one of whom was Stamboloff) to make sure that no treachery was intended. They were to whistle three times if there was anything wrong, but only once if all was well. A few minutes after their departure we heard a single whistle, and we entered the village singing the revolutionary hymn, which had been forgotten since the previous evening. The whole village came out to meet us, accompanied by the dogs, who barked as if we had revolted against them. We were taken to a threshing-ground where supper really had been provided for us. Here we planted our banner and sat down to food, being waited on most assiduously by bare-headed peasants, with candles in their hands, who one by one kissed our banner with deepest reverence. The village pope explained to his flock what was the significance of our black kalpaks, which he called Russian, and why our flag was embroidered with a lion and not any other animal. Another old peasant, sixty or seventy years of age, who had lived long in Greece and taken part in revolutions there, continued to declaim during the whole of our meal Greek poetry, in which the word "patrida" recurred very frequently. He was full of enthusiasm, as were all those present, so long as it was merely a question of welcoming and complimenting us. The moment we mentioned the forty men they had promised us to assist in setting fire to Stara Zagora, the pope slunk out at the doorway, and the old peasant who had recited the poetry disappeared; the faces of our hosts lost their joyful look, and groups of twos and threes began to form; whatever: firstly, because their village would remain defenceless, surrounded by Turkish villages; and, secondly, because we should not get a single man from any other village. Meanwhile, we learned that the Turks of Stara Zagora were all armed and on the alert, and that the town was surrounded by a strong patrol, which allowed no Bulgarian to pass either in or out. Villages who had arrived from Hain reported that all was quiet there, and had no knowledge of Dédo Nikola, our terrible voivode, the leader of seven hundred rebels.

Again despair reigned in our ranks, and also among the villagers, who were evidently on the point of asking us to be gone. Mikhail Jékoff, whom I have already described as one of the most resolute of our party, and who had sacrificed all he had in the world to our cause, lost consciousness and fell fainting to the ground. We determined to make for Hain, and if we really found that Dédo Nikola had done nothing, to try and reach Tirnovo, which we were convinced had long since shaken off the Turkish yoke. Jékoff, who was unable to walk, was hoisted on a horse which we took from the village.

About an hour and a half after sunset we left Nova Mahala, not with songs as we had entered it, but in utter despair. We gave out at first that we were returning to Stara Zagora, but when we were out of sight of the village we took the path towards the Hain pass. The rest of the band, who had not known of our decision, were much dissatisfied, many saying that they preferred to die in their native town to wandering thus aimlessly from village to village.

They were quite right, for it was easy to guess that no revolt had taken place either at Zagora or anywhere else. . . .

Meanwhile, from every side news came of the wholesale arrests which the Turks were making. At Stara Zagora the number of prisoners was variously stated at from a thousand to five thousand. Most of these were eventually released, but numbers of those who remained in prison were hanged the following spring, when the April rebellion broke out. The brothers Jékoff, whom we had left at Elkhovo, were destined to perish there. When their presence became known to the authorities—probably through treachery—they concealed themselves in a well, but upon the Turks surrounding their hiding-place Mikhail Jékoff first shot his brother dead and then blew out his own brains, rather than fall into the hands of their enemies.

Such was the inglorious end of the Stara Zagora insurrection, not a shot being fired by the insurgents either in that town or in any other of the revolutionary centres, from which such ready boasts of resolution had been made previously. . . .

CHAPTER 50

The Massacre of Bulgarians

The following is an account written by a close observer of Turkish affairs who was one of the first to report the atrocities committed against the Bulgarians in 1876. Because British interests seemed to dictate that the Porte be preserved against Russian interference, Prime Minister Disraeli was loath to believe the stories about massacres since British public opinion might be embarrassingly aroused. But as eyewitnesses testified, the atrocity stories were relatively accurate. And the monstrous character of the deeds seemed magnified by the absence, at least in 1876, of a Bulgarian rising. Of course, the Turks knew that revolt would come sooner or later and thought to intimidate the Bulgarians by giving them a lesson. The whole thing backfired, and within a decade, Bulgaria was independent.

Sir Edwin Pears, FORTY YEARS IN CONSTANTINOPLE, 1973– 1915 (New York: D. Appleton and Co., 1916), pp. 16–19.

Mr. Disraeli was then Prime Minister, and treated the matter very lightly. He declared, in reply to a statement that persons had been tortured as well as killed, that he doubted whether torture was practised among a people "who generally terminated their connection with culprits

in a more expeditious manner." He spoke of the Circassians
who had taken a large share in the plunder and killing
of the Bulgarians as "settlers with a great stake in the
country." His light manner of speaking on the subject irritated Members on both sides of the House, who recognised
that if my statements were true they constituted a damning
charge against Turkish methods of government in Bulgaria,
and demanded at least serious examination. My old friend,
Professor Hunter, in the House of Commons said that he
knew me as a "slow-minded man, who would not make
statements of that kind without being satisfied of the
truth."

Mr. (afterwards Sir John) Robinson, of the *Daily News,*
sent me a telegram reporting what Mr. Disraeli had said
and adding that he desired full explanations. Thereupon
I saw various friends, and especially Dr. Long and Dr.
Washburn, who furnished me with translations of a mass
of correspondence, from which I wrote a second and longer
letter to the Daily News. In my first letter I gave the
names of thirty-seven villages which had been destroyed
and whose inhabitants had been tortured or killed. In the
second letter, written on June 30th, I brought the number
of destroyed villages up to sixty, and stated that I had
seen an official report which estimated the number of persons killed at 12,000.

It should be understood that at this time there was no
revolt in Bulgaria, though there had been considerable
expression of discontent. The idea of the Turks was to
crush out the spirit of the Bulgarian people, and thus prevent revolt. In the two letters mentioned I had given the
names of the sixty villages which had been destroyed. One
London journal, which got into trouble with Mr. Labou-
chere of Truth, boldly asserted that the names of these
villages did not figure in any known map. The statement
may have been true of English maps, because the declaration of Mr. Schuyler, the United States Consul-General,
was not without a basis of truth, that for the United States
and the British Empire I was the discoverer of the existence of Bulgaria. I replied to the statement that the villages were as easily identified as if I had given the names
of Yorkshire or Devonshire villages, and I urged that a

Commission should be sent out by H.M. Government to make a report on the matter. The publication of the second letter still further aroused the British people. These letters, in the words of Mr. Glastone, "first sounded the alarm in Europe."

Meanwhile at my request, Mr. Robinson sent Mr. Macgahan, an Irish-American of great experience and fine character, to Bulgaria to report more fully than I had been able to do. There was no question of my going, and that for two reasons. First, that I was then fully occupied with professional work, and secondly, that beyond doubt difficulties would have been placed in my way by the Turkish Government; probably they would even have refused to give me the necessary local passport. The selection of Mr. Macgahan was a happy one. He was a friend of Mr. Schuyler's. Both of them had been in Central Asia and knew something of Russia, and neither of them could be charged with having any prejudice against the Turks. Mr. Schuyler went on behalf of his Government to make a report, and Mr. Macgahan accompanied him.

One of the first places they visited was Batak, the destruction of which had been mentioned in my first letter. From thence Macgahan sent me by private messenger a telegram, which came as a thunderbolt to the British public. Its contents were so horrible that I recognised at once Constantinople. I therefore sent it by letter to be dispatched from Bucarest. It was followed a day or two afterwards by a letter which I sent likewise by Bucarest.

This letter, which was dated 2nd August, and appeared in the *Daily News* about a week later, created a profound sensation, not only in Great Britain but throughout Europe. It was at once a series of pictures describing with photographic accuracy what the observers had seen and a mass of the most ghastly stories they had heard on trustworthy authority. They had seen dogs feeding on human remains, heaps of human skulls, skeletons nearly entire, rotting clothing, human hair, and flesh putrid and lying in one foul heap. They saw the town with not a roof left, with women here and there wailing their dead amid the ruins. They examined the heap and found that the skulls and skeletons were all small and that the clothing was that of women and girls. Macgahan counted a hundred skulls immediately around him. The skeletons were headless, shewing that these victims had been beheaded. Further on they saw the skeletons of two little children lying side by side with frightful sabre cuts on their little skulls. Macgahan remarked that the number of children killed in these massacres was something enormous. They heard on trustworthy authority from eye-witnesses that they were often spiked on bayonets. There was not a house beneath the ruins of which he and Mr. Schuyler did not see human remains, and the streets were strewn with them. When they drew nigh the church they found the ground covered with skeletons and lots of putrid flesh. In the church itself the sight was so appalling that I do not care to reproduce the terrible description given by Mr. Macgahan.

Batak, where these horrors occurred, is situated about thirty miles from Tartar Bazarjik, which is on the railway and on a spur of the Rhodope Mountains. It was a thriving town, rich and prosperous in comparison with neighbouring Moslem villages. Its population previous to the massacres was about 9,000. Macgahan remarks that its prosperity had excited the envy and jealousy of its Moslem neighbours. I elsewhere remark that, in all the Moslem atrocities, Chiot, Bulgarian, and Armenian, the principal incentive has been the larger prosperity of the Christian population; for, in spite of centuries of oppression and plunder, Christian industry and Christian morality everywhere make for national wealth and intelligence." . . .

CHAPTER 51

The Constitution of the Ottoman Empire, December 1876

The Ottoman Constitution of 1876 was auspiciously timed. The Bulgarian massacres had lost the Turks the good will of Western Europe, and both the aspirations of

Russia and the Balkan peoples faced little opposition. In this year of great Turkish embarrassment, when the European holdings seemed virtually lost, the "sick man of Europe" made a startling comeback. Mainly at the instigation of the very able Midhat Pasha, the Empire adopted some aspects of parliamentary government. But while Midhat Pasha's constitution used the word liberty, still Article I forbade any subtraction from the Empire's territory. The new Sultan, Abdul Hamid II, never intended to abide by the Constitution, and once the Turks assuaged the outraged public opinion of Western Europe, the Constitution was completely ignored. In early 1877, Midhat Pasha, who sincerely wanted to limit the Sultan's power, was dismissed from his position as the Grand Vizier.

Reprinted in Edward Hertslet, THE MAP OF EUROPE BY TREATY (London: Harrison and Sons, 1891), Vol. IV, pp. 2532–2537.

The Ottoman Empire.

Art. I. The Ottoman Empire comprises present territory and possesions, and semi-dependent (*privilégiés*) provinces.

It forms an indivisible whole, from which no portion can be detached under any pretext whatever.

Art. II. Constantinople is the capital of the Ottoman Empire. This city possesses no privilege or immunity peculiar to itself over the other towns of the Empire.

Sultan, "Supreme Caliph."

Art. III. The Ottoman Sovereignty, which includes in the person of the Sovereign the Supreme Caliphat of Islamism, belongs to the eldest Prince of the house of Osman, in accordance with the rules established *ab antiquo.*

Art. IV. His Majesty the Sultan, under the title of "Supreme Caliph," is the protector of the Mussulman religion. He is the Sovereign and Padisha of all the Ottomans.

Art. V. His Majesty the Sultan is irresponsible; his person is sacred.

Art VI. The liberty of members of the Imperial Ottoman Dynasty, their property, real and personal, and their Civil List during their lifetime, are under the guarantee of all.

Sovereign Rights of Sultan.

Art. VII. Among the Sovereign rights of His Majesty the Sultan are the following prerogatives:—He makes and cancels the appointments of Ministers; he confers the grades, functions, and insignia of his Orders, and confers investiture on the chiefs of the privileged provinces, according to forms determined by the privileges granted them; he has the coining of money; his name is pronounced in the mosques during public prayer; he concludes Treaties with the Powers; he declares war and makes peace; he commands both the land and sea forces; he directs military movements; he carries out the provisions of the Cheri (the sacred Law), and of the other laws; he sees to the administration of public measures; he respites or commutes sentences pronounced by the Criminal Courts; he summons and prorogues the General Assembly; he dissolves, if he deems it necessary, the Chamber of Deputies, provided he directs the election of new members.

Public Law of the Ottomans.
Personal Liberty.

Art. VIII. All subjects of the Empire are called Ottomans, without distinction, whatever faith they profess; the *status* of an Ottoman is acquired and lost, according to conditions specified by law.

Art. IX. Every Ottoman enjoys personal liberty on condition of not interfering with the liberty of others.

Art. X. Personal liberty is wholly inviolable. No one can suffer punishment, under any pretext whatsoever, except in cases determined by law, and according to the forms prescribed by it.

Religion.

Art. XI. Islamism is the State Religion.

Religious Liberty.

But, while maintaining this principle, the State will protect the free exercise of all faiths professed in the Empire and uphold the religious privileges granted to various bodies, on condition of public order and morality not being interfered with.

The Press.

Art. XII. The press is free, within limits imposed by law.

Commercial and other Companies.

Art. XIII. Ottomans have the power of forming commercial companies, industrial or agricultural, within limits imposed by law and statute.

Right of Petition.

Art. XIV. One or more persons of Ottoman nationality have the right of presenting petitions in the proper quarter relating to the breaking of law and regulation, done either to their own or public detriment, and may likewise present in protest signed petitions to the General Ottoman Assembly, complaining of the conduct of State servants and functionaries.

Education.

Art. XV. Education is free.
Every ottoman can attend public or private instruction on condition of conforming to the law.

Schools.

Art. XVI. All schools are under State supervision.

Proper means will be devised for harmonizing and regulating the instruction given to all the Ottomans, but without interfering with the religious education in the various districts.

Equality before the Law. Public Offices.

Art. XVII. All Ottomans are equal in the eye of the law. They have the same rights and owe the same duties towards their country, without prejudice to religion.

Art. XVIII. Eligibility to public office is conditional on a knowledge of Turkish, which is the offical language of the State.

Art. XIX. All Ottomans are admitted to public office, according to their fitness, merit, and ability.

Taxes.

Art. XX. The assessment and distribution of the taxes are to be in proportion to the fortune of each taxpayer, in conformity with the laws and special regulations.

Property.

Art. XXI. Property, real and personal, of lawful title, is guaranteed. There can be no dispossession, except on good public cause shown, and subject to the previous payment, according to law of the value of the property in question.

Inviolability of Domicile.

Art. XXII. The domicile is inviolable. The authorities

cannot break into any dwelling except in cases prescribed
by law.

Tribunals.

Art. XXIII. No one is bound to appear before any other
than a competent Tribunal, according to statutory form
of procedure.

Property. Forced Labour. Contributions in Time of War.

Art. XXIV. Confiscation of property, forced labour
("corvée"), and mulcting ("djéruné"), are prohibited. Nevertheless, contributions lawfully levied in time of war, and
measured rendered necessary by the exigencies of war, are
exempt from this provisions.

Taxes and Imposts.

Art. XXV. No sum of money can be exacted under the
name of a tax or impost, or under any other title whatever, except by virtue of a law.

Torture and Inquisition.

Art. XXVI. Torture and inquisition, under any form,
are wholly and absolutely forbidden. . . .

CHAPTER 52

The Accession of Abdul Hamid

This selection gives a detailed account of the events surrounding Abdul Hamid's acceptance of a Constitution in 1876. As Pears observes, the granting of parliamentary government was a temporary expedient, and Abdul Hamid quickly showed that he was unwilling to relax his control over the Turkish Empire.

Sir Edwin Pears, FORTY YEARS IN CONSTANTINOPLE, 1873–1915 (New York: D. Appleton and Co., 1916), pp. 57–59.

Abdul Hamid ascended the throne August 31, 1876. During the next nine months he was feeling his way to actual power. A project of Constitution which was drawn up mainly by Midhat Pasha was submitted for his approval, and whether he liked it or not he had to consent to its promulgation. Probably that which influenced him to give it sanction was the serious political difficulty in which he found himself. His mind was always tricky. There had assembled, December, 1876, in Constantinople, the Conference of the Representatives of the Powers, already mentioned, and the Sultan well knew that a project of reforms was to be submitted which would lessen the Imperial Prerogative and diminish his reputation in the eyes of his subjects. The problem before him was how to defeat the plans of the European Delegates. Rumours of what he proposed to do were widespread at the time. Midhat, who was then Grand Vizier, probably saw a chance of obtaining the grant of a Constitution by playing up to the Sultan's desire to checkmate the Powers. Accordingly a *coup* was played.

The Conference met in the Admiralty Buildings on the Golden Horn. A few days after they disclosed their plans, their sittings were interrupted by the booming of a hundred guns, fired from the Turkish ships in the Golden

Horn and the Bosporus. Thereupon Sir Henry Elliot, the British Ambassador, proposed to the Delegates that they should discontinue their sittings because those guns meant that the Sultan had issued a Constitution, which granted more privileges to the whole of the Empire than those which they had proposed to grant only to Serbia, Bulgaria, and Montenegro, the disaffected provinces. Thereupon, after a little hesitation, General Ignatiev expressed his opinion that he and his colleagues were there, charged with a specific mission by their respective Governments, and had nothing to do with any proclamation of the Sultan. Lord Salisbury supported the same view, and the sittings of the Conference continued.

The most important article in Midhat's Constitution provided for a Chamber of Representatives from all parts of the empire. It was an honest, bold and praiseworthy attempt to substitute a constitutional form of Government for absolutism. Its proclamation failed in its endeavour to put an end to the Conference, but it was welcomed by the more thoughtful of the subjects of the Sultan of all races. The Chamber met, and its deliberations filled friends of Turkey with hope that the new form of government would put an end to the great abuses in Turkey and give her a new chance of life. Many of the deputies were really able men desirous and hopeful of national progress. Of course there were no traditions of parliamentary government, and many of the speeches provoked merriment, but the general tone was serious and businesslike. They attacked abuses and the Pashas who were or ought to have been responsible for them. Their earnestness and the keen senses of what the country needed were very striking.

The existence of abuse was largely a revelation to the deputies themselves. The member for Jerusalem or for Salonica, or other distant places, spoke as if he believed that the district from whence he came was exceptional in the rankness of corruption. The discussions shewed us outsiders, as well as the members themselves, that the Government from one end of the country to the other required the most radical reforms. The members became so serious that the Pashas became alarmed, and I remember writing to the *Daily News* that the Chamber would shortly get rid of the offending Pashas or the Pashas of the Chamber. Its President was a certain Ahmed Vefyk, who was a neighbour of mine, and whom I knew well. He had been Ambassador in France, a favourite of Napoleon III., and considered himself, as he was, very much superior in education to the mass of the deputies. But as Speaker he was amusingly despotic. From the presidential chair he constantly stopped members, telling them that they knew nothing at all of what they were talking about. Dr. Washburn was present when a Saracli, a white-turbaned Mollah who was prosing along in somewhat dismal fashion, was suddenly brought up by a stentorian shout from the Speaker of, "Shut up, you donkey!" (*Sus eschek!*)

Nevertheless, in spite of many shortcomings and of ignorance of parliamentary usage, the attempt at legislation was an honest one. It was brought abruptly to an end by Abdul Hamid, who gave us, perhaps for the first time, a sample of how he wished to govern. A debate had taken place one day, in which certain charges were made against two Ministers whom the Chamber asked to be brought before it to give explanations. Next morning we learnt that all the deputies had been packed off during the night to the places they represented. No more was heard of attempts to govern Turkey constitutionally until 1908.

CHAPTER 53

Manifesto of the Prince of Serbia, Proclaiming a Renewal of the War with Turkey, December, 1877

The Serbian declaration of war against the Turks was prompted by the desire for more territory and the news that Russian troops, on December 10, 1877, had taken the almost impregnable Turkish fortress of Plevna, thus opening the way to Adrianople. Throughout the long siege of Plevna, Russia appealed to Serbia for assistance. However, Russia could promise Serbia very little in return, since this war of 1877 had commenced only after Austria had been given the promise of Bosnia-Herzegovina, the chief territory covetted by Serbia. Thus, Serbia was outwitted by the two major powers, both of which were not in favor of a large Serbian state in 1877.

Serbia achieved very little through armed intervention. But the Treaty of San Stefano (March 3, 1878) between Russia and the Turkish Empire did formally recognize the independence of Serbia. Still, Serbia opposed the Treaty and protested to Russia. Serbia was treated no better by the Treaty of Berlin (July 13, 1878). Although small parcels of land were conferred on Serbia, Austria, like Russia fearful of a strong Balkan state, took the Sanjak of Novi Bazar, a strip of land that separated Serbia from Montenegro. The union of Serbia and Montenegro was thus to be prevented. The events of 1877 and 1878 forcefully demonstrated the inability of new Balkan states to achieve significant advances if they did not have an advocate among the major powers. At the same time, despite the grandiose rhetoric of Milan in his declaration of war, his timing was so patently opportunistic that the Russians felt no necessity to express their gratitude.

Reprinted in Edward Hertslet, THE MAP OF EUROPE BY TREATY (London: Harrison and Sons, 1891), Vol. IV, pp. 2648–2650.

To my beloved People,

In my Proclamation of 21st February (5th March) of this year, I announced to my beloved people that the defence of the holy cause, for which we were last year obliged to draw the sword, had passed into more powerful hands. But since the time that Servia concluded peace with the Ottoman Porte, the Turkish race has enriched its history with new unheard-of horrors. Rapine, waste, and slaughter to-day fill all the provinces of the Turkish Empire, but more especially do the Turks vent their wrath on all who bear the Servian name. The Mussulman fanaticism, inflamed with vengeance, vents itself especially on those suffering brethren of ours who at the time of the war found refuge and protection in Servia, although by Article II of the Treaty we concluded on 16th (28th) February with the Ottoman Porte a complete amnesty is stipulated for them. Relying on the good faith of the International Convention, we induced the greater part of the martyrs to return to their hearths; but having returned with confidence in our advice they were, alas! under various pretexts, subjected anew to tortures and violence by their Mahommedan oppressors. In vain were the steps my Government took at Constantinople against this flagrant infraction of the Treaty. The Ottoman Porte left the fresh acts of violence unpunished, and trampled on the solemn promise it had made us.

Servians! after such a breach of the Treaty which the Porte concluded with us we are no longer obliged to remain in the trying condition which changed us from champions of freedom to patient spectators of those ruthless endeavors by which the Porte is evidently bent on extirpating the Servian race. The measure of the Turkish atrocities is such that Servia will now no longer remain a quiet looker-on, neither can she, without abasement, remain any longer bound to a Power which derives its might from devastation, fire, and blood, and which in the fury of its fanaticism, already threatens our Principality.

Although Servia has preserved amost correct attitude towards Turkey, the Ottoman Porte again begins to prepare new dangers for our country. Besides secret conspiracies which it fosters against our internal security, the Ottoman Minister for Foreign Affairs openly threatens us, saying that the Porte has innumerable ways of harming Servia, although she may not be *pro forma* at war with us.

Servians! since the Porte assumes such a threatening tone towards us at the moment when it is hard pressed by the army of one of the most powerful States, it is evident that we must not let the present opportunity pass without trying once and for all to insure our future. No; the struggle with our hereditary foe was not concluded with last year's campaign. It would neither be glorious nor profitable for us were we to occupy ourselves with the works of peace instead of endeavouring so far as lies within our power, to remove the dangers which beset the Servian race and to fulfil our national task.

And although the brave Russian army needs not our assistance to crown with success the holy cause which the Emperor Alexander has taken under his mighty protection, nothing in the world can free us from the duty which the Servian nation has to fulfil as a member of the community of Eastern Christian nations, which Servia must fulfil towards herself and her race.

Nations cannot attain true freedom until they have purchased it by their own exertions, and if necessary, by their blood. Great deeds like that undertaken last year by us are not begun in order to stop half-way. That were indeed a pusillanimous policy and a luke warm patriotism, for which posterity would blame us, for which our suffering brethren would execrate us, and of which we ourselves should hereafter repent.

The blessed spirits of our heroes who fell in last year's war would renounce us when they saw from above that we were indifferent whilst rivers of blood were shed on our frontier, that we undertook nothing to fulfil their legacy of fighting the enemy who devastated our beautiful and fertile land when the exigencies of war did not demand it.

Only by steadfastness and perseverance can we reap the fruits of the noble and courageous attempt which cost us such extra-ordinary efforts and enormous sacrifice. We have had time given us to rest until now, and we were entitled to take it. If the enemy could bring superior forces last year against the Servian Principality, to-day, taking the field, we find there a Russian army crowned with glory, we find there our heroic Montenegrin brethren, and our valiant Roumanian neighbours, who have crossed the Danube, and fight gallantly for their independence and the liberty of the oppressed Christians.

Servians! we take up arms to-day in a holy, national, and Christian cause. After the example of my grandfather, behold I place myself again at the head of the armed Servian nation. On the banner which Obrenovits IV unfurls

again are written, "Liberty and National Independence."
Under this banner you have already given splendid proofs
of your patriotism and self-devotion.

We now take a bold step; let us join hands with those
of our brethren from whom we have been separated since
the day of Kossovo.

To-day or never has struck the hour in which we must,
once and for all, complete the great national task which
the heroes of Takova so gloriously began, and which we
last year recommended.

And so, heroes, forward, beside the victorious banners
of the Czar liberator, with faith in God Almighty, the Protector of Right, for the liberation of our oppressed brethren
and for the independence of our country Servia!

Forward, heroes; it is the will of God.

MILAN M. OBRENOVITS IV, c.p.

Prince of Servia

Belgrade 13th December, 1877

CHAPTER 54

The Treaty of Berlin

The Treaty of Berlin constitutes one of the most important documents in the history of Eastern Europe. Bulgaria
began its national existence in the modern world while
Turkey lost much of its European holdings.

Reprinted in R. B. Mowat, SELECT TREATIES AND DOCU-
MENTS TO ILLUSTRATE THE DEVELOPMENT OF THE MODERN
EUROPEAN STATES-SYSTEM (London: Oxford University
Press, 1915), pp. 79–83.

TREATY BETWEEN GREAT BRITAIN, AUSTRIA-HUNGARY, FRANCE, GERMANY, ITALY, RUSSIA, AND TURKEY. (BERLIN) JULY 13, 1878.

Article 1. Bulgaria is constitued an autonomous and tributary Principality under the Suzerainty of His Imperial Majesty the Sultan, it will have a Christian Government and a national militia.

Article XXIII. The Sublime Porte undertakes scrupulously to apply in the Island of Crete the Organic Law of 1868 with such modifications as may be considered equitable.

Similar laws adapted to local requirements, excepting as regards the exemption from taxation granted to Crete, shall also be introduced into the other parts of Turkey in Europe for which no special organization has been provided by the present Treaty.

The Sublime Porte shall depute special Commissions, in which the native element shall be largely represented, to settle the details of the new laws in each province.

The schemes of organization resulting from these labours shall be submitted for examination to the Sublime Porte, which, before promulgating the Acts for putting them into force, shall consult the European Commission instituted for Eastern Roumelia.

Article XXV. The Provinces of Bosnia and Herzegovina shall be occupied and administered by Austria-Hungary. The Government of Austria-Hungary, not desiring to undertake the administration of the Sanjak of Novi-Bazar, which extends between Servia and Montenegro in a south-easterly direction to the other side of Mitrovitza, the Ottoman Administration will continue to exercise its functions there. Nevertheless, in order the assure the maintenance of the new political state of affairs, as well as freedom and security of communications, Austria-Hungary reserves the right of keeping garrisons and having military and commercial roads in the whole of this part of the ancient Vilayet of Bosnia. To this end the Governments of Austria-Hungary and Turkey reserve to themselves to come to an understanding on the details.

Article XXVI. The independence of Montenegro is recognized by the Sublime Porte and by all those of the High Contracting Parties who had not hitherto admitted it.

Article XXXIV. The High Contracting Parties recognize the independence of the Principality of Servia, subject to the conditions set forth in the following Article.

Article XXXV. In Servia the difference of religious creeds and confessions shall not be alleged against any person as a ground for exclusion or incapacity in matters relating to the enjoyment of civil or political rights, admission to public employments, functions, and honours, or the exercise of the various professions and industries, in any locality whatsoever.

The freedom and outward exercise of all forms of worship shall be assured to all persons belonging to Servia, as well as to foreigners, and no hindrance shall be offered either to the hierarchical organization of the different communions, or to their relations with their spiritual chiefs.

Article XLIII. The High Contracting Parties recognize the independence of Roumania, subject to the conditions set forth in the two following Articles.

Article XLIV. In Roumania the difference of religious creeds and confessions shall not be alleged against any person as a ground for exclusion or incapacity in matters relating to the enjoyment of civil and political rights, admission to public employments, functions, and honours, or the exercise of the various professions and industries in any locality whatsoever.

The freedom and outward exercise of all forms of worship shall be assured to all persons belonging to the Roumanian State, as well as to foreigners, and no hindrance shall be offered either to the hierarchical organization of the different communions, or to their relations with their spiritual chiefs.

The subjects and citizens of all the Powers, traders or others, shall be treated in Roumania, without distinction of creed, on a footing of perfect equality.

Article XLV. The Principality of Roumania restores to His Majesty the Emperor of Russia that portion of the Bessarabian territory detached from Russia by the Treaty of Paris of 1856, bounded on the west by the mid-channel of the Pruth, and on the south by the mid-channel of the Kilia Branch and the Stary-Stamboul mouth.

Article LII. In order to increase the guarantees which assure the freedom of navigation on the Danube which is recognized as of European interest, the High Contracting Parties determine that all the fortresses and fortifications existing on the course of the river from the Iron Gates to its mouths shall be razed, and no new ones erected. No vessel of war shall navigate the Danube below the Iron Gates with the exception of vessels of light tonnage in the service of the river police and Customs. The 'stationnaires' of the Powers at the mouths of the Danube may, however, ascend the river as far as Galatz.

Article LVIII. The Sublime Porte cedes to the Russian Empire in Asia the territories of Ardahan, Kars, and Batoum, together with the latter port, as well as all the territories comprised between the former Russo-Turkish frontier and the following line:—

(*Here follow the limits.*)

Article LIX. His Majesty the Emperor of Russia declares that it is his intention to constitute Batoum a free port, essentially commercial.

Article LXII. The Sublime Porte having expressed the intention to maintain the principle of religious liberty, and give it the widest scope, the Contracting Parties take note of this spontaneous declaration.

In no part of the Ottoman Empire shall difference of religion be alleged against any person as a ground for exclusion or incapacity as regards the discharge of civil and political rights, admission to the public employments, functions and honours, or the exercise of the various professions and industries.

All persons shall be admitted, without distinction of religion, to give evidence before the tribunals.

The freedom and outward exercise of all forms of worship are assured to all, and no hindrance shall be offered either to the hierarchical organization of the various communions or to their relations with their spiritual chiefs.

Ecclesiastics, pilgrims, and monks of all nationalities travelling in Turkey in Europe, or in Turkey in Asia, shall enjoy the same rights, advantages and privileges.

The right of official protection by the Diplomatic and Consular Agents of the Powers in Turkey is recognized both as regards the above-mentioned persons and their religious, charitable, and other establishments in the Holy Places and elsewhere.

The rights possessed by France are expressly reserved, and it is well understood that no alterations can be made in the *status quo* in the Holy Places.

The monks of Mount Athos, of whatever country they may be natives, shall be maintained in their former possessions and advantages, and shall enjoy, without any exception, complete equality of rights and prerogatives.

Article LXIII. The Treaty of Paris of March 30, 1856, as well as the Treaty of London of March 13, 1871, are maintained in all such of their provisions as are not abrogated or modified by the preceding stipulations....

CHAPTER 55

The Life of a Polish Serf

The following is a quaint description of peasant life in Poland during the nineteenth century. Slomka had seen in his lifetime such progressive developments as the use of clocks and chimneys. Peasant life was very harsh and at the outset of the century seemed unchanged from what it had been centuries before. But the increased flow of products resulting from industrialization had a perceptible effect on peasant life in the later nineteenth century, even if it meant their use of the most elementary accoutrements of civilization.

Jan Slomka, FROM SERFDOM TO SELF GOVERNMENT, MEMOIRS OF A POLISH VILLAGE MAYOR, 1842–1927, Translated by William John Rose (London: Minerva Publishing Co., 1941), pp. 14–30.

During serfdom days Dzikov belonged to the 'demesne', i.e. to the lords of Dzikov. This had been from long ago the home of the Counts Tarnowski, whose chief seat was the manor house in our village. In addition there were other villages belonging: Miechocin, Zakrzov, Sielets, Wielowies, Trzesn, Sobov, Furmany, Zupava, Jeziorko, Tarnovska village, Demba, Rozalin.

Towards the end of serfdom the total number of cottagers in Dzikov was forty-two, of whom twelve were owners, twenty-three tenants and seven day-labourers.

The first named had eighteen acres each, and did their dues six days a week for the lord of the manor, with team or yoke of oxen and implements, e.g. wagon, plough, harrows, disc, etc. For this they had, in addition to the pasture for cattle used by the whole village, a special fifty acres near Zwierzyniets and six acres on the Vistula. The latter, known as the 'Jewish Shrubbery', was for the use of three farmers from the hamlet Podlenze. The tenants had six-acre lots in each case, and did their dues three days a week with hand tools—flail, sickle, hoe, spade, etc. The labourers had only huts, and were not bound to any dues at all. They went to work for farmers engaged in doing their dues, but who often could not overtake them. The master in each case would give directions for the morrow's work, appointing the foreman under whom each hired helper was to work.

As the folk who knew this system and remembered it used to tell of it, no worse punishment could be found for men and women than serfdom was. People were treated worse then than cattle are today. They were beaten both at work and at home for the merest trifle. What I have heared from them could not be written down. It is unbelievable how men could thus torture their fellows!

Every farmer had first to do his dues at the manor house, whether with his team or on foot. Only then could he work his own land, sowing and reaping at night. No excuse as to pressing needs at home was of any use. If one did not appear as ordered, at once the overseer would come. If he found the wife busy cooking he would throw a pail of water on the fire, or in winter would carry off the windows or the doors.

In case that did not work, and men were needed for service, the overseer would come with his foremen and eject the farmer from home and homestead. Another would be put in his place. Nor was there any appeal anywhere, since that was the usage and at bottom the lord of the manor was owner of everything. His was both land and water, yes even the wind; since only he was allowed to build a wind-mill to grind corn.

Only when all his compulsory dues were done could the peasant sing the old song:

> *I'm not afraid the landlord will molest me,*
> *My dues are done, I'll set me home and rest me!*

Our Dzikov masters were esteemed as kindly and humane folk, yet no one dared go to the manor with any complaint about the manor servants: for the latter would find excuses and then afterward make trouble for us. The result was that all gave up the thought of just dealing. Running away would have done no good, for elsewhere it was no better— rather worse.

As already noted, the number of houses in the whole of Dzikov was something like seventy, each as like the other as two peas. They stood by the roadside, with backs to the street. If there was a grove round about, it was of wild trees, oak, elm or lime, which came up for the most part from the roots, and without any special care on anyone's part.

The farmyard would be fenced in, either with a willow hedge or with a picket fence made of splints from pine or spruce; or with a rail enclosure two, three or four rails high. Even the manor house park was surrounded by a hedge that was tended yearly: and not until about 1880 was this replaced by the present brick wall or by iron pickets. The last named, so common now, were formerly not known at all.

The village area of Dzikov was divided into several parts, each with its own name: the High Street, the Sands, the Bottom, and the hamlet Podlenze. As a whole its appearance was that of days long gone by, far different from what we see now. So, too, during the decades it had grown enormously; partly for the reason that it lies close to the county town, Tarnobrzeg, which is growing all the time. As a result Dzikov is today four times as large as fifty years ago.

The cottage of the peasant or the hired labourer was made up of a single living-room, alongside of which was a large shed and store room. The peasant had besides this his stable for horses, cattle and pigs, and his granary. All such buildings were built of round logs, laid almost as they grew, and with little trimming. At the corners the ends projected a couple of feet, so that when wood was scarce they could be cut off for fuel. Many, however, built this way in order to get a finer appearance.

In neighbouring villages, especially farther from the Vistula and set in the woods on sandy beaches, the cottages were almost all 'smoke' ones: i.e. the fire was built on a broad drum, made of packed clay, called an 'old woman'. The smoke went through the whole room, and out through the door to the shed, and so out the roof. The door had to be open when cooking went on, and everybody had to sit on the ground or go about stooped in order not to be choked. The walls were covered with soot, never white-washed. The people were blackened and saturated with smoke.

In Dzikov we had for the most part chimneys carried through the roof, but they were made of clay, mixed with straw. Here and there were chimneys made of a hollowed-out tree trunk, and in that case they were lined with clay. Not until about 1870 did the peasants begin to build proper brick chimneys, when the iron cooking stoves came in, which are now used everywhere in the kitchens.

Of old we used for cooking only the open hearth, on which the pots with food were set either close to or on the fire, according as we were in a hurry or not. Here and there folk used tripods or other iron fixtures to hold the pot. In addition there was in every house a bake-oven, big enough so that one could bake at one time the bread from a half-a-sack of flour. There was also a heater, into which the fuel was put from the outside passage, through an opening called the 'shoot'. These ovens were built of raw brick, and they took up a lot of room. The top surface of the oven and the heater together, faced off with stucco, was big enough so that four people could sleep on it. Right through the winter the children and the hired girl slept there all the time; and any one of the family who felt miserable or got a chill crawled up on the oven, to stretch out and toast himself. Between the oven and the wall was a space, which was called the 'oven-corner', where the children would also sleep.

The house furnishings were of the simplest. For furniture we had tables (though not in every house), a couple of benches, a chest that took the place of drawers, and beds or bunks. In addition the cottage had a hand-mill for grinding, a mortar for cracking up meal for porridge, or linseed for oil; and a block for splitting wood. All these were hewn of wood with a hatchet but no plane. Still all the walls were hung with pictures—a thing everyone loved. Once a year the walls would be whitened—mostly at Easter.

In every living-room there would be two beams just under the ceiling, called 'poles'. On them wood was put to dry, or flax or hemp was hung. On them the loaves of bread were laid. There were no floors, except in the manor house. When the cow was to calve in winter, they would bring her into the house, so that she would be warmer.

For cooking we had mostly earthenware pots. Only in later times, more or less with the coming of iron stoves, did iron utensils and kettles come in (from far-away Tarnov); the kettles being used to heat mash for the pigs. Dishes, jugs and bowls were of earthenware. For spoons we had wooden ones, much larger than the metal ones we now use.

There wasn't a clock in the village. In every house, however, there was a rooster, whose shrill crowing told you in winter when to get up. And he would crow with the greatest regularity; the first time at midnight, the second about three in the morning, the third time 'for the day' about four. It was the wife's business to keep track of his crowing, for she would waken the household after the second, or at the latest right after the third crow. Apart from this the farmer would step out to the yard and look at the stars to see how near it was to the morning.

From the start I did not like the idea of getting out in the cold and observing the stars in winter time, so as to see when to get up. At times the rooster made a mistake, or when he crowed for midnight one thought it was the second or third. I therefore decided to have a clock in the house. In order, however, not to have unpleasantness from our neighbours as a result (for clocks at that time were thought of as a curiosity and an extravagence!), I consulted the wife, and we decided for as long as possible to hide it from the village. We went together to the watchmaker in Tarnobrzeg and bought a clock for four ducats, with the understanding that he was to bring it over in the evening and hang it for us.

This was done. But the cat was soon out of the bag, for the children while playing in the street in front of the house heared the striking of the hours. 'Slomkas have a clock!' was the cry, and we soon had all the children at the door. They would listen for the ticking under the window; and in time their elders began to come, too, to look at the clock. They were amazed that I could pay four ducats for it, and more than one made the remark that I thought myself quite a person!

Later on the nearer neighbours, who had some date to keep, would come to the window day or night and ask what time it was. In time everyone came to the conclusion that a clock is a useful thing in a house, and today there isn't a cottage in Dzikov without one. Even watches became the fashion with the farmers.

In those times feather ticks and pillows were seen only in the better situated and kept peasant homes. The poor did not have them at all, and the household would use as covers at night, according to the time of year, sheepskin coats, cloaks or jackets—in a word, the same things they wore in daytime. The children or servants, who slept on the oven or behind it in a warm place, needed only a sheet or a jacket. The beds for the most part lay all in confusion during the day, a thing that can still be seen with careless housekeepers; only more diligent wives made them up for the day—and in time there came to be pride in doing this. Fair bed-linen became then one of the aims of all the best housewives, who would put out the bedding on the line during the day, both to air it and to show it to the neighbours. This they held as something to boast of before others....

CHAPTER 56

The Disposition of Bosnia and Herzegovina

Bosnia and Herzegovina had long been oppressed provinces of the Turkish Empire. Although forty per cent of the population followed Islam, still their lot was almost as bad as their Christian neighbors. With much feeling directed to emancipation from the Ottoman yoke, and with such a large Mohammedan population, union with Serbia was not universally popular. Austro-Hungarian diplomats realized that there were possibilities of expansion here, and in 1875, various ploys were used to foment unrest, including an ostentatious visit of the Emperor Franz Josef to the Adriatic coast.

In July of 1875, a revolt against Ottoman rule broke out in Herzegovina and led to European complications—The Russo-Turkish War and the Congress of Berlin (1878). At the Congress of Berlin, it was a foregone conclusion that Ottoman rule was finished in Bosnia and Herzegovina. But neither Austria-Hungary nor the Ottoman Empire wanted Serbia to profit. Therefore, the odd arrangement was made whereby Austria-Hungary would occupy Bosnia and Herzegovina but not annex the provinces. The Convention of April 21, 1879, well illustrates the delicate balance that was reached. Austria-Hungary had thwarted Serbia, and Ottoman pride was somewhat mollified by the few empty ceremonies such as raising the flag that were still allowed. Austro-Hungarian troops also occupied the Sanjak of Novi-

Bazar, and thus separated Serbia from the other South Slav state of Montenegro. Union of the two states was thus prevented.

Reprinted in Edward Hertslet, THE MAP OF EUROPE BY TREATY (London: Harrison and Sons, 1891), Vol. IV, pp. 2855–2859.

The Governments of Austria-Hungary and Turkey, having reserved to themselves the right of coming to an understanding with regard to the details of the occupation stipulated for by Article XXV of the Treaty of Berlin, and the fact of the occupation of Bosnia and the Herzegovina in no way affecting the rights of Sovereignty of his Imperial Majesty the Sultan over these provinces, the two Governments have named for the Plenipotentiaries:

Austria-Hungary, on the one part, His Excellency M. le Comte F. Zichy, c.; and Turkey, on the other part, His Excellency Al. Carthéodory Pasha, &c., and His Excellency Munif Effendi, &c.;

Who, after having exchanged their full powers, found in good and due form, have agreed upon the following Articles:—

Administration of Bosnia and the Herzegovina.

Art. I. The administration of Bosnia and the Herzegovina shall be carried on by Austria-Hungary, conformably to Article XXV of the Treaty of Berlin; the Austro-Hungarian Government, however, does not object to retain all those existing functionaries who may possess the necessary aptitude for the good administration of their departments. In filling up vacancies, preference will be given by the Austro-Hungarian Government to natives of these provinces.

Religious Liberty.

Art. II. The freedom and outward exercise of all existing religions shall be assured to persons residing or sojourning in Bosnia and the Herzegovina. Especially, entire freedom is assured to Mussulmans in their relations with their spiritual chiefs.

The commanders of the troops of His Majesty the Emperor and King, and the administrative authorities, shall continue to take the greatest care that no injury be done to the honour, to the customs, to the freedom of religion, to the security of the persons, or to the property, of Mussulmans. All aggression against Mussulmans, their property or their religion, shall be severely punished. The name of His Majesty the Sultan shall continue to be used in the public prayers of the Mussulmans as in times past.

Hoisting of Ottoman Flag on Minarets.

Wherever it shall have been the custom to hoist the Ottoman flag on the minarets, this custom shall be respected.

Administration of Revenues.

Art. III. The revenues of Bosnia and the Herzegovina shall be exclusively appropriated to the needs, to the administration of, and to the improvements deemed necessary in, those Provinces.

Current Ottoman Money.

Art. IV. The Ottoman currency shall continue to have free circulation in Bosnia and the Herzegovina.

Disposal of War Material, &c.

Art. V. The Sublime Porte shall dispose as it thinks fit of the arms, war-like stores, and other articles belonging to the Ottoman Government, and which were found in the fortified places or in the garrisons. For this purpose inventories shall be prepared with the intervention of Commissioners of the two Governments.

Treatment of Inhabitants when outside the Provinces.

Art. VI. The question of the treatment of the inhabitants of Bosnia and the Herzegovina sojourning or travelling outside these provinces, shall be regulated subsequently by a special arrangement.

Mode in which Article XXV of the Treaty of Berlin is to be carried out.

Sandjak of Novi-Bazar.

Art. VII. To attain, in a common interest, the political and military object that Article XXV of the Treaty of Berlin has in view concerning the Sandjak of Novi-Bazar, the two Governments have resolved to regulate the mode in which it shall hence forward be carried into execution. For this purpose the Government of His Majesty the Emperor and King undertakes to give notice beforehand to the Government of His Majesty the Sultan of the time when the entrance of the Imperial and Royal troops shall take place.

In order to prevent all unnecessary delay, the two Governments, each in so far as it is itself concerned, undertakes, should occasion arise, to furnish their authorities and commanders, without delay, with the full powers necessary to settle directly among themselves the questions connected with the subsistence of the Imperial and Royal troops, as well as to their quartering, and other details relating thereto. Moreover it is understood that all expenses incurred under this head shall be borne by the Austro-Hungarian Government.

Presence of Troops in Sandjak of Novi-Bazar.

Art. VIII. The presence of the troops of His Majesty the Emperor and King in the Sandjak of Novi-Bazar, will not interfere with the functions of the Ottoman administrative authorities, judicial or financial, of every kind, which will continue to be exercised as in former times under the exclusive and direct orders of the Sublime Porte.

Maintenance of Troops in Garrisons and Positions of
Sandjak of Novi-Bazar.

Art. IX. Should the Sublime Porte wish to maintain regular troops at the places in the Sandjak of Nov-Bazar where the Austro-Hungarian troops shall be garrisoned, no obstacles shall be raised to it. The troops of the two States shall be placed on a footing of perfect equality with regard to their number and military advantages, and the freedom of their movements.

Non-employment by Porte of Irregular Troops.

The Sublime Porte engages to maintain no irregular troops throughout the Sandjak of Novi-Bazar.

Power of Austria to maintain Troops in Garrison.

Art. X. It is nevertheless understood that the power of Austria-Hungary to maintain a sufficient number of troops, as circumstances may require, at the places where it is intended to keep garrisons, in conformity with the stipulations of Article VII, is not to be restricted by these arrangements.

In faith of which the Plenipotentiaries of Austria-Hungary and of Turkey, have signed the present Convention, and have affixed to it the seal of their arms.

Constantinople, 21st April, 1879.

                          (L. S.) ZICHY.
                          (L. S.) AL. CARATHEODORY
                          (L. S.) MUNIF.

CHAPTER 57

Declaration of War by Serbia—1885

In 1885, newly-created Bulgaria, led by its ambitious Prince Alexander of Battenburg, was intent on absorbing the Bulgarian-populated province on her southern frontier, Eastern Rumelia. The Treaty of Berlin (1878) had given Eastern Rumelia to the Turks on British insistence since it was thought that the province could be a bulwark against Russian expansion toward the Bosporus.

However, in September of 1885, Turkish rule in Eastern Rumelia was overthrown, and the major powers had to decide whether the provisions made at Berlin should be upheld. Britain reversed its former stand while Russia did not wish to give Eastern Rumelia to Bulgaria. The Serbian ruler, Milan, was embarrassed by Bulgaria's seeming good fortune, and also prompted by Austrian advice, he declared war on Bulgaria. The reasons given in his Declaration of War are to be taken only as a feeble expression of xenophobia.

The war, which all expected Serbia to win, turned out to be a great Bulgarian victory. On November 19, the Serbians were defeated at Slivnitza, and on November 26, the Bulgarian army entered Serbian territory. Only Austrian threats prevented further Serbian disasters, and on March 3, 1886, the Treaty of Bucharest ended the war with nothing gained by Serbia. Bulgarian patriotism impressed Europe, and despite Russian objections, on April 5, 1886, Eastern Rumelia, for all practical purposes, became a part of Bulgaria. This acquisition nearly doubled the territorial extent of Bulgaria.

Reprinted in Edward Hertslet, THE MAP OF EUROPE BY TREATY (London: Harrison and Sons, 1891), Vol. IV, pp. 3141–3142.

The King hereby declares that, in consulting the Skupt-china, he has taken all the necessary measures to show clearly that Servia cannot remain a disinterested spectator of the change which has taken place amongst the people of the Balkans, and, above all, cannot allow it when it is to the advantage of a State which has employed all its liberty to prove itself a bad neighbour towards Servia, and to be unwilling to respect wither the rights, or even the territory of Servia.

The unjustifiable Customs regulations which Bulgaria has introduced against Servia, and which have put a stop to all commercial intercourse between the two countries, have had, on the part of Bulgaria, for their exclusive object to give evidence of its unfriendly disposition towards Servia, dating from the commencement of Bulgaria's existence.

The forcible and unlawful seizure of the district of Bregovo, and the protection granted to the refugees in their intrigues against the internal order of the Kingdom, I have pardoned, as I wished to give a proof of the patience which becomes a State which has bought its liberty with its own blood, which—assisted by the sympathy of Europe—has made progress, and which, at each step of its development, has preserved and respected the rights of others as if they had been its own.

But the ill-treatment of our subjects in Bulgaria, the closing of our frontiers, the gathering of undisciplined masses on our frontiers, their acts of aggression against our border population, and even against our Army, to which is entrusted the defense of the Servian territory, all constitute a provocation to which I cannot remain indifferent, having regard to the great interests of the country, to the dignity of the people, and to the honour of the Servian arms. For these reasons, I have accepted the state of an open rupture which the Bulgarian Government has commenced, and I have therefore ordered my faithful and heroic Army to cross the Bulgarian frontier.

The just cause of Servia is to-day intrusted to the decision of arms, to the heroism of the Army, and to the mighty protection of God.

In addressing this Proclamation to my dear people, I rely with confidence, in this grave moment, on the love of the people towards their country, and on their devotion to the holy Servian cause.

Nisch, November 2 (14), 1885

MILAN

CHAPTER 58

Bulgarian Political Attitudes in the 1890's

Dicey's analysis of Bulgarian viewpoints is seemingly quite perceptive. Although he minimizes the potentiality of Bulgarian agressive tendencies, he gives the reasons why Bulgarian leaders had to take a rather cautious view toward any development that might upset the balance of power in the Balkans. Dicey notices the ambivalent attitude of the Bulgarians toward Russia. Although Russia was their champion in the past, still the Bulgarians wanted independence rather than incorporation in a large state. Dicey is especially perceptive in posting out that if Bulgarians wanted expansion, it would be expansion that would give them ports on the Aegean. Inside of two decades, this observation of Dicey would be borne out. But even in the Balkans Wars, 1912–13, Bulgaria failed to achieve this objective.

Edward Dicey, THE PEASANT STATE, AN ACCOUNT OF BULGARIA IN 1894 (London: John Murray, 1894), pp. 143–151.

It is very difficult to understand the national policy of any country except your own. Nor is it always easy to understand that. It is, therefore, with some hesitation I venture to explain what, in my view is the national policy of Bulgaria, in as far as she has at present any definite policy, other than that of waiting the course of events.

Putting together the many different opinions I have heard from natives and foreign residents in the country, and after making due allowance for the bias of my informants, I have arrived at one or two conclusions which, if not quite the truth, are, I fancy, very near the truth. I am convinced that for the time being the national ambition of the country is confined within very reasonable limits. There may be Bulgarian enthusiasts who, inspired by the traditions of the doubtful glories of a somewhat hypothethical past... look forward to the day when a Bulgarian empire might be re-established with Constantinople as its capital. But I do not believe that any such aspirations are entertained by the great mass of the people. Amongst the Bulgarians there is no dominant sentiment analogous to the *grande idée* of the Greeks. Every Bulgarian entertains the belief that within the lifetime of the generation now growing into manhood the Ottoman Empire in Europe will become a thing of the past. There is a very general desire that the ultimate solution of the Eastern Question should prove such as to secure the independence of Bulgaria, but there is no desire that Bulgaria should succeed to the inheritance of the Ottoman Empire. I quite admit that such an aspiration would be even more unreasonable in the case of the Bulgarians than it is in that of the Greeks. The Hellenic nation has a great past, a grand literature, and has also large colonies of fellow-Greeks settled over the whole face of the Levant. Bulgaria can put forward no pretensions of any equal value. Her people have not—and, I think know that they have not—the qualities of a ruling race. No more for that matter have the Greeks, but they fancy that they have, which makes all the differences. The Bulgars are brave soldiers, but they are not—which is by no means the same thing—a military nation. A peasant State of small proprietors can never, as a community, be actuated by a blind desire of conquest. By character, by custom, and by tradition, the interests of Bulgaria are confined pretty well within her own borders; and the prospect of ruling over foreign countries and alien races, even if such a prospect were realizable, would have little attraction for the sober, matter-of-fact Bulgarian character.

Thus it is a mistake to imagine that the Bulgarians,

as a nation, have any particular desire to bring about the fall of the Ottoman Empire. In common with all the Rayah races, which have been subject to Turkish domination, they have an hereditary antipathy, partly racial, partly theological, to the rule of Islam. Whenever the Cross replaces the Crescent over the mosque of St. Sophia, the sympathies of the Bulgars will be with the victors, not with the vanquished. But, as I have already remarked, fanaticism of creed is far less marked amidst the Bulgarians than amidst other Sclavonic races. They are in no particular hurry to see their own faith rendered triumphant by the fall of Islam, and they are perfectly content that the Turks should remain at Constantinople so long as their presence there affords any protection to Bulgaria against Russian aggression. Whatever may be the real truth about the Bulgarian atrocities, it is obvious that they have left behind no such bitter resentment in the minds of a people, slow to forgive or forget injuries, as to render the idea of co-operation with Turkey distasteful to the national sentiment.

In my opinion the aspirations of Bulgarian statesmanship look rather towards the Aegean than towards the Bosphorus, that is, towards the formation of a Sclav State, composed of Servia, Montenegro, Macedonia, and Bulgaria, rather than towards any reconstitution of the Byzantine Empire. But even this aspiration is not, I gather, very widely or very seriously entertained. No doubt, the Bulgarians, if they had to merge their individual existence in any larger community, would prefer incorporation with a great Sclav State to any other modification of their existing status. Pan-Sclavism, however, never made much progress south of the Balkans, and the influence of the Pan-Sclav agitation has declined in a very marked way since the emancipation of Bulgaria from Turkish rule. What the Bulgarians most desire at heart is to preserve their independence, and to be governed by their own people, according to their own ideas, customs, and sentiments. Education and material progress may possibly enlarge their aspirations, but for the present an autonomous peasant community, comprising the whole Bulgar-speaking race within its bounds, forms the ideal of the Bulgarian people. It is because this ideal is consistent with the maintenance of Turkey in Europe, and inconsistent with the establishment of Russia upon the Bosphorus, that the settled policy of the Bulgarian Government is to uphold the *status quo* is Eastern Europe. It is for this reason that the policy of the Government, though modified by hereditary dislike of Islam, commends itself on the whole to popular opinion in the Principality.

I do not believe, therefore, that an attempt to effect the general emancipation of the Rayah races under Turkish rule would meet with any enthusiastic support in Bulgaria, except under one particular contingency to which I shall refer presently. A crusade, for instance, for the emancipation of Armenia from Turkish rule would not in any case be actively encouraged by the Bulgarians; and if this crusade was conducted—as in all likelihood it would be—under the lead, and in the interest of Russia, it would probably be confronted by the active opposition of Bulgaria. For the time being Russia constitutes the chief danger of Bulgaria; and the Bulgarians, to speak the plain truth, care much more about the preservation of their own independence than they do about the immediate emancipation of their co-religionists under the rule of the Crescent, so long as these co-religionists are not men of their own race. It may be said that this is not a very magnanimous or elevated policy. My answer would be that I am discussing, not what the policy of Bulgaria ought to be upon abstract principles, but what it is as a matter of fact. I may add further, that no other policy could reasonably be expected from her. A community of small landed proprietors is the last one in the world in which altruistic sentiments are ever likely to obtain a footing. The French proverb that the shirt is nearer than the coat expresses tersely the view taken by a peasant community in all public as well as private affairs. In the present instance the shirt is independence; the coat is the substitution, elsewhere than in Bulgaria itself, of the rule of the Cross for that of the Crescent.

CHAPTER 59

Slavic National Feeling

The quest for national identity is well illustrated in the following selection from Oswald Balzer's "Slavic and German Culture," an open letter written in 1897 that defended the right of the Slavic peoples to the same understanding and appreciation accorded to the Germans. Although one might easily detect too much defensiveness in Balzer's words, still the Polish and other Slavic peoples had suffered a great number of frustrations in the nineteenth century. A more aggressive spirit, solidly based on the glorification of past cultural achievements, was ready to renew the quest for national identity in the twentieth century.

Manfred Kridl, Wladyslaw Malinowski, and Jozef Witlin (editors) FOR YOUR FREEDOM AND OURS (New York, 1943), pp. 147–157. By permission of Frederick Ungar Publishing Co., Inc.

The Slavs whom you have in mind and who supposedly intend to establish in Austria a reign of barbarism and ignorance are mainly large groups of Western Slavs, especially the Czechs and the Poles. Before going on I might point out here that even the groups of Southern Slavs who are part of the (Austrian) Empire have in the main belonged to the realm of Western Civilization for centuries. However, to simplify matters, I shall confine myself to Western Slavic nations.

There are two external elements which contributed to the civilization of Western Slavs: Christianity and the lay Western Culture. Thus, our Slavic civilization is not completely indigenous; it has been permeated with foreign elements though these were neither exclusively nor slavishly accepted. The third factor at work was the native genius which modified the other elements according to its own needs and peculiarities and united them into an organic whole. German civilization had exactly the same origins and character; it, too, grew out of Christianity and the Western lay culture as received by the Germans at their birth and as later transformed by them in their own national way. Neither of the tribes is, therefore, the creator of a completely original culture; both started out on borrowed capital and it is doubtful whether either has any right to claim superiority on that account. The sole difference lies in the fact that while the Germans availed themselves directly of the ancient civilization we profited additionally by whatever developments they subsequently added to it. On that particular account the Germans merit the gratitude of the Slavs, which we do not mean to deny—but on the same account let the Germans be consistent and not accuse us of lacking in culture. Such accusation could be justified only if we had been unable and unwilling to reap the fruits of the civilization we found at our historical inception.

In the period of our growth and up to the present day we have profited in many ways by the achievements of German culture, though not by them alone, for in the meantime the powerful Latin civilizations had developed and we did not remain strangers to them. The same is true of Germany itself. It is a well known fact that the development of urban life, which was to play so vital a role in the economic and social growth of Germany and, accordingly, in the intellectual life of that country, was based on Lombardian models. The great spiritual rebirth of the nation, which occurred at the close of the Middle Ages and at the beginning of modern times, brought about the study of old as well as of newly discovered treasures of ancient literature and art; yet even this Renaissance did not spring up in Germany itself but was brought there from Italy. In the 17th and 18th centuries petty German rulers were not the only ones to model their courts on French patterns—German literature, which in the 17th century could not produce a Moliere or a Corneille, and in the 18th century could not boast of a Voltaire or a Montesquieu, fed freely on French examples. Surely you remember, sir, what opinion was held on that subject by

Frederick II. And in the field of material culture—to quote but one instance let me remind you how unattainable, for years and even to this day, has been the standard of perfection set by French artistic industry, and how much Germany owes France in its own recent achievements in that field. Yet, I should like to see the countenance of any German, were a Frenchman or an Italian on that account to fling in his face the derisive accusation that he comes of a low-grade civilization, let alone that he is utterly lacking in culture.

How are we to determine whether the Slavs took part in the development of culture or whether they were at all capable of so doing? Let me remind you of a few facts. Here is one, fairly typical: Of the first two universities founded in Central Europe one was built in Prague and the other in Cracow—the two capitals of Western Slavs. True, it is commonly said that the Prague University was German, but it is yet to be proved that it was so in the Middle Ages. Education in those days was thoroughly cosmopolitan. Among the professors there were Germans as well as Czechs—for that matter, Italians and Frenchmen too—so it was not the Germans alone who carried the torch of knowledge. The University was founded by a prince who, though elected King of Rome, was at the same time hereditary King of the Czechs and he was not one to subordinate the welfare of the Czechs to that of the Germans. Indeed he was jokingly called the "father of the Czech Nation and arch stepfather of the Holy Roman Empire of the German Nation". The Czech character of the university became so apparent at the beginning of the 15th century that German professors began to leave it in droves. And the greatest personality produced by the Prague University in the Middle Ages—a man far exceeding in stature the common rank and file of professors—was a Slav by origin and name, Jan Hus. But let up proceed with our review. In the 15th century we find Dlugosz in Poland, writing his great history. In spite of the legendary yarn he wove around the prehistoric origins of his nation, as was the custom in those days, in spite of his obvious partiality in the presentation of contemporary events, he surpassed by far, both in scope and in his broad outlook on historical matters, the narrow attitudes of the Central European chroniclers of his times. Germans would be hard put to it to mention a single name among their own Middle Age chroniclers fit to be placed alongside that of Copernicus rising over the whole of Europe; and may we recall that Copernicus studied astronomy at a Polish university and under the expert tutelage of a Polish professor. The same century boasts of two other illustrious names: That of the statesman Modrzewski and that of the great poet Kochanowski. In the 18th century the Czechs produced an educational reformer renowned throughout the civilized world —Komensky, and in the present century the Western Slavic nations have contributed to the world of science such names as: Palacky, Safarik, Sniadecki, Szujski and Kalinka; to the world of poetry: Mickiewicz, Slowacki, Krasinski, Neruda, Halek, Vrchlicki and Sienkiewicz; to other fields of art: Grottger, Matejko, Siemiradzki and Chopin. Here are but a few of the names I could mention; but they will serve our purpose, for some of them are so great that many a pseudo-great cries that Slavs have no culture at all.

If the nations who claim a monopoly on culture and civilization had had the good fortune to be able to count these men among their own, without a doubt they would have placed them among their most prominent national figures. One fact should be emphasized, namely, a large number of those pioneers of civilization not merely Slavonic but European, appeared in the last century, at a time when the national progress of Western Slavs was hampered from every direction, as for that matter it still is today. The cultural impulses and abilities of these nations must indeed have been indomitable if, in spite of all these handicaps, they were able to contribute as much as they did to the progress of civilization. For all these great men, quick or dead, bear ample witness to the fact that their nations are civilized, they are living refutations of the malicious accusation of barbarism; barbarism could never have contributed what those men have contributed to the common treasure of civilization.

To go back, I wish to make it quite clear that I have not the slightest intention of concealing the historical faults

of the Western Slavonic nations. The faults most often
mentioned, sometimes with undue emphasis, refer to the
social and political structures of these nations; the privileges of the upper classes, the weakness of the government's
authority and its inability to maintain a strong political
organization. I am ready to admit that this was true in
certain historical periods. But I would not dream of insulting you, sir, an expert historian, by explaining at length
that such momentary weaknesses and even downfalls may
occur in the lifespan of any nation which has contributed
and may still contribute to the progress of civilization, and
that such downfalls are not necessarily final but may be
followed by periods of Renaissance. And I need not remind
you that many of these deplorable phenomena were not
peculiar to Slavonic nations alone, that we find them elsewhere among people who consider themselves leaders of
civilization. The privileges of the upper classes were not
abolished throughout Europe until the French Revolution;
at that time the Czech state had for almost three centuries
been without its independence, and Poland was just being
partitioned. In certain small states belonging to the German Empire, serfdom was abolished only at the end of
the 18th century. At the same time, though her fall was
imminent, Poland, for all her weakness, announced the complete equality of all citizens in the Constitution of May
3rd, 1791. On the other hand there was never a Polish
or Czech ruler who would sell human flesh, leasing whole
detachments of his army to foreign powers for money, as
did certain German princes as late as the end of the 18th
century. German residents in Polish cities were allowed
to use their own language in official documents as long
as they wished to do so; when they adopted the Polish
tongue it was of their own accord, without special laws
and without the coercion of the Poles. German children
were taught in primary schools in German; their language
was not systematically eliminated from the curriculum. The
ill famed Liberum Veto—the right of minorities to break
up parliaments,—was partly restricted by Poles themselves
in 1768, and completely abolished in 1791, and there is
not a single Pole today who does not condemn that practice;
yet now, at the end of the 19the century it has been revived

in its essential form by those very people who advance the theory of the cultural inferiority of the Slavs...

Not only did these Slavs strive to develop culture within their own borders, they also were forced to defend it against attacks from the east.

They gave their lives for it, whenever the necessity arose. On the battlefields of Lignica died a Polish prince whose task had been not simply to defend his own country but to save the whole of Central Europe from the Tartar flood that threatened it. And when in 1683 a Polish King came to the rescue of besieged Vienna he was nobly fulfilling his duty to the entire Western civilization. From the 14th century to the 18th century, Poland, in constant and ever renewed conflicts with the Tartars and Turks, lived through a glorious epic of its own, and not once did the Western world come to its aid, though this Western world was willing enough to give generous help to a German Order when the latter was fighting with Poland.

What is more, Western Slavs were eager to carry Western culture into lands where it had not yet penetrated; they were conscious of the obligations and duties they had assumed upon entering the orbit of Western civilization. Heathen Poland received Christianity from the Czechs; the son of the first Christian ruler of Poland, as far back as the end of the 10th century, sponsored the propagation of the faith among pagan Prussians; and he found a zealous executive for plan in the person of a saintly Czech bishop who was himself a descendant of Slavonic princes.

The Germans and the Slavs embarked upon their respective cultural tasks under totally different conditions. The young German states were rising at a time when the rotten structure of the old Roman Empire was crumbling, and when its direct heir, the Eastern Roman Empire was too feeble to assume any serious undertaking. It had already been defeated once by the barbaric tribes of Visigoths on the battle fields of Adrianople, and the later victories of Belisarius and Narses were to have only a temporary effect. The ancient culture which has engendered the German civilization was not represented by a large and powerful state which, on the strength of its cultural superiority could attempt to subdue the newcomers politically and nationally.

Beginners as they were, the Germans became at once independent; there was no one to hamper them, no one to dominate them; they were free to develop Western Civilization as they pleased, and, indeed, for a while they developed it single-handed. This was their good luck, not their merit. The Slavs, on the other hand, found themselves in totally different conditions at the start of their cultural development. They were not building on the ruins of an old order; it was from their own lands which they had settled many centuries before (or had occupied after the German tribes had voluntarily left) that the Slavs wished to, and in fact did, join the orbit of Western civilization. Next to them they have always had the powerful and civilized German nation with its older cultural past. Thus emerged, I would say not two different civilizations, for both are founded on the same basis, but two cultural centers, each focusing the efforts of its respective people. The trouble was that the "older brother" was determined to draw the "younger brother" into the sphere of his influence, and if possible, conquer him and incorporate him into his own possessions. And, as we know, he was ready to do it by hook or by crook. Perhaps, on purely formal ground, German actions may be justified with regard to some of the Slavic tribes; the Cis-Elbean Slavs, for instance, were obdurate pagans, and paganism was the negation of culture, which therefore had to be introduced by force. But how can one justify the German attempts against those Slavic nations which, once they embraced the principles of Christianity and Western culture, openly adhered to them and signified a willingness to cooperate in them? Even these, however, the Germans would not spare. The Czech King Venceslas I, who laid down his life for Christianity and Western culture, was the first to be subjugated by the Reich; the Polish King Boleslaw the Brave, who converted Prussians and helped the Germans in their conquest of the heathen Cis-Elbean Slavs, was forced into a long and bitter war with Germany to preserve his nation's independence. Were those Slavic people, simply on account of their cultural youth incapable of progress without outside supervision? When the Germans themselves emerged from barbarism they pursued their cultural apprenticeship unaided and would undoubtedly have resented any similar unsolicited control. Yet they were able to produce a great civilization. Perhaps, then, the Slavs lacked the necessary ability? But we have demonstrated in the preceding paragraph that they did not. In fact, it was precisely those Slavic nations which escaped total German subjugation, like the Czechs, who were but loosely bound to Germany, and the Poles, who early established their absolute independence, that were most successful in achieving a higher degree of civilization; other Slavic tribes such as the [Lusatian] Sorbs, for instance, who fully enjoyed the advantages of the German rule, show little progress. German guardianship and interference were, therefore, both unrequisite and inexcusable, and, from the standpoint of cultural progress, indifferent since, without them, civilization would have progressed just as well, if not better.

Besides, did cultural motives actually play the leading part in Germany's attempts at domination? Here is a small but very significant fact recorded by a German chronicler. When a section of the Elbean Slavs, defeated by the Germans, finally accepted both Christianity and German rule, and it seemed that from that time forward everything would proceed according to the desires of the culture-missionary, quite unexpectedly the tribe reverted to paganism. Christianity, in the minds of these simple people had become identified with the German rule, and they renounced it because they were sick of the Saxon greed ("avaritia"). As we see, besides sponsoring the great cause of civilization, these missionaries also pursued certain private ends which they did not even take the trouble to conceal.

But far more significant and illuminating than this little incident are other facts which show that even when the Slavs had progressed considerably along the road of civilization and were determined to carry Western ideals further East—thus serving the very principle of which Germans consider themselves the most faithful exponents—the same Germans not only did not help them but in many cases threw obstacles in their path...

None of us Slavs would make the slightest objection if Germans were to praise this, that, or the other of their actions as a great achievement, as a triumph of wise and foresighted diplomacy, as a victory of the valiant Germans arms and spirit. All we ask is, do not wrap all this in the cloak of special services rendered to culture and civilization. For the great majority of German tribes the interests of culture always coincided with political motives, and incidentally, political interests took precedent over cultural ones. For the sake of political gains they were ready to carry Western civilization to the Slavic East but they did not hesitate to abandon the cause whenever it interfered with these selfish political aims. Their primary motive was to conquer and Germanize, not to civilize, yet they identified culture with their own state; they believed and even attempted to convince the world that the road to civilization leads through Germany and that other people should consider themselves fortunate if allowed to travel that way to the upper strata of civilization.

CHAPTER 60

The Austro-Hungarian Monarchy Absorbs Bosnia and Herzegovina

The annexation of Bosnia and Herzegovina caused one of a half-dozen great crises that preceeded World War I. Serbia had hoped to annex Bosnia and Herzegovina, but had to stand by helplessly when Austria-Hungary absorbed the province. Russia was also upset, but when the crisis reached its peak, it appeared that there might be a war that Russia did not want. Finally, despite many protests, including one from Turkey, Austria-Hungary held the provinces.

R. B. Mowat (editor) SELECT TREATIES AND DOCUMENTS TO ILLUSTRATE THE DEVELOPMENT OF THE MODERN EUROPEAN STATES-SYSTEM (London: Oxford University Press, 1915), pp. 120–123.

DENUNCIATION BY AUSTRIA-HUNGRY OF ARTICLE XXV OF THE TREATY OF BERLIN. (Vienna) October 3, 1908.

In order to ensure the pacific development of the territories situated to the south of the frontier of the Monarchy, the Treaty of Berlin confided to Austria-Hungary the administration of Bosnia and Herzegovina with, in addition, the right of garrison in the Sanjak of Novi-Bazar, reserving to the governments of Austria-Hungary to come to an understanding with each other on this subject.

This understanding was brought about by the Convention of Constantinople signed on April 21, 1879, which provided for the simultaneous presence of Austro-Hungarian and Ottoman garrisons in certain localities of the Sanjak.

The object intended by this amicable co-operation of Austro-Hungarian and Ottoman troops has been fully attained. We have succeeded in maintaining order and ensuring the peace of Europe, which a conflagration in these regions would easily have been able to endanger.

Since, then the situation has undergone a radical change. Turkey, then enfeebled by the consequences of the sanguinary war, powerless by herself alone to ensure order and tranquillity in the Sanjak, has recovered herself during the thirty years which followed the signing of the Convention of Constantinople.

Above all the political movement which is manifesting itself there at this moment, under the auspices of His Majesty the Sultan, affirms the idea of the Ottoman State, and through that, a consolidation of the bases of the Empire itself.

In these circumstances, the Cabinet of Vienna is pleased to hope that the Ottoman Government will succeed, without other support, in maintaining order in the Sanjak and in fulfilling alone in these countries the task which there rested upon it, up till now, through the co-operation of the two governments.

Accordingly the Imperial and Royal Government has not hesitated to inform the Sublime Porte that it renounced to make use for the future of the rights which the Convention of Constantinople has conferred with regard to the Sanjak of Novi-Bazar.

With regard to the Imperial and Royal troops, the Ottoman Government has likewise been informed that they have received orders to evacuate the localities which they are garrisoning.

By this fact of high importance, the Cabinet of Vienna means not only to give to the Imperial Ottoman Government a striking proof of its confidence and of its sincerely amicable sentiments, it opposes by this, at the same time, the most formal denial to the rumours which ascribe to it selfish ambition and territorial covetousness.

In bringing to the knowledge of the Imperial Ottoman Governments its intention not to appeal to the dispositions of the Convention of Constantinople, in so far as they apply to the Sanjak of Novi-Bazar, the Cabinet of Vienna believes it necessary at the same time to make clear its point of view with regard to the other questions specified in the same Convention.

The mission which the Treaty of Berlin has confided to her in Bosnia and in Herzegovina, Austria-Hungary has fulfilled for the good of the populations, and in the interest also of the Ottoman Empire.

In fact, it is only the situation created in Bosnia and Herzegovina by the Treaty of Berlin and maintained in a condition of stability by Austria-Hungary, that has enabled Turkey to concentrate her forces for safeguarding the territorial integrity of the Empire.

Bosnia and Herzegovina have arrived to-day—thanks to the assiduous work of the Austro-Hungarian administration—at a high degree of material and intellectual culture; accordingly the moment appears to have come to crown the work undertaken, by granting to these provinces the benefits of an autonomous and constitutional system of government, which is ardently desired by the entire population. The Imperial and Royal Government ought, however, in order to realize these generous intentions, to regulate in a precise fashion the situation of these two provinces and to provide an effective guarantee against the dangers which would be able to menace the stability of the system established in 1878. The Cabinet of Vienna accordingly finds itself under the imperious necessity of freeing itself from the reserves contained in the Convention of

Constantinople, and of recovering, with regard to Bosnia and Herzegovina, its complete liberty of action.

The Austro-Hungarian Government has taken care to inform the Sultan, through the intermediary of the Imperial and Royal Embassy at Constantinople, of the point of view herein exposed; it has at the same time expressed the hope that the relations of the two countries, freed from the uncertainty of the situation in Bosnia-Herzegovina and in the Sanjak, will only gain by the presence of the well-defined and normal state of things which we wish to establish.

The Ottoman Government having examined, with all the attention that it merits, the considerations exposed in this Note, is bound to declare that it is unable to participate in the point of view of the Imperial and Royal Government.

In effect, the administration of Bosnia-Herzegovina, in its actual form, is based on Article XXV of the Treaty of Berlin as well as on the Convention of Constantinople of 1879, which is the development of it.

The diplomatic acts defined explicitly the character of the Austro-Hungarian occupation and administration of the aforesaid provinces, and the maintenance of the Ottoman sovereignty.

Any derogation from these acts cannot be brought about without the unanimous agreement of Turkey, the sovereign of these countries, and of the other High Contracting Powers.

Accordingly the Ottoman Government finds itself under the necessity of reserving all the rights which result in its favour from the international treaties, and of protesting against the violation of these acts by the Imperial and Royal Government....

CHAPTER 61

The Balkan Wars

The First Balkan War was caused by Turkey's inability to satisfy the demands of the Macedonians along with the desire of Serbia, Bulgaria and Greece to obtain territory at the expense of Turkey. The war started on October 8, 1912 when Montenegro declared war on Turkey. The other three states quickly followed suit, and on December 3, Turkey had no choice but to accept an armistice.

At the London Conference called to settle the problems of Southeastern Europe, it was decided that the Balkan states should carve up most of what remained of European Turkey. Albania was to be created as an independent state. The Austrians advanced the Albanian cause hoping thereby to stop Serbian expansion to the Adriatic.

The Second Balkan War found Bulgaria as its victim. The Bulgarians would not meet territorial demands made by Roumania and Serbia. At the same time, Bulgaria demanded territory held by Greece. And Turkey was ready for any possibility to claim lost territory. With almost unbelievably poor diplomacy, Bulgaria started the war, hoping to quickly defeat Serbia and Greece. If Roumania or Turkey then caused trouble, they too could be defeated.

On July 1, 1913, the Bulgarians began their attack upon the Serbs and Greeks in Macedonia. But on July 11, the Roumanians attacked Bulgaria, and on July 12, the Turks attacked Bulgaria. On July 30, Bulgaria had to agree to an armistice. The Treaty of Bucharest, as seen below, was most unfavorable to Bulgaria.

R. B. *Mowat* (editor), SELECT TREATIES AND DOCUMENTS TO ILLUSTRATE THE DEVELOPMENT OF THE MODERN EUROPEAN STATES-SYSTEM (London: Oxford University Press, 1915), pp. 120–123.

TREATY OF PEACE BETWEEN GREECE, BULGARIA, MONTENEGRO, SERBIA ON THE ONE PART AND TURKEY ON THE OTHER PART. (London) May 17/30, 1913.

Article I. There will be from the date of the exchange of the ratifications of the present treaty, peace and friendship between His Majesty the Emperor of the Ottomans on the one part, and their Majesties the Allied Sovereigns on the other part, as well as between their heirs and successors, their States and respective subjects in perpetuity.

Article II. His Majesty the Emperor of the Ottomans cedes to their Majesties the Allied Sovereigns all the territories of his Empire on the continent of Europe to the west of a line drawn from Enos on the Aegean Sea to Midia on the Black Sea with the exception of Albania. The exact line of the frontier from Enos to Midia will be determined by an international commission.

Article III. His Majesty the Emperor cf the Ottomans and their Majesties the Allied Sovereigns declare that they remit to His Majesty the Emperor of Germany, His Majesty the Emperor of Austria, the President of the French Republic, His Majesty the King of Great Britain and Ireland, and His Majesty the Emperor of All the Russias the care of settling the delimitation of the frontiers of Albania and all other questions concerning Albania.

Article IV. His Majesty the Emperor of the Ottomans declares that he cedes to their Majesties the Allied Sovereigns The Isle of Crete, and that he renounces in their favour all the rights of sovereignty and other rights which he possessed on that Isle.

Article V. His Majesty the Emperor of the Ottomans and their Majesties the Allied Sovereigns declare that they confide to his Majesty the Emperor of Germany, His Majesty the Emperor of Austria, the President of the French Republic, His Majesty the King of Great Britain and Ireland, His Majesty the King of Italy, and His Majesty the Emperor of All the Russias the task of deciding the destiny of all the Ottoman isles of the Aegean sea excepting Crete, and the Peninsula of Mount Athos.

Article VI. His Majesty the Emperor of the Ottomans and their Majesties of the Allied Sovereigns declare that they remit the task of regulating questions of a financial kind resulting from the state of war just finished and from the territorial cession above mentioned, to the International Commission convened at Paris, to which they have deputed their representatives.

TREATY OF PEACE BETWEEN ROUMANIA, GREECE, MONTENEGRO, SERBIA, AND BULGARIA. (Bucharest) July 28/ August 10, 1913.

Article I. There will be from the date of the day of the exchange of the ratification of the present treaty, peace and friendship between His Majesty the King of Roumania, His Majesty the King of the Hellenes, His Majesty the King of Montenegro, His Majesty the King of Servia, His Majesty the King of the Bulgarians, as well as between their heirs and successors, their States and respective subjects.

Article II. Between the Kingdom of Bulgaria and the Kingdom of Roumania, the old frontier between the Danube and the Black Sea is, conformably with the proces-verbal drawn up by the respective military delegates and annexed to the Protocol No. 5 of the 22nd of July (August 4th), 1913, of the Conference of Bucharest, rectified in the following manner:

The new frontier will start from the Danube above Turtukaia and terminate at the Black Sea to the South of Ekrene.

Between these two extreme points the line of the frontier will follow the line indicated on the maps 1/100.000 and 1/200.000 of the Roumanian General Staff, and according to the description annexed to the present article.

It is formally understood that Bulgaria will dismantle within two years at latest the existing fortifications, and will construct no others at Roustchouk, at Schoumla, in the country between, and in a zone of twenty kilometres round Baltchik.

Article III. Between the Kingdom of Bulgaria and the Kingdom of Serbia, the frontier will follow conformably with the proces-verbal drawn up by the respective military delegates and annexed to the Protocol No. 9 of the 25th of July (August 7th), 1913, of the Conference of Bucharest, the following line:

The frontier line will start from the old frontier from the summit of Patarcia, will follow the old Turco-Bulgarian frontier and the line of the watershed between the Vardar and the Strouma, with the exception of the upper valley of the Stroumitza, which will remain on Serbian territory; it will terminate at the Belasica Mountain, where it will bend back to the Graeco-Bulgarian frontier. A detailed description of this frontier and its indication on the map 1/200.000 of the Austrian General Staff are annexed to the present alticle.

Article IV. The questions relative to the old Serbo-Bulgarian frontier will be regulated according to the understanding agreed upon by the two High Contracting Parties stated in the Protocol annexed to the present article.

Article V. Between the Kingdom of Greece and the Kingdom of Bulgaria the frontier will follow conformably with the proces-verbal drawn up by the respective military Delegates and annexed to the Protocol No. 9 of the 25th of July (August 7th), 1913, of the Conference of Bucharest, the following line:

The frontier line shall start from the new Serbo-Bulgarian frontier on the summit of Belasica planina, to terminate at the mouth of the Mesta on the Aegean Sea.

It is formally understood that Bulgaria desists from henceforth, from every pretension to the Isle of Crete.

CHAPTER 62

The Austro-Hungarian Note to Serbia, July 23, 1914.

For decades, Austria-Hungary had thwarted the expansionist desires of Serbia, and the annexation of Bosnia and Herzegovina in 1908 especially embittered the Serbians. Secret organizations were formed in Serbia, and their aim was to take any possible action against Austria-Hungary. The plan to assassinate the Archduke Ferdinand, heir to the

Hapsburg crown, was conceived and carried out by one such organization, the *Narodna Odbrana*. After the assassination at Sarajevo on June 28, 1914, the Austrians cast about for appropriate action.

The ultimatum of July 23 was aimed at making the demands on Serbia so high that she would either not submit, or if she did, the country would be humiliated. Serbia sent back a somewhat conciliatory response, but since the demands of the ultimatum were not met, Austria-Hungary declared war on Serbia, July 28, 1914. Within a few days Britain, France, Germany and Russia became belligerents, and World War I had begun.

Max Montgelas and Walter Schucking (editors) OUTBREAK OF THE WORLD WAR: DOCUMENTS COLLECTED BY KARL KAUTSKY (New York: Carnegie Endowment For International Peace, 1924) Supplement I, 603–606.

The Austro-Hungarian Minister for Foreign Affairs, Berchtold, to the Minister at Belgrade, von Giesl

Vienna, July 22, 1914

Your Excellency will present the following note to the Royal Goverment on the afternoon of Thursday, July 23:

On the 31st of March 1909, the Royal Serbian Minister at the Court of Vienna made, in the name of his Government, the following declaration to the Imperial and Royal Government:

Serbia recognizes that her rights were not affected by the state of affairs created in Bosnia, and states that she will accordingly accommodate herself to the decisions to be reached by the Powers in connection with Article 25 of the Treaty of Berlin. Serbia, in accepting the advice of the Great Powers, binds herself to desist from the attitude of protest and opposition which she has assumed with regard to the annexation since October last, and she furthermore binds herself to alter the tendency of her present policy toward Austria-Hungary, and to live on the footing of friendly and neighborly relations with the latter in the future.

Now the history of the past few years, and particularly the painful events of the 28th of June, have proved the existence of a subversive movement in Serbia, whose object it is to separate certain portions of its territory from the Austro-Hungarian Monarchy. This movement, which came into being under the very eyes of the Serbian Government, subsequently found expression outside of the Kingdom in acts of terrorism, in a number of attempts at assassination, and in murders.

Far from fulfilling the formal obligations contained in its declaration of the 31st of March, 1909, the Royal Serbian Government has done nothing to suppress this movement. It has tolerated the criminal activities of the various unions and associations directed against the Monarchy, the unchecked utterances of the press, the glorification of the authors of the assassination, the participation of officers and officials in subversive intrigues; it has tolerated an unhealthy propaganda in its public instruction; and it has tolerated, finally, every manifestation which could betray the people of Serbia into hatred of the Monarchy and contempt for its institutions.

This toleration of which the Royal Serbian Government was guilty, was still in evidence at that moment when the twenty-eighth of June exhibited to the whole world the dreadful consequences of such tolerance.

It is clear from the statements and confessions of the criminal authors of the assassination of the twenty-eighth of June, that the murder at Sarajevo was conceived at Belgrade, that the murderers received the weapons and the bombs with which they were equipped from Serbian officers and officials who belonged to the *Narodna Odbrana,* and, finally, that the dispatch of the criminals and of their weapons to Bosnia was arranged and effected under the conduct of Serbian frontier authorities.

The results brought out by the inquiry no longer permit the Imperial and Royal Government to maintain the attitude of patient tolerance which it has observed for years toward those agitations which center at Belgrade and are spread thence into the territories of the Monarchy. Instead, these results impose upon the Imperial and Royal Government the obligation to put an end to those intrigues, which constitute a standing menace to the peace of the Monarchy.

In order to attain this end, the Imperial and Royal Government finds itself compelled to demand that the

Serbian Government give official assurance that it will condemn the propaganda directed against Austria-Hungary, that is to say, the whole body of the efforts whose ultimate object it is to separate from the Monarchy territories that belong to it; and that it will obligate itself to suppress with all the means at its command this criminal and terroristic propaganda.

In order to give these assurances a character of solemnity, the Royal Serbian Government will publish on the first page of its official organ of July 26/13, the following declaration:

"The Royal Serbian Government condemns the propaganda directed against Austria-Hungary, that is to say, the whole body of the efforts whose ultimate object it is to separate from the Austro-Hungarian Monarchy territories that belong to it, and it most sincerely regrets the dreadful consequences of these criminal transactions.

"The Royal Serbian Government regrets that Serbian officers and officials should have taken part in the above-mentioned propaganda and thus have endangered the friendly and neighborly relations, to the cultivation of which the Royal Government had most solemnly pledged itself by its declarations of March 31, 1909.

"The Royal Government, which disapproves and repels every idea and every attempt to interfere in the destinies of the population of whatever portion of Austria-Hungary, regards it as its duty most expressly to call attention of the officers, officials, and the whole population of the kingdom to the fact that for the future it will proceed with the utmost rigor against any persons who shall become guilty of any such activities to prevent and suppress which, the Government will bend every effort."

This declaration shall be brought to the attention of the Royal army simultaneously by an order of the day from His Majesty, the King, and by publication in the official organ of the army.

The Royal Serbian Government will furthermore pledge itself:

1. to suppress every publication which shall incite to hatred and contempt of the Monarchy, and the general tendency of which shall be directed against the territorial integrity of the latter;

2. to proceed at once to the dissolution of the *Narodna Odbrana,* to confiscate all of its means of propaganda, and in the same manner to proceed against the other unions and associations in Serbia which occupy themselves with propaganda against Austria-Hungary; the Royal Government will take such measures as are necessary to make sure that the dissolved associations may not continue their activities under other names or in other forms;

3. to eliminate without delay from public instruction in Serbia, everything, whether connected with the teaching corps or with the methods of teaching, that serves or may serve to nourish the propaganda against Austria-Hungary;

4. to remove from the military and administrative service in general all officers and officials who have been guilty of carrying on the propaganda against Austria-Hungary, whose names the Imperial and Royal Government reserves the right to make known to the Royal Government when communicating the material evidence now in its possession;

5. to agree to the cooperation in Serbia of the organs of the Imperial and Royal Government in the suppression of the subversive movement directed against the integrity of the Monarchy;

6. to institute a judicial inquiry against every participant in the conspiracy of the twenty-eighth of June who may be found in Serbian territory; the organs of the Imperial and Royal Government delegated for this purpose will take part in the proceedings held for this purpose;

7. to undertake with all haste the arrest of Major Voislav Tankosic and of one Milan Ciganovitch, a Serbian official, who have been compromised by the results of the inquiry;

8. by efficient measures to prevent the participation of Serbian authorities in the smuggling of weapons and explosives across the frontier; to dismiss from the service and to punish severely those members of the Frontier Service at Schabats and Losnitza who assisted the authors of the crime at Sarajevo to cross the frontier;

9. to make explanations to the Imperial and Royal Government concerning the unjustifiable utterances of high Serbian functionaries in Serbia and abroad, who, without regard for their official position, have not hesitated to express themselves in a manner hostile toward Austria-

Hungary since the assassination of the twenty-eighth of June;

10. to inform the Imperial and Royal Government without delay of the execution of the measures comprised in the foregoing points.

The Imperial and Royal Government awaits the reply of the Royal Government by Saturday, the twenty-fifth instant, at 6 p.m., at the latest.

CHAPTER 63

The Austro-Hungarian Occupation of Serbia in World War I

This selection comes from a Memorandum presented to the Socialist Conference at Stockholm in November, 1917. Its authors were the Serbian Socialists, Dushan Popovitch and T. Katzlerovitch. The Memorandum, while it was part of the propaganda war, held greater authority because the Serbian Socialists had no love for their own government-in-exile. As happened to the Poles, the Serbian people were victims of the first total war, and many of the Austrian deprivations created permanent economic problems. The Austrian treatment of a conquered people also demonstrated how they regarded the Serbians as inferior people, a view actuated by antiquated imperialism and prophetic of Nazi racism.

Dushan Popovitch and T. Katzerovitch, A NEW LIGHT ON CONDITIONS IN SERBIA (New York: The Serbian Relief Committee of America, 1918), pp. 4–10.

THE ECONOMIC SITUATION

Even before the occupation the economic life of Serbia

had been more gravely disorganised than that of any other belligerent State.

And what did the "bearers of Kultur" do under these circumstances? To the already formidable exactions of war weighing so heavily upon the population, they added the weight of an unjust economic policy.

The first act of the authorities of occupation consisted in interning in Austria-Hungary, for no reason and from no political or military necessity, more than 150,000 persons belonging to the civil population. Serbia was thus stripped of the last reserves in the way of labour which she still possessed and countless families lost their last resources.

Hundreds of thousands of children, women and old men were in this fashion condemned to die of starvation. An even more horrible fate was in store for those who were interned, and the country was drained completely of the working population which might have helped it to carry on. This was the first and most important act on the part of the invaders, in so far as their activity bears upon the economic, social, and intellectual reconstruction of occupied Serbia.

After the military authorities had made themselves masters of all that was left in the way of labour, they proceeded to requisition every article which either they could use, or fancied that they could use, and this process continues. Everything indispensable to production, all working material, without which the future development of productive resources is impossible, was requisitioned. Serbia's most important factories no longer exist; the machinery has been taken down and transported to the other side of the frontier. The peasants were deprived of their last carts, their horses and their oxen. There have been cases where small freehold farmers were compelled to hand over fifteen oxen to the authorities within the space of a year and a half. They had to deliver these oxen, whether they possessed them or not. In the latter case they were compelled to buy them at top prices or to obtain them as contraband at the risk of their lives, from the other side of the Morava, in Bulgarian territory.

The axe likewise constitutes a very important instrument of propaganda in Austro-German culture. The way in which the forests, those most vital assets of a country like ours, are being treated to-day in Serbia, not only represents excessive depredation but actual total destruction. To take but one example, the forest of Ragot, the property of the State, was one of the most beautiful, and one of the oldest forests in the heart of Serbia. It was worth several millions. To-day this forest is a thing of the past. It has been felled to the last tree. An empty desolate waste has taken its place. The rest of the Serbian forests, some—like the forests of Kopaonik, Tara and Rudnik—even larger and more valuable, have suffered the same fate. The sullen blows of the Austrian axe resound in the depths of the forests of Shumadia like the blows of a hammer upon an anvil.

And while the destruction of the forests goes on apace, we have on the other hand a systematic and uninterrrupted expropriation of all that belongs to the native population. This is called "requisition." Almost all the products of the country, including even metal utensils indispensable in every household, have been requisitioned under the pretext that they were required for military needs. Ridiculous payments were given in exchange. As a matter of fact, this is only a covert form of expropriation; in the same way, the whole of a harvest is commandeered.

As regards the forcible depreciation of Serbian money, this also is neither more nor less than robbery. No sooner had Serbia been conquered than an order appeared directing, under pain of the severest penalties, that the Serbian franc (dinar) was worth no more than half a krone (5d.). As the native population possessed no other money, it was obliged to circulate Serbian money, which in this way fell at absurdly low rates into the hands of the Germans and Bulgars.

In short, the economic losses sustained by Serbia during the course of the war, and above all, in consequence of the disastrous occupation, are so great that the reconstruction of the country will not be possible without generous public assistance from the Allies after the war.

THE FOOD POLICY

And what is the compensation offered by the Austro-

Hungarian authorities to the Serbian population as indemnification for the sufferings endured? Have they at least, after requisitioning everything, left it the minimum necessities to life? Not at all! All has been organised and calculated in such a way as to condemn the population to die of starvation. The district chiefs possess unlimited powers as regards food distribution. In this matter they are dependent upon no one, not even their own Government. The result is that the indispensable interchange of foodstuffs between the different parts of Serbia is rendered impossible. All surplus produce from one part of the country, which could and should be used to meet the needs of another part, is immediately exported to Austria-Hungary. Moreover, an artificial famine has thus been created, which is then exploited by the agents of the Government and their friends, who indulge in the most shameless speculation. In this way certain Austro-Magyar officers and civilians grow richer day by day, while hundreds of thousands of Serbian women, children and old men, are deprived of the primary necessities of life and threatened with the most appalling famine.

The desperate plight of the native population in Belgrade induced Dr. Veljkovitch, mayor of the city, Mr. Peritch, professor at the University and several other personages to present a memorandum on the distress of the people to Colonel Kerschnave, chief of staff of the Military Government. The requests put forward in this memorandum were quite modest; namely, the simplification of the regulations for obtaining permission to travel to the interior of the country, the present methods being very complicated and difficult to comply with. It was requested that such permission should be granted to all who needed it for the purpose of procuring provisions, and not only for a few privileged speculators. The administration was furthermore petitioned to modify its policy of minimum prices . Finally, the petitioners asked for the corporation of Belgrade itself permission to purchase a certain number of cattle, which would serve to check the speculation indulged in by the military commissariat of Belgrade. Yet this exceedingly modest memorandum was considered by the Austro-Hungarian authorities a highly suspicious document....Mr.

Veljkovitch was so badly treated that he found himself obliged to tender his resignation.

Naturally, the Socialists meet with even less consideration. When one of our comrades, Mika Spasoyevitch, town councillor permitted himself last year in very moderate terms to criticise this policy of inaction, and demanded bread for the people, *he was immediately arrested and interned in Hungary, although he was over seventy years of age.*

This intolerable state of affairs has been rendered even worse by the unscrupulous behaviours of the Austro-Hungarian authorities and their banks. Serbia is at present deprived of all economic life, every one in the country lives entirely on help received from abroad. People live on relief received from Switzerland and France, from relations and various charities. *But Alas! Serbia is now almost forgotten by all.* Twice only in 1916, did missions arrive in Belgrade, one a Swiss mission, and one an American, to distribute food and clothing among the inhabitants of Belgrade. The money received by the inhabitants from their relations is therefore their only resource; but the sums despatched hitherto are very small in proportion to the most elementary needs. Within two years about twenty million (francs) have been sent. Still, this sum represents a great deal for many families, which, but for it, would have nothing to live on. The Austro-Hungarian banks and authorities, however, are so cruel and devoid of conscience that they often delay payment of these sums for months together. In some cases sums despatched from Switzerland or France in September, 1916, were not paid out in Belgrade until March or April, 1917.

It is superfluous to point out once more that the plight of the population of Belgrade will be truly terrible this winter and next spring, if all these people are left without money. Hitherto they have managed to live, or rather to exist, under great privations, and with very great detriment to bodily health. The grave consequences of this state of things will not become apparent until after the war. But this winter and next spring the Serbian population will be faced by still greater suffering. The military authorities have organised a special system to deprive the Serbian peasants of the last grain of their crops. *All, absolutely all, in the literal sense of the word,* is now being exported, so that there will be nothing left for the population but to fold its hands and die of hunger. *Swift and extensive help is necessary,* both in money and in food, if this people, possessed though it is of an amazing vitality, is not doomed to die of starvation under the most atrocious conditions.

CHAPTER 64

The Situation in Bukovina

Written with some of the prejudice one would expect in time of war, Miss Bates tells of the great legends that still inspired the people at the beginning of this century. Bukovina, more so than many areas of Eastern Europe, had such a mixed population that no nation had a clear-cut claim to it. After World War I, the province passed from Austrian hands to become part of a greatly enlarged Roumania.

Jean Victor Bates, OUR ALLIES AND ENEMIES IN THE NEAR EAST (London: Chapman and Hall Ltd., 1918), pp. 81– 94.

How many people who have scanned reports of fierce fighting in the Sereth Valley, in the north-west of Moldavia, know anything about this little country? To the majority it becomes visualised as a place of utter desolation, of devastated villages, of dreary, muddy roads over which artillery lurch to and fro on their mission of death and torture, over which drift doomed and maddened multitudes of war-smitten peasants, over which the raw-headed vultures wing by, scenting the dead and dying that they may devour them.

Once upon a time, in the reign of Stefan Domn cel Mare

—Stephen the Great, Prince of Moldavia—when the Bukovina was the richest province of that sturdy ruler's dominions, Albrecht, King of Poland, thought fit to pitch his camp and graze the horses of his army on the great open plain lying along the river Pruth. Whereupon Stefan Domn cel Mare sallied out with all his forces and put the intruders to flight after having slain half their host and taken twenty-five thousand prisoners, of whom many were haughty and dissolute nobles. Fearing greatly, the Polish king made overtures to Stefan and offered a large ransom for the release of his subjects. But the Moldavian prince was not a man who did things half-heartedly. He refused his enemy's offer, and ordered many ploughs to be made. To these he harnessed the Poles and sent them out to till the lands of the Bukovina, after which he obliged them to sow in the furrows which they had ploughed the seeds of the beech tree.

In time these seeds grew up into great stretches of forest, and so the country came to be called the "Dumbreville Roshe"—which is, being interpreted, The Land of the Bloody Beech Forest. Legend declares that a terrible curse, the curse of blood has laid upon the country from that day to this; that the murmur of dead voices sounds through the rustling branches of its woodlands; that the sighing of the slain may be heard through its softest breezes; and the fact remains that the shadow of the sword has never through long centuries departed from the fields and forests of the Bukovina.

Stefan died, and much of the Roumanian power and liberty died with him. His dominions came under the rule of the Sultan, and the free descendants of the Veterans of the Emperor Trajan and Decebalus the Dacian learnt the bitterness of foreign oppression. In the year 1775 the Sublime Porte, having for long held in thrall this Roumanian Land of the Beeches, ceded it to the Imperial Court of Austria "as an unequivocal proof of friendship, affection, and good neighbourliness," or, to speak truly, ceded it because Austria, discontented with its slice of partitioned Poland, put a pistol to the head of the Unspeakable Turk and demanded the gift. On that midnight, so the Roumanian legend relates, in the old monastery of Putna, in the

Bukovina, where rest the bones of the Roumanian princes, the great Buga (bell) began to toll by itself, and tolled louder and louder. And the monks awoke in fright and rushed into the church, which they found bright with a strange and terrible light not of earth, which light went suddenly out and left them groping in thick darkness. Then the holy men brought flaming torches and oil-lamps, but the torches went out, although there was no wind, and the lamps did likewise, although they were full of oil, and from the tomb of Stefan Domn cel Mare came an angry and awful voice calling curses upon the spoilers of his country, and the monks fled in terror. Next morning when they returned it was to find the portrait of the great prince fallen to the ground and blackened out of recognition, as if by smoke, and a coldness as of death filled all the building....

Dotted all over the many pooled plains between the Dniester and the Pruth, through the gloomy primaeval forests of Luczyna; on the pleasant undulating country about Suczawa; in the romantic valley of the Putna; along the fruitful well-cultivated banks of the Sereth; over the melancholy rocky wildernesses of the Raren and Szumalen; on the lower slopes of the chalk mountains in the north; round the extinct volcano of Ouschor in the south, are villages where dwell the representatives of many past and present nationalities, the adherents of many past and living religions. These contrasting and bitterly opposed peoples may meet and trade in the public market-places; but only when it is a matter of business do they make the slightest attempt to fraternise. Take the Roumanian villages of the Bukovina first. Despite every effort on the part of the Teutonic Government, they still retain their Roumanian characteristics. There homesteads are the same white-washed, red-painted, wooden constructions; have the same cross-surmounted gables, the same sloping thatched roofs, the same shrine-frescoed walls, inset with the same little crude pictures of unfamiliar, soup-plate-haloed saints; each small *casa* is surrounded by the same high wicker work fence; and each dwelling is quaintly, roughly beautiful, with the beauty which seems to belong to everything the Roumanians are possessed of. Needless to remark, no self-respecting Teuton would dream of condescending to reside alongside "the Wallach swine," so they build for themselves small replicas of the villages of the distant Fatherland. In these, each prim, two-storied stone house stands complacently secure in the centre of an immaculately clean, flagged, or cobbled courtyard, set about by a forbiddingly solid and lofty stone wall. Indeed, everything connected with the German villages of the Bukovina is solid, from their red-tiled pointed roofs and their closely-latticed, neatly-curtained windows, to their fortress-like churches and well-guarded orchards and gardens. The Wallachs are content to construct their villages along either side of the public road. Not so the Germans. In their settlements there are invariable three or four so-called streets running in the form of a cross or triangle in the midst of which is the church. Along the German gutters there is never any garbage, and no scantily-attired infants sport amongst friendly geese and amiable porkers; yet, judging by the unsavoury odours which emanate from both German and Roumanian Bukovina villages, with respect to sanitation the ideas of both races are evidently the same. At intervals here and there between the Roumanian and German hamlets may be found those of the Jews and Ruthenians.

Jewish villages are never by any chance salubrious or lovely, but these in the Bukovina are extraordinarily horrible. Sordid clusters of wretched wooden hovels, plastered with mud and cow-dung and smeared over with glaring blue paint, they are, like their inhabitants, indescribably loathsome. The reek of cabbage stew and garlic, offal, and verminous humanity meets the nostrils in every direction. In the open doorways lounge and sprawl black-kaftaned men, gaudily-turbaned women, and their lice-infested offspring. Until one has learnt the little ways of the Israelites it seems incomprehensible why in open, sparsely-populated lands like Galicia, Moldavia, and the Bukovina, human beings should be obliged to compress about five families, a couple of cows and pigs, not a few turkeys, and a considerable number of fowl into two low-roofed rooms, which are lighted and ventilated only by a three-inch-wide slit in the wall! Every one to their taste, however, for, as the rustic Jew hereabouts cannot claim poverty as an excuse, it must be their natural instinct which prompts them to exist in this state of filthiness and intimacy. As for the habitations of the Ruthenians, they, too, are so many tiny offshoots of Little Russia. The wooden, or clay, and brushwood, straw-thatched huts of which they are composed stand, as do those in the Roumanian and Jewish villages, along both sides of the highway. To the English eye there is something rather familiar in their aspect, for each small homestead is encircled by a low hedge of briers or willows, and has a pretty flower garden in front and vegetable garden in the rear. Moreover, there is always a triangular goose green at the end of the hamlet near the church, which is of the Eastern faith, and a pond shaded by alder bushes, where congregate the ducks and babies, and in the vicinity of which are wooden benches where the old cronies sit on warm evenings, exchanging the latest local scandals...

CHAPTER 65

The Formation of Yugoslavia—The Pact of Corfu

The Pact of Corfu served as one of the most important foundation stones for the newly-created Yugoslavia that emerged after World War I. By the Summer of 1917, it was evident that the Austrian Empire would probably collapse with the end of the war. A new South Slavic state would emerge. The question was whether that state would be an enlarged Serbia or a state based on a federal principle giving equal rights to Croats and Slovenes as well as Serbs.

In 1917, the Serbian government-in-exile hoped for an enlarged Serbian state, but the non-Serbians, led by Dr. Ante Trumbić, president of the Yugoslav Committe, wanted a federated state. Some sort of modus vivendi had to be reached. Otherwise, the door would be open to Italian dreams of expansion on the Dalmatian coast. The Pact of

Corfu allowed the two Yugoslavian factions to effectively counter-balance Italian ambitions and show a united voice to the western powers. But though the Pact of Corfu solved religious and linguistic problems (both the Cyrillic and Latin alphabets were accepted), at the instance of Pasic, the Serbian Prime Minister, the Pact did not promote the idea of a federated state. If Dr. Trumbic had won more concessions in the Pact, many later problems caused by Serbian nationalism might have been avoided.

Reprinted in THE JUGO-SLAV MOVEMENT, Foreign Office, Historical Section, No. 14 (London: H. M. Stationery Office, 1920), pp. 35–38.

At the conference of the members of the late Coalition Cabinet and those of the present Cabinet, and also the representatives of the Jugoslav Committee in London, all of whom have hitherto been working on parallel lines, views have been exchanged in collaboration with the President of Skupstina, on all questions concerning the life of the Serbs, Croats, and Slovenes in their joint future State.

We are happy in being able once more on this occasion to point to the complete unanimity of all parties concerned.

In the first place the representatives of the Serbs, Croats, and Slovenes declare anew and most categorically that our people constitutes but one nation, and that it is one in blood, one by the spoken and written language, by the continuity and unity of the territory in which it lives, and finally in virtue of the common and vital interests of its national existence and the general development of its moral and material life.

The idea of its national unity has never suffered extinction, although all the intellectual forces of its enemy were directed against its unification, its liberty, and its national existence. Divided between several States, our nation is in Austria-Hungary alone split up into eleven provincial administrations coming under thirteen legislative bodies. The feeling of national unity, together with the spirit of liberty and independence, have supported it in the never-ending struggles of centuries against the Turks in the East and against the Magyars in the West.

Being numerically inferior to its enemies in the East and West, it was impossible for it to safeguard its unity as a nation and a State, its liberty and its independence against the brutal maxim of 'might goes before right' militating against it both East and West.

But the moment has come when our people is no longer isolated. The war imposed by German militarism upon Russia, upon France and upon England for the defence of their honour as well as for the liberty and independence of small nations, has developed into a struggle for the Liberty of the World and the Triumph of Right over Might. All nations which love liberty and independence have allied themselves together for their common defense, to save civilization and liberty at the cost of every sacrifice, to establish a new international order based upon justice and upon the right of every nation to dispose of itself and so organize its independent life; finally to establish a durable peace consecrated to the progress and development of humanity and to secure the world against a catastrophe similar to that which the conquering lust of the German Imperialism has provoked.

To noble France, who has proclaimed the liberty of nations, and to England, the hearth of liberty, the Great American Republic and the new, free, and democratic Russia have joined themselves in proclaiming as their principal war aim the triumph of liberty and democracy and as basis of the new international order the right of free self-determination for every nation.

Our nation of the three names, which has been the greatest sufferer under brute force and injustice, and which has made the greatest sacrifices to preserve its right of self-determination, has with enthusiasm accepted this sublime principle put forward as the chief aim of this atrocious war, provoked by the violation of this very principle.

The authorized representatives of the Serbs, Croats, and Slovenes, in declaring that it is the desire of our people to free itself from every foreign yoke and to constitute itself a free, national, and independent State, a desire based on the principle that every nation has the right to decide upon its own destiny, are agreed in judging that this State should be founded on the following modern and democratic priciples:

1. The State of the Serbs, Croats, and Slovenes, who are also known as the Southern Slavs or Jugoslavs, will be a free and independent kingdom, with indivisible territory and unity of allegiance. It will be a constitutional, democratic, and Parliamentary Monarchy under the Karageorgevitch Dynasty, which has always shared the ideas and the feelings of the nation, placing liberty and the national will above all else.

2. This State will be named 'The Kingdom of the Serbs, Croats, and Slovenes'. And the style of the sovereign will be 'King of the Serbs, Croats, and Slovenes'.

3. The State will have a single coat-of-arms, a single flag, and a single crown. These emblems will be composed of the present existing emblems. The unity of the State will be symbolized by the coat-of-arms and the flag of the Kingdom.

4. The special Serb, Croat, and Slovene flags rank equally and may be freely hoisted on all occasions. The special coats-of-arms may be used with equal freedom.

5. The three national designations—Serbs, Croats, and Slovenes—are equal before the law throughout the territory of the Kingdom, and every one may use them freely upon all occasions of public life and in dealing with the authorities.

6. The two alphabets, the Cyrillic and the Latin, also rank equally and every one may use them freely throughout the territory of the Kingdom. The Royal authorities and the local self-governing authorities have both the right and the duty to employ both alphabets in accordance with the wishes of the citizens.

7. All recognized religions may be freely and publicly exercised. The Orthodox, Roman Catholic, and Musulman faiths, which are those chiefly professed by our nation, shall rank equally and enjoy rights with regard to the State.

In consideration of these principles the legislative will take special care to safeguard religious concord in conformity with the spirit and tradition of our whole nation.

8. The calendar will be unified as soon as possible.

9. The territory of the Kingdom of the Serbs, Croats, and Slovenes will include all the territory inhabited compactly and in territorial continuity by our nation of the three names. It cannot be mutilated without detriment to the vital interests of the community.

Our nation demands nothing that belongs to others. It demands only what is its own. It desires to free itself and to achieve its unity. Therefore it consciously and firmly refuses every partial solution of the problem of its national liberation and unification. Its put forward the proposition of its deliverance from Austro-Hungarian domination and its union with Serbia and Montenegro in a single State forming an indivisible whole.

In accordance with the right of self-determination of peoples, no part of this territorial totality may without infringement of justice be detached and incorporated with some other State without the consent of the nation itself.

10. In the interests of freedom and of the equal rights of all nations, the Adriatic shall be free and open to each and all.

11. All citizens throughout the territory of the Kingdom shall be equal and enjoy the same rights with regard to the State and before the Law.

12. The election of the Deputies to the National Representative body shall be by universal suffrage, with equal, direct, and secret ballot. The same shall apply to the elections in the Communes and other administrative units. Elections will take place in each commune.

13. The Constitution, to be established after the conclusion of peace by a Constituent Assembly elected by universal suffrage, with direct and secret ballot, will be the basis of the entire life of the State; it will be the source and the consummation of all authority and of all rights by which the entire life of the nation will be regulated.

The Constitution will provide the nation with the possibility of exercising its special energies in local autonomies delimited by natural, social, and economic conditions.

The Constitution must be passed in its entirety by a numerically defined majority in the Constituent Assembly.

The Constitution, like all other laws passed by the Constituent Assembly, will only come into force after having received the Royal sanction.

The nation of the Serbs, Croats, and Slovenes, thus unified, will form a State of about 12,000,000 inhabitants. This State will be the guarantee for their independence and national development and their national and intellectual progress in general a mighty bulwark against the German thrust, an inseparable ally of all the civilized nations and States which have proclaimed the principle of right and liberty and that of international justice. It will be a worthy member of the new Community of Nations.

Drawn up in Corfu, July 7/20, 1917.

The President of the Jugoslav Committee, (Sgd.)
DR. ANTE TRUMBIC.
Advocate, Deputy and Leader of the Croatian National Party in the Dalmatian Diet, late Mayor of Split (Spalato), late Deputy for the district of Zadar (Zara) in the Austrian Parliament.
The Prime Minister of the Kingdom of Serbia and Minister for Foreign Affairs,
(Sgd.) NIKOLA P. PASIC.

CHAPTER 66

Polish Independence

Although Polish independence had already been proclaimed on October 7, 1918 at Warsaw by the Regency Council, the Manifesto of November 7 is of note since it outlined the future policies of a Polish national state. There would be war with Russia, trouble with minority groups, and inability to solve economic questions in the first years of independence. It was not until 1924 that the Polish government was able to implement the social program outlined in the Manifesto of November 7. If no other problems were solved, post-war Poland could claim one of the best records in the field of social legislation.

Manfred Kridl, Wladyslaw Malinowski, and Józef Wittlin, FOR YOUR FREEDOM AND OURS (New York, 1943), pp. 219–221. Reprinted by permission of Frederick Ungar Publishing Co., Inc.

To the Polish People! Polish workers, peasants and soldiers! Over blood-drenched, tortured humanity rises the dawn of peace and freedom. . . .

By order of the people's and socialist parties of the former Congress Kingdom and of Galicia we proclaim ourselves the Provisional People's Government of Poland and until the convening of the Constitutional Sejm we take over complete and full authority, pledging ourselves to exercise it justly for the good and benefit of the Polish people and state, not shrinking, however, from severe and absolute punishment of those who will not recognize in Poland the authority of Polish democracy. As the Provisional Polish People's Government we decree and proclaim the following laws binding the whole Polish nation from the moment of the issuance of the present decree:

The Polish state, embracing all lands inhabited by the Polish people, with a sea coast of its own, is to constitute for all times a Polish People's Republic whose first President will be elected by the Constitutional Sejm.

The Constitutional Sejm shall be convoked by us during the current year on the basis of general, equal, direct, secret, and proportional suffrage for both sexes. Electoral regulations will be announced within the next few days. Every citizen who has reached twenty-one years of age will have the right to vote or to be elected.

From this day we proclaim in Poland full equality of political and civic rights for all citizens irrespective of origin, faith and nationality, freedom of conscience, press, speech, assembly, procession, association, trade-unionization and freedom to strike.

All donations and majorats in Poland are hereby declared state property. Special prescriptions will be issued to counteract land speculation.

All private as well as former government forests are declared state property; the sale and cutting of forests without special permission is prohibited from the time of the publication of the present decree.

In industry, handicrafts and commerce we hereby introduce an eight-hour working day.

After we shall have finally constitutionalized ourselves we shall at once proceed to the reorganization of community councils, county assemblies and municipal local governments, as well as to the organization in towns and villages of a people's militia which will insure to the population order and safety, obedience to and execution of the orders of our legislative organs, and the proper settling of the problems of food supply for the population.

At the Constitutional Sejm we shall propose the following social reforms:

Forceful expropriation and abolition of big and medium landed property and its transference to the working people under state supervision;

Nationalization of mines, salt-mines, the oil industry, roads of communication and other branches of industry where this can be done at once;

Participation of workers in the administration of those industrial plants which will not be nationalized at once;

Protection of labor, unemployment, sickness and old age insurance;

Confiscation of capital accumulated during the war through criminal speculation with articles of primary necessity and supplies for the army;

Introduction of universal, obligatory and free lay school education.

We call upon the Poles living in the lands of the former Grand Duchy of Lithuania to strive in brotherly harmony with the Lithuanian and White Ruthenian nations for the reconstruction of the Lithuanian state on its old historical boundaries, and upon the Poles in Eastern Galicia and in the Ukraine to settle peacefully all controversial questions with the Ukranian nation until they are ultimately regulated by competent agents of both nations. . . .

We consider it to be one of our most important and most urgent tasks to organize a regular people's army. We trust that the peasant and working youth will gladly join the ranks of the revolutionary Polish army, emanating from the people, defending the political and social rights of the working people, faithfully and completely devoted to the People's Government, subject only to its orders.

Polish People, The hour of your action has struck. Take into your worn, powerful hands the great task of liberating your land which is soaked with the sweat and blood of your fathers and forefathers and bequeath to subsequent generations a great and free and united homeland. Rise united to action, do not spare wealth or sacrifice or life for the great task of Poland's and the Polish workers' liberation.

We call upon you brotherly Lithuanian, White Ruthenian, Ukranian, Czech and Slovak nations to live in harmony with us and to support each other mutually in the great work of creating an association of free and equal nations.

> The Provisional People's Government
> of the Polish Republic
> Lublin-Cracow, November 7, 1918

CHAPTER 67

The Coup d'État at Prague on October 28, 1918

The events of October 28, 1918 are described as a coup d'état by Dr. Benes, the future foreign minister of Czechoslovakia, but from his description, the inevitability of throwing off the Austro-Hungarian yoke is evident. Vienna knew the end of its power had come and generally tried to handle the Empire's dissolution in a peaceful fashion. Of course, long years of patient work and terrible frustration preceded the day when the Czechs regained the freedom lost to the Hapsburgs in 1526. In the elation of victory, all the tragic problems of the next three decades were hardly apparent to those who celebrated the independence of Czechoslovakia.

Eduard Benes, MY WAR MEMOIRS, translated by Paul Selver (New York and Boston: Houghton Mifflin Co., 1928), pp. 451–454.

The events at Prague between October 28th and 30th formed a connecting link in the great chain of circumstances constituting the downfall of the Habsburg Empire. Each of those who took part in this huge drama played his part as the instrument of a destiny which some interpret as the irresistible development of historical forces, others as the divine purpose of Providence. And as regards the events in Prague their relation to our national cause is that of a logical conclusion to the vast struggle which demanded so much exertion and sacrifice, self-denial, and firmness of will. This last phase had been so well prepared by the preceding events that, at the moment when the time came to act, there could be no doubt of immediate success, provided that sufficient skill and determination were brought to bear upon the task. The results show that this was indeed the case.

On October 25th a meeting was held at the Hotel Continental in Vienna between our Geneva delegates and the Poles and Jugoslavs. On the same day the delegation proceeded to Geneva and Dr. Rasin returned to Prague. This was the time when news had reached our politicians and, in fact, all persons of authority in the Empire, that an Austro-Hungarian military collapse was imminent. On October 26th Rasin refused the appeal for help which General Boroevic had made to the Prague National Committee, his answer being that Austria-Hungary must first capitulate. On the same day the Austro-Hungarian Ministry of War was negotiating with the National Committee on the subject

of joint action concerning the food supply, and the National
Committee decided to co-operate with the Corn Exchange.
On the evening of October 27th Tusar telephoned to Dr.
Rasin about the disastrous situation on the Italian front,
whereupon Rasin immediately settled with Scheiner that
arrangements should now be made because on the next
day "things were going to happen." The Germans in Bohemia, being also aware of the critical situation of the
Empire, held a meeting at Dresden on the same day to
discuss the question of help for German Bohemia in case
there should be a catastrophe and a revolution in Bohemia.
Early on the morning of October 28, 1918, the chief
members of the National Committee learnt the contents
of Andrássy's note (Tusar had telephoned about it to Rasin
during the night and the newspaper *Bohemia* had brought
out a special early morning edition containing full details)
as well as the capitulation of Vienna. This news at once
became the starting-point for decisive action on the part
of the National Committee. Svehla, together with Dr. F.
Soukup, on behalf of the National Committee, took charge
of the Corn Exchange, which formed the headquarters of
the food supply for the whole country. Immediately afterwards the Vaclav Square, where the inhabitants of Prague
learnt the joyful news in front of the offices of the Národ-
ní Politika, was filled with cheering crowds and the houses
were decorated with flags. In this atmosphere of excitement the National Committee met at 11.30 a.m., and at
noon Svehla, Rasin, Soukup, and Stribrny proceeded to the
Governor's residence and to the central administrative offices, where they demanded that the administrative authority should be surrendered to the National Committee.

The news of these events reached Vienna shortly after
midday at the moment when Lammasch, the new Prime
Minister, was taking his vow of loyalty to the Emperor
at the Hofburg. The Emperor at once began to discuss
the situation with Lammasch and Andrássy, and these discussions were continued at the first meeting of the Lammasch Cabinet which was held on the same day at five-
o'clock in the afternoon. Coudenhove, the Governor of Bohemia, was present, and from the Council Chamber telephoned to his deputy, Vice-President Kosina, instructing

him to refuse to hand over the administration to the National Committee.

Meanwhile, in Prague, during the afternoon, the military authorities endeavoured to moderate the excitement of the crowds, who had already begun to pull down the Austrian emblems. The Magyar troops who were garrisoned in Prague were sent to patrol the streets. The military commander, however, who had been instructed to co-operate with the national committees for the maintenance of peace, acceded to the request of the National Committee in Prague and recalled the troops. The National Committee thereupon undertook the task of maintaining order in the city, largely with the help of the Sokols. The enthusiasm of the people was thus allowed free play, and October 28th was duly celebrated as the first day of national liberty. In accordance with the prevailing mood the National Committee, at seven o'clock in the evening, issued the first law of the Czechoslovak State. It runs as follows:

The independent Czechoslovak State has come into being. In order that continuity should be preserved between the juridicial order hitherto existing and the new regime, in order that no confusion may arise and that there may be an undisturbed transition to the new life of the State, the National Committee, as executor of the State supremacy, enacts as follows on behalf of the Czechoslovak nation:

Article I

The State form of the Czechoslovak State will be decided by the National Assembly in agreement with the Czechoslovak National Council in Paris as bodies expressing the unanimous will of the nation. Before this is done, the State supremacy will be exercised by the National Committee.

Article II

All imperial and provincial laws will continue to remain in force until further notice.

Article III

All autonomous bodies, all State, district, municipal, and local institutions are answerable to the National Commitee, and until further notice they will continue to carry out their duties in accordance with the existing laws and regulations.

Article IV

This law comes into force from to-day onwards.

Article V

The presidential board of the national Committee will be responsible for the carrying out of this law.

PRAGUE, *October 28, 1918.*
 ANTONIN SVEHLA.
 DR. F. SOUKUP
 DR. ALOIS RASIN.
 DR. VAVRO SROBAR.
 JIRI STRIBRNY.

At the same time the National Committee issued a proclamation to the people, calling upon them to maintain order and to show themselves worthy of the freedom which had crowned their efforts.

CHAPTER 68

The Yugoslav—Italian Dispute Over Dalmatia, 1919

Lieutenant Colonel Sherman Miles was sent to Croatia in January, 1919, to gather data for the American Commission to Negotiate Peace. By the Treaty of London (April 26, 1915), Italy had been promised Adriatic territories as the price for entrance into World War I on the Allied side. At the war's end, the Italian government pressed for even more territory, thus causing endless squabbles at the Paris Peace Conference. Miles' reports were quite unfavorable to Italian pretentions, and President Woodrow Wilson favored the Yugoslavian claims. The Treaties of San Germain and Trianon did not settle all the outstanding questions, especially the problem of which state would receive the important port of Fiume. Finally, in 1924, after Italian troops had already occupied Fiume, the city was assigned to Italy by an agreement with Yugoslavia (January 27, 1924). The Yugoslavs tried to build a rival port at Susak, but had little success. Fiume, cut off from the Yugoslav hinterlands, also declined. Neither side gained anything, and the whole affair represented one of the chief failures of the diplomats at the Paris Peace Conference.

Jerome Jareb (Editor) "Sherman Miles' Reports from Croatia March to April 1919" (JOURNAL OF CROATIN STUDIES 1962–1963), Vols. III and IV, pp. 148–151. Reprinted by permission of the editor of the JOURNAL OF CROATIAN STUDIES.

Subject: *The Dalmatian Coast—*
Question of Future Nationality

1. The three factors of self determination, economics and geography seem to be in agreement in the Dalmatian question—all in favor of Jugoslavia.

2. Even in the small town of Zara [Zadar], which the Italians point out as being the center of Italian colonization on the coast, the people are divided, and it is by no means certain than an unprejudiced vote would be in favor of Italy, I am told by Americans and Englishmen who have been there frequently in the past months that, in spite of the Italian occupation and the repressive measures taken by them, the Jugoslavs are very much in evidence, and by no means consist solely of the lower strata of society.

3. In Sebenico [Sibenik] the Jugoslavs certainly predominate. It is a Jugoslav town in every sense of the word.

4. South of Sebenico [Sibenik] the predominance of the Jugoslavs, even in the coast towns, is still more marked.

5. All along the coast the hinterland is purely Jugoslav.

6. One of the most striking features of the present situation is the fact that is in the so-called purely Italian towns now strongly occupied by Italian troops that trouble in the form of imprisonment and deportation occurs, while

south of the Pact of London Line, though the Jugoslav military occupation is very light, no trouble occurs save that directly attributable to Italian attempts to extend their control. The disturbances at Spalato [Split], for instance, were found by Allied investigation to have been due to Italian sailors on shore leave attempting to arrest civilians of the town.

7. The difference, from the military point of view, between the Italian and the Jugoslav occupation is very marked. At Fiume, for instance, the Italians have practically a whole division of troops, and they are composed of some of the picked regiments of the Italian Army. In Istria their force, particularly in the Slav interior, is very strong (I noticed three division headquarters in motoring from Fiume to Pola [Pula]). In the Zara [Zadar] and Sebenico [Sibenik] districts it is the same story. On the Jugoslav side of the line (as I have personally observed in three most important points and have had reports from American officers who have crossed the line at others) the Jugoslav forces are very light. In the city of Spalato [Split], for instance, there are in all only some 800 Jugoslav troops, and this in spite of the fact that it is the most important point on the coast for them and that they are faced by a much stronger Italian force only 30 kms. away.

8. There is overwhelming proof, well known to the unprejudiced American and British naval officers on this coast, that the Italian authorities are going to great lengths in their propaganda. At present a favorite form seems to be bribery by food and fuel. They have repeatedly landed food and fuel and given it away to anyone who would sign a written receipt (which was also a vote for Italy). Unfortunately they have not limited themselves to this humanitarian form of propaganda, but have gone in for deportations and imprisonment on an extensive scale. There has also been the usual suppression of newspapers, clubs, etc. Their activities extend well beyond their own line of occupation. The American Admiral in command at Spalato [Split] recently received a letter from the Italian Admiral saying openly that he would continue to exert his influence ashore in the form of propaganda. This same Italian Admiral, so our Admiral tells me, was prepared to land in

Spalato [Split] a month ago, and the Italian Government undoubtedly hoped to seize the town on the same pretext they used at Fiume.

9. In view of the force and oppression of the Italian occupation of a large part of Dalmatia, and of the means to which they go to exert their influence over the rest of the province, the difficulties they are experiencing in preserving order even in their so-called Italian towns is very indicative of the predominantly Slav nature of the province.

10. On the side of economics, it is difficult to follow the Italian arguments. About the best they can say is that they have the ships in which to export the produce of Dalmatia. But, aside from lumber, which must [sic] of the world needs, there is nothing in Dalmatia which can profitably be exported to Italy. It is a notoriously poor land, which has been wasted for centuries, and the cost of production of its wine and other products is higher than in Italy. Under Italian control it is difficult to see how it could prosper, and it might well starve. For what it has to export, other bottoms are certainly as good as Italian.

11. The Jugoslav arguments on the point of economics are obvious and sound. They are based on the fact that the Dalmatian coast is the sea-outlet not only for Jugoslavia but also of the Hungary of the future. When Spalato [Split] is connected by railroad with the interior, much of the trade of the Save [Sava], Drave [Drava] and Danube basins will naturally be diverted from Fiume to Spalato [Split]. (This point is admitted even by the merchants of Fiume who would most suffer). It is true that it will take a great deal of money and time to develop Canale Castelli [Kastelanski Zaljev] (the large bay behind the town of Spalato [Split] and to complete its railroad connections with the interior. But this fact is in itself an argument for the Jugoslav side, for it means that only if the coast and the hinterland are under the same control can both be developed, and that if a large part of the coast be given to Italy the development of the hinterland must suffer. If Italy should get, for instance, the territory given her by the Pact of London, Spalato [Split] would not only be cut off from its railroad connections to the

north (such as they are), but the town and all other possible railroad connections would be so close to the Italian
frontier as to be indefensible, and therefore a commercial
risk. In addition to this, the loss of the islands of Lesina
[Hvar], Lissa [Vis], Cursola [Korcula] and Lacosta [La-
stovo] (as per the Pact of London) would completely block
Spalato [Split] from a naval point of view. To a lessor
[sic] degree the ceding to Italy of the district of Zara
[Zadar] and the islands to the north west of it would
cut into the natural economic life of Jugoslavia (though
not so much as would the loss of Fiume). The present
embittered relations (commercial as well as every other)
and the intolerent attitude of both sides leaves little to
be expected in the way of satisfactory commercial relationships, even after long years of peace. In fact, it is the
opinion of most American and British officers who have
had a recent opportunity to study the situation on the spot
that the ceding of Dalmatia to Italy (in addition to the
loss of the Slavs of Istria and of the hinterland of Trieste)
would inevitably lead to war, sooner or later.

12. Geographically, the Italian claims run into the va-
garies of strategical speculation. The defense of Italy from
a possible enemy of the future is only the military problem
of Rome all over again. Like Rome, Italy, in her present
way of thinking, can really logically admit of no fixed
bounds of safety. The Jugoslav side of the case—the geo-
graphical unity of Dalmatia—is, on the other hand, obvious
and undisputable.

13. The Italian historical argument harks back to the
Venetian Republic and Roman Empire. Wherever two or
three Italians and a Roman ruin are gathered together,
there is Italy. But even this side of the question, if really
taken seriously, is all in favor of the Jugoslavs, for the
undisputable fact is that they are here in predominant numbers, and have been so for many generations.

SHERMAN MILES, Lieutenant Colonel, General Staff

CHAPTER 69

Dissolution of the Hapsburg Empire

The Treaty of St. Germain-en-Laye, signed on September 10, 1919, was most unfavorable to Austria. At Vienna, Austria had been proclaimed as a republic on November 12, 1918. While their empire was lost, Austrians were dismayed that the final settlement deprived them of one-third of their German population. Approximately 3,500,000 German Austrians were placed under Czechoslovakia and 250,-000 were lost to Italy. There had been agitation in Austria for union (Anschluss) with Germany, but this was also forbidden.

Reprinted in Lawrence Martin (editor), THE TREATIES OF PEACE, 1919–1923 (New York: Carnegie Endowment For International Peace, 1924), Vol. I, pp. 297–299.

Treaty Between the Allied and Associated Powers and Austria, signed at St. Germain-en-Laye, Sept. 10, 1919

GENERAL PROVISIONS

Article 88
The independence of Austria is inalienable otherwise than with the consent of the Council of the League of Nations. Consequently Austria undertakes in the absence of the consent of the said Council to abstain from any act which might directly or indirectly or by any means whatever compromise her independence, particularly, and until her admission to membership of the League of Nations, by participation in the affairs of another Power.

Article 89
Austria hereby recognises and accepts the frontiers of Bulgaria, Greece, Hungary, Poland, Roumania, the Serb-

Croat-Slovene State and the Czecho-Slovak State as these frontiers may be determined by the Principal Allied and Associated Powers.

Article 90

Austria undertakes to recognise the full force of the Treaties of Peace and additional conventions which have been or may be concluded by the Allied and Associated Powers with the Powers who fought on the side of the former Austro-Hungarian Monarchy, and to recognise whatever dispositions have been or may be made concerning the territories of the former German Empire, of Hungary, of the Kingdom of Bulgaria and of the Ottoman Empire, and to recognise the new States within their frontiers as there laid down.

Article 91

Austria renounces, as far as she is concerned, in favour of the Principal Allied and Associated Powers all rights and title over the territories which previously belonged to the former Austro-Hungarian Monarchy and which, being situated outside the new frontiers of Austria as described in Article 27, Part II (Frontiers of Austria), have not at present been assigned to any State.

Austria undertakes to accept the settlement made by the Principal Allied and Associated Powers in regard to these territories, particularly in so far as concerns the nationality of the inhabitants.

Article 92

No inhabitant of the territories of the former Austro-Hungarian Monarchy shall be disturbed or molested on account either of his political attitude between July 28, 1914, and the definitive settlement of the sovereignty over these territories, or of the determination of his nationality effected by the present Treaty.

Article 93

Austria will hand over without delay to the Allied and

Associated Governments concerned archives, registers, plans, title-deeds and documents of every kind belonging to the civil, military, financial, judicial or other forms of administration in the ceded territories. If any one of these documents, archives, registers, title-deeds or plans is missing, it shall be restored by Austria upon the demand of the Allied or Associated Government concerned.

In case the archives, registers, plans, title-deeds or documents referred to in the preceding paragraph, exclusive of those of a military character, concern equally the administrations in Austria, and cannot therefore be handed over without inconvenience to such administrations, Austria undertakes, subject to reciprocity, to give access thereto to the Allied and Associated Governments concerned.

Article 94

Separate conventions between Austria and each of the States to which territory of the former Austrian Empire is transferred, and each of the States arising from the dismemberment of the former Austro-Hungarian Monarchy, will provide for the interests of the inhabitants, especially in connection with their civil rights, their commerce and the exercise of their professions.

CHAPTER 70

Hungary's Losses after World War I—Treaty of Trianon

Hungary's most famous treaty of peace was signed at the Trianon on June 4, 1920. The signing of the Treaty had been delayed by the Allies' unwillingness to deal with the leftist regime of Bela Kun in 1919. Hungary, after the overthrow of Kun, received an ultra-rightist regime that had little choice but to accept the terms imposed by the Allies. Of the territory that had been included in Historic Hungary, two-thirds was lost, mainly to Roumania,

Czechoslavakia and Yugoslavia. Based on the census of 1910 the loss in population was more than one-half—eighteen million in 1910, seven and one-half million after Trianon. The Treaty of Trianon was bitterly resented in Hungary and contributed to the strength of Hungarian nationalism during the inter-war years.

Lawrence Martin (editor), THE TREATIES OF PEACE, 1919–1923 (New York: Carnegie Endowment For International Peace, 1924), Vol. I, pp. 478–484.

Treaty Between the Allied and Associated Powers and Hungary, signed at Trianon, June 4, 1920

Section II.

SERB-CROAT-SLOVENE STATE.

Article 41.

Hungary, in conformity with the action already taken by the Allied and Associated Powers, recognises the complete independence of the Serb-Croat-Slovene State.

Article 42.

Hungary renounces so far as she is concerned in favour of the Serb-Croat-Slovene State all rights and title over the territories of the former Austro-Hungarian Monarchy situated outside the frontiers of Hungary as laid down in Article 27, Part II (Frontiers of Hungary) and recognised by the present Treaty, or by any Treaties concluded for the purpose of completing the present settlement, as forming part of the Serb-Croat-Slovene State.

Article 43.

A Commission consisting of seven members, five nominated by the Principal Allied and Associated Powers, one by the Serb-Croat-Slovene State, and one by Hungary, shall be constituted within fifteen days from the coming into force of the present Treaty to trace on the spot the frontier line described in Article 27 (2), Part II (Frontiers of Hungary).

Article 44.

The Serb-Croat-Slovene State recognises and confirms in relation to Hungary its obligation to accept the embodiment in a Treaty with the Principal Allied and Associated Powers such provisions as may be deemed necessary by these Powers to protect the interests of inhabitants of that State who differ from the majority of the population in race, language or religion, as well as to protect freedom of transit and equitable treatment of the commerce of other nations.

The proportion and nature of the financial obligations of Hungary which the Serb-Croat-Slovene State will have to assume on account of the territory placed under its sovereignty will be determined in accordance with Article 186, Part IX (Financial Clauses) of the present Treaty.

Subsequent agreements will decide all questions which are not decided by the present Treaty and which may arise in consequence of the cession of the said territory.

Section III

ROUMANIA.

Article 45.

Hungary renounces, so far as she is concerned, in favour of Roumania all rights and title over the territories of the former Austro-Hungarian Monarchy situated outside the frontiers of Hungary as laid down in Article 27, Part II (Frontiers of Hungary) and recognised by the present Treaty, or by any Treaties concluded for the purpose of completing the present settlement, as forming part of Roumania.

Article 47.

A Commission composed of seven members, five nominated by the Principal Allied and Associated Powers, one by Roumania, and one by Hungary, will be appointed within fifteen days from the coming into force of the present Treaty to trace on the spot the frontier line provided for in Article 27 (3), Part II (Frontiers of Hungary).

Article 47.

Roumania recognises and confirms in relation to Hungary her obligation to accept the embodiment in a Treaty with the Principal Allied and Associated Powers such provisions as may be deemed necessary by these Powers to protect the interests of inhabitants of that State who differ from the majority of the population in race, language or religion, as well as to protect freedom of transit and equitable treatment for the commerce of other nations.

The proportion and nature of the financial obligations of Hungary which Roumania will have to assume on account of the territory placed under her sovereignty will be determined in accordance with Article 186, Part IX (Financial Clauses) of the present Treaty.

Subsequent agreements will decide all questions which are not decided by the present Treaty and which may arise in consequence of the cession of the said territory.

Section IV.

CZECHO-SLOVAK STATE.

Article 48.

Hungary, in conformity with the action already taken by the Allied and Associated Powers, recognises the complete independence of the Czecho-Slovak State, which will include the autonomous territory of the Ruthenians to the south of the Carpathinas.

Article 49.

Hungary renounces, so far as she is concerned, in favour of the Czecho-Slovak State all rights and title over the territories of the former Austro-Hungarian Monarchy situated outside the frontiers of Hungary as laid down in Article 27, Part II (Frontiers of Hungary) and recognised by the present Treaty, or by any Treaties concluded for the purpose of completing the present settlement, as forming part of the Czecho-Slovak State.

Article 50.

A Commission composed of seven members, five nominated by the Principal Allied and Associated Powers, one by the Czecho-Slovak State, and one by Hungary, will be appointed within fifteen days from the coming into force of the present Treaty to trace on the spot the frontier line provided for in Article 27 (4), Part II (Frontiers of Hungary).

Article 51.

The Czecho-Slovak State undertakes not to erect any military works in that portion of its territory which lies on the right bank of the Danube to the south of Bratislava (Pressburg).

Article 52.

The proportion and nature of the financial obligations of Hungary which the Czecho-Slovak State will have to assume on account of the territory placed under its sovereignty will be determined in accordance with Article 186, Part IX (Financial Clauses) of the present Treaty.

Subsequent agreements will decide all questions which are not decided by the present Treaty and which may arise in consequence of the cession of the said territory.

Section V.

FIUME.

Article 53.

Hungary renounces all rights and title over Fiume and

the adjoining territories which belonged to the former Kingdom of Hungary and which lie within the boundaries which may subsequently be fixed.

Hungary undertakes to accept the dispositions made in regard to these territories, particularly in so far as concerns the nationality of the inhabitants, in the treaties concluded for the purpose of completing the present settlement.

Section VI.

PROTECTION OF MINORITIES.

Article 54.

Hungary undertakes that the stipulations contained in this Section shall be recognised as fundamental laws, and that no law, regulation or official action shall conflict or interfere with these stipulations, nor shall any law, regulation or official action prevail over them.

Article 55.

Hungary undertakes to assure full and complete protection of life and liberty to all inhabitants of Hungary without distinction of birth, nationality, language, race or religion.

All inhabitants of Hungary shall be entitled to the free exercise, whether public or private, of any creed, religion or belief whose practices are not inconsistent with public order or public morals.

Article 56.

Hungary admits and declares to be Hungarian nationals *ipso facto* and without the requirement of any formality all persons possessing at the date of the coming to force of the present Treaty rights of citizenship (pertinenza) within Hungarian territory who are not nationals of any other State.

Article 57.

All persons born in Hungarian territory who are not born nationals of another State shall *ipso facto* become Hungarian nationals.

Article 58.

All Hungarian nationals shall be equal before the law and shall enjoy the same civil and political rights without distinction as to race, language or religion.

Difference of religion, creed or confession shall not prejudice any Hungarian national in matters relating to the enjoyment of civil or political rights, as for instance admission to public employments, functions and honours, or the exercise of professions and industries.

No restriction shall be imposed on the free use by any Hungarian national of any language in private intercourse, in commerce, in religion, in the press or in publications of any kind, or at public meetings.

Notwithstanding any establishment by the Hungarian Government of an official language, adequate facilities shall be given to Hungarian nationals of non-Magyar speech for the use of their language, either orally or in writing before the Courts.

Hungarian nationals who belong to racial, religious or linguistic minorities shall enjoy the same treatment and security in law and in fact as the other Hungarian nationals. In particular they shall have an equal rights to establish, manage and control at their own expense charitable, religious, and social institutions, schools and other educational establishments, with the right to use their own language and to exercise their religion freely therein.

Article 59.

Hungary will provide in the public educational system in towns and districts in which a considerable proportion of Hungarian nationals of other than Magyar speech are resident adequate facilities for ensuring that in the primary schools the instruction shall be given to the children of such Hungarian nationals through the medium of their own language. This provision shall not prevent the Hungarian Government from making the teaching of the Magyar language obligatory in the said schools.

In towns and districts where there is a considerable proportion of Hungarian nationals belonging to racial, religious or linguistic minorities, these minorities shall be assured an equitable share in the enjoyment and application of sums which may be provided out of public funds under the State, municipal or other budgets for educational, religious or charitable purposes.

Article 60.

Hungary agrees that the stipulations in the foregoing Articles of this Section, so far as they affect persons belonging to racial, religious or linguistic minorities, constitute obligations of international concern and shall be placed under the guarantee of the League of Nations. They shall not be modified without the assent of a majority of the Council of the League of Nations. The Allied and Associated Powers represented on the Council severally agree not to withhold their assent from any modification in these Articles which is in due form assented to by a majority of the Council of the League of Nations.

Hungary agrees that any Member of the Council of the League of Nations shall have the right to bring to the attention of the Council any infraction, or any danger of infraction, of any of these obligations, and that the Council may thereupon take such action and give such direction as it may deem proper and effective in the circumstances.

Hungary further agrees that any difference of opinion as to questions of law or fact arising out of these Articles between the Hungarian Government and any one of the Allied and Associated Powers or any other Power, a Member of the Council of the League of Nations, shall be held to be a dispute of an international character under Article 14 of the Covenant of the League of Nations. The Hungarian Government hereby consents than any such dispute shall, if the other party thereto demands, be referred to the Permanent Court of International Justice. The decision of the Permanent Court shall be final and shall have the

same force and effect as an award under Article 13 of
the Covenant. . . .

CHAPTER 71

A Rationale of the Little Entente

In this statement, Benes outlines the events that led to
the formation of the Little Entente. Fear of reaction against
Czechoslovakia, Roumania, and Yugoslavia led to the forma-
ion of the Little Entente, and as can be seen from the
words of Benes, he had hopes that it would serve as the
basis for greater stability in Eastern Europe. Such would
not be the case in the 1930's.

Eduard Benes, FIVE YEARS OF CZECHOSLOVAK FOREIGN
POLICY (Prague: Orbis Publishing Co., 1924), pp. 12–19.

It is evident from what has been said that our foreign
policy has from the beginning endeavoured to take into
account the realities and to work accordingly, But it has
never dropped from its high moral ideals; it wanted to
be and, I think it really and truly was, idealistic and
founded entirely upon moral principles.

It is from this point of view that one should judge all
that has been accomplished by the Ministry of Foreign
Affairs since September 1919.

On leaving the Peace Conference and having in December 1919 the opportunity once more of returning to Paris,
I made in company with the representatives of Yugoslavia
the first preparations for the formal treaty between Yugoslavia and Czechoslovakia. The arguments were not merely
of a sentimental character and dictated by the traditional
policy held in common by the two countries: they resulted
also from the European disorder owing to the reasons which
I have already mentioned. Against the universal alarm in

our neighbourhood, the monarchistic plots, the threatened
trouble from the East, and the reproaches levelled at our
heads by Western Europe to the effect that we had "bal-
kanized" Central Europe, we had to give a clear proof
that we knew how to build up and maintain our States.
This was the origin of the Little Entente. The Kapp
"putsch" and the Charles Habsburg affair were the external cause, but the real causes lay deeper; they are and
were more lasting and will not cease to be so, as long
as these two States exist. Hence right from the beginning
everything that has been said on the dissensions within
the Little Entente has been ridiculous, and this is truer
today than ever. Such reports are a proof either of naiveté
and ignorance of the actual conditions, or else of an absence of good-will.

The signing of the first treaty of alliance on August
14, 1920 and of the second on August 31, 1922 was merely
the external and formal side of a policy which was based
on the logic of events; this conclusion of treaties happened
at a time when external events made it psychologically
possible and politically opportune. Formally and essentially
it was a preeminently peaceful action; it confirmed the
Peace Treaties and guaranteed, both externally and in accordance with the deep needs of the two nations, the security of the people who needed peace in the highest degree and desired to stabilize conditions and follow the aims
of the League of Nations.

In connection with this act I went to Bukarest in August
1920 where, as is well-known, I negotiated the protocol
of our aggreement with M. Take Jonescu, whereby Rumania
adhered in principle to that alliance, reserving to herself
the right to give her formal signature on the earliest occasion. On April 23, 1921 the treaty was formally signed
because of the impression produced by the first affair in
connection with Charles of Habsburg, and last year the
alliance was renewed with the same aims and the same
ideas. Thus the Little Entente was formally created.

You know yourselves that this policy was criticized, be-
littled, and distorted from its true meaning. At first it
was not welcomed in Western Europe. We quietly went
on, and later events have proved that we were acting on

the right lines. One section of the Opposition at home said that the Little Entente was imperialistic and militaristic; another section saw in it a weapon for European reaction against Soviet Russia; some considered it to be hostile to Italy, others said that it meant discord with France, declaring nevertheless, when it was convenient to say so, that the Little Entente was in vassalage to France; finally, others thought that it was merely out for self-advertisement and was no more than a piece of bluff. This is what was said to me here on one occasion even in the Czechoslovak Commission for Foreign Affairs.

Today after three years the group of these three States has shown great vitality; it has shown an example of close cooperation, loyalty and genuine friendship and has achieved considerable results in its policy; it has preserved the peace of Central Europe in the most critical moments, acted as a moderating influence in a series of conflicts, and brought about such a degree of consolidation in its neighbourhood and within its own States that there is no important international statesman today who would not openly recognize its value. I do not want to give to this group a greater or different significance than it really has and I do not wish to exaggerate its merits, but I am only stating facts and I appeal to the objectivity and sense of justice of all those who possess good-will.

If I speak of these matters I only do so in order that those who today will criticise the treaty with France may recall to mind that they were unjust in regard to our policy when I was striving to reach an aggreement with Austria and signed it, also when I signed the treaties with Yugoslavia and Rumania, and also when I made three attempts to reach an aggreement with Hungary or Poland. Our policy was at last understood in the West, especially in England, then in Germany, and finally today in Russia. Without all these explanations and these references to criticisms on the one hand and to the results of our policy on the other, it is impossible to form a correct judgment on the whole of our treaty policy.

As early as in January 1920 I invited Dr. Renner, the Austrian Chancellor, to come to Prague; we spoke together on the common interests of the two countries and on the question of mutual help and we aggreed upon a policy of political and economic cooperation. We have followed the same policy with all the successors of Dr. Renner and I declare today that all the successive representatives of the foreign policy of Austria have accepted without any reservations the principles adopted in January 1920 as the basis for their future policy in regard to us. When Herr Schober was Chancellor this basis was made still wider; we arrived at still closer cooperation in the economic sphere and we concluded a friendly political treaty between the two republics. These ideas were deepened by collaboration at the Genoa Conference and in consequence of the visits exchanged by the two Presidents in Austria and in Czechoslovakia (at Lány).

The friendly treaty with Austria, which was concluded and signed on December 16, 1921, is a manifestation of our political ideas: peace with our neighbours, economic cooperation, the recognition of the legal status quo in Central Europe, friendship in the future and the obligatory settlement before a Court of Arbitration of any disputes which might occur. For us the idea of a Court of Arbitration is important: it is the idea of the League of Nations and by its gradual extension there will be established permanent peace in accordance with the ideas of modern democracy. I draw attention to the fact that we appealed to this principle on the first occasion, that of the first treaty with a State which was formerly unfriendly and with which conflicts might have occured. In our further political actions we followed this principle and shall continue to follow it.

Our further actions regarding Austrian affairs are well-known; our loan to Austria at a time when nobody wished to help, our decisive intervention in the League of Nations on behalf of the protection and the financial sanitation of Austria, our financial guarantees and the signing of the Geneva protocols all that can be criticised, but one thing cannot be denied, namely that we showed good will to our neighbour and applied the ideas of peace and the policy of reconstruction. I know the criticisms which have been made in connexion with this action: those who voted against it are the very same people who reproached us for years with being unfriendly towards Austria; I mean our German Opposition and those who wished to see in our policy a support for reaction. Today this already belongs to history and history will speak in another way about the matter. Moreover the Czechoslovak Government received from the Austrian Government, and from European public opinion without exception, nothing but expressions of thanks and justified gratitude.

You are well aware, Gentlemen, that we have not ceased our efforts in following this policy of conducting aggreements with all our neighbours, our Allies in the War, and our former enemies. Ever since the time of the creation of the Little Entente—formally directed against Magyar irredentism and nationalism, in reality against post-War disorder, attempted "putsches", unrest, uncertainty and all the excesses from the Right and the Left—we have not ceased to negotiate with Hungary precisely on the basis of these principles. I have attempted three times by direct negotiations with the Hungarian Governments to arrive at an aggreement both on disputed points and also on the whole of our political relations in general so as to have peace and quietness for the future. The memory is still fresh of our meeting with the Ministers, MM. Teleki and Gratz at Brück on the Leitha on March 14, 1921. The first attempt of Charles of Habsburg at a coup d'état destroyed the results of our negotiations. A few months later, on June 24, 1921, we had a meeting at Marianské Lazné with Minister Banffy and made a little more progress than on the former occasion.

The results of the negotiations were threatened once again by the insurrection in the Burgenland, yet even at that critical moment I maintained the peaceful line of our policy. I warned the Allies and entered into negotiations with Austria and Hungary in order that the matter might be settled satisfactorily and without recourse being had to war which was then much nearer than many people realized. Perhaps I can safely say today that on the occasion of this third attempt I endeavoured at the meeting at Brno on September 26, 1921 to settle with Minister Banffy, once and for all and in a friendly fashion, the question of the Habsburgs. What I feared soon happened: war with

Hungary on account of the Habsburg question. Before our negotiations were concluded—we had already arrived at an agreement in principle—Charles of Habsburg came for the second time. The events of November 1921—the mobilization and the well-known diplomatic conflict—are still fresh in the memory of all.

In spite of this grave conflict we did not swerve from our policy. In the question of the Habsburgs we did not yield to the Magyars just as we could not yield to the insistant demands of our Western Allies. Our struggle—and it was a struggle for future tranquility and peace—ended on the whole successfully. Our democratic policy, having for its object the consolidation and peace of Central Europe, but also our policy of treaty-making, has entirely justified itself. And Europe has at last recognized this. Those who were irritated with us during the time of the conflict have also recognized it.

Meanwhile during the years 1922-1923 we did not cease to negotiate with Hungary: in spite of great difficulties we solved one after the other the questions arising from the Peace Treaties, we got rid of the disputed points one by one, till finally last summer managed to clear away almost all the obstacles and to establish between the two countries almost normal relations. There still remain, however, certain disputed points, but I firmly hope that they will not cause any harm to our present normal relations.

The question of the reconstruction and the financial sanitation of Hungary then came to the front. We immediately adopted in this respect the same point of view as in the Austrian problem. At the last meeting of the League of Nations in September 1923 we agreed in principle with Count Bethlen, the Hungarian Prime Minister, on the course of action to be taken, and we ourselves together with the two other representatives of the Little Entente sent in a request on our own initiative to the League of Nations, asking this body to begin negotiations for the financial sanitation of Hungary.

And again we were criticized from both sides. Some considered it to be too much, whilst others thought it to be too little; as far as we were concerned, it was merely a continuation of our policy from which we shall not diverge even an inch. It is precisely this policy that gained us international significance and respect in the world. We cannot renounce any of our rights and claims in regard to the Magyars, nor any of our democratic principles. We cannot give up the general line of this policy even in the Hungarian question.

I have mentioned on various occasions that all of the members of the Little Entente are anxious to see a change in the relations with Hungary and that the moment is approaching when a reasonable agreement can be concluded with this country too and when the Little Entente will no longer be directed against Hungary, just as it has ceased to be directed against Austria. Thus will be realized the organization of Central Europe upon which we have so often insisted, an organization consisting in the creation of a new political and economic system in which all the countries of Central Europe would preserve their full sovereignty; it is an organization, in which, let us hope, all the present divergences of opinion will disappear in order to make room for collaboration. There is no reason why the present solidarity of the members of the Little Entente should not remain unchanged.

Our conception of the policy of agreements in Central Europe has not stopped also in face of another difficult question, that of our relations with Poland. The whole of 1919 and six months of 1920 were occupied with the dispute about the Tesin district; the Conference at Spa and the decision of the Conference of Ambassadors of July 28, 1920 formally put an end to the dispute, but the consequences of the conflict continue to a certain degree to this day. However, since 1920 and 1921 we have again attempted in accordance with our policy to arrive at political and economic cooperation. We have concluded a series of conventions and on the basis of the Peace Treaties we began to negotiate a political convention which was signed in November 1921.

Its contents are well-known and it again incorporates all our political principles which have been applied on other occasions: the recognition of the Peace Treaties, their loyal application, neutrality in the case of a conflict with a third party, and the obligatory arbitration of the League of Nations in the case of a conflict between us.

It is impossible to express more clearly the policy contained in the Pact of the League of Nations.

You all know that this treaty has not been put into operation. I regret this and meanwhile it remains merely as a document of our foreign policy. There was not enough understanding either amongst ourselves or in Poland. The last echoes of the whole of this political action were recently heard at the Hague on the occasion of the Javorina dispute and again in Paris before the Council of the League of Nations at its session of December 1923. Both these institutions declared in our favour of our legal standpoint in the whole dispute.

I will today say openly why I regret that we have not been able to arrive at a Czechoslovak-Polish treaty earlier. People have spoken, and from time to time they still speak, of the entrance of Poland into the Little Entente. That is not correct. That is the way to hurt the sensibilities of Poland and it does not have any material bearing upon the situation either. Between the Little Entente and Poland there has several times been close cooperation in questions common to both, and especially at the Genoa Conference.

This collaboration is desirable and good and it will certainly be put again strongly into practice. I wish it sincerely. But that has meant and will always mean the formula: Poland and the Little Entente. This is in a way an obstacle to an agreement on mutual interests being arrived at by each group—Czechoslovakia and Poland, etc. separately, and then, on this basis, each adjusting for the future their relations with the others.

But if one takes into account the general line of policy followed so far by Poland and the members of the Little Entente, one can see that no negotiations have ever been undertaken concerning the creation of a great territorial combination and allied *block*, but only of a limited understanding based on real interests and following concrete aims This has always been expressed by the provisional formula: "Poland and the Little Entente". I have always considered this formula as just and realizable in spite of various difficulties.

I do not doubt that finally we shall come to an agreement with Poland regarding a formula of pacific collaboration, I only regret, as I have already said, that this agreement has not yet been realized; my aim has always been to come to an understanding with Poland before the entrance of the new Russia into European politics. The situation is such that an understanding will be so much more difficult when Russia intervenes more actively in European politics and it will be more difficult for all of us, for ourselves, for Poland and for Russia. It seems that this has not been understood in time and sufficiently, either in Czechoslovakia or in Poland.

Hence we have the intention today to resume as soon as possible the interrupted work and finally to come to an agreement. If this agreement is formulated once and for all in a convention—and I do not see why this could not be done—there will be contained in it once more only the principles of our policy as incorporated in the Pact of the League of Nations.

CHAPTER 72

Greek Politics in the Twentieth Century

As a specialist on the earlier history of Greece, the author of this selection spent many years there in which he came to understand the contemporary political situation. Miller refers to the atomization of Greek politics in the early twentieth century as one of the major reasons why parties found it difficult to obtain large followings. The consequent fragmentation of political allegiance among a multiplicity of parties made it almost impossible to avoid episodes of dictatorship.

William Miller, GREECE, (New York: Charles Scribner's Sons, 1928) pp. 139–146.

"Man," said Aristotle, "is a political animal," and his saying is especially true of the Greeks. Just as Englishmen open a conversation by a remark about the weather, so in Greece the question, "What is your view of the situation?" is a quite usual beginning. In towns and villages, in clubs and monasteries, politics form the most natural theme of conversation. To people with acute minds and a love of dialectics public affairs have always been a favourite subject for discussion. Ancient Athens was intensely political; in Roman Athens, when there were no politics, University questions took their place, and parties rallied round this or that celebrated professor; just as in medieval Byzantium they discussed theology, and to-day in the Dodekanese the ordinary people, cut off from politics, are keenly interested in the question whether or no the Church shall be autocephalous. Even in the Turkish days, as travellers have recorded, there were parties in the then small world of Christian Athens, and with the dawn of freedom, and still more after the abolition of Bavarian autocracy by the September revolution of 1843, politics became an all engrossing topic. Three parties, the "English," the "French," and the "Russian," were formed under leaders, approved and sometimes inspired by the Ministers of the three protecting Powers, and Athens became the battle ground for British, French, and Russian intrigues, the favourite British leader being Mavrokordatos, the French Kolettes, and the Russian Metaxas. The French diplomatist Thouvenel is recorded to have sometimes actually composed the declaration of Ministerial policy, when the French protege was in office, and Sir Edmund Lyons and his Russian colleague, Catacazy, openly took part in internal politics. This unfortunate practice finds parallels in the cases of the rival Austrian and Russian parties in Serbia under Milan, the Russian intervention in Bulgaria under Alexander, and the Austro-Italian squabbles at Durazzo during the reign of William of Wied. Greece, like Jugoslavia and Bulgaria, has long outgrown this system of foreign parties. The Barlaioi, as the "English" partisans were called, from a Herculean Anglophil delegate to the Assembly of Hermione; the Moschomangai, as Kolettes' adherents were named, from the "hooligans" who frequented the "bastion of Moschos" near the harbour of Nauplia; and the Napaioi, as the "Russians" were nicknamed after the Moreote Napas, although there were German and Entente parties and leaders, including the Communists, are neither "English," "French," nor "Russian," but Greek.

Those who knew Greece some years ago notice, however, a decline in political interest among young people. The rising generation has seen so many and such drastic political changes that it has become surfeited of politics. Besides, the capital, now a big cosmopolitan city, offers diversions from politics which Othonian and even Georgian Athens could not present. Social functions are numerous; sport, especially football, tennis, and golf, has become acclimatised; horse-racing is an institution; the cinematograph occupies a large place in the public eye. As for the people, they are weary of politics, and only want peace to go on with their work. This was the explanation of the indifference with which they looked on at the departure of George II., the proclamation of the Republic, the coups d'etat which made and unmade Pangalos. This was the reason why at a recent municipal election in some places there were no candidates for the mayoralty, whereas at Pylos years ago the late Dr. Burrows found 123 candidates standing for 15 seats on the Municipal Council. Moreover the growing industrialisation of Greece offers more remunerative and attractive careers than place-hunting.

A generation ago Greek Governments were fairly stable, for Trikoupes remained three and again four and a half years in power, and Theotokes also three, just as Kolettes and Miaoules had done half a century earlier, while Kriezes was nearly five years Premier. Mr. Venizelos beat all records by remaining once five years and then three continuously in office; but since 1920 Cabinets have come and gone with rapidity. The young Republic has known already seven Prime Ministers, but this is not a special characteristic of the Republican regime, for in the early times of the second Monarchy there were nine Cabinets in thirteen months. At present thirteen politicians have filled the Premiership — Messrs. Zaimes, Skouloudes, Venizelos, Trianaphyllakos, Charlampes, Gonatas, Kaphandares, Papanastasiou, Sophoules, Michalakopoulos, Pangalos,

Eutaxias, and Kindyles—the first six times and the third thrice. There seemed, therefore, no need for the article embodied in the draft Constitution forbidding the tenure of the Premiership for more than a year, just as the first Greek Constitution, that of Epidauros in 1822, limited that of the Executive. However short be the Premier's term of office, he is styled Kyrie Proedre ("Mr. President") for the rest of his life—a form of address highly prized in the absence of all titles (except the old Venetian titles of nobility still used locally in the Ionian Islands), and after the recent abolition of decorations (except for medals) for Greek subjects. Since the introduction of constitutional government in 1843 there have been forty-seven different Prime Ministers (many of whom held the office repeatedly) and eighty-seven Ministers of Foreign Affairs, likewise recurrent, since 1829. The causes of these frequent changes are the personal character of Greek political parties, mostly based upon men rather than measures, and consequently liable to crumble away according to the feelings of the followers towards their leaders, and still more the individualism (atomismos) deeply engrained in the Hellenic character. When Kleon, as reported by Thucydides, said that "he, and not the other fellow, ought to be general," he expressed an eternal truth of Greek politics. George I., when an unknown Greek was presented to him, used to ask where he was "president." The very laudable ambition to be first makes team work difficult; but there are notable exceptions, such as the loyal outside support given by Mr. Kaphandares to the Michalakopoulos Premiership, and the heroic self-sacrifice of General Kondyles in 1926. It is not material gain, but rather the love of power that makes Greek politicians desire the Premiership. Deligiannes, after his repeated tenure of that office, left little more than his top hat and frock-coat behind him when he died. One of his rivals spent a considerable part of a considerable fortune on politics. A recent Premier remarked to me that Greek history contained no example of a Prime Minister who had enriched himself. Many of the heroes of the War of Independence lived in poverty, and one of the few commemorative tablets in Athens informs the passer-by that in a certain insignificant house in the then suburb of Kypsele "lived and died" Constantine Kanares, the most famous of them all.

Another cause of the fluidity of parties and the consequent changes of Cabinet is the lack of a party caucus, which in our Parliament makes the private member toe the party line or lose his seat, and the absence of party "whips." Hence the reader of the Athenian press becomes accustomed to such announcements as that "Mr. So-and-So has made declaration of his political friendship to such-and such a leader," or that several deputies belonging to a particular party have "skipped off." The individualism above mentioned makes parties fissiparous; proportional representation, introduced at the elections of 1926, further favours this tendency, and 65 parties entered the lists then for 286 seats! These parties consisted, however, in two notorious cases of one candidate each, and a party leader once said to me that at a meeting of chiefs one "leader" present "had no need to leave the room in order to consult his party"! it was himself! In practice, however, parties have simplified themselves into two main groups—Republicans and Royalists—each containing several subdivisions. The Republicans consists of a "Conservative" a "Progressive," and an advanced group (the "Republican Union"), under Messrs. Michalakopoulos, Kaphandares, and Papanastasiou respectively. There are also a few independent Republicans like Mr. Sophoules, the Speaker of the Chamber. The Royalists include a moderate and an advanced wing—viz., the party of "Free Thought" under General Metaxas, and the "popular" party under Mr. Tsaldares. The latter, however, contains certain intransigent Royalists, who must at times try the patience and require all the diplomacy of its leader. They are the "die-hards" of Greek politics, the men who still look to the "king over the water," as our Jacobite ancestors said, and who will have no compromise with the Republic. There are also independent Republicans from Mytilene and independent moderate Royalists, like Mr. Demertzes. Outside the Chamber, General Kondyles has recently re-entered politics and made a political tour of the Peloponnese. At the extreme back of the Chamber sit the nine Communists—now for the first time appearing in Parliament as a party, mostly young men

with a large dose of theoretical principles, whose leader
is Mr. Maximos, but whose god is Marx. Owing to the
individualism of the Greek character, the cutting-up of the
large estates in Thessaly, and the wide diffusion of small
properties, Greece would seem to be an unfavourable soil
for the growth of Communism. The Communist party is
chiefly recruited from the "new" provinces, where there
are many refugees, and notably from the tobacco workers
at Kavalla; but there was a big Communist poll at Larissa
(of which the President's would-be assassin was a native),
due it is said, to the personal influence of one apostle.
Greek Communism has its journal and its historian, Mr.
Koradatos; it fishes in troubled waters, as on 9 September,
1926, and in the strike of 10 March 1927; a few University students have made demonstrations against "capitalist"
professors, and the University Senate proposes to exact
a written statement from every undergraduate that he will
join no Communist organisation, under pain of expulsion.
Other more stringent measures have been invoked in consequence of the attempt on the President; but Bolshevik
propaganda, despite the exaggerated staff of the Soviet
Legation, seems likely to fail in "atomistic" Hellas, where
at the last election only 40,988 Communist votes were polled
out of 961,437.

The vehement feud between Republicans and Royalists
has died down. Royalist and Republican ladies—the ladies
were usually more intransigent than their husbands—play
cards together, and Royalist damsels find Republican part-
ners at dances. Athens—thank heaven!—is no longer divided up into an Elysee and a Faubourg-St-Germain. The
"Ecumenical" Government was at once a sign, and a cause
of this much-desired and most desirable "reconciliation."
Royalists are now seen at the parties of Government House,
just as the Jacobites went to the Court of George III.

Besides, the feud was not so much between Republicans
and Royalists as between Venizelists and anti-Venizelists.
The Greeks in politics are usually rather "anti" than "pro";
the Republicans are not so much enamoured of the ideal
beauties of a Republic as opposed to the House of Glucks-
burg; the Royalists are less enthusiastic about George II,
than resentful of Mr. Venizelos and General Plastiras. At

the elections of 1926 in some constituencies the contest was over a dead issue—Constantine versus Venizelos—and the electoral literature was what English politicians would call "ancient history." Now that Constantine is physically and Mr. Venizelos politically dead, all of the life has gone out of this historic controversy. One past event, the execution of "the Six," still casts a malign shadow over the political situation and causes Ministerial crises. Nor is this remarkable; for that terrible affair is barely five years old, and in Athens, where relationships have wide ramifications, the number of persons connected with the executed men is legion, and the brother of one of them is an influential deputy. The practice of the newspapers to publish frequent articles on the history of yesterday tends to revive smouldering disputes, and the return of Mr. Venizelos in 1927 to reside in Greece, even as a private individual, immediately made the Royalists suspicious. They would never believe that he had come back merely to bask in the Cretan sun or to translate Thucydides, but would scent some political intrigue in his presence among them, just as they saw another military plot in the sojourn of General Plastiras at Kephissia. Nor were the Royalists alone offended at the return of the Cretan, even to his native Crete. New political vested interests have grown up within his own party; new men have arisen with new claims to the leadership, and not at all disposed to be kept in leading strings; and there are stalwart Republicans who regard him as a tepid adherent who would have preferred a really constitutional monarchy which reigned, but let an all-powerful Premier govern. Mr. Venizelos belongs to history; as far as politics are concerned, he is *magni nominis umbra*.

CHAPTER 73

The Minorities in Roumanian Transylvania

The cession of Transylvania to Roumania by the Treaty of Trianon (1920) almost necessarily created grave problems for the non-Roumanians involved. Had the Roumanian government assumed a more enlightened attitude, it would probably not have aroused so much resistance to assimilation among minorities, especially among the Hungarians.

Jules Jezequal, ROUMANIA TEN YEARS AFTER (Boston: The Beacon Press, 1928), pp. 132–138.

The victory of Roumania's allies brought her several vast provinces which really beonged to her, for their population was undoubtedly in a large majority, Roumanian. Transylvania, one of these provinces, was part of Hungary before the war. She had been colonized by her conqueror who had established himself firmly. Important German groups had also established themselves in certain parts of Transylvania. Of the five million inhabitants of Transylvania, when she was given back to Roumania, 57.5% were Roumanians, 25.53% Magyars and Szeklars, 10.45% were Germans (Saxon and Swabs). There were also 3.60% Jews, 2.92% Ruthenians, Serbs, Bulgarians, etc. This made a very mixed population, as far as race was concerned, and not less so from the viewpoint of religion.

The Roumanians are Greek Orthodox; the Hungarians are Roman Catholics numbering about a million, Protestants, divided into Reformed, more than 700,000, and Unitarians about 74,000. Those of the population who are German by extraction, but have become Hungarian subjects, are Lutherans, numbering 260,000. To these about 200,000 Jews should be added. Relations between the Government of Old Roumania and the Orthodox Roumanians of Transylania were easily established. In the meantime, a Transylvanian peasant party has been formed which is not always in harmony with the Central Government. Serious difficulties however, are not likely to occur on this hand. But the relations with the Magyar, the Germans, and the Jews, were at once found to be very intricate.

Of the Jews, I will say nothing. The lot of the Jews of Transylvania is that of the Jews of the rest of Roumania. Of the Germans, there is not much to say, as they are treated in the same way as the Magyars, and when I speak of the Magyars I am also speaking of the Germans. It should however, be noted that the authorities are perhaps a little less severe with the latter than with the other minorities. This is perhaps because they have behind them Germany, a more imposing power than Hungary. It is quite natural that the Magyar minorities are the most disturbing element the Roumanian Government has to deal with. They were torn from their country by force. This force, it is true, was that of justice. It was right that a province, in which the large majority was Roumanian, should be returned to Roumania. But this justice was none the less hard for the Magyars of Transylvania. It was naturally sad for them to be torn from their mother country. They are in this way, it is said, expiating an old sin. But because a sin was committed far back in the past, one can hardly hold the present Transylvanian Magyars responsible, and one cannot hold a grudge against them for not rallying with enthusiasm and without regret to the new regime.

On the other hand, one cannot hold it against the Roumanian Government for regarding these newcomers with some mistrust. The situation is one of great delicacy. The Roumanians are in the majority in Transylvania, but these Roumanians are peasants. Their ancient masters left them systematically, one might say, in total ignorance. It is true that in old Roumania the directing class did not trouble itself to teach the miserable peasant. But this statement is not an excuse for the Magyars, however much they pride themselves on a superior civilization to their neighbors. Established in the towns, when they were not in their chateaux, the Magyars of Transylvania, great landowners, officials, industrials and merchants reigned for their own profit alone.

Now, by a sudden turn of affairs, the disdained and despise Roumanian peasants take precedence over the superb Magyar. It is the Roumanian who has become master. The Magyar must bow before the uneducated and rough Roumanian gendarme. It is perfectly comprehensible that this gendarme, and the government for whom he acts, cannot wholeheartedly believe in the loyalty of these enforced Roumanians. Mistrusting their loyalty, and moreover, annoyed by the deep-rooted as well as irritating habits of these people, the Government has taken a distrustful and vexatious attitude toward the Magyars.

The different Hungarian religious denominations deeply resent this feeling. They have raised bitter complaints. Their lamentations are not, properly speaking, about ecclesiastical questions alone. They include also questions of instruction and of property. On these two questions they are most bitter.

The Central Government in matters ecclesiastical has respected things as it found them, equally for Roman Catholics, as for Protestants. But the Greek Orthodox Church is the church of the State. Other churches are only tolerated. All the Orthodox archbishops and bishops have a constitutional right to sit in Parliament, but only one Catholic bishop has been admitted. But that is only a small inconvenience. The essential point is that liberty of creed should be respected. And it seems that it is so respected. The Churches, provided they confine themselves strictly to their religious functions, seem to have all the liberty that they can legitimately expect.

This however, does not mean that the religious minorities do not suffer from the new regime. From the first they were hit, and often hard hit, by the agrarian reform. Before the annexation, they possessed vast lands, whose revenues contributed to their maintenance. I believe that with the old regime, certain churches enjoyed bigger revenues than their needs demanded, but today it is certain that their revenues are insufficient. In many cases they did not have anything left because the expropriation laws were applied to them without mercy.

Have they the right to complain? The principle of expropriation was just. The peasant who cultivated the land, in the old Roumania, as well as in the new, did not possess a bit of ground. It was all in the hands of the great landowners, of the officials and of the Churches. To avoid a threatened peasant-uprising after the war, the Government took over the lands for distribution to the peasants. It was right in so far as principle was concerned. But the application was not always so. The State took into consideration itself and its friends, but it struck heavily at those whom it considered its enemies—namely, Magyar land owners, and the Churches of the minorities. As far as the latter were concerned, the blow was particularly heavy, as it also struck the church schools. Now in Hungary, all the schools are church schools. They were equally so in Transylvania. Thus in a day these schools lost the most valuable of their resources. And the churches, impoverished themselves, had so much less for the support of their schools. And they needed more than ever, because in these schools alone could suitable religious instruction be given in their own language. Another example of the complexity of Roumanian affairs! The Churches and the schools, left to their own devices, are thrown back on themselves, and for better or worse have become centers of Hungarian culture. Hotbeds of "Irredentism," says the Government.

Would it not have been wiser on the Government's part to have become the protector of these churches and schools? It has not thought so. It has preferred to adopt an antagonistic attitude.

It has tolerated the creation and functioning of private church schools, but has surrounded them with a meddling supervision. It has subjected them to annoyances and vexation. For example: no Roumanian child is allowed to attend a private church school. If any official discovers in one of these schools, a child whose name has a Roumanian sound, even though it is proved to him over and over again that the child is a Magyar or German by extraction, the child has to leave his school to go to the Roumanian public school where the Orthodox religion is taught. And it is only by good fortune that the private school he has left is not closed. I was told with such sincerity of an instance of this kind that I was obliged to believe it. A Roman Catholic orphanage had taken in Roumanian children afflicted with ophthalmia, for treatment. It has imprudently accepted for the care of these children, a subsidy from the Government which thereupon took the opportunity of taking over the orphanage. I gathered evidence of a number of acts of this sort. I cannot guarantee that they are all true, but they are too numerous not to be insignificant.

Here is another instance of hardship. It is asserted that the secondary church schools, of which many are very important, have not the right to give graduating diplomas to the universities. The Government denies this. What is true, and this possibly explains the contrary statements of both parties, is that pupils, in order to acquire diplomas, have to pass examination before professors, who belong to the Department of Public Instruction, and are appointed for this purpose by the State. It is true, this system is not illiberal in itself. It can be justified with good reason. The minorities are wrong to complain of it. But, if, as they assert in all seriousness, the authorities profit by the system to disqualify as a foregone conclusion, the candidates drawn from the church schools, then the minorities have a right to protest.

These lamentations and recriminations are not voiced by just this or that minority. This fact in itself gives them additional weight. All agree in denouncing the bad spirit of the Government toward them. The harmony between Roman Catholics and Unitarians, which I observed everywhere in Transylvania, would not be so close if they did not both suffer from the same vexations and annoyances. If these annoyances affected individuals only, it would be a small matter, but they affect the most cherished convictions and most essential principles of the minorities. It is not surprising that after treatment of this kind these minorities are rebellious and restless, and that they do not always strive for an adjustment which should be their special work. . . .

CHAPTER 74

A Montenegran Conversion to Communism

Milovan Djilas (1911–   ) has proved himself to be one of the most interesting intellects produced by Eastern Europe in the twentieth century. Born in Montenegro while that country was still an independent state, he attended the University of Belgrade where he was won over to Marxism. In 1933, the authorities arrested him for organizing anti-monarchist demonstrations, and he spent the first of many detentions in the prison at Sremska Mitrovica. During World War II, he fought in the resistance movement. He was already high in the Communist hierarchy, having been placed in the Yugoslavian Politburo in 1940.

After the war and Tito's seizure of power, Djilas held many important posts in the government. In January of 1953, he became one of four vice-presidents under Tito. He acted quite independently and had already attracted the critical attention of many doctrinaire Communists. In Janury of 1954, he was removed from all his positions.

A long series of imprisonments followed, and Djilas became so outspoken that he virtually turned into an anti-Communist. His book, *The New Class*, caused a sensation when it was published in 1957. The selection below comes from an autobiography that was published a year after *The New Class*.

Milovan Djilas, LAND WITHOUT JUSTICE, Introduction and Notes by William Jovanovich (New York, 1958), pp. 349–357.   1958, by Harcourt, Brace & World, Inc. and reprinted with their permission.

It was classical and humanistic literature that drew me to Communism. True, it did not lead directly to Communism, but taught more humane and just relations among men. Existing society, and particularly the political movements within it, were incapable even of promising this.

At that time I was reading Chernyshevsky. He and his clumsy novel could not make any particular impression on me, certainly because it was so completely unconvincing and shallow as a literary work. He might have been able to rear a series of revolutionary generations in Russia, and to have significant influence even in our country until modern times, but for the generation under the dictatorship he was without any significance. Such utopian musings, sentimental stories, and the like left no lasting traces. *Uncle Tom's Cabin* and Hugo's *Les Miserables* caused only a temporary impress, albeit a very strong one, which was forgotten when the book was laid aside. Marxist or socialist literature of any kind did not exist at all in

Berane at the time, nor was it to be had. The only thing that could exert any influence, and indeed did, was great literature, particularly the Russian classics. Its influence was indirect, but more lasting. Awakening noble thoughts, it confronted the reader with the cruelties and injustices of the existing order.

Yet it was the state of society itself that provided the prime and most powerful impulse. If anyone wished to change it—and there are always men with irresistible desires—he could do so only in a movement that promised something of the kind and was said to have succeeded once through a great revolution. The guardians of the *status quo* only made something like this attractive to a young man by their stories about the Communist specter and by their panicky preservation of old forms and relations.

This was a desire for a better and happier life, for change, which is inborn in every creature, and which in certain concrete conditions could not take on any but the Communist form. Communism was a new idea. It offered youth enthusiasm, a desire for endeavor and sacrifice to achieve the happiness of the human race.

Ilija Markovic knew that I felt drawn to Communism and that I was in love with a girl toward whom he had more serious intentions than those of a high-school student. I could tell by the kind and considerate way he treated me. This would have been gratifying, for it showed his generosity, had it not struck me as being a contrived pity, which I had never asked from anyone.

I was beset by questions that shook all of my previous moral, emotional, and intellectual conceptions. Was it honest for an older man, moreover a sick man, to entice —even with intentions of marriage—a girl of sixteen or seventeen years? And his pupil at that! True, there had already been marriages between instructors and pupils in the school. But such things were not done by the bearers of such great ideas as Communism, which was supposed to bring not only justice and an end to misery, but a new morality among men.

And what was I to do, if that is how it was? Was I to love or to hate this man? Was I to hold him in contempt or to admire him as a contender for the same ideal? The posing of these and similar questions did not at all affect actual relationships, but had vast importance for my inner life and further development. On the answer depended the growth of my inner moral personality. Of course, I answered straight away: There is no real reason to hate him; this would be selfish and unmanly on my part. Yet from this answer to a corresponding reality within myself there was a very long and painful path full of mental twists and turns and visions that could only excite moral repugnance and even jealousy. Feeling that I hated this man, I suppressed the hate.

I succeeded even in liking him, though without warmth, even more than was required by our tie, either personal or ideological. Through this I got over my love. That inner metamorphosis, which ended in my stifling within myself both jealousy and love, quickened my vague progress toward Communism and conscious turning to literature.

It was as though my adherence to Communism, too, depended on my success in mastering myself in this personal morality play. This was my first great sacrifice, in the name of nobility, even a pretended one.

My last year in high school was full of painful and complex inner conflicts. This was followed, finally, by a certain clarity, at least in the form of the question to write or to fight. Even then, future lines and tendencies made their appearance and left their mark in the midst of troubled psychological conflicts, social discontent, and an overtaxing nostalgia. From this moral and emotional crisis I emerged strengthened, with some bitterness inside myself, but with an ethical principle—that one should not hate men for personal reasons, and that one should not mix personal needs and problems with one's ideology.

At the end of the school year, on St. Vitus's Day, the majority of my schoolmates appeared with canes and ties. These were considered the signs of maturity of the graduating students. It all seemed to me too common and formalistic. I also put on a tie, but a different kind—a red one. I thought about it a long time before I did it, for a tie of that color was the badge of a Communist, and none dared to wear it. If I am a Communist, I thought, and I am, then I must be publicly true to that conviction. There was childish bravado in this, but also defiance at a time and in a place where no one was defiant.

There existed—and perhaps still exists—a picture of myself just after graduation, in a Russian-style peasant shirt and a sash, with my arm hanging over the back of a chair. I had recalled even before sitting in front of the camera, that Tolstoy held his arm in the same way in a certain picture and that he, too, wore a peasant shirt. I was consciously imitating him. The shirt—its cut and everything—was designed by me in imitation of Tolstoy, of the Russians. Later it caught my fancy, both for its originality and practicality, and I wore it as a university student. Despite such imitations of every kind, which I carried to an extreme, there was then, and after, and in these very imitations, a dark inner turbulence, a profound dissatisfaction with the existing state of affairs and with the limitations they placed on human and social potentialities. A vague inner spiritual and intellectual torment beset me even then and would not let me go.

Marković came up to me after the diplomas were presented, obviously as man to man because of Dusanka, and as comrade to comrade because of Communism. He walked with me from the school to town, telling me, sagely and gently, how in Belgrade, at the university, everything would be nicer and better: many new friends, a life of greater ease, a more progressive and developed environment. But there was no need either to console or to encourage me. I had already made my peace with many things —with sentimental love and with helping the world through charity. Things and human relations presented themselves in ever harder and harsher forms. It was still a land without justice.

I spent the summer in Bijelo Polje, where my family had already resettled. Bijelo Polje was similar to Berane in many ways, except that the Moslem population in and around it was more numerous. Its way of life was still patriarchal, its houses poorer, and the uncleanliness even greater. There was not even a dirt road to connect it with any other town except Plevlje. Here was a remote region, rich in fruit that rotted away unused, godless, filled with the halt and the blind. The rebellious and overweening Vasojević tribe had poured into the Lim plain and had taken over both it and the little town of Berane. Here, however, the Montenegrins were interlopers who had forced their way into a town that was not theirs. The former Turkish landlords of Berane were hardly noticed, but here their adversity filled every little corner of life—their songs and stories, evening gatherings under the old pear trees, and the desperate nightly carousing.

But this did not concern me then. I was preparing myself for a new world, with my eyes already opened to comprehend it and with a troubled soul, fearful of becoming lost in it....

CHAPTER 75

Causes of the Autonomist Movement in Slovakia

Nationalism can hardly be answered with any sort of genteel argument, but here a Slovak tries to explain and destroy the Slovak autonomists. The ancient heritage of the Slovaks and their thousand year union with Hungary are stressed. Of course, Derer's arguments are somewhat sophistic and illustrate the harsh difficulties of East European nationalism.

Ivan Derer, THE UNITY OF THE CZECHS AND THE SLOVAKS— HAS THE PITTSBURGH DECLARATION BEEN CARRIED OUT? (Prague: "Orbis" Publishing Co., 1938), pp. 74–78.

The conception of Czechoslovak national unity upheld by the so-called centralist Slovaks is based on the view that only the closet possible intellectual, cultural and political unity between Czechs and Slovaks can ensure full development for Czech and especially Slovak life. Czechoslovak national unity means that the Slovaks can feel themselves to be the State nation everywhere throughout the whole country, not merely in Slovakia, but also in the Czech territories, that the Slovak language can find full and free application not only in the restricted limits of its own home but also in all the other parts of the Republic. In other words, the Czechoslovak conception gives the Slovaks an all-State, more universal consciousness. This conception makes us a 10-million strong nation and not a mere 2-million fraction.

How is it possible that there should be Slovaks who do not understand this conception, and accept a different conception—the autonomistic conception? Why is it that in place of seeing to it that the Slovak language and the Slovak element should take a full and expanding part in the all-State affairs, they prefer to content themselves with the modester position offered by autonomy.

On this occasion I cannot go into all the causes of this phenomenon. One of the causes is *Hungarianism,* a Hungarian mentality. For nearly a thousand years the Slovaks were part and parcel of the Hungarian State. In the sixteenth and seventeenth centuries when the Magyars fell under the Turkish yoke, Hungary consisted really only of Slovakia and one or two smaller territories. The Slovaks in those days had no importance whatsoever. They lived in economic, social and political subjugation. Hungary was represented in the economic, social and political spheres by the free classes, the gentry, the nobles, the priesthood and the townspeople. When serfdom was abolished in 1848, these ruling classes attempted to dominate the liberated masses by means of Magyarisation. It was only this Hungarianism that separated the Slovaks from the Bohemians and Moravians. The Hungarian State therefore directed its energies not merely towards maintaining a Hungarian spirit in the ruling and upper classes but systematically inculcating such a spirit in the broad masses of the Slovak people. The autonomist efforts, directed as they are towards an artificial separation of the Slovaks from the Czechs, are in substance relics of the thousand-year-old Hungarianism. This Hungarianism, despite the tremendous harm it did the Slovaks, never succeeded in breaking up the national unity of the Czechs and Slovaks. It produced, however, in the numbers of Slovaks, the desire to see Slovakia separated at least to a certain extent from the Czech lands. This gave rise to the demands for autonomy. The autonomy movement is a relic of the thousand-year-old Hungarianism.

As I have already indicated *Hungarianism meant the dominance of the ruling classes and the subjugation of the masses*. In the days when Hungarianism manifested itself in the process of Magyarisation this meant the predominance of not only the nobility and gentry but also of the townspeople, the bulk of the priesthood and the intelligentsia who had been Magyarised in the schools, over the Slovak masses, totally neglected spiritually and mentally as they were and living a wretched existence. This process of Magyarisation, of implanting a Hungarian mentality in the Slovaks, was so intense throughout many centuries in former Hungary, and so completely dominated generation after generation, that *even the breaking up of Hungary and the liberation of Slovakia has not entirely freed the Slovaks from the moral consequences of the thousand years of subjugation and serfdom.*

These conditions are finely described by the Slovak authoress Timrava in her novel entitled "Two Ages". She there portrays the life of a Slovak village before the War. She draws a plastic picture of the moral and mental degradation of the Slovak masses who allow themselves to be the object of every possible provocation on the part of the denationalised intelligentsia, for the thousand-year yoke has blunted them so that they are no longer conscious of human and national dignity. Indeed they have sunk so low that they laud their own murderers and abuse these who make a stand against tyranny. The authoress has found the right expression for that aspect of Slovak life when she exclaims with a pained cry: "Slaves!"

The authoress goes on to describe this same village at another epoch, after the War, after the triumph of the Slovak cause and the Slovak language, after the attainment of all that the best men of the nation had formerly dreamed of in vain. She describes how the masses were helped not merely by the inculcation of self-respect and self-consciousness, by the making of their language the official language and the making of their interests the interests of the State, but also by a cultural, economic and social uplift. With admirable cogency she depicts the characters who have only by pretence or superficially changed their former attitude of enemies to the people, who exploit the slightest possible mistake or shortcoming on the part of the new regime for indulging in ironical, spiteful and trouble-stirring criticism. And the masses, in whose interest the great change has taken place, succumb to these seducers and abuse their own freedom. The one-time apathetic spirit who used to take the greatest oppression as quite a natural thing today passionately criticises and exaggerates the most insignificant faults; he is satisfied with nothing, and all is too little for him. Again the authoress relieves her feelings with the cry of "Slaves!"

Yes, many of the former Slaves are only nominally free, for the servile spirit is still within them. The autonomist movement is the expression of this survival of servile spirit. The child which awakes out of a long and sound sleep rubs its eyes and does not yet realise that it is no longer asleep, it would like to roll over for another sleep and is angry when its parent rouses it up to greet the bright and happy yet work-filled day. Such is still the state of many Slovaks. That is the very substance of the autonomist and separatist movement. It is a passing condition. I have already pointed out from the results of the elections that the greater part of Slovakia has already arisen from its sleep to the fulness of Czechoslovak life. But there is a minority of the Slovaks who would continue their barren autonomist dreaming. Yet this relic of a thousand-year-old servitude will also disappear. Things proceed slowly of course in the life of nations, and so we shall have to do with the autonomy movement for some considerable time yet to come.

The process must be solved by us Slovaks ourselves. It is our affair. We shall also solve it. I have not the slightest doubt that the Czechoslovak idea will triumph.

CHAPTER 76

Munich Agreement

The capitulation of Britain and France at Munich became the classic example of appeasement. For many years, German propaganda had held that the Germans of the Sudetenland were being unfairly treated by the Czech government. At the same time, the material successes of Hitler's government encouraged the nationalism of the Sudeten Germans. Prime Minister Chamberlain along with many others regarded the possibility of war over the Sudeten problem as inadmissible. But while the Munich Agreement could have been defended on tenuous grounds, Czechoslovakia was virtually destroyed as an independent state. On March 14, 1939, German troops began to occupy the rest of Czechoslovakia; a separate Slovak state, allied to Germany, had already been set up, and both Hungary and Poland took slices of territory in the eastern part of Czechoslovakia.

FURTHER DOCUMENTS RESPECTING CZECHOSLOAVKIA, Presented by the Secretary of State for Foreign Affairs to Pol. Misc #8 (London: His Majesty's Stationery Office, 1938), pp. 3–4.

Agreement Concluded at Munich on September 29, 1938

Germany, the United Kingdom, France and Italy, taking into consideration the agreement, which has been already reached in principle for the cession to Germany of the Sudeten German territory, have agreed on the following terms and conditions governing the said cession and the measures consequent thereon, and by this agreement they each hold themselves responsible for the steps necessary to secure its fulfilment:—

1. The evacuation will begin on the 1st October.

2. The United Kingdom, France and Italy agree that the evacuation of the territory shall be completed by the 10th October, without any existing installations having been destroyed and that the Czechoslovak Government will be held responsible for carrying out the evacuation without damage to the said installations.

3. The conditions governing the evacuation will be laid down in detail by an international commission composed of representatives of Germany, the United Kingdom, France, Italy and Czechoslovakia.

4. The occupation by stages of the predominantly German territory by German troops will begin on the 1st October. The four territories marked on the attached map will be occupied by German troops in the following order: the territory marked No. I on the 1st and 2nd of October, the territory marked No. II on the 2nd and 3rd of October, the territory marked No. III on the 3rd, 4th and 5th of October, the territory marked No. IV on the 6th and 7th of October. The remaining territory of preponderantly German character will be ascertained by the aforesaid international commission forthwith and be occupied by German troops by the 10th of October.

5. The international commission referred to in paragraph will determine the territories in which a plebiscite is to be held. These territories will be occupied by international bodies until the plebiscite has been completed. The same commission will fix the conditions in which the plebiscite is to be held, taking as a basis the conditions of the Saar plebiscite. The commission will also fix a date, not later than the end of November, on which the plebiscite will be held.

6. The final determination of the frontiers will be carried out by the international commission. This commission will also be entitled to recommend to the four Powers, Germany, the United Kingdom, France and Italy, in certain exceptional cases minor modifications in the strictly ethnographical determination of the zones which are to be transferred without plebiscite.

7. There will be a right of option into and out of the transferred territories, the option to be exercised within six months from the date of this agreement. A German-

Czechoslovak commission shall determine the details of the option, consider ways of facilitating the transfer of population and settle questions of principle arising out of the said transfer.

8. The Czechoslovak Government will within a period of four weeks from the date of this agreement release from their military and police forces any Sudeten Germans who may wish to be released, and the Czechoslovak Government will within the same period release Sudeten German prisoners who are serving terms of imprisonment for political offences.

> ADOLF HITLER.
> NEVILLE CHAMBERLAIN.
> EDOUARD DALADIER.
> BENITO MUSSOLINI.

Munich,
September 29, 1938.

CHAPTER 77

The Nazi-Soviet Alliance of 1939

As a prelude to its attack on Poland, the Hitler Government arranged this treaty with Soviet Russia. Stalin acted out of realistic motives bent on gaining Baltic and Polish land while postponing confrontation with Nazi Germany. The alliance of the two inveterate foes proved to be a difficult pill for non-Russian Communists to accept.

Paul R. Sweet, Margaret Lambert, Maurice Baumont, et al. (editors), DOCUMENTS ON GERMAN FOREIGN POLICY, 1918–1945, (Series D, 1937–1945), Vol. VII, THE LAST DAY OF PEACE, AUGUST 9—SEPTEMBER 3, 1939 (Washington Government Printing Office, 1956), pp. 245–247.

Treaty of Non-Aggression between Germany and the Union
of Soviet Socialist Republics and the Secret Additional
Protocol

The Government of the German Reich and the Government of the Union of Soviet Socialist Republics, desirous
of strengthening the cause of peace between Germany and
the U.S.S.R., and proceeding from the fundamental provisions of the Treaty of Neutrality, which was concluded
between Germany and the U.S.S.R. in April 1926, have
reached the following agreement:

Article I

The two Contracting Parties undertake to refrain from
any act of violence, any aggressive action and any attack
on each other either severally or jointly with other Powers.

Article II

Should one of the Contracting Parties become the object
of belligerent action by a third Power, the other Contracting Party shall in no manner lend its support to this third
Power.

Article III

The Governments of the two Contracting Parties will
in future maintain continual contact with one another for
the purpose of consultation in order to exchange information on problems affecting their common interests.

Article IV

Neither of the two Contracting Parties will join any
grouping of Powers whatsoever which is aimed directly
or indirectly at the other Party.

Article V

Should disputes or conflicts arise between the Contracting Parties over questions of one kind or another, both
Parties will settle these disputes or conflicts exclusively

by means of a friendly exchange of views or if necessary by the appointment of arbitration commissions.

Article VI

The present Treaty shall be concluded for a period of ten years with the proviso that, in so far as one of the Contracting Parties does not denounce it one year before the expiry of this period, the validity of this Treaty shall be deemed to be automatically prolonged for another five years.

Article VII

The present treaty shall be ratified within the shortest possible time. The instruments of ratification will be exchanged in Berlin. The treaty shall enter into force immediately upon signature.

Done in duplicate in the German and Russian languages.

Moscow, August 23, 1939.

> For the Government of the German Reich:
> V. RIBBENTROP
>> With full power of the Government of the U.S.S.R.:
>> V. MOLOTOV

Secret Additional Protocol

On the occasion of the signature of the Non-Aggression Treaty between the German Reich and the Union of Soviet Socialist Republics, the undersigned plenipotentiaries of the two Parties discussed in strictly confidential conversations the question of the delimitation of their respective spheres of interest in Eastern Europe. These conversions led to the following result:

1. In the event of a territorial and political transformation in the territories belonging to the Baltic States (Fin-

land, Estonia, Latvia, Lithuania), the northern frontier of Lithuania shall represent the frontier of the spheres of of interest both of Germany and the U.S.S.R. In this connection the interest of Lithuania in the Vilna territory is recognized by both Parties.

2. In the event of a territorial and political transformation of the territories belonging to the Polish State, the spheres of interest of both Germany and the U.S.S.R. shall be bounded approximately by the line of the rivers Narev, Vistula, and San.

The question whether the interests of both Parties make the maintenance of an independent Polish State appear desirable and how the frontiers of this State should be drawn can be definitely determined only in the course of further political developments.

In any case both Governments will resolve this question by means of a friendly understanding.

3. With regard to South-Eastern Europe, the Soviet side emphasizes its interest in Bessarabia. The German side declares complete political *désintéressement* in these territories.

4. This Protocol will be treated by both parties as strictly secret.

MOSCOW, August 23, 1939.

> For the Government of the German Reich:
> v. RIBBENTROP
> With full power of the Government of the U.S.S.R.:
> V. MOLOTOV

CHAPTER 78

Persecution of Czech Cultural Life after March 15, 1939

This report illustrates how the Nazis tried to thoroughly oppress the Czechs. The cultural oppression was soon followed by the creation of the extermination camps that swallowed up not only the Jews but anyone designated by the capricious condemnations handed out by German authorities.

Czechoslovak National Committee, CULTURAL OPPRESSION IN CZECHOSLOVAKIA (London: George Allen and Unwin, Ltd., 1940), pp. 8–12. Reprinted by permission of George Allen and Unwin, Ltd.

The German entry into Prague on March 15th, 1939, allowed Germany, fortified as she was by all the means of repression, spying and torture, to proceed towards the realisation of the plans of domination of which we have spoken. Apart from complete political enslavement and unexampled economic spoliation, Germany inaugurated a policy of unmerciful spiritual suffocation of the Czechoslovak nation. The territory taken under German "protection" which, even according to the German census, contained 94.78 per cent of Czech population and only 3.66 per cent of German population was, it was said, to receive German colonists brought from the South Tyrol, the U.S.-S.R. and the Baltic countries. One part of the Czechoslovak population was to be literally exterminated or scattered in various different parts of the Reich, while the other part was to remain as a mass of labourers deprived of all political willpower and of all intellectual curiosity. The author of the remarkable articles which appeared in *The Times* in November 1939, under the title "Martyred Czechs," reports that one of the Sudeten German chiefs had informed him that the aim of Nazi policy in Bohemia

was to "smash the brains out of the Czechs," to destroy
the intellectual strata which had "disturbed the desirable
relationship which used to exist between German employer
and Czech employee." "The Czechs had a young educated
class that is much too numerous. We must prevent a too
large number of their young people from studying at Universities, and see that they practise commerce and trades
to a greater extent," wrote the *Völkischer Beobachter*, the
chief organ of the National Socialist Party. It is in this
fashion that the German régime treats a people which has
the smallest percentage of illiterates of any nation
in Europe, which has built up a magnificent network of
cultural organisations, which possesses a public library in
every commune, large or small, and a country in which
the finest buildings of every town and village are the school
buildings. "The Czech people has nothing to do but to work
and produce children," Protector von Neurath's official
newspaper, *Der Neue Tag*, declared a few weeks after the
invasion. And it is this motto that directs the entire attitude
of the German régime to the Czechoslovak people and which
explains the atrocities committed especially against the University students and the representatives of Czechoslovak
intellectual life.

The *furor teutonicus* has been raging ever since the very
inception of the German régime against all branches of
Czechoslovak culture. The works of artists long dead have
been submitted to a censorship no less severe than those
of living authors. Everything that in the literature, music
and plastic arts of the past hundred years was inspired
by the will of the reawakened nation to live its own independent life—and all the great works of art were imbued
with this ideal—was forbidden. The Germans went so far
as to have removed from the répertoire of the National
Opera House certain works of Smetana in which the nation
sees the musical incarnation of its inmost soul, and from
the répertoire of instrumental concerts Dvorak's Slavonic
Dances—doubly suspect, because of their title and their
enchanting rhythm. In certain villages the German authorities forbade the singing of Czech popular songs and of
the national anthem "Kde domov muj?" (Where is my
home?). The works of the greatest poets and novelists had

to undergo an examination by the experts of the Gestapo in order to ascertain whether they did not contain anything dangerous for the security of the Reich. The foreign authors —French, English, Russian and German—read in Bohemia-Moravia before Hitler's arrival were eliminated even more rigorously than in Germany itself. Representative works of the Czech drama as well as those of French and British authors have had to disappear from the répertoire of the National Theatre; the gap thus created has been filled by insipid works in which even the Nazi censorship has found nothing to complain of. In many towns the tasks of policing the Czech theatres has been given over to the German authorities. The film censorship has been handed over to a German group dependent on the German administration. Numerous films which had already been authorized by the Czech censorship have been confiscated by the Gestapo authorities. In October 1939 the number of Czech films forbidden reached 240—practically the entire output of the Czech talking-film industry. Disguised agents of the Gestapo attend all cinema performances and arrest on the spot any persons who dare to demonstrate, however timidly, against the régime. The film studios at Barrandov where so many French films were made, have been confiscated and handed over to an agent of the Gestapo, Freiherr von Gregory, whose task it is to superintend Czech film production.

When Germany had suppressed all the Czech political parties and reduced to silence all the organisations of a national character she was mistaken in hoping that this veritable assassination of Czechoslovak culture would take place almost without a murmur of protest. This was not the case at all. The National Solidarity organisation which had been created with the permission of the German régime as an *Ersatz* for the suppressed political parties found the necessary courage to protest in May 1939—without result—against the prohibition of the sale of the works of the nationalist poet, Viktor Dyk, of the organisation of a concert which was to include a performance of the cantata "Prayer to St. Wenceslas not to forget his Czech people," against the "purging" of school libraries, etc. The National Solidarity organisation recalled to the Protector Hilter's solemn promise that the Reich would guarantee the Czechs their intellectual autonomy and the free development of their culture. This promise was worth no more, in the Führer's mind, than all the other promises he had given and not kept. The real ideas of Hitler and his party were expressed at that time by a certain Herr Holler, the representative of the Nazi Party at a meeting of the district propaganda chiefs (*Gaupropagandaleiter*). In the presence of all the official German personages at Prague he declared that the Czechs must become accustomed to the idea that they were living at the very heart of German civilisation. Prague must become the centre of German intellectual expansion towards the South and East. When inaugurating the "Exhibition of the German Book" at Prague in November 1939, Herr Giessagen, who was delegated by the Protector to represent him at this ceremony, again claimed Prague for German culture: "Prague is a great German book whose pages bear witness to German creation and German passion, to German struggles and victories." At the same exhibition the Czech books on the history of the art or the literature of Bohemia were completely excluded. Where the organisers of the exhibition were compelled to use a foreign language they chose Latin.

At the same time the plundering of Czechoslovak treasures of science and art began. Hitler's nocturnal visit to the Royal Castle of Prague was followed by the dispatch to Berlin of ten precious tapestries which adorned the rooms of the Castle. From the museums of Prague, especially from the Czechoslovak National Museum and from that of the National Revolution all the documents have disappeared which might inconvenience the new masters. The Czech University of Prague was deprived of all the documents which proved its direct descent from the University founded at Prague by King Charles IV in the fourteenth century. All these documents attesting the nobility and ancient character of Czechoslovak learning were transferred to the German University of Prague. The Czech professors and students were forbidden to use the venerable precincts of the Carolinum which recall to the Czechoslovak nation certain moving episodes of its history—such as the period when Jan Hus was Rector of the University. The celebrated Theatre of the Estates, founded by the Bohemian nobility at the end of the eighteenth century and dear to the Czechoslovak nation as the cradle of dramatic art in the country, has been taken away from the Czechs and declared a German theatre. As the small German minority in Prague—5 per cent of the population—already possessed two theatres of which one was subsidised by the State, it now has three, while the 95 per cent of Czech population in Prague have only two theatres at their disposal. In certain large Czech provincial towns—at Ceske Budejovice, Olomouc, Moravska Ostrava—the running of the theatres has been made impossible because of the total or partial occupation of the theatre buildings. At Brno, capital of Moravia, the Czech provincial theatre was simply taken over by the Germans who permit four Czech performances each month for the Czechs who number 85 per cent of the population of the town. In many towns the "Masaryk Houses"—which for the most part contain libraries, halls for the showing of educational films, for the performance of plays and concerts, etc.—have been confiscated and transformed into barracks or offices for the Gestapo. The monuments they contained, sometimes of great artistic worth, were defiled and broken, and in most cases completely demolished—especially those of Masaryk or those recalling the exploits of the Czechoslovak volunteers during the Great War....

CHAPTER 79

Polish Resistance after Nazi Conquest

This Manifesto of Freedom circulated throughout Poland in November of 1939, following the defeat at German and Russian hands. The document was highly critical of the pre-war regime and blamed the defeat on that government as much as on German expansionism. The pleas for resistance were of a socialist and democratic character, and the condemnation of anti-Semitism quite explicit.

Manfred Kridl, Wladyslaw Malinowski, and Józef Wittlin,
FOR YOUR FREEDOM AND OURS (New York, 1943), pp. 330–
333. Reprinted by permission of Frederick Ungar Publishing Co., Inc.

At the years of independent political existence, Poland has fallen victim to the imperialism and unprecedented aggression of Nazi Germany.

At the moment of greatest strain, the fate of Poland was disastrously burdened with errors in foreign policy, infiltrations of reactionary ideologies, with the existing government itself, with its negligence in the economic and social fields and its policy of oppression of national minorities. During the first twenty years of her independence, Poland failed to fulfill her obligations to the masses of working people, who were not permitted to exercise any influence on the fate of the country.

The chief aim of the régime in power had been to perpetuate itself and to oppose any expression of the independent aspirations of the masses of the people. The regime had betrayed the tradition of the struggle for independence and had accepted a reactionary fascist ideology. The standard slogan of Hitlerism—anti-Semitism—became the bridge between the régime in power and the nationalist fascist groups....The territory of the Republic has been occupied by foreign armies bringing violence and injustice. As long as the struggle continues, however, Poland has not lost her independence.

Europe has been thrown into the abyss of war, the first act of which was the sacrifice of Poland's blood. Nazi Germany has imposed this war upon the world in the name of her imperialistic aspirations, which conflict with the imperial interests of England and France. Besides its imperialist character, this war has, however, still another aspect: it is a war between Hitlerism and democracy, between totalitarianism, barbarism, cultural and moral savagery and the ideas of Freedom and Justice. Such is the meaning of the present war, as understood by the masses of the working people of oppressed Poland as well as those of England and France.

Hitlerism must be defeated in this war; however, the victory of the allies should not induct the hegemony of one group of nations over others. From the chaos, there must rise a new Europe organized on the principles of political freedom and social justice. Such a Europe is the desire of millions of workers, peasants, and intellectuals, as well as of the soldiers who fight on all fronts.

Poland, in spite of military defeat, continues to fight. On Polish soil the people carry on a daily heroic struggle against the occupation, preparing themselves for the moment when the final battle will take place. In the West the Polish army fights in cooperation with the armies of France and England.

In order that the sacrifice of blood so freely given through so many years shall not again be in vain, we formulate our aims as follows:

1. The chief aim of the struggle of the Polish working masses is the reconstruction of the full political freedom and independence of Poland, and the establishment of her existence on the principles of democracy and social justice.

2. In the New Poland the decisive influence of the masses of the people on the future of the country, the influence of the peasants, the workers, and the intellectuals must be secured. The political constitution and the social and economic structure of Poland must once and for all preclude the possibility of the existence of privileged social groups which strive to seize power and economic supremacy.

3. The political constitution of Poland must be based on the principles of political democracy guaranteed by: a democratic representation of the people elected on the basis of equal, secret, universal, direct and proportional suffrage; responsibility of the government before Parliament; independence of the Courts of Justice; extensive democratic self-government; freedom of speech, of the press, of assembly, and of association; and personal immunity of the citizens.

Under these conditions the political and social aspirations of the working masses will find their expression in the emergence of a workers' and peasants' government, endowed with the confidence of the people and representing the interest of all working men.

4. The influence of big capitalist and landlord groups on the fate of Poland must be removed through the abolition of large landed estates by means of a thorough and immediate agrarian reform, through socialization or through the subjection to strict social control of the credit system and of large scale industrial establishments, and through the abolition of monopolistic organizations such as cartels, syndicates, etc.; and through support of small-scale agriculture, of the cooperative movement, and the protection of small business men.

5. The military forces of Poland must be based on democratic organization which precludes any caste systems.

6. All nationalities living in Poland must be guaranteed full political, economic and cultural equality. Race doctrines and anti-Semitism must be eliminated from public life in Poland.

7. Universal and free education must be provided for all citizens, particularly for the children of peasants and workers.

8. The freedom of science and of religion must be guaranteed.

9. All citizens of the New Poland must be guaranteed the right to work, the protection of labor and health. It is necessary to expand social insurance on the basis of democratic self-government.

10. The foreign policy of Poland must be based on full cooperation and mutual understanding with all free peoples of the world, and particularly with the nations with which Poland must live in good neighbourly relations.

The struggle for such a Poland is a struggle for Freedom, Justice, and Peace. In this struggle the masses of the working people are not isolated. It coincides with the struggle of the masses of the working people in the whole world against totalitarianism which brings slavery and destruction to the people of Europe. Fighting for the Freedom of Poland, we fight for the fate of all oppressed nations. We fight under the noble slogan: "For Your Freedom and Ours!"....

November 7, 1939

"FREEDOM"
Executive Committee

CHAPTER 80

The Suicide of Teleki

In February of 1939, Pál Teleki became prime minister of Hungary, succeeding the neo-fascist, Gyula Gömbös. Teleki made some overtures to the Axis powers. And he won a major victory with the Vienna Award of August 30, 1940. Hungary's claims on Transylvania were partially satisfied by the absorption of more than 16,000 square miles of territory with a population of 2,557,260.

With his many successes, Teleki also arranged for a treaty with a perennial foe, Yugoslavia. On December 12, 1940, a "Pact of Eternal Friendship" was signed. In March of 1941, Hitler decided to attack Yugoslavia. Teleki became despondent because it was impossible for him to stop the transit of German troops through Hungary. At the same time, since Germany would gain so much, it was decided that Hungary should try to retrieve from Yugoslavia the Voivodina, prized because it had a large Magyar population.

When Great Britain showed hostility to Teleki's arrangements, and it became obvious that Hungary would be classified as a belligerent, Teleki came to the end of his rope. On April 2, 1941, he committed suicide. Others carried through the planned attack, and the Regent, Miklós Horthy, was left the task of explaining Teleki's suicide.

Miklós Szinai and Laszlo Szucs (editors), THE CONFIDENTIAL PAPERS OF ADMIRAL HORTHY (Budapest, 1965), pp. 175–179. Reprinted by permission of the Corvina Press.

April 3rd, 1941

Farewell Letter of Prime Minister Pál Teleky to Miklós

Horthy Before His Suicide

Your Highness,

We have become faithless—out of cowardice—to the Pact of Everlasting Friendship based on the address of Mohacs. The nation is feeling it, and we have thrown away the nation's honour.

We have taken stand by the side of backguards—for there is not a word true of the trumped-up atrocities! Neither against Hungarians, nor against Germans! We shall become robbers of corpses! the basest of nations.

I have not detained you.

I am guilty

Pál Teleki

April 3rd, 1941

Letter of Prime Minister Pál Teleki to Miklós Horthy Tendering His Resignation

Your Highness,

I am tendering my resignation herewith for the event I should fail to succeed completely and should I be still living.

With profound respect,
Pál Teleki

April 3rd, 1941

Letter of Prime Minister Pál Teleki to Miklos Horthy Tendering Suicide

Your Excellency,

I have the honour to inform Your Excellency of the repercussions on Hungarian politics and the situation in Hungary of the outcome of the change that had taken place in the Yugoslav government on March 27th.

At 9:30 a.m. on March 27th, Chancellor Hitler asked for my minister in Berlin in order to communicate to him that in consequence of the events in Yugoslavia perhaps the moment had arrived in which Hungary might make good her claims for a revision of the frontier to Yugoslavia and in the way it suited the Germans we might raise the Yugoslav problem.

Minister Sztójoy flew to Budapest on the same day, and rendered account to me of this communication made by the Chancellor of the Reich.

To the message directed to me by the Chancellor of the

Reich I replied by a letter dated March 28th, a copy and translation of which I am enclosing. In this letter I expressed my gratitude for the message and, emphasizing that we had maintained our territorial claims in every respect, I referred to the rapprochement to Yugoslavia at the suggestion of the Chancellor of the Reich, which rapprochement had come to expression in the form of a Pact of Friendship, yet I had once again drawn the attention of the Chancellor not to lose sight of the danger which threatened us on the part of the Russians and Rumanians.

After this letter had been posted, a German general came to Budapest with the purpose to discuss with the Hungarian general staff the details of a direct Hungarian intervention in Yugoslavia. In the cabinet council held in my presence on April 1st we discussed the extremely difficult moral situation of Hungary in particular, which presented itself in consequence of the Pact of Everlasting Friendship which had come into force only little before, further the circumstances of a possible Hungarian intervention, when particular attention was given to the great difficulties caused by the adverse weather conditions in the foodstuff situation, and their effects in the event of a mobilization of the army. In this cabinet council no decision had been taken, yet the necessity presented itself of taking up the details of such an intervention on the part of Hungary with the Germans.

A day after this cabinet council Prime Minister Count Teleki, who esteemed and honoured Your Excellency so greatly, took his own life. The tragic death of Count Teleki, for which only an extreme crisis of conscience could account, has moved me as well as the entire Hungarian nation. Count Teleki in a letter addressed to me before his suicide mentioned the circumstances that in consequence of the Pact of Friendship signed with Yugoslavia seemed to burden his conscience.

Your Excellency who is so well acquainted with the Hungarian mentality will appreciate that Count Teleki's suicide is an expression of this conflict of conscience which had not only been the cause of his death, but which together with him is felt by the entire nation. With these reflections and with a deep sense of responsibility which in these grave times rests on me and each member of my government, I have addressed to Chancellor of the Reich Hitler the letter a copy and translation of which I am enclosing. I request Your Excellency to show to my country and me the same benevolence in these difficult times as Your Excellency deigned to harbour before.

Pray accept, Your Excellency, the assurance of my sincere esteem.

CHAPTER 81

Hitler Honors General Antonescu

Hitler always showed great favor to his Roumanian puppet, General Antonescu. The oil fields of Ploesti were a grave concern to the Nazi leader, and Antonescu kept sufficient order in Roumania that Hitler allowed him a free hand even when it was a question of suppressing the fascist Iron Guardists. As the Russian compaign developed, Hitler was solicitous for the southern front lest a Russian counter-offensive imperil German control of Roumanian oil. Antonescu's successful use of his Roumanian troops on the Russian front thus elicited the warm congratulations of Hitler.

Howard Smyth, Margaret Lambert, Maurice Baumont, et al. (editors), DOCUMENTS ON GERMAN FOREIGN POLICY, 1918–1945 (Series D, 1937–1945), Vol. XIII, THE WAR YEARS JUNE 23—DECEMBER 11, 1941 (Washington: Government Printing Office, 1964), pp. 296–299.

Record of the Bestowal of the Knight's Cross on General Antonescu by the Führer in the School At Berdichev (Ukraine) on August 7, 1941.

The Führer personally presented the Knight's Cross to General Antonescu in the presence of Field Marshals Keitel and von Rundstedt, General Jodl and their immediate staff. Antonescu was accompanied by his Chief of Staff and an aide.

Before presentation of the decoration the Führer stated that when he decided a year ago to give a guarantee of the inviolability of the Rumanian frontiers he had been aware that this measure as well as others which followed later would cause Russia sooner or later to become the implacable enemy of Germany. In the further course of the developments Russia had made more and more attempts at blackmail, so that he (the Führer) had to make up his mind to act quickly in order to anticipate the enemy who, as one now knew, was unbelievably well armed. In this connection he (the Führer) had asked himself what attitude Rumania would be likely to adopt. The fact that that country was today fighting on the German side, after having overcome its own internal crisis within a short time, was exclusively due to General Antonescu, whose courage, determination, devotion, and will to work represented values which were not measurable, to be sure, but which had had an extraordinary influence on the course of things. From the very beginning Antonescu has possessed the Führer's personal trust.

Since the weapons had begun to speak the General had shown courage and the qualities of a leader. Without hesitation he had immediately placed himself at the side of Germany, and it turned out that in the short time he had been governing Roumania he had accomplished astonishing things. In these circumstances it had given the Führer pleasure and deep satisfaction to know that German units, too, were under the command of General Antonescu.

The liberation of Bessarabia represented Antonescu's first success, and he (the Führer) wanted to use this occasion to award General Antonescu the decoration with which the German nation rewarded the courage, heroism, and the qualities of leadership of its men.

General Antonescu thanked the Führer most sincerely for the accommodating attitude which he had always shown toward him. He gladly accepted the decoration on behalf of the Rumanian Army and the Rumanian people. In so doing he repeated the assurance which he had already given the Führer at this first meeting with him, namely, that Germany could count on the Rumanian people fully and entirely; for after all it had not been General Antonescu alone who had marched with Germany; the entire people had stood behind him. Germany could place her trust in the brave and honest Rumanian nation in the future, too. Rumania felt honored to be able to fight against the common foe side by side with Germany, and in this way to contribute her share toward the defense of civilization.

Thereupon the Führer presented General Antonescu with the Knight's Cross as well as the Iron Cross first and second class.

In a short conversation in the presence of Field Marshal Kietel and Colonel Schmundt, which followed the bestowal of the decoration, the Führer stated that the quick clarification of the relationship with Russia had been very important. At the beginning of June he had gained the conviction that every further effort to reach such a clarification had merely been treated in a temporizing manner by the Russians, so that the unavoidable conflict could only have been postponed for 1 or 2 months at the most. Thereby the conflict would have happened at a time that was highly unfavorable for Germany; for after the middle of August and the beginning of September it was difficult for reasons of climate to start a military operation against Russia.

After long deliberations and after a thorough examination of his own conscience he (the Führer) had reached the conviction that the fight was unavoidable. He thanked Rumania for having immediately recognized this situation for her part and for not having made any kind of difficulties.

The problems that had to be solved were the same ones as at the start of the Russian campaign, that is, first the destruction of the living strength of the foe and second the destruction or capture of the important industrial centers and raw material bases of Russia. As far as the first question, i.e., the destruction of the living strength of the foe, was concerned, the Russians themselves had answered it by doing what the Führer had always hoped, to be sure, but what was by no means certain. They had accepted battle near the frontier. Considering their own tremendous concentration probably nothing else had been left for them to do, as a retreat by the strongly concentrated masses of troops had no longer been possible. In this manner essentially the major part of the Army had suffered crushing defeat, and had been taken prisoner or dispersed. Only fragments of the Army had succeeded in establishing a new front. These, however, were already forces of lesser quality.

The results of the German advance could be seen in the numbers of prisoners and amount of booty: 900,000 prisoners, 10,000 planes, 13,000 tanks, 1,400 guns and very considerable amounts of other material had been captured. Because according to World War experience there were at least two casualties to one prisoner, and the Russians had this time fought with particular fanaticism, one could probably assume that 3 to 4 million Russian soldiers had been put out of action. The fact that the Russians had suffered heavy losses was also indicated by the combining of troop units. Thus the first objective could be considered to have been attained. As regards the second objective, namely, the capture or destruction of the industrial centers and raw material bases, he (the Führer) hoped that in the coming month it would be possible to occupy Leningrad with its industrial center, the ore regions in the southern Ukraine, the industrial area around Kharkov, and the industrial area of Moscow. He hoped to achieve these objectives by the beginning of the bad weather season.

The Führer termed the next major objective the attack on Leningrad, which was to begin day after tomorrow, the straightening of the bulges still existing in the front, and the mopping up of the troop units which were still surrounded in the pockets. Furthermore, an advance had to be made in the south toward the ore areas, and finally, as the last operation, Moscow had to be taken.

Even with still greater achievement than had actually been attained it would not have been possible to accelerate the advance because supplies would not have kept up. In these circumstances it was a triumph for Germany that she could put into operation again practically the entire

Russian railroad network in the portions of Russia occupied by her, in part with Russian rolling stock but partly also with German rolling stock after changing the gauge. However, supplies had to be assured in all circumstances, before the further advance could be begun, if one did not want to fall into the same error that another famous man had committed in his operation against Russia.

In the further course of the conversation the Führer then discussed with Antonescu a few strategic questions as to how to proceed in the Ukraine, especially with regard to the possibility of driving the Russian forces in the southern Ukraine into a pocket by having several tank divisions wheel around them.

Antonescu affirmed this possibility and explained with the aid of the map the plans which he had in regard to the army group placed under his command. He mentioned in this connection that in the area which he was now facing he would have cleared out all nests of resistence within 2 weeks; and stressed repeatedly that after the various pockets had been sealed off too many troops were assembled there, so that supply difficulties were to be feared. He suggested that above all the Italian divisions which were now being brought up be shifted farther to the north so that the concentration of troops might be prevented.

The Führer replied that the necessary orders for shifting Italians and also for the general directing of troops to the north had already been issued.

Antonescu stated further that in the south he wanted to occupy not only Odessa, but also Sevastopol and the Crimea, in order thus to seize the air bases of the Russians from which the Russian Air Force with its new bombers, which had a speed of 500 kilometers, was making heavy bombing attacks on Constanta.

With the aid of the map Antonescu also described his further plans concerning the advance in the Ukraine to the east and south by the troops under his command, without however providing precise data in this connection. He merely indicated with gestures of his hand the general direction of the advance planned by him.

After the conclusion of the conversation with the Führer, the latter had a conference with Field Marshal von Rundstedt, whereas Antonescu was informed in a room nearby of the further German intentions regarding Kiev, etc., by the responsible members of Field Marshal von Rundstedt's staff.

SCHMIDT
Minister

CHAPTER 82

Slovak Relations With the Hitler Government

This memorandum gives some idea of how Nazism and the war could create an extremely complex situation in so small a state as the new Slovakia. Adalbert Tuka, before the Slovak "declaration of independence" from the Prague government (March 14, 1939), had played a long and seemingly unsavory role. In 1921, even though he was more Magyar than Slovak, he began to play a significant role in the Hlinka Party, the promoter of Slovak exclusivism. After many intrigues, he was found gulty of espionage in 1929 and sentenced to fifteen years imprisonment. In 1939, Tuka, who had been amnestied in 1936, emerged as an extremist leader in the movement for Slovak separatism. Monsignor Joseph Tiso, President of the new independent state of Slovakia, also had a long record of Slovak extremism dating back to the Hlinka Party. But Tiso enjoyed a higher reputation, and as early as 1927, had been allowed to hold office in the Czechoslovakian government.

Karel Sidor, the Slovakian ambassador to the Vatican, who is mentioned slightingly in this memorandum, played a role in the crisis that preceded the "declaration of independence" on March 14, 1939. Aware of a conspiracy to break up Czechoslovakia, the Slovak ministers, led by Tiso, were dismissed from office on March 11 by the Prague government. For the next two days, Karel Sidor held office in the Slovaks' chief city, Bratislava. On March 13, Tiso, after having visited Hitler to obtain his blessing, returned to Bratislava and easily perpetrated the coup d'état. Sidor was sent to the Vatican, and obviously was a thorn in the side of the Tiso-Tuka clique. Sidor represented that large group of Slovaks who wanted national identity but not at the cost of subservience to Nazi Germany.

Smyth, Lambert, Baumont, et. al. (editors) DOCUMENTS ON GERMAN FOREIGN POLICY, 1918–1945 Vol. XIII, pp. 823–825.

Record of the Reception of the Slovak Minister President Tuka by the Foreign Minister in Berlin on November 25, 1941.

At first the Slovak Minister President presented the Foreign Minister with the highest Slovak decoration, together with a chain, and stated in an address that the Slovak Government actually gave this rank of decoration only to Heads of State. However, on consideration of the especially great services of the Foreign Minister it had felt impelled to make an exception and had awarded him this decoration. Furthermore, M. Tuka stated in his address that being a teacher of international law he had to note that the German policy in recent years had brought about a new epoch in international law, and was striving finally to establish a true legal order, whereas formerly a policy devoted to interests and exploitation had dominated the life of nations and had to be presented to their listeners as international law. The name of the Foreign Minister was inseparably connected with this new epoch of international law.

The Foreign Minister thanked M. Tuka warmly and in his reply pointed out that for every German the name of Tuka had become the very enbodiment of the sincere and militant Slovak element.

In the following discussion M. Tuka first pointed out that the Slovak people had immediately understood the meaning and the necessity of the National Socialist movement. To be sure, the intelligentsia still held back and was often uncertain, as he had been able to observe also among the student youth in the lectures which he was now giving once more. Thus it was asserted, for example, that National Socialism was not entirely Christian, and more of the like, a critical attitude that was naturally also promoted by church influences.

To the Foreign Minister's question whether M. Sidor was still at the Vatican as Slovak Minister, M. Tuka replied that he had to leave him there, in the first place in consideration of M. Tiso, and then also for the reason that he would be compelled to have him imprisoned at once if he brought him back to Slovakia.

The Foreign Minister then dealt with the participation of the Slovak troops in the struggle in the east, and emphasized how happy we were about the attitude which Slovakia displayed in this struggle. M. Tuka had been right when in his address in the morning he had termed the accession to the Anti-Comintern Pact as being of only formal significance for Slovakia. For the rest, the situation in the east was such that Soviet Russia was as good as finished today. To be sure, bad luck with the weather in recent weeks had prevented us from advancing more rapidly, but practically speaking we would have attained our objective in Soviet Russia by the end of this year. The Russians could not recover from these blows, and would be entirely finished off next year. In summary, one could therefore be only exceedingly satisfied with the balance sheet of this year. The battle in Africa now in progress, regarding which our latest reports were favorable, was in no way decisive for the outcome of the war. Once the Führer had time to occupy himself more intensively with Africa, a way would be found there, too, to master the situation in accordance with our wishes. In fact, the war had already been won, and today it was primarily a question of bringing it to a close with as few losses as possible.

With regard to a question by the Foreign Minister concerning Slovak-Hungarian relations, M. Tuka stated that the Hungarians were somewhat nervous and there was constant friction with them. The people in Slovakia were prejudiced against the Hungarians, and this fact could not simply be set aside with logical reasons.

The Foreign Minister replied to this that it was at any rate desirable that a settlement be reached if possible between Slovakia and Hungary. In any case there were always rumblings between Hungary and Rumania. We, of course, had an interest that these things not be stirred up during the present great struggle and that the awards that had been made be maintained. In Hungary, they were already asserting that the former Little Entente was already being revived. Germany, however, had an interest in stable conditions. After the war had been brought to a victorious conclusion, there would be such great tasks of reconstruction that at that time, too, no questions should be brought up that could interfere with reconstruction. Rather, one should let things be consolidated.

M. Tuka stated that he for his part would do everything to bring about a détente in the relationship with Hungary. Subsequently he spoke briefly of M. Durcansky, remarking that the latter wished to take over a top position as general manager of a Slovak farmers' bank, in which he wanted to participate purely financially. Since at the time he had promised the Foreign Minister to keep an eye on Durcansky, he wanted to ask whether the Foreign Minister had any objections to this.

The Foreign Minister replied that he had no objections if it was purely a matter of private business activities. However, Durcansky must not play again any kind of political note.

To a final question from the Foreign Minister regarding Tuka's relations with Tiso, M. Tuka replied that he and the State President simply lived in two different worlds, but avoided a conflict with one another and in any case did not want to fight it out now.

In conclusion the Foreign Minister asked M. Tuka to transmit to State President Tiso his best thanks for the decoration as well as his best regards.

CHAPTER 83

Cominform Resolution Condemning Titoism

Yugoslavian Communism's path to victory differed from that of other East European parties in that Soviet aid played a minimal role. Tito's partisans suffered many vicissitudes during World War II, but managed to attract many followers, thus supplanting the Chetniks, a group loyal to the Yugoslavian monarch, Peter II. While Tito's government adhered to the Stalinist line during the first years after World War II, still there were some signs of independence. And because Tito ruled the nation without Soviet troops, he did not have to rely on Stalin to prop up his regime. Mild disagreements in the post-war years assumed awesome proportions in 1948, and on June 28 of that year, the Yugoslavian Communist party was expelled from the Cominform. Undoubtedly, Stalin was intent on holding absolute control over the East European states, and decided that Yugoslavia must be isolated lest the independent spirit of Tito infect other Communist leaders. The expulsion caused Tito to take a more experimental road to socialism, and his reliance on Western aid also prompted revisionist tendencies inasmuch as Western economic experts gave advice that was sometimes followed.

The Cominform Resolution of November, 1949, is typical of the propaganda war that followed Tito's fall from Stalin's favor. In the following document, the accusations clearly underscored Stalin's position which inspired wide-spread purges in the other East European states. Of note is the fact that in 1966, Rankovic, heir apparent to Tito and head of the Yugoslav secret police, was also purged for overly-zealous activities.

WHITE BOOK ON AGGRESSIVE ACTIVITIES OF THE USSR, POLAND, CZECHOSLOVAKIA, HUNGARY, RUMANIA, BULGARIA, AND ALBANIA TOWARDS YUGOSLAVIA (Beograd:

Ministry of Foreign Affairs of the Federal People's Republic of Yugoslavia, 1951), pp. 174–178.

The Cominform Resolution, "The Communist Part of Yugoslavia in the Power of Murderers and Spies," Passed at the Cominform Session in the Second Half of November, 1949, in Hungary

The Information Bureau, consisting of representatives of the Communist Party of Bulgaria, Rumanian Workers' Party, Working People's Party of Hungary, United Workers' Party of Poland, Communist Party of the Soviet Union (Bolsheviks), Communist Party of France, and the Czechoslovak and Italian Communist Parties, having considered the question "The Yugoslav Communist Party in the power of murderers and spies," unanimously reached the following conclusions:

Whereas, in June 1948 the meeting of the Information Bureau of the Communist Parties noted the change-over of the Tito-Rankovic clique from democracy and socialism to bourgeois nationalism, during the period that has elapsed since the meeting of the Information Bureau this clique has travelled all the way from bourgeois nationalism to fascism and outright betrayal of the national interests of Yugoslavia.

Recent events show that the Yugoslav Government is completely dependent on foreign imperialist circles and has become an instrument of their aggressive policy, which has resulted in the liquidation of the independence of the Yugoslav Republic.

The Central Committee of the Party and the Government of Yugoslavia have merged completely with the imperialist circles against the entire camp of socialism and democracy; against the Communist Parties of the world; against the New Democracies and the USSR.

The Beograd clique of hired spies and murderers made a flagrant deal with imperialist reaction and entered its service, as the Budapest trial of Rajk–Brankov made perfectly clear.

This trial showed that the present Yugoslav rulers, having fled from the camp of democracy and socialism to the camp of capitalism and reaction, have become direct accomplices of the instigators of a new war, and, by their treacherous deeds, are ingratiating themselves with the imperialists and kow-towing to them.

The change-over of the Tito clinque to fascism was not fortuitous. It was effected on the order of their masters, the Anglo-American imperialists, whose mercenaries, it is now clear, this clique has been for long.

The Yugoslav traitors, obeying the will of the imperialists, undertook to form in the People's Democracies political gangs consisting of reactionaries, nationalists, clerical and fascist elements and, relying on these gangs, to bring about counter-revolutionary coups in these countries, wrest them from the Soviet Union and the entire socialist camp and subordinate them to the forces of imperialism.

The Tito clique transformed Beograd into an American centre for espionage and anti-Communist propaganda.

When all genuine friends of peace, democracy and socialism see in the USSR a powerful fortress of Socialism, a faithful and steadfast defender of the freedom and independence of nations and the principal bulwark of peace, the Tito-Rankovic clique, having attained power under the mask of friendship with the USSR, began on the orders of the Anglo-American imperialists a campaign of slander and provocation against the Soviet Union, utilising the most vile calumnies borrowed from the arsenal of Hitler.

The transformation of the Tito-Rankovic clique into a direct agency of imperialism, and accomplices of the warmongers, culminated in the lining up of the Yugoslav Government with the imperialist bloc at UNO, where the Kardeljs, Djilases and Beblers joined in a united front with American reactionaries on vital matters of international policy.

In the sphere of home policy, the chief outcome of the activity of the traitorous Tito-Rankovic clique is the actual liquidation of the People's Democratic system in Yugoslavia.

Due to the counter-revolutionary policy of the Tito-Rankovic clique which usurped power in the Party and in the State, an anti-Communist police State—fascist type regime—has been installed in Yugoslavia.

The social basis of this regime consists of kulaks in the countryside and capitalist elements in the towns.

In fact, power in Yugoslavia is in the hands of anti-popular reactionary elements. Active members of the old bourgeois parties, kulaks and other enemies of People's Democracy, are active in central and local government bodies.

The top fascist rulers rely on an enormously swollen military-police apparatus, with the aid of which they oppress the peoples of Yugoslavia.

They have turned the country into a military camp, wiped out all democratic rights of the working people, and trample on any free expression of opinion.

The Yugoslav rulers demagogically and insolently deceive the people, alleging they are building socialism in Yugoslavia.

But it is clear to every Marxist that there can be no talk of building socialism in Yugoslavia when the Tito clique has broken with the Soviet Union, with the entire camp of socialism and democracy, thereby depriving Yugoslavia of the main bulwark for building socialism and when it has subordinated the country economically and politically to Anglo-American imperialists.

The State sector in the economy of Yugoslavia has ceased to be people's property, since State power is in the hands of enemies of the people.

The Tito-Rankovic clique has created wide possibilities for the penetration of foreign capital into the economy of the country, and has placed the economy under the control of capitalist monopolies.

Anglo-American industrial-financial circles, investing their capital in Yugoslav economy, are transforming Yugoslavia into an agrarian-raw materials adjunct of foreign capital.

The ever-growing slavish dependence of Yugoslavia on imperialism leads to intensified exploitation of the working class and to a severe worsening of its conditions.

The policy of the Yugoslav rulers in the countryside bears a kulak-capitalistic character.

The compulsory pseudo-cooperatives in the countryside are in the hands of the kulaks and their agencies and represent an instrument for the exploitation of wide masses of working peasants.

The Yugoslav hirelings of imperialism, having seized leadership of the Communist Party of Yugoslavia, unleashed a campaign of terror against genuine Communists loyal to the principles of Marxism and Leninism and who fight for Yugoslavia's independence from the imperialists.

Thousands of Yugoslav patroits, devoted to Communism, have been expelled from the Party and incarcerated in jails and concentration camps. Many have been tortured and killed in prison or, as was the case with the well-known Communist, Arso Jovanović, were dastardly assassinated.

The brutality with which staunch fighters for Communism are being annihilated in Yugoslavia, can be compared only with the atrocities of the Hitler fascists or the butcher Tsaldaris in Greece or Franco in Spain.

Expelling from the ranks of the Party those Communists loyal to proletarian internationalism, annihilating them, the Yugoslav fascists opened wide the doors of the Party to bourgeois and kulak elements.

As a result of the fascist terror of the Tito gangs against the healthy forces in the Yugoslav Communist Party, leadership of the party is wholly in the hands of spies and murderers, mercenaries of imperialism.

The Communist Part of Yugoslavia has been seized by counter-revolutionary forces, acting arbitrarily in the name of the Party. Recruiting spies and provocateurs in the ranks of the working class parties is, as is well-known, an old method of the bourgeoisie.

In this way the imperialists seek to undermine the Parties from within and subordinate them to themselves. They have succeeded in realising this aim in Yugoslavia.

The fascist ideology, and fascist domestic policy, as well as the perfidious foreign policy of the Tito clique, completely subordinated to the foreign imperialist circles, have created a gulf between the espionage fascist Tito-Rankovic clique and the vital interests of the freedom-loving peoples of Yugoslavia.

Consequently, the anti-popular and treacherous activity of the Tito clique is encountering ever-growing resistance from those Communists who have remained loyal to Marxism-Leninism, and among the working class and working peasantry of Yugoslavia.

On the basis of irrefutable facts testifying to the complete change-over of the Tito clique to fascism and its desertion to the camp of world imperalism, the Information Bureau of the Communist and Workers' Parties considers, that:

1. The espionage group of Tito, Rankovic, Kardelj, Djilas, Pijade, Gosnjak, Maslaric, Bebler, Mrazovic, Vukmanovic, Koca Popovic, Kidric, Neskovic, Zlatic, Velebit, Kolisevski and others, are enemies of the working class and peasantry and enemies of the peoples of Yugoslavia.

2. This espionage group expresses not the will of the peoples of Yugoslavia, but the will of the Anglo-American imperialists, and has therefore betrayed the interests of the country and abolished the political sovereignty and economic independence of Yugoslavia.

3. The "Communist Party of Yugoslavia," as at present constituted, being in the hands of enemies of the people, murderers and spies, has forfeited the right to be called a Communist Party and is merely an apparatus for carrying out the espionage assignments of the clique of Tito-Kardelj-Rankovic-Djilas.

The information Bureau of Communist and Workers' Parties considers therefore that the struggle against the Tito clique—hired spies and murderers, is the international duty of all Communist and Workers' Parties.

It is the duty of Communist and Workers' Parties to give all possible aid to the Yugoslav working class and working peasantry who are fighting for the return of Yugoslavia to the camp of democracy and socialism.

A necessary condition for the return of Yugoslavia to the socialist camp is active struggle on the part of Revolutionary elements both inside the Yugoslav Communist Party and outside its ranks, for the regeneration of the revolutionary, genuine Communist Party of Yugoslavia, loyal to Marxism-Leninism, to the principles of proletarian internationalism, and fighting for the independence of Yugoslavia from imperialism.

The loyal Communist forces in Yugoslavia who, in the present brutal conditions of fascist terror, are deprived of the possibility of engaging in open action against the Tito-Rankovic clique, were compelled in the struggle for the cause of Communism, to follow the path taken by the Communists of those countries where legal work is forbidden.

The Information Bureau expresses the firm conviction that, among the workers and peasants of Yugoslavia, forces will be found capable of ensuring victory over the bourgeois-restoration espionage Tito-Rankovic clique; that the toiling people of Yugoslavia led by the working class will succeed in restoring the historical gains of People's Democracy, won at the price of heavy sacrifice and heroic struggle by the peoples of Yugoslavia, and that they will take the road of building socialism.

The Information Bureau considers one of the most important tasks of the Communist and Workers' Parties to be an all-round heightening of revolutionary vigilance in Party ranks; exposing and rooting our bourgeois-nationalist elements and agents of imperialism no matter under what flag they conceal themselves.

The Information Bureau recognizes the need for more ideological work in the Communist and Workers' Parties; more work to train Communists in the spirit of loyalty to proletarian internationalism; irreconcilability to any departure from the principles of Marxism-Leninism, and in the spirit of loyalty to Peoples' Democracy and Socialism.

CHAPTER 84

The Treaty of Warsaw—May 14, 1955

Russia promoted the Warsaw Pact in order to ease its own military burden in Europe. The Pact was also an attempt to bring cohesiveness to the Communist states of Europe and to stop any overly nationalistic tendencies that had appeared after the death of Stalin in 1953. The Pact has had mixed success. Poland has been cooperative, but the

Balkan states, especially Roumania, have made a meager contribution. Albania has remained totally aloof from the Pact, and for the most part, has hurled steady streams of abuse at the Russians. Moscow's hopes for the Pact have been frustrated to a great degree.

Reprinted in the AMERICAN JOURNAL OF INTERNATIONAL LAW (Washington, D.C., 1955), Vol. 49, pp. 195–199. By permission of the AMERICAN JOURNAL OF INTERNATIONAL LAW.

Article 1

The Contracting Parties undertake, in accordance with the Charter of the United Nations organization, to refrain in their international relations from the threat or use of force, and to settle their international disputes peacefully and in such manner as will not jeopardize international peace and security.

Article 2

The Contracting Parties declare their readiness to participate in a spirit of sincere cooperation in all international actions designed to safeguard international peace and security, and will fully devote their energies to the attainment of this end.

The Contracting Parties will furthermore strive for the adoption, in agreement with other states which may desire to cooperate in this, of effective measures for universal reduction of armaments and prohibition of atomic, hydrogen and other weapons of mass destruction.

Article 3

The Contracting Parties shall consult with one another on all important international issues affecting their common interest, guided by the desire to strengthen international peace and security.

They shall immediately consult with one another whenever, in the opinion of any one of them, a threat of armed attack on one or more of the parties of the Treaty has arisen, in order to ensure joint defense and the maintenance of peace and security.

Article 4

In the event of armed attack in Europe on one or more of the Parties to the Treaty by any state or group of states, each of the Parties to the Treaty, in the exercise of its right to individual or collective self-defense in accordance with Article 51 of the Charter of the United Nations Organization, shall immediately, either individually or in agreement with other Parties to the Treaty, come to the assistance of the state or states attacked with all such means as it deems necessary, including armed force. The Parties of the Treaty shall immediately consult concerning the necessary measures to be taken by them jointly in order to restore and maintain international peace and security.

Measures taken on the basis of this Article shall be reported to the Security Council in conformity with the provisions of the Charter of the United Nations Organization. These measures shall be discontinued immediately after the Security Council adopts the necessary measures to restore and maintain international peace and security.

Article 5

The Contracting Parties have agreed to establish a Joint Command of the armed forces that by agreement among the Parties shall be assigned to the Command, which shall function on the basis of jointly established principles. They shall likewise adopt other agreed measures necessary to strengthen their defensive power, in order to protect the peaceful labours of their peoples, guarantee the inviolability of their frontiers and territories, and provide defense against possible aggression.

Article 6

For the purpose of the consultations among the Parties envisaged in the present Treaty, and also for the purpose of examining questions which may arise in the operation of the Treaty, a Political Consultative Committee shall be set up, in which each of the Parties to the Treaty shall be represented by a member of its Government or by another specifically appointed representative. The Committee may set up such auxiliary bodies as may prove necessary.

Article 7

The Contracting Parties undertake not to participate in any coalitions or alliances and not to conclude any agreements whose objects conflict with the objects of the present Treaty.

The Contracting Parties declare that their commitments under existing international treaties do not conflict with the provisions of the present Treaty.

Article 8

The Contracting Parties declare that they will act in a spirit of friendship and cooperation with a view to further developing and fostering economic and cultural intercourse with one another, each adhering to the principle of respect for the independence and sovereignty of the others and noninterference in their internal affairs.

Article 9

The present Treaty is open to the accession of other states, irrespective of their social and political systems, which express their readiness by participation in the present Treaty to assist in uniting the efforts of the peaceable states in safeguarding the peace and security of the peoples. Such accession shall enter into force with the agreement of the Parties to the Treaty after the declaration of accession has been deposited with the Government of the Polish People's Republic.

Article 10

The present Treaty is subject to ratification, and the instruments of ratification shall be deposited with the Government of the Polish People's Republic.

The Treaty shall enter into force on the day the last instrument of ratification has been deposited. The Government of the Polish People's Republic shall notify the other Parties to the Treaty as each instrument of ratification is deposited.

Article II

The present Treaty shall remain in force for twenty years. For such Contracting Parties as do not at least one year before the expiration of this period present to the Government of the Polish People's Republic a statement of denunciation of the Treaty, it shall remain in force for the next ten years.

Should a system of collective security be established in Europe, and a General European Treaty of Collective Security concluded for this purpose, for which the Contracting Parties will unswervingly strive, the present Treaty shall cease to be operative from the day the Genral European Treaty enters into force.

Done in Warsaw on May 14, 1955, in one copy each in the Russian, Polish, Czech, and German languages, all texts being equally authentic. Certified copies of the present Treaty shall be sent by the Government of the Polish People's Republic to all the Parties of the Treaty.

In witness whereof the plenipotentiaries have signed the present Treaty and affixed their seals.

For the Presidium of the People's Assembly of the People's Republic of Albania:
MEHMET SHEHU

For the Presidium of the People's Assembly of the People's Republic of Bulgaria:
VYLKO CHERVENKOV

For the Presidium of the Hungarian People's Republic:
ANDRAS HEGEDUS

For the President of the German Democratic Republic:
OTTO GROTEWOHL

For the State Council of the Polish People's Republic:
JOZEF CYRANKIEWICZ

For the Presidium of the Grand National Assembly of the Rumanian People's Republic:
GHEORGHE GHEORGHIU-DEJ

For the Presidium of the Supreme Soviet of the Union of Soviet Socialist Republics:
NIKOLAI ALEXANDROVICH BULGANIN

For the President of the Czechoslovak Republic:
VILIAM SIROKY

Establishment of a Joint Command of the Armed Forces of the Signatories to the Treaty of Friendship, Cooperation and Mutual Assistance

In pursuance of the Treaty of Friendship, Cooperation and Mutual Assistance between the People's Republic of Albania, the People's Republic of Bulgaria, the Hungarian People's Republic, the German Democratic Republic, the Polish People's Republic, the Rumanian People's Republic, the Union of Soviet Socialist Republics and the Czechoslovak Republic, the signatory states have decided to establish a Joint Command of their armed forces.

The decision provides that general questions relating to the strengthening of the defensive power and the organization of the Joint Armed Forces of the signatory states shall be subject to examination by the Political Consultative Committee, which shall adopt the necessary decisions.

Marshall of the Soviet Union, I.S. Konev, has been appointed Commander-in-Chief of the Joint Armed Forces to be assigned by the signatory states.

The Ministers of Defense or other military leaders of the signatory states are to serve as Deputy Commanders-in-Chief of the Joint Armed Forces, and shall command the armed forces assigned by their respective states to the Joint Armed Forces.

The question of the participation of the German Democratic Republic in measures concerning the armed forces of the Joint Command will be examined at a later date.

A Staff of the Joint Armed Forces of the signatory states will be set up under the Commander-in-Chief of the Joint Armed Forces, and will include permanent representatives of the General Staffs of the signatory states.

The Staff will have its headquarters in Moscow.

The disposition of the Joint Armed Forces in the territories of the signatory states will be effected, by agreement among the states, in accordance with the requirements of their mutual defense.

CHAPTER 85

Assessment of the Hungarian Revolution—1956

The Hungarian Revolution of 1956 was the most memorable event in the post-war history of Eastern Europe. World attention was attracted to what at first appared to be a successful emancipation from Soviet control. But the hopes of the revolutionists and the western democracies died. Hungary remained in the Soviet camp: on November 4, Soviet troops occupied most of the large towns and arrested Imre Nagy, the progressive premier.

It is difficult to choose an illustrative document from the mass of published material on the uprising. But the following interview with Bela Kovács tells much of the story, and the interviewer, Leslie Bain, was one of the most accurate journalists who tried to report events from Hungary in the very confusing situations of October and November, 1956.

Leslie B. Bain, "Budapest: Interview in a Basement Hideaway," THE REPORTER (New York, December 13, 1956), pp. 13–15. Reprinted by permission of THE REPORTER.

Late in the evening of Sunday, November 4—a night of terror in Budapest that no one who lived through it will ever forget—I met Béla Kovács, one of the leaders of Hungary's short-lived revolutionary government, in a cellar in the city's center. Constant thunder sounded from the pavement above us as Soviet tanks rumbled through the streets, firing heavy guns and machine-gunning house fronts. All day long, Soviet troops had been re-entering the city after their feigned withdrawal, and they had already arrested Premier Imre Nagy along with most of his Ministers and embarked on large-scale reprisals.

Kovács, as a Minister of State of the Nagy régime, had started off for the Parliament Building early that morning, but he never reached it. Soviet tanks were there ahead of him. Now he squatted on the floor opposite me, a fugitive from Soviet search squads.

The cannonade continued all night as we huddled there in the foul air of the small space under dripping pipes. The sound was louder when we cautiously opened a small window. It told us only too clearly that all hope for the uprising against the Soviets had gone. After two weeks of the heroism of an aroused people, nothing was left but a destroyed dream. For several hours Kovács sat plunged in a depression too deep for talk. Then at last he began to recount what he had been through on that fateful day.

The dim light deepened the heavy lines of his face. A hunched, stocky man, with a thin mustache and half-closed eyes, Béla Kovács was only a shadow of the robust figure he once had been. Now in his early fifties, he had risen to prominence after the war as one of the top leaders of the Hungarian Independent Smallholders Party. Back in 1947, when Mátyás Rákosi began taking over the government with the support of the Soviet occupation forces, Kovács had achieved fame by being the only outstanding anti-Communist Hungarian leader to defy Rákosi and continue open opposition. His prestige had become so great among the peasantry that at first the Communists had not molested him. But the Soviets themselves stepped in, arresting him on a trumped-up charge of plotting against the occupation forces and sentencing him to life imprisonment. After eight years in Siberia, Kovács was returned to Hungary and transferred to a Hungarian jail, from which he was released in the spring of 1956, broken in body but not in spirit by his long ordeal. After what was called his "rehabilitation," Kovács was visited by his old enemy Rákosi, who called to pay his respects. Rákosi was met at the door by this message from Kovács: "I do not receive murderers in my home."

The Defiance of Mr. Bibo

So long as Nagy's government was still under the thumb of the Communist Politburo, Kovács refused to have anything to do with the new regime. Only in the surge of the late October uprising, when Nagy succeeded in freeing himself from his former associates and cast about to form a coalition government, did Kovács consent to lend his name and immense popularity to it. He himself had not been in Budapest when the revolt broke out, but at his home in Pécs, a southern city near the Yugoslav border. In fact, he told me, he was made a member of the new Nagy government before he even had a chance to say "Yes" or "No," but, understanding the situation and what Nagy was trying to do, he had agreed to go along. The name of Kovács among the Ministers of State was to many Hungarians a guarantee of a new era in which the government would carry out the mandates of the victorious revolution.

At about six o'clock in the morning of November 4, when Soviet tanks were already pouring into the city, Kovács had received a message from Nagy calling an immediate meeting of the Cabinet. When he reached Parliament Square the Russians had already thrown a tight cordon around it. One of Nagy's new Ministers, Zoltan Tildy, who had been ousted from the Presidency in 1948, came out of the building and told Kovács that he had just negotiated a surrender agreement with the Russians whereby civilians would be permitted to leaved the building unmolested in exchange for surrendering the seat of the government. However, Tildy reported, State Minister Istvan Bibo refused to leave and had entrenched himself with a machine gun on the second floor. Tildy begged Kovács to get in touch with Bibo by telephone and order him to leave. Then Tildy himself left.

Kovács called Bibo from a nearby phone and tried to persuade him to leave. He was unable to move the aroused Minister, whose argument was that if the Russians moved against him, this would serve as a clear demonstration before the world that Soviet forces had been employed to crush the independent Hungarian government. Bibo declared that the Russians intended to install Janos Kadar and his clique as a new government, and by not yielding, he wanted to demonstrate that the exchange of governments was accomplished by armed force.

I told Kovács that as late as four in the afternoon, I had been in touch with the beleaguered Bibo by telephone. He was still holding out, but an hour later his private line did not answer. By that time Premier Nagy himself was in custody, and the Ministers who had not been arrested were in hiding. Kovács voiced his admiration of both Bibo and the Premier. "My fondest memory of Nagy," he said to me, "will always be his transformation from an easygoing, jolly, studious professor into a flaming revolutionary."

"What do you think caused the Russians to change their tactics and come in again?" I asked Kovács.

"Two things. First, we went too fast and too far, and the Communists panicked. Second, the Russians felt deeply humiliated." He went on to explain that he felt that all the goals of the revolution could have been attained if there had been a way to slow down the process. In a free election, he estimated, all the left-of-center parties would not command more than thirty per cent of the vote. But a free election was what the Communists were afraid to risk.

"Wouldn't such an election have brought in the extreme Right and possibly a new reign of White Terror?" I asked.

Kovács admitted there might have been a possibility of that, but he was convinced it could have been checked in time. He went on to say that in his estimation there was no chance of reconstituting large landholdings in the hands of their former owners or of the workers' permitting the return of the mines and factories to their former owners. "The economic salvation of Hungary lies in a mixed economy, combining capitalism, state ownership, and co-operatives," he said. Politically, there had been the likelihood of a strongly rightist development, but, in the absence of economic power, after a few short months the extremists would have been silenced.

As for the Russians, Kovács thought that their pride had run away with their common sense. "When Pal Maleter (Nagy's Minister of Defense and commander of all armed forces) reported about his first contact with the Russian high command only yesterday, he said the Russians made just three demands—the restoration of destroyed Red Army memorials and desecrated Russian cemeteries, a guarantee that the resting places of Soviet soldiers would in future be respected by the Hungarians, and finally that the Soviet Army when leaving Hungary should be accorded full military honors."

The Nagy government had felt that these demands were reasonable and that their fulfillment was a small price to pay for getting rid of the Russians. Yet when Maleter had gone to meet again with the Soviet commanders later that Saturday evening, he had never come back—and now their tanks were shooting up the city.

"They Will Fail"

I asked Kovács whether he felt the Nagy government's declaration of neutrality had aroused the Soviet leaders to action. No, he thought that the decision to crush the Hungarian revolution was taken earlier and independently of it. Obviously the Russians would not have rejoiced at a neutral Hungary, but so long as economic co-operation between the states in the area was assured, the Russians and their satellites should not have been too unhappy.

In that regard, Kovács assured me, there was never a thought in the Nagy government of interrupting the economic co-operation of the Danubian states. "It would have been suicidal for us to try tactics hostile to the block. What we wanted was simply the right to sell our produce to the best advantage of our people and buy our necessities where we could do it most advantageously."

"Then in your estimation there was no reason why the Russians should have come in again and destroyed the revolution?"

"None unless they are trying to revert to old Stalinist days. But if that is what they really are trying—and at the moment it looks like it—they will fail, even more miserably than before. The tragedy of all this is that they are burning all the bridges which could lead to a peaceful solution."

He went on in the semi-darkness to say that after today there would be no way to bring about a reapproachment between Hungary and the Soviet Union. The wound the Russians were inflicting on Hungary was so deep that it would fester for generations. "Yet we can't pick up Hungary and take it somewhere else. We have to go on living with our ancient neighbors who are now in the Soviet grip."

We discussed the revolution itself. Kovác's somber eyes lit up. "It has brought modern history to a turning point," he said. "It has exposed totalitarian fallacies more sharply than any event before. Our people were beaten, cowed, and for years lived in abject surrender, yet when the hour struck they all streamed out of their homes, Communists and non-Communists alike, to regain their self-respect by defying their tormentors. And look what happened to the Communist Party! It disappeared overnight—not forced to dissolve, but by common consent! Have you ever heard of a ruling party voting itself out of existence? Once the revolution touched them, all became Hungarians—all except those whose crimes were too many to be forgiven. These are the ones who now serve their Russian masters.

As to Janos Kadar, the Russian favorite just being installed as Premier, Kovács was reserved. He was not sure that Kadar agreed with all that his masters had dictated. Kovács knew, as we all did, that on Friday, November 2, while still serving the Nagy government, Kadar had disappeared from Budapest. All efforts to locate him failed, and it was widely thought that he had been kidnaped by the Russians. Whether this was true was hard to say in the light of subsequent developments, but Kovács thought he might be acting under compulsion. "Compulsion or no, he has an impossible task."

What seemed to depress Kovács more than anything else was the immediate future of the people of Hungary. He detailed the damage to the country's economy (this was on a day when the damage was only half as great as it became in the following six days) and said that without large and immediate deliveries of coal and wood everything in the country would break down. Food would be scarce and later unobtainable except in minute quantities through rationing. He estimated that the physical damage in Budapest would take anywhere from ten to fifteen years to repair. "Don't forget," he added, "the wreckage of the Second World War is still with us because of the crazy economic planning of the Communists."

"Tell Your People"

Now and then the sudden staccato of machine guns was heard nearby, amid the artillery. Kovács said that he wanted to leave "so as not to embarrass my host." I begged him to wait until morning when more people would be on the streets and he would not be so conspicuous. He agreed to stay on.

The talk moved toward the crucial pooint: How much truth was in the Russian assertion that the revolution had become a counter-revolution and that therefore Russian intervention was justified?

"I tell you," said Kovács, "this was a revolution from inside, led by Communists. There is not a shred of evidence that it was otherwise. Communists outraged by theïr own doings prepared the ground for it and fought for it during the first few days. This enabled us former non-Communist party leaders to come forward and demand a share in Hungary's future. Subsequently this was granted by Nagy, and the Social Democratic, Independent Smallholders, and Hungarian Peasant Parties were reconstituted. True, there was a small fringe of extremists in the streets and there was also evidence of a movement which seemed to have ties with the exiled Nazis and Nyilas of former days. But at no time was their strength such as to cause concern. No one in Hungary cares for those who fled to the West after their own corrupt terror régime was finished—and then got their financing from the West. Had there been an attempt to put them in power, all Hungary would have risen instantly."

I told Kovács that this analysis agreed with my own observation during the first phase of the revolution. For the first time during the night Kovács smiled. He told me:

"I wish you could convince the West and make them keep the reactionaries out of our hair. Many of the exiles the Americans are backing are men who are marked because of their war crimes. Some of the voices that come to us over Radio Free Europe in particular are not welcome here. I understand the Americans' eagerness to fight Communism, but this is not the way to do it. As long as the West continues to maintain ties with Hungarian feudalists and fascists, we are handicapped in our effort to seek ties with you. Tell your people to help us by selling democracy to the Hungarians, rather than White reaction."

"What of the future?" I asked. After some hesitation Kovács said: "All is not lost, for it is impossible for the Russians and their puppets to maintain themselves against the determined resistance of the Hungarians. The day will come when a fateful choice will have to be made: Exterminate the entire population by slow starvation and police terror or else accept the irreducible demand—the withdrawal of Soviet forces from our country."

We parted, and I did not see Kovács again. The last thing I heard about him was an A.P. report from Budapest that Kadar had called him in for a three-hour conference. Maybe he was able to find out whether Kadar was acting under compulsion or whether he agreed with all that his masters dictated.

CHAPTER 86

The Understanding of Freedom in Poland

The following excerpts from a 1962 debate in the Polish Sejm show that while the government was willing to tolerate some loyal opposition, that opposition still had but a scant chance to obtain basic freedoms for all. The speech of Deputy Lubienski, a Catholic representative who opposed a new censorship bill, was answered by Deputy Stanewicz, representing the government. The censorship bill was passed and subsequent events have shown that the opportunities for pursuit of free expression have significantly diminished in Poland since 1962.

Hansjakab Stehle, THE INDEPENDENT SATELLITE: SOCIETY AND POLITICS IN POLAND SINCE 1945 (New York, 1965), Appendix II, pp. 297–305 (Translated by O.J.S. Thompson from NACHBAR POLEN, published by S. Fischer Verlag, Frankfurt am Main). By permission of Frederick A. Praeger.

Deputy Konstanty Lubienski (Znak-Catholic Club):

Mr. Sejm Marshal, high Sejm! In judging the bill before us, we must take the constitution as our starting point. Article 71 of the Constitution guarantees citizens freedom of assembly. Naturally, this is not an unlimited freedom, for—as someone rightly said—freedom, in order to be effective, must be tempered with justice.

In times such as ours, in which public life becomes more and more complex, regulations are absolutely necessary for the maintenance of order and public security. The Assembly Law is necessary for the same reason, because the previous one dates back to 1932. The Assembly Law must, however, be based on the constitutional principle of freedom of assembly. This fundamental right can only be taken away or restricted if special circumstances arise. Clause 2 of the bill gives the right to hold meetings not merely to various organizations but even to each adult citizen, who is legally competent and has not been deprived of his civil rights—in other words, very broad rights.

But let us consider how these rights are affected by subsequent provisions of the bill. Meetings of state institutions, of political and trade union organizations, are not included in the authorisation clauses of this bill. Such meetings require neither authorisation nor that prior notice should be given to the administrative authorities . . . Does this bill, therefore, raise any problem concerning the freedom of assembly? Unfortunately it does—and it is a problem, or rather they are problems, which are unimportant. Clause 1, paragraph 2, of the bill says that any group of people constitutes an assembly, if these are summoned 'for the purpose of common consultation or common manifestation of their viewpoint in connection with a specific question or matter'—in other words, a group consisting of a few persons, who wish to discuss any problem, is an assembly! There would be no objection to this if further provisions of the bill did not make it clear that any such assembly requires the approval of the Ministry of the Interior—that such meetings are tolerated as 'social gatherings' which are exempt from the law—are, in my view, open to fairly arbitrary interpretation. In the provinces this can give rise to misunderstandings, so that the matter requires either (1) a clear, legal definition or (2) that the present legal position should be maintained, whereby a meeting of persons known to the chairman calls neither for approval nor prior notification, or (3) a change in the definition of the word 'assembly', which could mean, for example, that only a group of ten people or more constitutes an assembly.

Clause 10, para 1, lays down that the state organs for internal affairs can forbid a meeting or refuse to give permission for it, if the meeting violates the provisions of this present bill or violates the penal laws, if the meeting is likely to endanger general security and order—or if it is 'contrary to the interests of society'. This last phrase arouses grave misgivings. The definition 'running counter to the interests of society' is not sufficiently precise and can be variously interpreted, which will effectively complicate the life of social organisations and is sure to give rise to a wave of protests. Is it even necessary to introduce such a condition if the interests of society are already protected by the existing penal law? Provincial authorities afraid of taking responsibility, might develop a tendency to apply it without discrimination and in this way stifle valuable initiative.

I would now like to touch upon certain religious questions, which are bound up with this bill. In clause 4, para 1, points 3 and 4, official assemblies and closed meetings of social organisations are exempted from the obligation of seeking approval. In principle this should also apply to closed meetings of the clergy. This was, in fact, the burden of statements made by the representatives of the Ministry of the Interior before the Sejm committee. That such statements were made is gratifying, but unfortunately they are not sufficient since in practice the church is to be regarded in this bill as a social organisation, as it should be; then this must be clearly said. But unfortunately all our proposed amendments, which were designed to clarify this problem were rejected. As things stand, it could happen that even diocesan and parish conferences, which are essentially closed meetings, will be classified as requiring official approval! I do not believe that the government wishes to carry its intervention quite so far. Nevertheless, the formal, legal position should be clarified.

In general, I must say that the legal status of the church has still not been settled. The church is denied the status of a public institution. The church is not considered to be a social organisation, and logic does not permit that it should be treated as a private one.

Following this analysis, I make the following objections to the bill:

Firstly, it limits—or at least it places in an ambiguous position—all groups of people and—says the bill—even small ones, if they meet to discuss social problems.

Secondly, it limits many social organisations, as it subjects their activities not only to the control but also to the constant influence of the authorities.

Thirdly, it can threaten or limit the existing privileges of the church.

Finally, a few remarks of a general nature. All that has been said about the development of public life in our country is quite correct. In fact, the social life in People's Poland is a full one. Undoubtedly, the events of October 1956 exercised a decisive influence. It is difficult to assess the effects of this revival. On the other hand, there is surely no doubt that many of the achievements in our economic, cultural and political life are the results of this dynamic activity by various social elements. If there were also negative results, they were, it seems to me, the exception rather than the rule.

The draft of the Assembly Law is, unfortunately, not based on any such estimate of the very recent past. The main principle governing assemblies, which are subject to the law, is that of compulsory authorisation. Cases where this obligation does not apply are exceptional. This is the reverse of the situation so far, in which the main principle was freedom of assembly and compulsory authorisation was the exception. I fear that his will slow down the development of social life and with it the process of consolidating social unity and integrating our socialist society.

The limited definition of assembly, with all the consequences that flow from it, can do serious harm to all—as I would describe it—spontaneous initiative. There is every reason to fear that the law will weaken the critical opposition of the citizen to cliques, patronage and other such symptoms.

In practice, the provincial authorities in particular can stifle any initiative that is unwelcome to the present leaders of our economic or cultural life, to people who wield a comparatively strong influence in the internal departments of the National Council Presidiums. A characteristic feature of this bill is mistrust of society and of the organisations which are legally in existence. It is a vote of no-confidence in the direction in which our social forces are developing. This is unjustified. The level of intelligence of our society, its political maturity and social discipline are steadily rising. And if there are also negative symptoms, then there are many ways of combating them. To do this by imposing more stringent regulations is to exact too high a price in social development and is furthermore ineffectual.

We are constantly hearing and reading about the fight against bureaucracy, and rightly so. But, at the same time, we should not provide fresh opportunities for this disease to spread. This bill will bring a fresh flood of paper which will circulate between the interested parties and the National Councils and much of which will also reach the Ministry of the Interior and perhaps even the Central Committee, because, as we know from the experience, many unimportant things can often be solved only by a decision at the highest level. I could give several examples to prove this.

High Sejm! We are living through a period in which the new, socialist system is being created. Not only party members but also the broad, non-party masses are playing their part. It is undoubtedly a great achievement by the party that it was able to get the non-party citizens actively involved in this reconstruction; for many non-party people this is no mere formality, nor are they motivated by opportunism but by a deep conviction that this is the right system, one in accordance with developments in the world at large and serving Poland's interests.

For all party members and non-party people who are taking a sincere and all active interest in building up the socialist system, the process of democratization is particularly important since it is fundamental to socialism. We attach great value to what has already been achieved in this respect and we want more. That is why this bill alarms us, for in our view it does not take us one step forward on the road to democratization but is rather a symptom of the opposite trend.

Many features of the modern, socialist democracy have not yet been clearly defined, yet some things appear to be certain; there is no doubt that the principle of freedom of assembly is inseparable from the concept of democracy.

I have said that a new law is necessary, but it is my profound conviction that a law such as this, which we are now considering in draft, is not necessary. If it is passed, its placing on the statute book will cause serious unrest amongst the general public.

I am bound to say, therefore, that this bill—as I have tried to show—contains many misleading and obscure provisions. In our deputies' club Znak, we are convinced that a revision of the bill could bring many improvements and that basic changes should be made to allay the fears and reservations which I have put before the High Sejm. On behalf of the deputies' club Znak, I accordingly move that the bill be referred back to the Committee of Internal Affairs for reconsideration.

Deputy Artur Starewicz, PZPR (communist)—then head

of the press Department in the Central Committee; since 1963 in the Party Secretariat:

High Sejm! I would not have prolonged today's debate and taken up the valuable time of my fellow deputies if Deputy Lubienski had not spoken. I think his was a dishonest, dogmatic performance, misrepresenting the substance of the bill under discussion. He had depicted in his speech the spectacle of some apocalyptic threat hanging over our Constitution, over the nation's democratic achievements and over the freedom of assembly. . . . All this is pure imagination, and has nothing to do with the real text of the bill before this High Sejm. . . . In his imaginary picture, Deputy Lubienski alleges that everything that is essential to the life of our nation takes place in a tiny section of our national life, represented by these casual meetings which are to be legally subject to a modest measure of control by the People's Government. Control, mark you, not an over-riding ban! According to what Deputy Lubienski has said, the real pulse of Poland's social and political life beats in a few casually attended meetings or gatherings which bring together a handful of those people who stand aloof and belong to none of the 30,000 organisations in present-day Poland. We, it seems to him, not only want to restrict this form of activity, but—worst still— to suppress it!

Are we really to believe that official control of these insignificant, unimportant meetings is a threat to our Constitution? I venture to say that this is sheer demagogy. The vital activity, social initiative, criticism of the authorities, the struggle against cliques and bureaucracy, of which Deputy Lubienski spoke—all these find their expression in Poland, not in small marginal areas for which he demands the right of uncontrolled activity, but in hundreds, thousands of political, trade union and professional meetings, meetings called by the most varied social organisations, national councils, national front committees, bloc committees, agricultural circles and mayors' councils. And the bill does not affect one of these countless meetings. These are the practical forum for the creative energy and initiative about which Deputy Lubienski is so concerned.

As previous speakers have pointed out, we are not yet

living in such idyllic times that we can afford to surrender all vestiges of intervention by state control in public
assemblies. The heart of the matter is that this particular
intervention only affects a very limited category of meetings which have no place in the broad and natural stream
of our country's social life.

Deputy Lubienski demanded the restoration of the old
assembly regulations. This is a senseless demand. What
was the object of these laws, including clause 18 of the
old law? It was no more than a trick in order to retain
some excuse for widespread police control of all mass-meet-
ings, in public, in the streets, all demonstrations by the
anti-fascist movement of the popular masses.

Deputy Lubienski mentioned that this bill does not solve
the problem of the church's status. But this seems to me
to be a misunderstanding. The bill lies before us. It can
pronounce upon meetings called by the church—in this case
religious services, ceremonies and processions—and it does.
But whether the church is a social organisation or not
is something upon which this bill cannot pronounce; that
is quite a different matter. In the legal sense it would
be illogical and incomprehensible if the problem were decided in this bill. It belongs in quite a different legal context.

Deputy Lubienski maintains that the bill limits
the church's privileges and demands that, instead of talking
about concrete forms of religious worship (such as divine
service or other religious ceremonies), which are not subject
to control, the bill should speak vaguely and indeterminate-
ly about 'religious meetings'. What does this really mean?
Under such a label, with such a vague, elastic phrase, any
kind of meeting could be convened. It would be enough
for the author or initiator to be a clergyman for the meeting to be given some ostensibly religious purpose, while
the substance of this 'religious meeting' could be quite un-
predictable. It might have some connection with divine service and ceremonies, or it might be concerned with something that went far beyond these natural functions of the
church and the clergy. This is not merely a theoretical
misgiving. Any such vague definition is unacceptable, for
in practice it could give rise to a great many misunder-

standings and could cause quite unnecessary conflict between the authorities and the church.

All processions, pilgrimmages and other outward manifestations are subject to the general regulations which concern public order and security. If we have so far been sixty years behind France in this respect, where these questions have been resolved by democratic civil law, is it not high time to make up the lost ground and bring the regulations into line with the requirements of our daily life? Only a malicious person could detect in this a restriction of the church's privileges . . . Do the policies so far pursued, the actions and the behaviour of the authorities give anyone grounds to fear that the rights vested in the authorities by the law will be exploited to restrict the freedom of assembly? Does our experience provide any excuse for the sort of demagogy Deputy Lubienski had displayed here?

I would add at this point, that what Deputy Lubienski has said suggests, to say the least, a lack of faith, a lack of confidence in the policy of the National Front parties, not to mention a lack of trust and faith in the real, profoundly democratic policy of the People's Government. For that reason I find that Deputy Lubienski's motion to refer the draft back for reconsideration is unjustified. I propose that his motion be rejected and the bill be adopted in its present form

Deputy Marian Kubicki, ZSL (Peasants' Party):

It appears that my fellow deputies from the Znak group are well aware that the social consequence of a traffic congestion by thousands of people—for example, of the road to Czestochowa—are infinitely more serious and more complicated in 1962 than they were in 1932, when the old law was in force. I presume that these same colleagues have had the opportunity to take part in a pilgrimage on foot. In that case they should have seen for themselves how much care and organisation is required to ensure that these people are properly looked after. There is also a problem of caring for the health and property of the local residents as well as that of the pilgrims.

Is it to be wondered, then, that the authorities should be informed? Is it to be wondered that these authorities require the opportunity to weigh every possibility and to consider whether they can reasonably expect to perform their duty to protect the citizens and public order? Should they not be allowed to consider such things before they approve specific functions of this kind?

The action taken so far by our administrative organs with regard to such meetings gives ground for no doubt as to the tact and sympathy with which they meet the needs and deal with the religious practices of believers in Poland. And what of the relationship with the church, of which Deputy Lubienski spoke? Let us remind him of the many reports and articles that have appeared in the French and even the West German press on church-building in our western territories, in Warsaw and other large cities which were destroyed during the war. That is the relationship of the state to the church and the relationship to the new churches and chapels which were built in Poland. That may be another matter which may have little to do with the bill under debate; but Deputy Lubienski ought not to forget such things.

CHAPTER 87

Church—State Relations in Poland

In 1956, events in Poland nearly developed along the lines followed in Hungary. However, a revolution did not occur, and the astute diplomacy of the Polish leader, Wladyslaw Gomulka, avoided a military confrontation with Soviet Russia. During the period of crisis, when it appeared that Poland would share the fate of Hungary, considerable popular support generated for Gomulka's apparent policy of an independent and national path toward socialism. The Catholic Church, embodied in the person of Cardinal Wyszynski, gave some support to Gomulka, and the following communique appears to have been a product of this brief détente between church and state. Good relations did not ensue, and many clashes have occurred since 1956, culminating in the various repressions and disorders that marred the observance, in 1966, of the thousandth anniversary of Poland's conversion to Christianity.

Hansjakab Stehle, THE INDEPENDENT SATELLITE: SOCIETY AND POLITICS IN POLAND SINCE 1945 (New York, 1965), Appendix III, pp. 309–310 (Translated by O.J.S. Thompson from NACHBAR POLEN, published by S. Fischer Verlag, Frankfurt am Main). By permission of Frederick A. Praeger.

Communiqué of the Joint Commission of Representatives of the Government and the Episcopate, December 7, 1956

The Joint Commission of representatives of the government and the episcopate discussed a number of unresolved questions concerning relations between the state and the church. In the course of the conversations the representatives of the government emphasized their readiness to remove the remaining obstacles to the realisation of the principle of full freedom for religious life.

The representatives of the episcopate stated that, as a result of changes in public life aimed at the consolidation of legality, justice, peaceful coexistence, the raising of social morality and the righting of wrongs, the government and the state authorities would find in the church hierarchy and clergy full understanding for these aims.

The representatives of the episcopate expressed full support for the work undertaken by the government aiming at concentrating the efforts of all citizens in harmonious work for the good of the country, for the conscientious observance of the laws of People's Poland and for the implementation by the citizens of their duties with regard to the state.

The Joint Commission examined and settled a number of questions of great importance for the state and the church.

Appointment of bishops

(1) In order to regulate juridically relations between

the state and the church administration, the Joint Commission will request the state authorities to annul the currently binding decree on the filling of church ecclesiastical posts. The new legal act regulating these matters will guarantee the influence of the state in the appointment of archbishops, diocesan bishops and coadjutors with the right of succession, as well as parish priests, preserving at the same time the requirements of church jurisdiction. The draft of the new legal act will be agreed in the Joint Commission.

Religious instruction in schools

(2) In order to regulate religious instruction in schools, the following principles have been established:

Full freedom is ensured and the voluntary character guaranteed of religious instruction in elementary and secondary schools for children whose parents express such a wish. Religious instruction will be conducted in schools as an extra-curricular subject. The school authorities are to make it possible for religious instruction to be followed through a properly drafted syllabus of lessons.

Teachers of religion will be appointed by the school authorities in agreement with the church authorities. The teachers of religion will be paid from the budget of the Ministry of Education. The programs of religious instruction as well as the religious instruction manuals must be approved by the church and educational authorities.

Inspections of religious instruction will be carried out by the church and educational authorities. The school authorities will endeavour to enable the children and youth to participate freely in religious practices outside school.

The school authorities and the clergy will ensure complete freedom and tolerance both to believers and to non-believers and will firmly counteract all manifestations of violation of freedom of conscience.

Religious care for the sick; prison chaplains

(3) Principles of ensuring religious care for the sick have been agreed upon. New directives of the Ministry of Health will be issued on the basis of these principles.

(4) The principles of religious care for prisoners and of the appointment of prison chaplains have been agreed upon.

Return of nuns and priests.

(5) The return of nuns moved in 1953 from the Opole and Wroclaw and Katowice Provinces has been allowed. Those among them who do not feel bound to Poland and express the desire to go abroad will be able to leave the country. A decision has also been made as to the return of priests moved from their parishes in the western provinces.

(6) An agreement has been reached between the episcopate and the government concerning the five new bishops appointed by the Holy See in the western territories.

CHAPTER 88

The Czech Crisis of 1968

World attention focused on Czechoslovakia on August 20, when Soviet, Bulgarian, East German, Hungarian and Polish forces occupied that country in order to combat the so-called force of "reaction and counter-revolution" which, it was alleged, threatened to take control.

Czechoslovakia, from the time of the 1948 Communist take-over until early 1968, appeared to have one of the more rigid regimes in Eastern Europe. But the regime of Antonin Novotny, the Czechoslovakian Communist party chief, had been gradually discredited by economic failures, and towards the end, opposition asserted itself among Communist economic planners, and in a more subtle form in the freer expression exhibited in cultural productions, especially among movie directors. With a certain degree of acquiescence on the part of the Soviets, a power struggle took place which led to the replacement of Novotny, on Janury 5, 1968, by the Slovak party chief, Alexander Dubcek.

On March 5, the Dubcek regime lifted press censorship, and on April 9, a Dubcek manifesto was issued promising fuller civil rights. It appeared that Dubcek wished to establish a truly democratic society where the tenets of Marx would dominate through popular acceptance, not through the use of force. There was strong reaction against Czech "democratization" in Russia and East Germany. On May 17, the Soviet Premier, Aleksei Kosygin, arrived in Prague for talks that led to subsequent Warsaw Pact maneuvers in Czechoslovakia. The maneuvers occurred, but on July 9, Czechoslovakia reacted to more pressure by refusing to attend a Warsaw Pact summit meeting. On July 15, the following five-party letter demanded an end to Czechoslovakia's liberalization. On July 18, the Dubcek regime rejected the rebuke from the Warsaw Pact nations and insisted that reform would continue. This document appears to be one of the best explanations for the whole process of events that had developed in 1968.

It appeared that Dubcek had scored a great triumph, and on July 29, Czech leaders started a series of meetings with the Soviet Politburo which appeared to result in resolution of the conflict. But the July meetings did not end the conflict. Popular sentiment for democratization had built up, and Dubcek had made no effort to curb this feeling. The propaganda campaign of the Soviets was renewed and on August 20, the invasion, which was not resisted militarily by the Dubcek regime, began. There was passive resistance by the Czechs, protests from the Italian and French Communist parties as well as the Yugoslavian and Rumanian regimes. In its embarrassment at being unable to form a puppet regime, the Soviets finally had to settle for acceptance of Dubcek, provided that there would be some curbing of the democratization process.

New York Times, Friday, July 19, 1968, pp. 12–13.
© 1968 by The New York Times Company. Reprinted by permission.

Five Party Letter

Dear comrades,

On behalf of the Central Committees of the Communist and Workers' parties of Bulgaria, Hungary, the German Democratic Republic, Poland and the Soviet Union we are applying to you with this letter prompted by a feeling of sincere friendship based on the principles of Marxism-Leninism and proletarian internationalism and by the concern for our common affairs, for strengthening the positions of Socialism and the security of the Socialist community of nations.

The development of events in your country evokes deep anxiety in us. It is our deep conviction that the offensive of the reactionary forces, backed by imperalism, against your party and the foundations of the social system in the Czechosolvak Socialist Republic threatens to push your country off the road of Socialism and that consequently it jeopardizes the interests of the entire Socialist system.

We expressed these apprehensions at the meeting in Dresden, during repeated bilateral meetings, as well as in letters which our parties sent in the recent period to the Presidium of the Central Committee of the Communist party of Czechoslovakia.

Recently, we offered the Presidium of the Central Committee of the Communist party of Czechoslovakia to hold a new joint meeting on July 14 this year so as to exchange information and opinions on the state of affairs in our countries, including the development of events in Czechoslovakia. Unfortunately, the C.P.C. Central Committee Presidium did not take part in this meeting and did not use the opportunity for a collective comradely discussion of the situation that has developed. That is why we thought it necessary to state to you in this letter, with complete sincerity and frankness, our common opinion. We want you to understand us well and assess correctly our intentions.

We neither had nor have an intention to interfere in such affairs which are strictly the internal business of your party and your state, to violate the principles of respect, independence and equality in the relations among the Communist parties and Socialist countries.

INTERFERENCE IN METHODS DENIED

We are not applying to you as representatives of the past who would like to interfere in the correction of mistakes and shortcomings, including the violations of Socialist law which had taken place.

We are not interfering in the methods of planning and

management of the Socialist national economy of Czechoslovakia and in your actions aimed at improving the structure of economy and developing Socialist democracy.

We shall hail the settlement of relations between Czechs and Slovaks on healthy foundations of friendly cooperation within the framework of the Czechoslovak Socialist Republic.

At the same time we cannot agree to have hostile forces push your country from the road of Socialism and create a threat of severing Czechoslovakia from the Socialist community. This is something more than your cause. It is the common cause of all the Communist and workers' parties and states united by alliance, cooperation and friendship. This is the common cause of our countries, which have joined in the Warsaw Treaty to ensure the independence, the peace and security in Europe, and to set up an insurmountable barrier for the intrigues of the imperialist forces, aggression and revenge.

At the price of tremendous losses the peoples of our countries gained victory over Hitlerite Fascism, won freedom and independence and an opportunity to follow the road of progress and Socialism. The frontiers of the Socialist world have moved to the center of Europe, to the Elbe and Sumava Mountains. And we shall never agree to have these historical gains of Socialism, independence and security of our peoples being put to threat. We shall never agree to have imperalism, using ways peaceful and non-peaceful, making a gap from the inside or from the outside in the Socialist system and changing in imperalism's favour the correlation of forces in Europe.

The might and firmness of our alliances depend on the inner strength of the Socialist system in each of our countries, on the Marxist-Leninist policy of our parties who discharge the leading role in the political and social life of their respective nations and states. Hamstringing of the leading role of the Communist party leads to liquidation of Socialist democracy and the Socialist system. There are thus imperiled the foundations of our alliance and the safety of the comity of our countries.

AN UNDERSTANDING IS RECALLED

You are aware of the understanding with which the fraternal parties treated the decisions of the January plenary meeting of the Central Committee of the Communist party of Czechoslovakia, as they believed that your party, firmly controlling the levers of power, would direct the entire process in the interests of Socialism and not let anti-Communist reaction exploit it to grind its own axe. We shared the conviction that you would protect the Leninist principle of democratic centralism as the apple of your eye. For the flouting of any aspect of this principle, democracy or centralism, inevitably serves to weaken the party and its guiding role by transforming the party into either a bureaucratic organization or debating club. We discussed all these matters time and again at the meetings we had, and received from you assurances that you are aware of all the dangers and are fully resolved to repulse them.

Unfortunately events have taken another course.

Capitalizing on the weakening of party leadership of the country and demagogically abusing the slogan of "democratization," the forces of reaction triggered off a campaign against the Communist party of Czechosolvakia and its honest and devoted cadres, clearly seeking to abolish the party's leading role, subvert the Socialist system, and place Czechoslovakia in opposition to the other Socialist countries.

The political organisations and clubs that have emerged of late outside the framework of the national front have become, in effect, headquarters of the forces of reaction. The Social Democrats are doggedly striving to establish their own party, are organizing underground committees, and are seeking to cleave to the working class movement in Czechoslovakia and to take over the leadership of the country in order to effect a bourgeois restoration. Anti-Socialist and revisionist forces have laid hand on the press, radio and television, making of them a rostrum for attacking the Communist party, disorienting the working class and all working folk, spewing forth uncurbed anti-Socialist demagogy and undermining the friendly relations between the Czechoslovak Socialist Republic and the other

Socialist countries. Some mass communication media are carrying on a systematic campaign of real oral terror against people opposing the forces of reaction or voicing anxiety over the trend of developments.

PLATFORM IS ASSAILED

Despite the decisions of the May plenary meeting of the Central Committee of the Communist party of Czechoslovakia, which indicated the threat emanating from rightwing and anti-Communist forces as the main danger, the increasing attacks that reaction has mounted have not met with any rebuff. This is precisely why reaction has been able to publicly address the entire country and to print its political platform under the title of "The 2,000 Words" which contain an outright call for struggle against the Communist party and constitutional authority, for strikes and disorders. This call represents a serious danger to the party, the national front and the Socialist state, and is an attempt to introduce anarchy. In essence, this statement is the organizational and political platform of counterrevolution. The claims made by its writers that they do not seek to overthrow the Socialist state, operate without the Communists or rupture alliances with the Socialist countries, should kid nobody. This is empty talk, the purpose of which is to legalize the platform of counterrevolution and hoodwink the vigilance of the party, the working class and all the working folk.

Far from being repudiated, this platform, being so extensively circulated at a responsible moment on the eve of extraordinary Congress of the Communist party of. Czechoslovakia, has, on the contrary, found obvious advocates in the party rank and file and leaderhsip, who second the anti-Socialist calls.

Anti-Socialist and revisionist forces smear all the activities of the Communist party, wage a slander campaign against its cadres, discredit honest and loyal-to-the-party Communists.

A situation has thus arisen which is absolutely unacceptable for a Socialist country.

It is in this atmosphere that attacks are also being made on the C.S.S.R. Socialist foreign policy, on the alliance and friendship with Socialist countries. Voices are heard demanding a revision of our common coordinated policy as regards the F.R.G., despite the fact that the West German Government invariably pursues a policy hostile to the interests of the security of our countries. The flirting of the F.R.G. authorities and revenge seekers meets with response among leading quarters of your country.

The entire course of events in your country in recent months shows that the forces of counterrevolution, supported by imperialist centers, have developed a broad offensive on the Socialist system without meeting due resistance on the part of the party and the people's power. There is no doubt that the centers of international imperialist reaction are also involved in these events in Czechoslovakia, and are doing everything to inflame and aggravate the situation, inspiring anti-Socialist forces to act in this direction. The bourgeois press, under the pretext of praising "democratization" and "liberalization" in the C.S.S.R. is waging an instigative campaign against the fraternal Socialist countries. F.R.G. ruling quarters are especially active, attempting to use the events in Czechoslovakia to sow discord between the Socialist countries, isolate the G.D.R. and carry out their revenge-seeking designs.

DANGERS ARE POINTED OUT

Don't you, comrades, see these dangers? Is it possible, under such conditions to remain passive, to limit oneself to mere declarations and assurances of loyalty to the cause of Socialism and allied observations? Don't you see that counterrevolution is wresting from you one position after another, that the party is losing control over the course of events and is further retreating under the pressure of anti-Communist forces.

Is it not for the purpose of sowing distrust and emrity towards the Soviet Union and other Socialist countries that the press, radio and television of your country unleashed a campaign in connection with the staff exercises of the armed forces of the Warsaw Treaty organization? Matters went as far as the joint staff exercises of our troops with the participation of several units of the Soviet Army, customary for military cooperation, are being used for groundless accusations of violating the sovereignty of the C.S.S.R. And this is taking place in Czechoslovakia, the people of which sacredly honor the memory of Soviet servicemen who gave their lives for the freedom and sovereignty of that country. At the same time near the western borders of your country exercises of military forces of the NATO aggressive bloc are being conducted with the participation of the army of revenge-seeking Western Germany. But not a single word is mentioned about this.

The inspirers of this unfriendly campaign apparently wish to confuse the minds of the Czechoslovak people, disorient them and undermine the truth that Czechoslovakia can retain her independence and sovereignty only as a Socialist country, as a member of the Socialist community. And only the enemies of Socialism can today speculate on the slogan "defending the sovereignty" of the C.S.S.R. from the Socialist countries, from those countries with whom alliance and fraternal cooperation create a most reliable foundation of the independence and free development of each of our peoples.

It is our conviction that a situation has arisen, in which the threat to the foundations of Socialism in Czechoslovakia jeopardizes the common vital interests of other Socialist countries. The peoples of our states would never forgive us for being indifferent and light-hearted in the face of such a danger.

SOCIALIST UNITY DEMANDED

We are living in such a time when peace, security and freedom of peoples more than ever demand the unity of the forces of Socialism. The international tension is not relaxing. American imperialism has not rejected its policy of strength and open intervention against the peoples, fighting for freedom: It continues its criminal war in Vietnam, supports Israeli aggressors in the Near East, hampers a peaceful settlement of the conflict. The arms race has not been slowed down. The Federal Republic of Germany, in which the neo-Fascist forces are growing, is attacking the status quo, demanding the revision of the borders, does not want to give up its aspirations either for seizing the G.D.R. or for getting access to nuclear weapons, and opposes the disarmament proposals. In Europe, where tremendous means of mass destruction have been accumulated, peace and security of peoples are maintained first of all thanks to the power, unity and peaceful policy of the Socialist states. All of us are responsible for this power and unity of the Socialist countries, for the destiny of peace.

Our countries are linked with one another by treaties and agreements. These important mutual obligations of states and peoples are based on the general aspiration to defend Socialism and ensure collective security of the Socialist countries. Historic responsibility rests on our parties and peoples for the revolutionary gains not to be lost.

Each of our parties is responsible not only to its working class and its people, but also to the international working class, the world Communist movement and cannot evade the obligations following from this. Therefore, we must be solid and united in defending the gains of Socialism, our security and the international positions of the whole of the Socialist community.

That is why we believe that the decisive rebuff to the anti-Communist forces and the decisive efforts for the preservation of the Socialist system in Czechoslovakia are not only your but also our task.

The cause of defending the power of the working class and all working people, of the Socialist gains in Czechoslovakia demands a decisive and bold offensive against the right wing and anti-Socialist forces, mobilization of all means of defense created by the Socialist state; the stopping of the activity of all political organizations coming out against Socialism; the mastery by the party of the means of mass information—press, radio, television—and the use of them in the interests of the working class, all working people and Socialism; the closing of the ranks of the party itself on the principled basis of Marxism-Leninism, and the undeviating observation of the principle of democratic centralism, the struggle against those who help the inimical forces by their activity.

We are aware that forces exist in Czechoslovakia that are capable of defending the Socialist system and inflicting defeat on the anti-Socialist elements. The working class, the toiling peasantry, the front rank intelligentsia and the overwhelming majority of the working people of the republic are ready to do everything necessary for the sake of the further development of the Socialist society. The task today is to provide these healthy forces with a clear-cut perspective, to stir them to action, to mobilize their energy for the struggle against the forces of counterrevolution in order to safeguard and consolidate Socialism in Czechoslovakia.

In the face of danger of counterrevolution and in response to the appeal of the Communist party the voice of the working class should ring out in full might. The working class, together with the toiling peasantry, exerted the greatest effort for the sake of the triumph of the Socialist revolution. They precisely cherish most of all the safeguarding of the gains of Socialism. We express the conviction that the Communist party of Czechoslovakia, conscious of its responsibility, will take the necessary steps to block the path of reaction. In this struggle you can count on the solidarity and all-around assistance of the fraternal Socialist countries.

CZECHOSLOVAK REPLY

The Presidium of the Central Committee of the Communist Party of Czechoslovakia has thoroughly studied the letter it received addressed to the Central Committee of our party from the meeting of the representatives of the parties of five Socialist countries in Warsaw.

In the letter it is stressed that it is motivated by anxiety over our common cause and the strengthening of Socialism.

On the basis of this fact and led by the same strivings, we wish to openly state also our own attitude to the question mentioned in the letter.

We are at the same time fully aware that an exchange
of letters cannot fully explain such a complex problem
which the subject of attention and our attitude does not
aim at such ends but on the contrary presumes direct mutual talks between parties.

The number of fears explained in the letter were also
expressed in the resolution of our May plenary session of
the Central Committee of the Communist party of Czechoslovakia.

However, we see the causes of the conflicting situation
mainly in the fact that these conflicts accumulated over
the years preceding the January plenary session of the Central Committee of the Communist party of Czechoslovakia.

These conflicts cannot be satisfactorily solved in a short
time.

In the process of the realization of the political line of
the action program of our party, it is, therefore, unavoidable that the wide mass stream of healthy Socialist activities is accompanied by extremist tendencies, that the
remnants of anti-Socialist forces in our society are also
trying to go along and that at the same time the dog-
matic-sectarian forces connected with the faulty policy of
the pre-January period are also spreading their activities.

PARTY AFFECTED BY DISPUTES

Not even the party itself can remain untouched by internal disputes which accompany this process of unification on the line of the action program.

One of the negative aspects of this process is also the
violation of the principles of democratic centralism in the
dealings of some Communists, which is mainly one of the
results of the fact that for many long years the old party
leadership applied bureaucratic centralism and suppressed
internal party democracy.

All these things prevent us from achieving only those
results in our political work which we ourselves wish.

We do not wish to hide these facts and we do not hide
them either from our own party and people.

For this reason also the May plenum of the Central Committee stated clearly that it is necessary to mobilize all forces to prevent a conflict situation in the country and the endangering of Socialist power in the Czechoslovak Socialist Republic. Our party has also unequivocally stated that if any such danger occurred that we should use all means to protect the Socialist system.

We therefore, ourselves saw the possibility of such danger. We understand that the fraternal parties of the socialist countries cannot be indifferent to this. We do not however, see any realistic reasons permitting our present situation to be called counter-revolutionary, statements on the immediate endangering of the basis of the Socialist system or statements that Czechoslovakia is preparing a change in the orientation of our Socialist foreign policy and that there is concrete danger of the separation of our country from the Socialist camp.

Our alliance and friendship with the U.S.S.R. and other Socialist countries is deeply rooted in the social system, the historical traditions and experience of our peoples, in their interests, their thoughts and feelings. The liberation from Nazi occupation and the entry onto the path of a new life is forever connected in the consciousness of our people with the historical victory of the U.S.S.R. in the Second World War, with respect to the heroes who laid down their lives in this battle.

This is also the basis of the action program of our party which proclaims this tradition to be its starting point.

The basic orientation of Czechoslovakia's foreign policy was born and confirmed at a time of the national liberation fight and in the process of the Socialist reconstruction of our country—it is the alliance and cooperation with the Soviet Union and the other Socialist countries. We shall strive for the friendly relations between our allies—the countries of the world Socialist system—to deepen on the basis of mutual respect, sovereignty and equality, mutual esteem, and international solidarity. In these senses we shall contribute more actively and with a worked-out concept to the common activities of the Council of Mutual Economic Assistance and the Warsaw Treaty.

SURPRISE IS EXPRESSED

In the letter there is a mention of the attacks against the Socialist foreign policy, on assaults against the alliance and friendship with Socialist countries, about voices calling for the revision of our common and coordinated policy in relation to the G.F.R. and it is even stated that attempts at making advances by the authorities of the G.F.R. revanchists are finding response in the leading circles of our country.

We are surprised at such statements because it is well known that the Czechoslovak Socialist Republic is applying a thorough Socialist foreign policy, the principles of which were formulated in the action program of the Communist party of Czechoslovakia and the program statement of the Government. These documents and the statements made by leading Czechoslovak representatives and also our further actions are consistently based on the principles of Socialist internationalism, alliance and the development of friendly relations with the Soviet Union and the other Socialist states.

We are of the opinion that these facts are decisive and not the irresponsible voices of the individuals which are sometimes heard.

With regard to the bitter historical experiences of our nations with German imperialism and militarism it is inconceivable that any Czechoslovak government could ignore these experiences and foolhardedly hazard the fate of our country, even less a Socialist government, and we must refute any suspicion in this direction.

As regards our relations with the G.F.R. it is universally known that although Czechoslovakia is the immediate neighbor of the G.F.R., it was the last to take definite steps toward the partial regulation of mutual relations, particularly in the economic field, while other Socialist countries adapted their relations to one or another extent much earlier without it causing any fears.

At the same time, we thoroughly respect and protect the interests of the F.D.R., our Socialist ally, and do all in our power to strengthen its international position and authority. This is definitely proved by all the speeches of the leading representatives of our party and state in the entire period after January 1968.

COMMITMENTS ARE RESPECTED

The agreements and treaties which connect the Socialist countries are an important factor of mutual cooperation, peace and collective security. Czechoslovakia fully respects its contractual commitments and further develops the system of treaties with Socialist countries, which is proved by the new friendship treaties which we recently concluded with the Bulgarian People's Republic, and also the prepared treaty on friendship and cooperation with the Rumanian Socialist Republic.

Together with the authors of the letter we shall not agree to the historic achievements of Socialism and the safety of the nations of our country being threatened or for imperialism either by peaceful or forceful means breaking down the socialist system and changing the balance of power in Europe to its advantage. The main content of our development after January is the struggle to increase our internal strength and the stability of the Socialist system and thus also our bonds of alliance.

The staff exercise of the allied forces of the Warsaw Treaty on the territory of Czechoslovakia are a a concrete proof of our faithful fulfillment of our alliance commitments.

In order to insure its smooth course we took the necessary measures on our side. Our people and the members of the army gave a friendly welcome to the Soviet and other allied soldiers on the territory of Czechoslovakia, the top representatives of the party and Government by their participation proved what importance we attach to it and the interest we have in it.

The obscurities and some doubts in the minds of our public occurred only after the repeated changes of the time of the departure of the allies' armies from the territory of Czechoslovakia at the end of the exercise.

The letter of the five parties also deals—with some internal problems of the present. We accept the assurance

that the aim of this interest is not to interfere into the
"methods of planning and management of the Socialist national economy in Czechoslovakia" and into our "measures
aimed at perfecting the structure of the economy and the
development of socialist democracy" and that the "settlement of the relations between Czechs and Slovaks on the
healthy principles of fraternal cooperation within the
framework of the Czechoslovak Socialist Republic" are welcomed.

INNER STRENGTH VITAL

We agree with the opinion that the strength and firmness
of our ties—which are undoubtedly the common vital interest of us all—depends on the inner strength of the Socialist system of each of our fraternal countries.

We do not doubt that the undermining of the leading
role of the Communist party would threaten the liquidation
of Socialist society. Just for this reason it is essential that
we should understand each other on the question of what
is the condition for the strength of the Socialist system
and the strengthening of the leading role of the Communist
party.

In the action program of our party we set down the
following on the basis of our previous experience.

In the present time it is especially essential for the party
to carry out such a policy that could fully merit it the
leading role in our society. We are convinced that under
the present circumstances it is a condition for the Socialist development of the country.

The Communist party depends on the voluntary support
of the people. It is not implementing its leading role by
ruling over the society but is faithfully serving its free,
progressive Socialist development. It cannot impel its authority, but must constantly acquire it by its actions. It
cannot force its line by orders, but by the work of its
members and the veracity of its ideals.

We do not hide the fact—and we stated this plainly at
the May Plenum of the Central Committee—that there ex-

ist today also tendencies aimed at discrediting the party, attempts to deny it its moral and political right to lead the society. But if we ask the question whether similar phenomena can be correctly judged as a threat to the Socialist system, as a decline of the political role of the Communist party of Czechoslovakia under the pressure of reactionary, counterrevolutionary forces, then we come to the conclusion that this is not so.

The leading role of our party gravely suffered in the past by the distortions of the fifties and the policy of their inconsistent removal by the leadership headed by A. Novotny He is even more responsible for the deepening of the social conflicts between the Czechs and Slovaks, between the intelligentsia and workers, between the young generation and older generations.

The inconsistent solution of the economic problems has left us in a condition in which we cannot solve a series of justified economic demands of the workers and when the effectiveness of the entire national economy is gravely disrupted.

FURTHER MISTAKES ACCUMULATE

Under that leadership the confidence of the masses in the party dropped and there were expressions of criticism and resistance, but all this was "solved" by interference from a position of power against justified dissatisfaction against criticism and against attempts to consistently solve the social problems in the interests of the party and in the interests of its leading role.

Instead of the gradual and well-considered removal of errors, further mistakes and conflicts accumulated as a result of subjective decision-making. In the years when Socialist democracy could objectively be developed gradually and scientific management could have been applied, the subject deficiencies sharpened and social conflicts and difficulties.

On the outside it seemed that everything was in order in Czechoslovakia and it was made to appear that developments were without conflict. In actual fact the decline in the confidence in the party was masked by exterior forms of directive party control. Although this regime was presented as being the firm guarantee of the interests of the entire Socialist camp, internal problems created suppression by forceful means of those advocates of new and creative approaches.

Any indication of a return to these methods would evoke the resistance of the overwhelming majority of party members, the resistance of the working class, the workers, cooperative farmers and intelligensia.

The party would by such a step imperil its political leading role and would create a situation in which a power conflict woud really arise. This would truly threaten the Socialist advances of the Socialist community.

We agree that one of the primary tasks of the party is to thwart the aims of right-wing and anti-Socialist force. Our party has worked out its tactical political plan and is solving the problems according to it. This plan is based on a system of measures which can be successful only if we have the conditions to gradually implement them over the course of several months.

MAIN AIMS SPECIFIED

We consider the conditions for success to be for the realization of the action program and the preparations of the party congress to take its course without any false step which could cause a power-political struggle in our country. The May plenum stated this quite plainly in its resolution.

The party considers the basic problem of the current situation is to prevent the threatening of the Socialist character of power and the social system from either side—either from the side of right-wing anti-Communist tendencies, or from the side of conservative forces, who were unable to insure the development of Socialism but who would wish for a return to the conditions before January, 1968.

Our party has laid down the following main aims and stages of political work.

1. To consistently separate the party as a whole from the distortions of the past for which specific persons of the old party leadershp are responsible. These specific people are justifiably being called to task.

2. To prepare the fourteenth extraordinary congress of the party which will evaluate the development and political situation during the January plenum and in accordance with the principles of democratic centralism will lay down the compulsory line for the entire party, will adopt an attitude to the federal arrangement of Czechoslovakia, will approve the new party statute and elect a new Central Committee so that it has the full authority and confidence of the party and the entire society.

3. After the fourteenth congress to launch the offensive for the solution of all the fundamental internal political questions: Toward the construction of a political system based on the Socialist platform of the National Front and social self government, the solution of the federal constitutional arrangement, the elections to the representative bodies of the state (federal national and local) and the preparation of a new constitution.

At present we are at the stage of the political fight to implement the line of the May plenum of the central Committee of the Communist party of Czechoslovakia. It is real fight and, therefore, we both win and suffer drawbacks.

It would not be correct to judge the outcome of the whole war, however, according to the results of the individual battles. Despite this we think that we have managed to consolidate the political situation since the May plenum.

In the past days, the extraordinary district and regional conferences have plainly shown that the party is becoming unified on the line of the action program.

Delegates have been elected to the congress, and their composition is a guarantee that the future fate of the party will not be decided by representatives of extremist opinions, but by the democratically-appointed progressive core of our party.

The representatives of the new leadership of the Communist party of Czechoslovakia who are associated with the line of the action program and the May plenum of the Central Committee, were all proposed by the regional conferences to the new Central Committee. Therefore, a certain stabilization is going on in the party and the basic steps for the preparations of the congress took place with success.

PLATFORM BEING CREATED

In accordance with the resolution of the May plenum of the Central Committee of the Communist party of Czechoslovakia, a binding political Socialist platform of the National Front is being created on the initiative of Communists. All the political components of the National Front adopted the program statement made on June 15, 1968, which clearly accepts the historically-won leading role of the Communist party of Czechoslovakia and which expresses the principles of a Socialist system, the Socialist internal and foreign policy.

The National Front is now discussing the proposal for its statute which is a binding form of organization insuring the Socialist political orientation of all parties and organizations.

We consider all these steps to be important results arising from the fulfillment of the line adopted at the plenary session of the Central Committee of the Communist party of Czechoslovakia, to be important features of the consolidation of political conditions and the strengthening not only of the declared but the genuinely leading influence of the party in our country.

In spite of this we see and do not want to conceal the fact that not all conclusions drawn at the May plenary session have been carried out satisfactorily. Now, too, it happens that voices and tendencies appear in the press and the radio and in public meetings which are outside the positive endeavors of the party, the state bodies and the National Front.

We consider the solution of these questions to be a long-term task and are guided by the resolutions of the May plenary session of the Central Committee according to which "political leadership cannot be imposed by the old, administrative and power structures." The Presidium of the Central Committee of the Communist party of Czechoslovakia, the Government and the National Front clearly rejected the appeal of the statement of the "two thousand words," which urges people to engage in anarchist acts, and to violate the constitutional character of our political reform. It should be noted that, following these negative positions, similar campaigns in fact did not occur in our country and that the consequences of the appeal of "two thousand words" did not threaten the party, the National Front and the Socialist state.

The campaigns and unjustified slanders against various functionaries and public officials—including members of the new leadership of the Communist party of Czechoslovakia—which are conducted from extremist positions both left and right, are still a negative aspect of our situation.

SECRETARIAT OPPOSES METHODS

The Secretariat of the Communist Party Central Committee and leading officials have unequivocally come out against these methods in specific cases.

We know that this situation is facilitated by the abolition of censorship in our country and the enactment of freedom of expression and of the press. What had been spread in the form of "whispered propaganda," etc. before can now be expressed openly .

By the law of judiciary rehabilitations we basically solved the painful problem of the illegal reprisals against innocent people which took place in the past years. This step has so clearly helped that the attention of the wide public and the mass communications media no longer concentrates on these questions.

In September—immediately after the party congress— other new important laws will be discussed: the constitutional law on the National Front, which is to confirm the permanent existence of the system of political parties within the National Front; and, further, a law on the right of assembly and association which sets forth the legal regulations for the birth and activities of various voluntary organizations, associations, clubs, etc.

This will give the opportunity to effectively face attempts of anti-Communist forces to gain an organizational basis for public activities.

The Communists have also taken the initiative, according to the resolution of the May plenary session of the Central Committee, to solve the important questions of the work of the trade unions and enterprise workers councils. In general, the party has been able to overcome political demagogy in these questions which attempted to utilize the justified demands of the workers to dis-organize our system and which fanned an impromptu movement in the name of "workers demands" in order to make the economic and political situation in the country more difficult.

At the same time, however, according to the means at our disposal, we are solving some urgent social and political problems such as the increase of low pensions and urgent wage increases.

The Government is gradually dealing with the fundamental economic problems of the country in order to give the impulse for the new development of production and in order to be able to move over to the further improvement of the living standard of our people.

We people have taken the necessary measures to insure the safety of our state borders. The party fully supports the consolidation of the army, security prosecutors and judiciary of the workers' militia whose nation wide meeting gave full support to the new leadership of the Communist party of Czechoslovakia and the action program. The importance of this step, as is known, was welcomed by the workers not only in this country, but also in the U.S.S.R.

ONLY A PART OF SITUATION

If we ask ourselves though whether it is correct to consider such phenomena as forfeiture of the leading political role of the Communist party of Czechoslovakia under pressure of reactionary counter-revolutionary forces, we reach the conclusion that this is not so. For all this is only part of our present political situation. There is also another, and in our opinion, decisive aspect to this situation. The rise of the authority of the new, democratic policy of the party in the eyes of the broadest masses of the workers, the growth of the activity of the overwhelming majority of the people. The overwhelming majority of the people of all classes and sectors of our society favor the abolition of censorship and are for freedom of expression.

The Communist party of Czechoslovakia is trying to show that it is capable of a different political leadership and management than the discredited bureaucratic-police methods, mainly by the strength of its Marxist-Leninist ideas, by the strength of its program, its just policy supported by all the people.

Our party can prevail in the difficult political struggle only if it has an opportunity to implement the tactical line of the May plenary meetings of the Central Committee and to settle basic political questions at the extraordinary fourteenth congress in the spirit of the action program.

We, therefore, consider all pressure directed at forcing the party onto another path, that is to settle basic questions of its policy elsewhere and at another time than at the fourteenth congress, the principal danger to the successful consolidation of the leading role of the party in the Czechoslovak Socialist Republic.

Pressure of this sort is being brought to bear by domestic extremist forces on the right as well as from the positions of the conservatives, the dogmatists and sectarians, endeavoring for a return to conditions before January, 1968.

In evaluation of the situation as contained in the letter of the five parties and the no doubt sincerely intended advice for our further activities do not take into account the entire intricacy of the dynamic social movement as it was analyzed by the May plenary meeting of the Central Committee of the Communist party of Czechoslovakia or the complexity of the conclusions that were adopted by this plenum.

Our policy, if it hopes to remain a Marxist-Leninist policy, cannot be based only on superficial phenomena which do not always reflect the precise and profound causes of social development but must determine the substance of the development and to be guided by it.

At the given time the interests of Socialism in our country can be served best by a ration of confidence in the leadership of the Communist party of Czechoslovakia and of full support of its policy by our fraternal parties. For this reason we have proposed, as a prerequisite of successful joint discussions, bilateral meetings of the representatives of our parties so that the joint talks may proceed from deep mutual consultations and factual information.

We sincerely regret that these proposals put forward by us were not implemented. It is not our fault that the meeting in Warsaw was held without us. We discussed the proposals of the five parties for holding this meeting at the Presidium of the Central Committee of the Communist Party of Czechoslovakia twice—on July 8 and 12—and each time we immediately conveyed our view on the method of this meeting was to be prepared as we believed to be most correct.

Unfortunately, our meeting of July 12 was already superfluous because, notwithstanding its outcome, the meeting had already been convened for July 14, a fact we learned only through Ceteka in the afternoon of July 13, at the time when the representatives of the five parties were already on their way to Warsaw.

In no statement that we sent to the five parties did we refuse on principle to take part in joint conferences. We only voiced our view concerning their suitability at the present time and on the method in which they were prepared so that they could really be in the point and based on more profound information about our complex problems.

From the contents of the letters of the five parties, sent to us between July 4 and 6, 1968, we had the impression that such information is absolutely vital if there was not to be a meeting, the success of which would be threatened by one-sided and sparse information of the large majority of the participants in the conference concerning the real situation in Czechoslovakia.

PURPOSE OF PROPOSAL EXPLAINED

This is the purpose of our proposal for preliminary bilateral meetings. We were motivated not by an effort to isolate ourselves from the community of our fraternal parties and countries, but on the contrary, by a desire to contribute to their consolidation and development.

We think that the common cause of Socialism is not advanced by the holding of conferences at which the policy and activity of one of the fraternal parties are judged without the presence of its representatives.

We consider the principle expressed in the declaration of the Government of the Soviet Union of Oct 30, 1956, which says, "The countries of the great community of Socialist nations united by the common ideals of the building of a Socialist society and the principles of proletarian internationalism, can build their mutual noninterference in their internal affairs" to be still valid.

This principle, as is generally known, was confirmed at the conference of the representatives of Communist parties in Moscow in November, 1957, and generally adopted. In our activity we wish to continue to strengthen and promote the deep internationalist tradition which, according to our conception, must include an understanding of the common interests and goals of the progressive forces of the world as well as an understanding of each nation's specific requirements,

We do not want our relationships to become worse and we are willing on our side to contribute to the calming of the situation in the interests of Socialism and the unity of the Socialist countries. On our side, we shall do nothing which would be against this aim. We expect however, that the other parties will aid these efforts of ours and will express understanding for our situation.

We see an important task in the implementation of the bilateral talks, which we proposed, in the nearest future, and which would also assess the possibility of a common meeting of the Socialist countries at which it would be possible to agree on its program and composition, the time and place of its convening.

We consider it to be decisive for us to agree on positive

steps in the near future, which would insure the continuation of our current friendly cooperation and which would convincingly demonstrate our common will to develop and strengthen mutual friendly relations.

This is in the interests of our common fight against imperialism, for peace and the security of nations, for democracy and Socialism.

DATE DUE

GAYLORD			PRINTED IN U.S.A.